D1563501

Helen Thomas' study opens a new avenue for Romantic literary studies by exploring connections with literature produced by slaves, slave owners, abolitionists and radical dissenters between 1770 and 1830. In the first major attempt to relate canonical Romantic texts to the writings of the African diaspora, she investigates English literary Romanticism in the context of a transatlantic culture, and African culture in the context of eighteenth-century Britain. In so doing, the book reveals an intertextual dialogue between two diverse yet equally rich cultural spheres, and their corresponding systems of thought, epistemology and expression. Showing how marginalised slaves and alienated radical dissenters contributed to transatlantic debates over civil and religious liberties, Helen Thomas remaps Romantic literature on this broader canvas of cultural exchanges, geographical migrations and identity-transformation, in the years before and after the abolition of the slave trade.

HELEN THOMAS is lecturer in English at Queen Mary and Westfield College, University of London. She has published an essay in *Gender and Catastrophe* (1997), various articles and reviews in *Wasafiri, Literature of the African World* and *Stand Magazine* and is currently preparing a book on Caryl Phillips.

This series aims to foster the best new work in one of the most challenging fields within English literary studies. From the early 1780s to the early 1830s a formidable array of talented men and women took to literary composition, not just in poetry, which some of them famously transformed, but in many modes of writing. The expansion of publishing created new opportunities for writers, and the political stakes of what they wrote were raised again by what Wordsworth called those 'great national events' that were 'almost daily taking place': the French Revolution, the Napoleonic and American wars, urbanisation, industrialisation, religious revival, an expanded empire abroad and the reform movement at home. This was an enormous ambition, even when it pretended otherwise. The relations between science, philosophy, religion and literature were reworked in texts such as *Frankenstein* and *Biographia Literaria*; gender relations in *A Vindication of the Rights of Woman* and *Don Juan*; journalism by Cobbett and Hazlitt; poetic form, content and style by the Lake School and the Cockney School. Outside Shakespeare studies, probably no body of writing has produced such a wealth of response or done so much to shape the responses of modern criticism. This indeed is the period that saw the emergence of those notions of 'literature' and of literary history, especially national literary history, on which modern scholarship in English has been founded.

The categories produced by Romanticism have also been challenged by recent historicist arguments. The task of the series is to engage both with a challenging corpus of Romantic writings and with the changing field of criticism they have helped to shape. As with other literary series published by Cambridge, this one will represent the work of both younger and more established scholars, on either side of the Atlantic and elsewhere.

For a complete list of titles published see end of book.

CAMBRIDGE STUDIES IN ROMANTICISM 38

ROMANTICISM AND
SLAVE NARRATIVES

ROMANTICISM AND SLAVE NARRATIVES

Transatlantic Testimonies

CAMBRIDGE
UNIVERSITY PRESS

PUBLISHED BY THE PRESS SYNDICATE OF THE UNIVERSITY OF CAMBRIDGE
The Pitt Building, Trumpington Street, Cambridge, United Kingdom

CAMBRIDGE UNIVERSITY PRESS
The Edinburgh Building, Cambridge CB2 2RU, UK
40 West 20th Street, New York NY 10011–4211, USA
477 Williamstown Road, Port Melbourne, VIC 3207, Australia
Ruiz de Alarcón 13, 28014 Madrid, Spain
Dock House, The Waterfront, Cape Town 8001, South Africa

http://www.cambridge.org

First published 2000
Reprinted 2001
First paperback edition 2004

Typeset in Baskerville 11/12.5pt [CE]

A catalogue record for this book is available from the British Library

Library of Congress cataloguing in publication data

Thomas, Helen, Dr.
Romanticism and Slave Narratives: Transatlantic Testimonies / [Helen Thomas]
p.   cm. (Cambridge Studies in Romanticism: 38)
Includes index.
ISBN 0 521 66234 6 (hardback)
1. English literature – 18th century History and criticism. 2. Slavery in literature.
3. American literature – Afro-American authors – History and criticism. 4. English literature –
Black authors – History and criticism. 5. English literature – 19th century – History and
criticism. 6. Slaves' writings, American – History and criticism. 7. Slaves' writings, English –
History and criticism. 8. Antislavery movements – History. 9. Slave trade in literature. 10.
Romanticism. I. Title. II. Series.
PR448.S55&48   2000
820.9′358 – dc21   00– 23186 CIP

ISBN 0 521 66234 6 hardback
ISBN 0 521 60456 7 paperback

Transferred to digital printing 2004

To Hugo, Felix and Claude

If not If not If
Not
If not in yours
In whose
In whose language
Am I

Marlene Nourbese Philip, 'Meditations on the Declensions of
Beauty by the Girl with the Flying Cheek Bones'

Contents

Illustrations

Acknowledgements

Over the past few years I have become increasingly convinced that research, in so far as I am involved in it, functions as a kind of displaced autobiography in which the boundaries between the subject who does the researching (myself) and the subject of the narrative (this study) are in fact permeable. Since we may assume that the self has no meaning without the concept of others, then this displaced 'autobiographical' study is indebted to the continued support, enthusiasm and expertise of several 'others', although I take full responsibility for any mistakes or errors contained herein.

For their professional help and generosity, especially during the late stages of this book, I would like to thank all the staff at the British Library, both at Bloomsbury and St Pancras. I would also like to thank Cora Kaplan, Alan Richardson, Moira Ferguson, Lucy Newlyn, Robert Young and Paul Hamilton for their invaluable comments, advice and suggestions for this work during its various, sometimes digressive, stages; and for their patience and good-humour, Geoff Cox, Victoria de Rijke and the staff and students at the School of Humanities at Oxford Brookes University, most especially, Ron Hammond, Nigel Messenger, Paul O'Flinn, Helen Kidd and John Perkins. For his unhesitating support throughout the various drafts of this book I would especially like to thank Hugo de Rijke. And finally, for patiently waiting before making their entrance into the world, I must thank my sons: Felix and Claude.

Introduction

A plan having been laid before the King, for sending out of this
Country a Number of Black Poor (many of whom have been
discharged from His Majesty's Naval Service at the Conclusion
of the Late War, and others after having been employed with
the Army in North America) who have since their Arrival in
England been reduced to the greatest distress, in order that a
Settlement may be formed in or near the River Sierra Leona,
in the Coast of Africa.[1]

In 1782, 350 British convicts were sent to the west coast of Africa and
used as soldiers on the huge slave fortresses where African captives
were detained before being shipped across the Atlantic. Four years
later, in an effort to relieve its overcrowded prisons, the British
government considered a plan to transport convicts to Sierra Leone.
Following the investigations of the Parliamentary Committee on
Convict Transportation, however, the plan was rejected, since given
the advice of the botanist and naval officer Henry Smeathman, it
was estimated that Sierra Leone's hostile climate would accelerate
the number of convict mortalities to a rate of 100 per month.[2]
Botany Bay was chosen in preference to Sierra Leone, thus establishing a route of involuntary transportation of criminals from
England to the Australian continent at a crucial moment in Britain's
colonial history.

But there soon occurred an unprecedented historical development
in the relations between England and Africa. The racial ideology
which had underpinned the capture, transportation and enslavement
of generations of Africans by British slavers was compounded by a
government plan to relocate Africans to the British colony of Sierra
Leone. Within a year of his contact with the Parliamentary Committee on Convict Transportation, Smeathman wrote to the Committee for the Relief of the Black Poor in February 1786, offering to

take responsibility for their charges and transport them at a cost of £14 per head to a settlement in Sierra Leone. At this time there were approximately 20,000 blacks in London, including a number of black loyalists (mainly runaway slaves) who had recently fought for Britain during the American War of Independence. Smeathman described the proposed Sierra Leone settlement, called the 'Province of Freedom', as 'fit and proper for their Establishment' within the 'pleasant and fertile' land of Sierra Leone.[3] What had been rejected as a fatal location for white convicts was, according to Smeathman, an excellent situation for those blacks presently residing in England. Emphasising the commercial viabilities of his scheme, Smeathman's *Plan of a Settlement to Be Made Near the Sierra Leona, on the Grain Coast of Africa* (1786) suggested that any initial financial outlay would be easily recompensed by the initiation of new channels of trade with Africa. Granville Sharp, founder of the Committee for the Relief of the Black Poor and also the Committee for the Purpose of Effecting the Abolition of the Slave Trade, approved the scheme. He went on to stipulate the advantages of the resettlement plan and its colonial implications in two of his publications: *Regulations for the New Settlement in Sierra Leone* (1786) and *Free English Territory in Africa* (1790). The Treasury, keen to cultivate colonialist commercial ventures that would yield the riches of Africa, duly agreed to the plan and accepted financial responsibility.

Sierra Leone was not entirely new territory to the British government. It had been 'mapped' over two centuries earlier in 1562 when Sir John Hawkins, the entrepreneur sponsored by Queen Elizabeth I, sailed to Sierra Leone and returned with 300 'borrowed' Africans. In subsequent years, more Africans were brought to England, where they became fashionable household accessories, servants, prostitutes and entertainers. A century later, in 1663, Charles II chartered the Royal Adventurers, who built forts in the Sherbo and on Tasso Island of Sierra Leone. In 1753, the slave trader John Newton (who later testified against the slave trade), passed a year of misery on the Plantain Islands, south-east of Sierra Leone. Henry Smeathman himself visited Sierra Leone in 1771 to gather botanical specimens for his collectors in London.

Despite the concerted efforts of the Committee for the Relief of the Black Poor to attract black settlers to the scheme, few signed up. Firmer action was decided upon and in October 1786 the Committee declared that it would only give financial aid to those 'volunteering' to resettle in Sierra Leone.[4] Eventually, orders were given by the Committee and the City authorities to round up black beggars and 'reconcile them to the plan proposed by the Government' by sending them to the new African colony where they would have the 'protection' of the British government.[5] As Moira Ferguson notes, this large-scale effort to remove Africans illustrated Britain's refusal to deal with the wider issues of blacks' right to freedom and other basic human rights recognised by the Court of the King's Bench in the landmark Somerset case of 1772, which held that the escaped slave, James Somerset, could not be forcibly returned by his master to the plantations in Jamaica.[6]

By the end of October 1786 the transport ships *Atlantic*, *Belisarius* and *Vernon* (escorted by HMS *Nautilus*) were commissioned by the Navy Board and were docked at Deptford in South London, ready to take the prospective settlers to Sierra Leone. Each settler had been given a document granting him/her free citizenship of the 'Colony of Sierra Leone or the Land of Freedom'. Yet of the 700 settlers who originally agreed to the scheme, only 259 were on board by the end of November. Seventy of these were white female prostitutes from London, who, it was claimed, had been intoxicated and tricked onto the ships. After an outbreak of fever in February 1787, the convoy of ships eventually set sail but a storm in the channel disabled two of the ships and forced the others to return to port. Those who continued their journey, including fifty-nine white and forty-one black women, eventually arrived at Frenchman's Bay in Sierra Leone in May 1787.[7]

Within three months of their arrival, a third of the party had died. By March 1788, only 130 were alive. The promises of abundant land and the prospects of lawful trade were replaced by the stark realities of disease, death, infertile soils and hostile attacks from native rulers who challenged the settlers' claims of land ownership. Determined to make the scheme a public success, Granville Sharp (who advised the defence counsel in the Somerset case) arranged to send out another party to Sierra Leone in 1791, two of whom were English doctors. 'Granville Town', named in honour of Sharp's pioneering work, was burnt down by the local ruler, Jimmy, in retaliation against the Sierra Leone Company's violations on his territory. In March 1792, assisted by Sharp and his replacement Henry Thornton (of the Sierra Leone Company) and funded by the British

government at a cost of £9,000, over 1000 former American slaves
sailed to Sierra Leone from Nova Scotia. These ex-slaves had been
moved to temporary homes in Nova Scotia, after having fought for
Britain in the American War of Independence, and were thereafter
lured to Sierra Leone by the promise of land.[8]

In 1787, the same year in which the first black 'British' party of
settlers arrived in Sierra Leone, two of a number of politically visible
Africans in London, Olaudah Equiano and Ottobah Cugoano,
published vehement criticisms of the scheme. Cugoano's *Thoughts and
Sentiments on the Evil and Wicked Traffic of the Slavery and Commerce of the
Human Species Humbly Submitted to the Inhabitants of Great Britain* (1787)
highlighted the fact that the prospect of setting up a free colony for
Great Britain had 'neither altogether met with the credulous
approbation of the Africans here, nor yet been sought after with any
prudent and right plan by the promoters of it'.[9] Even more critically,
in a letter to Cugoano which was published in the *Public Advertiser* of
4 April 1787, Equiano denounced the credibility of members of the
Committee who had replaced Smeathman after his death: 'I am sure
Irwin, and Fraser the Parson, are great villains, and Dr Currie. I am
exceeding much grieved at the conduct of those who call themselves
gentlemen. They now mean to serve (or use) the blacks the same as
they do in the West Indies'.[10] Likewise, two former Nova Scotian
black settlers, Cato Perkins and Isaac Anderson, made the journey to
Sierra Leone and later departed for London, where they criticised
John Clarkson over the false promises 'you [Clarkson] made us in
Nova Scotia' and bitterly complained about the pernicious misman-
agement of the Sierra Leone Company.[11]

By the late 1780s, therefore, local and parliamentary debates
concerning slavery, colonialist projects, land disputes and negotia-
tions, repatriation schemes, enforced transportations (of blacks,
whites, convicts and prostitutes) and programmes concerning racial
eradication, emancipation and resettlement, were high on the
agenda. Blacks themselves were contributing to these and to fundamental discourses over civil rights and liberties during the most
productive period of Romantic literature (1770–1830). By the late
1780s the migrations of peoples between Africa, the Americas and
Britain had been firmly established and texts produced by black and
dissenting authors had begun to penetrate the literary sphere. This
book attempts to open new vistas for Romantic studies by indicating
the ways in which it can be brought into contact with transatlantic

and black Atlantic studies. In this way, Mary Louise Pratt's sense of Romanticism as growing out of the 'contact zone' between Europe and the colonial frontier may be extended to include the space in which black Atlantic subjects and their texts met, 'clashed and grappled' with the worlds of Europe and the Americas.[12] Accordingly, this book endeavours to disclose a hitherto obscured dialogue of exchange and negotiation: that is, between the discourse of Romanticism as it emerged out of eighteenth-century dissent and enthusiasm, and the narratives of displaced subjects, the slaves from the African diaspora. As a consequence, it manifests a significant challenge to concepts of Romanticism which continue to hold the revolutions in France and America at their centre and endeavours instead to prioritise the slaves' rebellions, both literary and actual, upon the emerging autobiographical genre. By foregrounding the ways in which marginalised slaves and alienated radical dissenters contributed to transatlantic debates over civil and religious liberties, Romantic writing is recontextualised against a broader canvas of cultural exchanges, geographical migrations and displaced identities.

This book therefore investigates Romanticism in the context of transatlantic western culture and African culture in eighteenth-century Britain. Its predominant theme resides in the intersection, intervention and interaction between these two diverse, yet equally rich, cultural spheres and their corresponding systems of thought, epistemology and articulation: the transcultural, restless mutations and clashes of African and western philosophies, ideologies and practices which distinguished the late eighteenth century.[13] It investigates the ways in which such movements were negotiated, compromised and actualised by asking a series of linked questions. In what ways did Romanticism reflect or challenge Britain's participation in the slave trade? In what ways did the strategies employed by eighteenth-century radicals, misfits and/or the sociopolitically marginalised resemble those used by Africans upon their entry into the west? How did Africans articulate difference, dissidence or conformity in the years prior to and following the abolition of the slave trade? And finally, what is the connection between the seemingly disparate discourses of 'Romanticism' and the narratives published in England between 1770 and 1830 by ex-slaves from Africa and the colonies?[14]

A heterogeneous selection of canonical and marginalised untraditional works by white 'British', black 'British' and Anglo-American

authors are analysed in terms of their distinct and often challenging
efforts to construct and advance diverse formulations of identity.
Methodism's early transatlantic connections are set up alongside the
'black Atlantic', an entity which has been defined as the 'hybrid
sphere of black culture within Africa, America, the Caribbean and
Europe'.[15] Using a synthesis of archival material and theoretical
application, these works are presented as articulate expressions of
self/cultural-consciousness and located within the context of
eighteenth-century religious and political dissent. It is hoped that
this examination of the slave narratives within the context of
Romanticism will acknowledge the emergence of a culturally hybrid
black diaspora. Within the context of this book, the term 'diaspora'
is used to describe the common historical processes of dispersal,
fragmentation, displacement, enslavement and transportation experienced by African peoples and their descendants, experiences
which unified such peoples at the same time as cutting them off from
direct access to their past.[16] In this sense therefore, 'diaspora' as Jim
Clifford has argued, functions not simply as a signifier of historically
spatial fluidity and intentionality of identity but also of the endeavours to define a 'distinctive community' within historical contexts of
displacement.[17] This book accordingly investigates the literary
relationship between the black diaspora and its host community. It
revisits and extends definitions proposed by postcolonialist critics
and cultural theorists which suggest that all forms of culture are in
some way related to one another as 'symbol-forming' and 'subject-
constituting, interpellative practices'.[18] The liberating connotations
of cultural 'hybridities' here reciprocate the complex mechanisms of
'translation' and correlate with the interdependent processes of
'displacement' within the linguistic sign and the necessarily plura-
listic concepts of subjectivity:

If . . . the act of cultural translation (both as representation and as
reproduction) denies the essentialism of a prior given original or originary
culture, then we see all forms of culture are continually in a process of
hybridity . . . Hybridity to me is the 'third space' which enables other
positions to emerge.[19]

In other words, this study extends the concept of cultural hybridity
to the concept of cultural intertextuality. It is concerned with texts
which witness a process of movement and negotiation between
cultures. But in order for cultural intertextualities to succeed (that is,

in order that the works of ex-slaves were read) particular forms of discourse were adopted so as to advance not only a 'sign' of assimilation with the host culture but also transformation of it. For poststructuralist critics such as Michel Foucault and Paul de Man, the concept of 'discourse' registers an ordering, or transposition of 'reality' onto convenient constructions or representations that are not necessarily dependent upon that reality; the production of systems of language in which utterances and texts, regardless of their factual status, differ according to the social and cultural context from which they emerge.[20] In its provision of a free signifier, the protean quality of what I have termed the 'discourse of the spirit' initiated by radical dissenting Protestantism facilitated the slaves' entry into the dominant literary order, an entry otherwise obstructed by restrictive legal and socioeconomic conditions. Establishing a process by which the slave's identity was liberated from the conditions imposed upon it by others, the discourse of the spirit identified the role of the slave in the black diaspora as sanctioned by a spiritual entity whose power was considered both impregnable and absolute. This discourse not only denied the possibility of a straightforward literal use of language but also enabled a form of cultural exchange between Christian and African belief systems: whilst the slave-narratives were obliged to present an acceptable form of 'x' (evidence of the workings of the holy spirit as maintained by radical dissenting Protestantism), they simultaneously revealed 'y' (a raw but coherent form of self-conciousness in the diaspora). This process of literal 'displacement' thus presents a lucid manifestation of the predicament of eighteenth-century African/slave identity within the diaspora. Alongside the dynamics of 'cultural' migration and 'hybridisation', such anti-essentialist conceptions of identity redetermined configurations of history, language and culture as processes of becoming rather than being.[21]

Drawing from Freudian analysis, the linguist Emile Benveniste has argued that it is language which provides the possibility of subjectivity; it is through language that people constitute themselves as subjects: 'Consciousness of self is only possible if it is experienced by contrast . . . Language is possible only because each speaker sets himself up as a *subject* by referring to himself as *I* in his discourse'.[22] Since there is no other testimony to the identity of the subject other than via language, there is no other form of authentication other than whatever the subject articulates about him/herself. Yet the

speaking subject can only become such by 'conforming' his/her
speech to a system of linguistic prescriptions. Identity, therefore,
constitutes a complex matrix of sometimes contradictory subject
positions.[23]

The first part of this study is largely concerned with political and
autobiographical tracts published in Britain by abolitionists, millen-
arianist prophets, Romantic poets and evangelical revivalists. The
second part is concerned with works by slaves of African descent
published in England during the late eighteenth and early nineteenth century. Part I identifies the transatlantic discourse of the
spirit which emerged under the influence of eighteenth-century
radical dissenting Protestantism. It traces the development of spiritual autobiography as an heterogeneous medium of liberationist and
abolitionist ideology, and conversely, elucidates its appropriation by
advocates of territorial expansion and colonial ideology. Chapter 1
looks at the historical development of Britain's slave-trading and
colonial practice, the tensions arising from this and the emergence of
radical dissenting Protestantism on both sides of the Atlantic.
Chapters 2 and 3 present critical examinations of English traditions
of confessional writing by a selection of (white) literary predecessors
to the Romantics, 'tangential' Romantic writers and 'canonical'
poets. Within Chapter 2, relations are drawn between the narratives
of the former slave trader, John Newton, the writings of the
Devonshire visionary, Joanna Southcott, and the poetry of William
Cowper, an important precursor to the Romantic poets. Their
writings chart the rise of a self-conscious paradigm of counter-
hegemonic discourse which operates both within and without the
sociopolitical sphere. The writings of Joanna Southcott are examined
in terms of the explicit challenges they pose to both patriarchal and
non-conforming dissenting circles, via their strident demands for
self-authorisation and female emancipation. The poems of William
Cowper are seen to involve a complex fusion of spiritual discourse,
personal psychosis and abolitionist ideology, which is neither
unproblematic nor unambiguous. Likewise, the analysis of the
writings of Cowper's mentor, John Newton, highlights the ways in
which the liberationist model of spiritual salvation was strategically
employed in order to denounce the slave trade, yet remained isolated
from overt demands for black emancipation. Chapter 3 deals with
the writings of first generation Romantics in terms of their responses
to the slave trade. The popularised discourse of radical dissenting

Protestantism and abolitionist ideology is seen to provoke a conflicting range of responses in the writings of Mary Wollstonecraft, Samuel Coleridge, William Wordsworth and William Blake. At times, such writings urged the British public to challenge the colonial policies of empire-building; at other times, such writings, paradoxically framed by the discourse of liberation and individual autonomy, revealed a pronounced detachment from demands for black civil and political rights. The discussion of John Stedman's text in Chapter 4 identifies a significant departure in its synthesis of principal tenets of salvation/liberation with the dynamics of cross-cultural contact. Set against the author's expedition to Surinam to quell insurrectionist blacks, Stedman's text explodes cultural divisions in its exposure of interracial sexual relations and 'miscegenations', which confuse the boundaries between coloniser and colonised, enslaved and free. From this perspective, Stedman's narrative provides a fitting precursor to the discussion of the 'mutant' or 'creolised' strategies contained within the autobiographical narratives by slaves discussed in Part II.

At this point the book leaves the discussion of Romantic and non-conformist writings to examine a number of works by slaves of African descent. Here the materials are from texts published in England during the late eighteenth century, works which represent the emergence of the black diaspora amidst the crisscrossing of the Atlantic Ocean, from West Africa to the West Indies, from the Americas to the British Isles. The term 'slave narrative' as it is used in the context of this book, encompasses the important disclosures, poetical and prosaic, of the slaves' experience of cultural fragmentation and their emergence into the social and linguistic orders of the west. Chapters 5 and 6 demonstrate the ways in which the works by the ex-slaves John Marrant, Jupiter Hammon and James Albert Ukawsaw Gronniosaw prioritised the landscape of radical dissenting Protestantism and reinscribed the 'self' within a revised cultural/textual narrative. Chapter 7 charts the ambivalent appropriation of the evangelical redemptive model by the accomplished poet and slave, Phillis Wheatley. The continuation of African cultural beliefs and practices in Wheatley's work problematises the 'redemptive' Christian missionary ideology of the west and proffers an important paradigm of intermediate cultural and literary negotiation which destabilises the foundations of eighteenth-century racist/colonial ideology. The discussion of the works by Olaudah Equiano and

Robert Wedderburn in Chapters 8 and 9 posits such writings as 'hybridised' versions of fundamental African and Christian belief systems, akin to the syncretic linguistic process of creolisation. Equiano's focus upon divine election and 'spirit possession' imparts a correlation of non-conformist Protestantism with tenets of Ibo culture. This in turn highlights the penetration of the political sphere by the black voice and determines the condition of the diasporic identity as a state of hiatus, which both continues and interrupts the pervasive narrative of western hegemony. Anarchic to an extreme, Robert Wedderburn's vehement critique of the colonial narrative extends the paradigm of spiritual inspiration to a radical demand for socioeconomic compensation and 'black' deliverance from the law. Posed as a conscious evolution of 'creolised' discourse, Wedderburn's work establishes an astonishingly vivid model of consciousness in the black diaspora. For Wedderburn the oceanic emptiness of the Atlantic functions not only as a demarcation of absence, or 'nothingness', in which black subjects were 'erased' and redefined as cultural 'voids', but as a simultaneous and paradoxical signifier of infinite possibilities and transformations.

In writing this book certain terms have been used to convey the volatile dynamics of Britain's colonial practices. The terms 'creolisation' and 'miscegenation' endeavour to describe an historicised and continued process of geographical and cultural interactions and strategies by which new, vibrant mutations are (re)energised and produced. Linguists have used the term 'creolisation' to describe the creation of new languages during periods of linguistic crisis in response to urgent needs for communication. In terms of cultural displacement, the key words here are self-evident: crisis, communication and 'new' ways of speaking.[24] As a linguistic system therefore, a creole constitutes a sophisticated development of a pidgin language, the latter being a reduced or make-shift form of verbal communication which results from an extended contact between groups of people with no language in common. The creation of 'creole' thus attests to a language system which has pidgin in its ancestry, but which is spoken natively by an entire speech community whose ancestors have been displaced geographically and/or whose own sociohistorical identities have been partly disrupted. One of the predominant causes of such sociolinguistic upheaval was the unprecedented scale of black slavery. As Africans representing diverse ethnolinguistic groups were brought by Europeans to colonies in the New World, their urgent need for communication necessitated the development of intricate linguistic systems with their own phonology, syntax and word formations amidst a highly variable, chaotic linguistic environment. This process of creolisation is still not completely understood, but for linguists and cultural theorists alike it presents a fascinating model of expansion, elaboration and reorganisation during a period of trauma, resulting in the creation of a coherent and sophisticated verbal system.

Originating from the Latin term *'creare'*, to 'create', the term 'creolisation' offers an appropriate term to describe not only the linguistic, but the cultural, geographical and literary positions which Africans took up in the New World and continue to occupy within the African diaspora. Creolisation is thus a response to crisis and extreme upheaval, which operates upon a series of linguistic, psychological and ontological levels. In essence it attests to the overriding will to survive, a paradoxical process which endeavours towards expansion at the moment of reduction; towards speech at the moment of silence; and towards history at the moment a cultural continuum is broken. Likewise, my use of the term 'miscegenation', from the term to 'interbreed', to 'mingle', testifies in this context to the interaction (and indeed interdependence) between two otherwise contrasting cultural/subject positions. By this I refer to the fact that Europe and Africa have for centuries been shaped by each other, have extended their borders into each other; categorisation in terms of fixed racial, cultural, political or historical entities cannot therefore be coherently maintained.

Another term which I use is 'African epistemology', by which I refer to the spectrum of African based epistemologies and ontological practices existent at the moment of colonial contact. Notwithstanding the complexity and multiplicity of subnational languages and traditions which make up the construct known as 'Africa', the most persistent and consistent of these traditions were maintained by the new group formations of Africans (predominately the Yoruba peoples of West Africa) on board the slave ships, on the slave plantations of the new world, and within the widespread black communities.[25] Such traditions offered conceptual frameworks tangential to European, Christianised frameworks of time, space and subjectivity. Taking the first of these, African philosophical and metaphysical cultures prioritised a cyclic consciousness and configuration of time which dissolved /refused divisions between the

metaphysical and the physical tripartite aspects of reality: past –
present – future; ancestor – living – unborn. These systems, with
their correlating beliefs in immortality, spiritual presence and ver-
idical dreams, promoted a predominately vitalist rather than gnosio-
logical focus within which, in contrast to Cartesian ontology, the
metaphysical and the concrete were unified.[26] Whereas Western
subjectivism posits the subject as a self-sufficient, relatively 'free',
egocentric agent, African metaphysics and philosophy offer a com-
municentric view of the subject, whose status is affirmed via the
cultivation of contacts and exchanges with others. Within such an
existential framework, therefore, 'death' does not destroy the tissue
of human possibilities and aspirations but rather confers personal
immortality and continued existence via generations of descendants
and ancestors, the guardians of the community.[27] Differences such as
these can perhaps serve to register the counter-discourses to Western
subjectivism, colonial expansionism and imperial historical frameworks. The sites of cultural displacement and encounter may thus
be seen to offer, albeit chaotic and unguaranteed, revised definitions
of the self within a wider political, geographical and cultural
dimension.

In its examination of the intersection between African and
Western culture, the outlines of this study are broad, yet they begin
from a point of departure that is specifically marked in the late
eighteenth century by three interrelated movements. Exemplified by
England's interaction with Sierra Leone, these movements: (1) the
emergence of modern colonial ideology; (2) the emergence of
abolitionist discourse; and (3) the processes of writing the self, mark
the period 1770–1830 as one of intense (self-)consciousness on an
individual, national and cultural scale. These developments, as I
suggest in the chapter that follows, register the shift in England's
definition of itself and its relations with others (racial and colonial) in
the context of civil rights and liberties.

In summary, this book attempts to provide a new way of reading
both Romantic writing and the writings of blacks in British society
by demonstrating the feasibility of an intertextual dialogue between
Western and African culture within the slave narratives. It highlights
the continuous processes of identity-transformation and negotiation
within the diaspora, processes which disturb ideas of 'fixed' traditions, cultures or 'selves'.[28] By elucidating the mapping of African
epistemology on to the various English traditions of confessional

writing and the dynamics of radical dissenting Protestantism, this book locates the 'creolised' discourse of the slave narratives within a complex nexus of cultural history. For both the slaves and the prophetic writers alike, the transfiguration of the 'self' on to a spiritual mode of discourse provided a strategic release from the restraints of subjectivity as defined in terms of physical presence or sociopolitical status. Given the West's pervasive theories of cultural hierarchy and racial inferiority dominant during the late eighteenth and early nineteenth century, beliefs centred upon cultural coalescence or racial 'interplay' tended to be perceived as subversive threats to the established socioeconomic order. But it is exactly this 'interplay' which provides the prophets, poets, radicals and slaves alike with a form of credibility and critique: the word of the 'spirit' is counterpoised to that of the 'law'; identity, power and authority are made fluid and versatile. The dynamics of spiritual discourse thus provided an effective process of self-consciousness and self-authorising which challenged conceptual boundaries between 'selves' and racial 'others'. For the slaves, the narratives enabled a simultaneous articulation of assimilation and difference: it allowed them to speak of a 'self' beyond that prescribed by eighteenth-century slave laws, a 'self' determined by both African epistemological belief systems and culturally diverse historical codes; a self which simultaneously occupied a creative space of transformation and 'becoming'.

PART I

Fig. 1. Sir John Hawkins' Crest.

CHAPTER ONE

The English slave trade and abolitionism

Although it would be a further one hundred years before England had successfully wrested the body of the slave trade from Spain and Portugal, and a further seventy years before it succeeded in dominating the European slave market, John Hawkins' voyage from England to Africa in 1562 marked England's entrance onto the world market of transatlantic slavery and its subsequent ascendance as a global power supported by colonial expansion. During this 'historic' voyage, some 300 slaves were taken from Sierra Leone on the Guinea Coast and transported to the Caribbean island of Hispaniola (now Haiti and the Dominican Republic) where they were sold to the Spaniards for £10,000 worth of pearls, hides, sugar and ginger.[1] In 1607 England founded its first colony at Virginia and in the 1620s Barbados and the Leeward Islands in the West Indies were appropriated for this expanding empire.[2] Just over a decade later, in 1633, the English 'guinea' coin was struck to commemorate the foundation of the slave-trading company known as the Royal Adventurers and by the 1650s, demand for slave produce such as sugar, coffee and tobacco had reached an unprecedented intensity. In the period 1673–1689, over 70 per cent of the slaves imported by the Royal African Company (formerly the Royal Adventurers) came from the Guinea Coast, the remainder from the Senegambia region further north and from Angola in the south. The majority of slaves in the Caribbean originated primarily from the Windward Coast (modern Liberia), the Gold Coast (Ghana) and the Slave Coast (Togoland, Dahomey and Western Nigeria).[3] By 1770, Britain's status as one of the most powerful and dynamic states was established – its commercial vigour having created some of the most productive slave colonies in the world, with a total population of 878,000 slaves (450,000 in British North America and 428,000 in the British Caribbean).[4] By 1760, the British and French slave colonies were producing 150,000

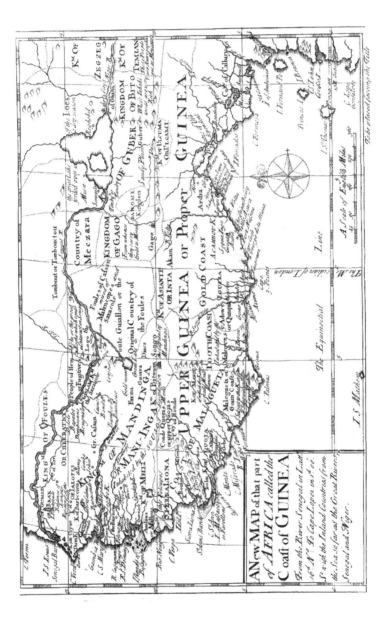

Fig. 2. Map of Guinea. William Snelgrave, *A New Account of Some Parts of Guinea and the Slave Trade* (London, 1734). Frontispiece.

tons of sugar per year, an amount which had almost doubled by the years 1789–1790.[5] The annual rate of slaves shipped by Britain to the West Indies and America during the latter half of the eighteenth century reached 45,000 per year, with Liverpool, Bristol and London functioning as England's most important slave ports. In the decade between 1783 and 1793, slave ships departing from Liverpool completed a total of 878 trips to the West Indies, resulting in a net profit of £15 million.[6] By 1807 the slave population of the British Caribbean had reached a total of 750,000 and by 1832 there were over 500 coffee plantations in Jamaica.[7]

By the end of the eighteenth century, the system of representational government and the system of slavery were firmly established in law and custom in the British Caribbean – the former based upon a monopoly of political power in the hands of a white elite dependent on the English Crown, and the latter, a slave system dependent on the legal concept of property on persons.[8] Yet despite the legal rationalisation of this economic system and its extension via subsequent West Indian Slave Codes, hostility towards the institution of slavery from a section of opinion in England continued to make itself heard. The decision of the Court of the King's Bench in 1772 over the rights of the escaped black Virginian slave, James Somerset (a slave who refused to serve his master while in England and who as a result was imprisoned on board a ship to be sold away to Jamaica) signalled an historic moment in the British abolition movement, in its identification of blacks as free individuals rather than slaves. In his *Commentaries on the Laws of England in Four Books* (1779), William Blackstone commented on the rights of man as follows:

If neither captivity, nor the sale of one's self, can by the law of nature and reason reduce the parent to slavery, much less can they reduce the offspring. Upon these principles the law of England abhors, and will not endure the existence of, slavery within this nation . . . And now it is laid down (Salk. 666), that a slave or negro, the instant he lands in England, becomes a freeman; that is, the law will protect him in the enjoyment of his person, and his property.[9]

The origins of the abolition movement were, however, heavily influenced by the appropriation of Enlightenment ideology and the emergence of a network of non-conformist religious groups informed by radical dissenting Protestantism, the central features of which I shall discuss below.[10] Although misconstrued as determining the illegality of slavery, Lord Mansfield's ruling in the Somerset case prescribed that the slave in question could not be removed from England against his will:

The power of a master over his slave has been extremely different, in different countries. The state of slavery is of such a nature, that it is incapable of being introduced on any reasons, moral or political; but only [by] positive law, which preserves its force long after the reasons, occasion, and time itself from whence it was created, is erased from memory: It is so odious, that nothing can be suffered to support it, but positive law. Whatever inconveniences, therefore, may follow from a decision, I cannot say this case is allowed or approved by the law of England; and therefore the black [James Somerset] must be discharged.[11]

Mansfield's judicial decision was not well received by planters, as demonstrated by Edward Long's satirical response, *Candid Reflections Upon the Judgement Lately Awarded by the Court of the King's Bench* (1772):

The invention of printing has been ascribed to a *soldier*, of gunpowder to a *priest*; perhaps the longitude may be discovered by a *taylor*; but the art of *washing the Black-a-moor white* was happily reserved for a *lawyer*... The name of **** M—[Lord Mansfield] shall henceforth become more popular among all the *Quacoes and Quashebas of America*, than that of patriot *Wilkes* once was among the porter-swilling swains of St. Giles.[12]

Long emphasised the fact that in the past Parliament had implicitly encouraged expansion of the slave trade as a traffic 'highly beneficial to the kingdom, and the colonies and plantations thereon depending' and had provided a definition of negro labourers as 'fit objects of purchase and sale, transferable like any other goods or chattels':

No blame can deservedly rest on the planter, who is ignorant of the means, and innocent of the guilt. That trade . . . has been carried on by this nation from time immemorial. Kings, Lords, and Commons, have shared in its profits, and concurred in various laws for supporting, regulating, and firmly establishing it.[13]

Others associated the consequences of the Mansfield decision with an unprecedented escalation in the number of black citizens in England and viewed it as a pernicious threat to national purity in terms of the resulting intermixture of 'racial blood':

It is therefore humbly hoped the Parliament will provide such remedies as may be adequate to the occasion, by expelling the Negroes now here, who are not made free by their owners, and by prohibiting the introduction of them in this kingdom for the future; and save the natural beauty of Britons from the Morisco tint.[14]

Jurists and moral philosophers had justified the legal basis of slavery according to the doctrine enunciated in Aristotle's *Politics*, a work which provided a detailed examination of the origins of society and government and included an analysis of the nature of servitude between master and servant. For Aristotle, the domestic slave was defined as 'merely the possession and property, or, as it were, the separable part of that master' to be used, not according to his own interest or caprice, 'but in subserviency to the general good, and suitably to reason'.[15] Likewise Aristotle defined the slave as a person 'naturally' fitted to such status:

Those men, therefore, whose powers are chiefly confined to the body, and whose principal excellence consists in affording bodily service; those, I say, are naturally slaves, because it is their interest to be so. They can obey reason, though they are unable to exercise it; and though different from tame animals, who are disciplined by means merely of their own sensations and appetites, they perform nearly the same tasks, and become the property of other men, because their safety requires it.[16]

Conversely, in his 'Essay Concerning the True Original, Extent, and End of Civil Government', the philosopher John Locke defined political power as a direct derivative of that state in which all men exist naturally, that is, 'a State of perfect Freedom to order their Actions, and dispose of their Possessions, and Persons as they think fit, within the bounds of the Law of Nature'.[17] According to Locke, man's natural state was one of equality, 'wherein all the Power and Jurisdiction is reciprocal, no one having more than another'.[18] Slavery was 'so vile and miserable an Estate of Man' and so directly opposed to the benevolent temper and spirit of the nation that it was 'hardly to be conceived, that an *Englishman*, much less a *Gentleman*, should plead for't'.[19] Since man, 'not having the power of his own life' could not enslave himself *to* any one, it followed that the natural liberty of man represented an inalienable freedom from absolute, arbitrary power.[20] No man had complete control over his own life, Locke argued, therefore no man could voluntarily deliver himself to the absolute power of another:

For a Man, not having the Power of his own Life, cannot, by Compact, or his own Consent, enslave himself to any one, nor put himself under the Absolute, Arbitrary Power of another, to take away his Life, when he pleases. No body can give more Power than he has himself; and he that cannot take away his own Life, cannot give another Power over it . . . This is the perfect condition of Slavery, which is nothing else, but the State of War continued, between a lawful Conquerour, and a Captive.[21]

However, as an investor in the Royal African Company and as a draftsman of the 1699 Constitution of Carolina, a text which prescribed the power of freemen *over* that of slaves, Locke's position was deeply ambiguous. Indeed, it was only by locating slavery *outside* the social contract that Locke could reconcile his belief in man's inalienable rights over his person to concepts of cultural inferiority.[22]

In 1748, the French philosopher Baron Montesquieu, Charles Louis du Secondat, published his *De l'espirit des lois* (1748), a work which ridiculed many of the conventional justifications for the enslavement of Africans.[23] The premise of Montesquieu's thesis, published in London in 1750 as *The Spirit of Laws*, was founded upon a deep rooted conviction in the existence of some underlying order (or 'law') within the social world, a system which paralleled the laws of nature. According to Montesquieu, the 'spirit' of a given system – that is, its common character or general disposition – was essentially interrelated to the complex conditions which allowed such laws – political, international, religious and otherwise – to arise. In the posthumous edition of 1756, the antislavery element of Book xv of *The Spirit of Laws* was reinforced and extended by means of an additional chapter. Slavery was classified as 'contrary to the spirit of the constitution', contravening the doctrines of natural law and liberal democracy in the sense that it served merely to give citizens a power and a luxury to which they were not entitled and deprived slaves of the opportunity to act independently. Yet even in the 1750 edition the antislavery momentum was clearly identifiable:

The state of slavery is bad of its own nature: it is neither useful to the master nor to the slave; not to the slave, because he can do nothing thro' a motive of virtue; not to the master, because he contracts all manner of bad habits with his slaves, he accustoms himself insensibly to the want of all moral virtues, he grows fierce, hasty, severe, choleric, voluptuous, and cruel.[24]

Although Montesquieu's remarks fell short of an unmitigated demand for abolition and suggested rather that in some circumstances slavery was a necessary evil, his work provided a suitable prototype for other eighteenth-century abolitionist texts. Furthermore, it hinted at the threat of rebellion presented by the slaves themselves and juxtaposed the deprived state of the slave's soul with the slave master's political and civil liberty:

> He sees the happiness of a society, of which he is not so much as a member; he sees the security of others fenced by laws, himself without protection. He sees his master has a soul, that can enlarge itself; while his own is constrained to submit to a continual depression . . . Nothing more assimilates a man to a beast, than living among freemen, himself a slave. Such people as these are the natural enemies of society, and their number must be dangerous . . . I would as soon say, that the right of slavery proceeds from the contempt of one nation for another, founded on a difference of customs.[25]

One of the most important, and indeed, the most persuasive counter-arguments to rational justifications of the slave trade resided in claims which advocated the *spiritual* potential of blacks. Whereas sociopolitical systems had defined slaves in terms of property and resisted the idea that slaves could obtain freedom by becoming Christians, others argued that since the Christian gospel was intended to be made available to *all* men, then blacks, although possibly culturally disadvantaged, were susceptible to the principal tenets of Christianity and, most importantly, to the workings of the spirit.[26] The dynamics of antislavery discourse thus emerged from a framework of spiritual salvation – a narrative which was used to prioritise a concern for the slaves' spiritual welfare and emphasise the potential spiritual deterioration of slave owners. Inspired by the arguments against slavery which had appeared in *The London Magazine* during the late 1730s, by Sir Hans Sloane's *A Voyage to the Islands Madera, Barbados, Nieves, S. Christophers and Jamaica* (1707) and the Royal Navy Surgeon, John Atkins' *A Voyage to Guinea, Brasil, and the West Indies in his Majesty's Ships the Swallow and Weymouth . . . With Remarks on the Gold, Ivory and Slave Trade* (1735), in 1755 the Scottish philosopher Francis Hutcheson published his *System of Moral Philosophy* (1755).[27] In this text, designed to 'unfold the several principles of the human mind as united in a moral constitution', Hutcheson declared that the aim of moral philosophy was to 'direct men to that course of action which tends most effectually to promote their greatest happiness and perfection'.[28] Hutcheson's *System* provided a detailed account of the ways in which slavery violated all sense of natural justice, Christian morality and any proper sense of liberty. Since no man was devoid of moral sense, nor of the desire for liberty, property and happiness, Hutcheson maintained that the slave trade contravened those very principles which had established each man as the 'natural proprietor of his own liberty':

The natural equality of men consists chiefly in this, that these natural rights belong equally to all . . . Every one is a part of that great system, whose greatest interest is intended by all the laws of *God* and nature. These laws prohibit the greatest or wisest of mankind to inflict any misery on the meanest, or to deprive them of any of their natural rights, or innocent acquisitions, when no publick interest requires it.[29]

Furthermore, Hutcheson identified the natural rights of each individual as a right to life, 'the connate desire of life and self-preservation' which existed alongside man's natural desire for happiness and an instinctive condemnation of any cruelty directed towards his fellow men.[30] In opposition to Aristotle's theory of innate principles, therefore, Hutcheson argued that since *all* men possessed an overpowering desire for liberty and a profound understanding of the concepts of property and justice, then neither natural nor acquired rights could give one the right to assume absolute power over others:

We must therefore conclude, that no endowments, natural or acquired, can give a perfect right to assume power over others, without their consent . . . This is intended against the doctrine of Aristotle, and some others of the antients, 'that some men are naturally slaves, of low genius but great bodily strength for labour'.[31]

According to Hutcheson, no men were born 'natural slaves', since despite their difference from each other in terms of wisdom, virtue, beauty or strength, 'the lowest of them, who have the use of reason, differ in this from the brutes, that by forethought and reflection they are capable of incomparably greater happiness or misery'.[32]

Five years later, in 1760, the Scottish jurist George Wallace published his *System of the Principles of the Law of Scotland*, a radical text which identified the doctrine of slavery as being 'so contrary to the feelings of humanity' as to make it incompatible with the Law of Scotland: 'I take it to be undeniable, that every man is born equal to every other . . . Hence Liberty is said to be a *natural* faculty, *naturalis faculdas*; and slavery is said not only to owe its original to the arbitrary constitutions of men but to be *contrary to nature*'.[33] Wallace's text, published twelve years before Lord Mansfield's famous verdict of 1772, identified slavery as an inhuman and unlawful institution and called for its abolition. Slavery, he argued, was neither essential to the subsistence of society, nor conducive to the happiness or well-being of society; rather, it introduced 'the greatest possible inequality among mankind' by stripping innocent members of society of all the property they owned and denying them spiritual potential:

It subjects them entirely to the dominion of their masters; it exposes them to all the insults, torture, cruelty, and hard usage, which inhumanity, avarice, pride and caprice can suggest: It makes the bulk of mankind dependent on the few . . . Are not slaves, as well as others, men? Have they not human souls, human faculties, and human passions? . . . I abhor the principles, upon which it [slavery] is either justified or founded.[34]

Moreover, Wallace suggested that Britain's continuing support of the slave trade was detrimental to its progressive (and hence spiritual) development: 'Set the Niggers free, and, in a few generations, this vast and fertile continent [Africa] would be crowded with inhabitants; learning, arts, and every thing would flourish among them'.[35]

Wallace's denunciation of slavery was later reiterated in the pamphlet published by the English-born Quaker, Antony Benezet. Benezet's *A Short Account of That Part of Africa Inhabited by Negroes* (1762), a text reprinted on both sides of the Atlantic, presented a series of essays directed exclusively towards the discourse of slavery, which contested the prejudiced misrepresentations of Africa advanced in the works by Michel Adanson, William Bosman and William Smith.[36] In his subsequent, comprehensive work, *Some Historical Account of Guinea* (1771), Benezet endeavoured to expose the iniquity of the slave trade and its 'inconsistency with every Christian and moral virtue'.[37] Heavily influenced by his Quaker upbringing, Benezet insisted upon the spiritual and intellectual equality of the Africans and criticised the devastating impact of Europeans upon the African continent:

Let the opulent planter or merchant prove that his Negroe slave is not his brother; or that he is not his neighbour, in the scripture sense of these appellations; and if he is not able to do so, how will he justify the buying and selling of his brethren, as if they were of no more consideration than his cattle? . . . Let him diligently consider whether there will not always remain to the slave a *superior* property or right . . . [that] which was given him by God, and which none but the giver can justly claim.[38]

In the introduction to his text, Benezet identified the purpose of his *Short Account* as a counter-argument to common vindications of the trade which had claimed that slavery had arisen from a natural desire to save the lives of African prisoners of tribal warfare who would otherwise have been 'sacrificed to the implacable revenge of their conquerors'.[39] In his *A Caution and Warning to Great Britain and Her Colonies, in a Short Representation of the Calamitous State of the Enslaved Negroes in the British Dominions* (1766), a work which collated the antislavery agenda of various authors and reiterated the claims made by George Wallace in his *System of the Principles of the Laws of Scotland* concerning the inalienable rights of liberty – 'To declare him[self] free – this is the law of nature, which is obligatory in all men, at all times, and in all places' – Benezet extended his narrative of spiritual development to produce a critique of the influence of slavery upon the spiritual status of planters and colonialists alike.[40] In this text he listed some of the most undesirable consequences of the trade, including the destruction of natural bonds of affection, 'whereby mankind in general love are united', the debauchment of morals and most importantly, the deterioration of the institution of marriage amongst Europeans resident in the British Dominion: 'Europeans forgetful of their duty, as men, and Christians . . . have led them [the negroes] into excess, into drunkenness, debauchery and avarice'.[41]

In his work, *A Philosophical and Political History of the Settlements and Trade of the Europeans in the East and West Indies* (1776), Benezet's friend and correspondent, Guillaume Raynal, condemned slavery's denial of the tenets of humanity, reason and justice:

He who supports the system of slavery is the enemy of the whole human race. He divides it into two societies of legal assassins; the oppressors and the oppressed. It is the same thing as proclaiming to the world, If you would preserve your life, instantly take away mine, for I want to have yours . . . My blood rises at these horrid images. I detest, I abhor the human species, made up only of victims and executioners, and if it is never to become better, may it be annihilated![42]

Drawing on drafts from several authors, including the radical utopian abolitionist and socialist, Jean de Pechmeja, Raynal's text went through fifty-five editions during the first thirty years of publication and was translated into five languages. His condemnation of slavery skilfully combined a detailed critique of Anglo-American territorial expansionism and British imperialism:

Slaves are to the commerce of Europeans in Africa, what gold is in the commerce we carry on in the New World. The heads of the Negroes represent the stock of the state of Guinea. Every day this stock is carried off, and nothing is left them, but articles of consumption.[43]

In anticipation of the mass slave revolt in St Domingue in 1791, Raynal's text identified the slaves' potential to precipitate a radical transformation of their condition and determine their own historical 'narratives':

Sooner or later, will any people, made desparate by tyranny, or the oppression of conquerors, always get the better of numerous and well-disciplined armies; if they have but resolution enough to endure hunger rather than the yoke, to die rather than live in bondage, and if they chuse to see their nation extinct rather than enslaved.[44]

Indeed Raynal's call was not without precedent: slave conspiracies and revolts, especially on the large estates of Jamaica, had already begun to unsettle the imposed social order of the slave colonies. In 1760–1761, during what became known as 'Tacky's Revolt', 400 slaves rebelled in St Mary's Parish on the north coast of Jamaica, an uprising which resulted in the execution of about 400 suspected slave rebels and the deportation of 500 others to British colonies.[45] Later slave insurrections included Gabriel Prossere's revolt in Virginia (1800), Bussa's rebellion in Barbados in 1816, Denmark Vesey's revolt in South Carolina (1822), the slave rebellion in Demerara (1823) and Nat Turner's revolt in Virginia (1831).

In the same year that witnessed the publication of Raynal's influential text and the American Declaration of Independence, Adam Smith's *Inquiry into the Nature and Causes of the Wealth of Nations* (1776) presented a powerful challenge to colonial slavery, premised on an argument which prioritised the productive superiority of free labour. According to Smith, slavery was an inefficient system of production: since slaves had no prospect of acquiring property, they possessed no real incentive to work. According to Smith, the establishment of international commerce, and hence the abolition of slavery, would augment the wealth of the British nation to unprecedented proportions:

The rulers of Great Britain have for more than a century past, amused the people with the imagination that they possessed a great empire on the west side of the Atlantic. This empire, however, has hitherto existed in imagination only. It has hitherto been, not an empire, but the project of an empire; not a gold mine, but the project of a gold mine; a project which has cost, which continues to cost, and which if pursued in the same way as it has been hitherto, is likely to cost immense expence, without being likely to bring any profit; for the effects of the monopoly of the colony trade, it has been shewn are, to the great body of people, mere loss instead of profit.[46]

John Millar's *The Origin of the Distinction of Ranks* (1771) similarly presented a systematic denunciation of the slave trade, focused specifically upon the unprofitability of the institution and its incompatibility with industry, population and moral integrity. In the third edition of 1779, Millar condemned the slave trade as inconvenient and retrograde: 'No conclusion seems more certain than this, that men will commonly exert more activity when they work for their own benefit, than when they are compelled to labour for the benefit merely of another'.[47] Extending his analysis to the effects on slave owners, Millar further suggested that slavery was harmful to the 'good morals of a people', since the debasement of servants had a direct influence upon the 'temper and disposition' of masters.[48] This focus upon the relation between slaves and their masters, and indeeed, between Africa and Europe, was an important step in acknowledging the relationship between the two races.

Heavily influenced by the ideas of Montesquieu, *An Essay on the Nature and Immutability of Truth, in Opposition to Sophistry and Scepticism* (1771) by James Beattie, Professor of Moral Philosophy at the University of Aberdeen, exposed the fallacies inherent in Aristotle's and Hume's theories of racial inequality.[49] Countering both Hume's assertions that 'there *never was* a civilised nation of any other complexion than white, *nor even any individual* eminent either in action or speculation', and Aristotle's claims that 'men of little genius' were 'by nature destined to serve', Beattie attempted to close the cultural gap between Africa and Britain, claiming that the former was merely at an earlier stage of development:

The inhabitants of Great Britain and France were as savage two thousand years ago, as those of Africa and America are at this day. To civilise a nation, is a work which it requires a long time to accomplish. And one may as well say of an infant, that he can never become a man, as of a nation now barbarous, that it never can be civilised.[50]

In keeping with this vindication Beattie argued that African cultural artifacts demonstrated a high level of creative invention which 'even Europeans would find . . . no easy matter to imitate'. More importantly, he celebrated the 'unwearied perseverance' of those enlightened persons who had vindicated the 'sacred rights of mankind':

Let it never be said, that slavery is countenanced by the bravest and most generous people on earth; by a people who are animated with that heroic passion, the love of liberty . . . [and] the unwearied, perseverance, in vindicating, at the expence of life and fortune, the sacred rights of mankind.[51]

Arguments outlined by moral philosophers such as Beattie, Hutcheson and Raynal disclosed the increasing antagonism between discourses founded upon concepts of slavery and those which emphasised man's natural rights to freedom. A key component of liberationist ideology, however, was the prioritisation of a narrative of individual autonomy alongside declarations of the *spiritual* equality of masters and slaves. The following section explores the multifarious development of the 'discourse of the spirit' within the sociopolitical context of England during the mid-eighteenth century; from its origins as a principal factor of radical dissenting Protestantism, its influence upon abolitionist and liberationist ideology, its mutant transformation via the literary works of slave narrators, Romantics and prophets alike and its success as a viable challenge to the legal and political agents of slave ideology.

ABOLITION AND RADICAL DISSENTING PROTESTANTISM

While condemnations of slavery were premised upon inalienable rights of liberty and concepts of spiritual equality, the Church of England as an institution remained defiantly impervious to growing antislavery agitation. Consequently, during the early phase of abolitionist propaganda, religious protest in England and America emerged mainly from nonconformist groups such as the Quakers and Evangelical Methodists. The discourse of spiritual salvation and radical dissent advanced by these groups provided a powerful rhetoric of liberation, the central features of which strategically influenced the success of the abolitionist movement during the late eighteenth and early nineteenth centuries. As David Bebbington notes in his study of the development of Protestant Christianity in modern Britain and America, 1734 witnessed one of the most important developments in the history of dissenting Protestantism, with the emergence of Evangelicalism and the success of the conversion and pastoral work of Jonathan Edwards at Northampton, Massachusetts during the spiritual revival of 1734–1735.[52] Linked with the Puritan movement of the sixteenth century, this form of religious dissent emphasised the dynamics of conversion (the concept of 'new' birth), biblicism (a reliance on the Bible as the ultimate religious authority), crucicentrism (a focus on Christ's redeeming work) and activism (an energetic approach to religious duties and social involvement), and ultimately became known as Evangelicalism.[53] Amongst its chief proponents were the American theologian and philosopher, Jonathan Edwards (1703–1758), the English clergyman and founder of Methodism, John Wesley (1703–1791) and the English evangelist and itinerant revivalist, George Whitefield (1714–1770).

From the earliest stages of its history, Methodism was a transatlantic phenomenon. Representatives of the evangelical movement, including John Wesley and George Whitefield, crisscrossed the Atlantic during a fertile period of exchange and reassessment. In 1729, Jonathan Edwards became a full minister in Northampton, New England. During the winter of that year his congregation experienced an extraordinarily intense crescendo of religious zeal, accounts of which spread to other communities throughout the American colonies and to Great Britain.[54] This religious fervour, which made Edwards something of a celebrity, was, however, short-lived. Its revival was reinstigated with the arrival of the enigmatic preacher, George Whitefield, who received his ordination in England in 1738 and who was inspired by the missionary labours of the Wesley brothers (John and Charles) in the newly founded colony of Georgia, North America. Preaching in open fields, Whitefield criticised the national clergy and claimed that he himself was a recipient of direct guidance from the Holy Spirit. Whitefield's mode of itinerant preaching and persuasive powers of oratory influenced scores of ministers and established the revivalist period of 'Great Awakening' wherein emotional outbursts were identified as the work of God's spirit and the harbingers of a millennial age. Whitefield, however, approved of black slavery and kept slaves himself. In 1748, he with others, urged the trustees of Georgia to introduce slavery into the colony, arguing that without it, Georgia would 'never prosper'.[55]

John Wesley, ordained in 1725, had served as his father's curate in Lincolnshire before taking over the leadership of a religious study group known as the 'Methodists'. In 1735 he agreed to assume spiritual leadership of the new colony of Georgia and from the time of his own spiritual experience of May 1738, a moment during which he claimed he felt his heart 'strangely warmed' ('An assurance was given me that He had taken away *my* sins, even *mine*, and saved *me* from the law of sin and death'), Wesley's wide-ranging missionary zeal took him to Oxford, London and Bristol, Wales, Cornwall and Scotland and Ireland.[56] Although Wesley claimed that he had set out to *revive* the spiritual life of the Church of England, his 'Methodism' quickly took on a character of its own and his preaching of 'salvation by faith' succeeded in establishing an independent 'connexion' of itinerant preachers and churches.[57] Wesley's style of preaching transgressed eighteenth-century taboos against extemporary prayer and lay-leadership and promoted a 'plain-style' of oral preaching.[58] As he commented in a sermon of 1746, this mode of plain-speaking translated into text was an attempt to write 'as I generally speak, *ad populum*, to the bulk of mankind'.

I design plain truth for plain people . . . I labour to avoid all words which are not easy to be understood, all which are not used in common life . . . I am persuaded that, on the one hand, this may be a means of enabling me more clearly to express the sentiments of my heart . . . without entangling myself with those of other men . . . I am not afraid to lay open what have been the inmost thoughts of my heart . . . I am a spirit come from God and returning to God.[59]

In terms of its immediacy and accessibility, Wesley's emphasis on plain oracy and self-reflection provided an important model for literary expressions of identity employed by Methodists, Romantics and slaves alike.

QUAKERS AND SHAKERS

The Religious Society of Friends, or 'Quakers' as they were called by their first leader, George Fox, emerged in seventeenth-century England and America, during the Puritan Commonwealth under Oliver Cromwell, as an inward intensification of the radical and spiritual forms of Puritanism. According to Fox, within all men, including heathens, there resided a principle of God capable of leading one to salvation. A central feature of Quakerism therefore was its concern with personal conviction and the possibility of 'truth' inwardly revealed. For Fox, Quakerism embodied a 'spiritual move-ment', a movement which highlighted the innate capacity of the human soul and advocated a belief in the purely inward nature of true baptism and communion, and the fulfilment of biblical events within the duration of an individual's lifetime. Influential Quaker theological texts included George Fox's *Journal, or an Historical Account of the Life, Travels, Sufferings, Christian Experience and Labour of Love in the Ministry of George Fox* (1694); John Woolman's *Journal of the Life, Gospel Labours and Christian Experience* (1776); William Penn's *No Cross, No Crown* (1669) and Robert Barclay's *Apology for the True Christian Divinity, As the Same is Held Forth by the Quakers* (1678).[60]

Across the Atlantic, the Philadelphian Quakers John Woolman and Anthony Benezet played a crucial role in persuading the Friends to disassociate themselves from both the slave trade and slaveholding itself. In 1753, the tailor and scribe Woolman made the assertive gesture of refusing to transcribe wills for those Quakers who intended to bequeath slave property. In a letter to the Philadelphia Society Yearly Meeting, Woolman rearticulated his concern over the Quakers' increasing involvement in slavery and published his text, *Some Considerations on the Keeping of Negroes* (Philadelphia, 1754) accordingly. In this tract, Woolman extended the Quaker concept of the brotherhood in Christ to a critique of slavery – 'To consider Mankind otherwise than Brethren . . . plainly supposes a Darkness in the understanding' – and in an even more radical gesture, coalesced the concept of salvation with that of the Divine's imminent deliverance of the slaves: '*Negroes* are our Fellow Creatures . . . The Parent of Mankind . . . gives deliverance to the oppressed'.[61] As a response to Woolman's text and his criticism, the Philadelphia Society sanctioned a motion prohibiting slaveholders from acquiring positions of authority within the Church, a move that was similarly supported by the London Quakers in 1761. This strategic severance from slave ideology in the context of spiritual guidance played an important role in Woolman's autobiographical *A Journal of the Life, Gospel Labours and Christian Experience of that Faithful Minister of Jesus Christ, John Woolman* (1776), a text in which the expression of identity was fused with literary and polemical tactics. In this text, Woolman described his personal spiritual development, including the visitations of what he termed his blessed 'experience of the goodness of God', and elucidated his ultimate rejection of the slave trade in terms of its incompatibility with Christianity – 'I said . . . that I believed Slave Keeping to be a practice inconsistent with the *Christian* religion'.[62] More importantly perhaps, the author ascribed the Pennsylvania and New Jersey Friends' resolution to actively withdraw themselves from the trade as a direct manifestation of spiritual guidance:

We . . . have found it to be our duty to cease from this national Contest productive of misery and Bloodshed, and submit our Cause to him . . . And we, through the gracious Dealings of the Lord our God, have had Experience of that Work which is carried in, 'not by *earthly* Might, nor by Power, but by my Spirit', saith the Lord of Hosts.[63]

In his tract, *The Case of Our Fellow-Creatures, the Oppressed Africans, Respectfully Recommended to the Serious Consideration of the Legislature of Great Britain* published in London in 1784, Anthony Benezet, speaking as a representative of the 'People called Quakers', similarly stressed the Society's obligation to 'bear a public testimony' against a species of oppression 'long exercised upon the natives of Africa'.[64] Benezet condemned the commercial motives of the English nation's 'system of tyranny' and argued that it would have been more in keeping with the 'avowed principles of Englishmen' had they advanced a national programme aimed at establishing the heathen's conversion to Christianity: 'to incline them to receive the glad tidings of the gospel'.[65] Although the underlying suggestion of Benezet's work prescribes an advancement of expansionist colonialism these 'Quaker' texts demonstrate the emergence of a significant strain of antislavery ideology set within the framework of radical dissenting Protestantism. In May 1783, Quakers in London presented a petition against the trade to the Houses of Parliament. In 1787, with the aid of members from other dissenting groups, the Quakers founded the Society for Effecting the Abolition of the Slave Trade, possibly because many Quaker families had profited substantially from their involvement in the trade and considered their participation in the abolitionist campaign a means of alleviating their guilt.[66]

One splinter group of the Quakers, known as the 'Shaking Quakers' or 'Shakers', highlighted a more enigmatic form of the Quaker commitment toward 'spiritual' regeneration. Led by two Quakers, Jane and James Wardley, who embraced the millennial teachings of the biblical prophets, the Shakers were established in Manchester in 1747. As their name implied, the Shakers encouraged uninhibited participation in their unstructured, emotional forms of worship and interpreted the spiritual visitation experienced during such meetings as confirmation of Christ's imminent second coming. Heralding celibacy as an essential requirement of salvation, the nucleus of the Shaker community moved to America in 1774. There, under the charismatic leadership of Anne Lee, a former Manchester

factory worker who had joined the Shakers at the age of twenty-
three, the Shakers set up a self-contained community in Watervleit,
New York. Although they never specifically aligned themselves to
any overt demands for abolition, the philosophical and practical
ideologies of the Shaker communities were essentially founded upon
a belief in sexual and racial equality and their belief in prophetic
forms of spiritual manifestation provided a more extreme articulation of the self-conscious expression characterised by radical dissenting Protestantism. Anticipating feminist critiques of religious
institutions, in 1778 Lee declared herself to be 'the first *Mother*, or
spiritual parent in the line of the female' within whom the 'Word'
dwelt spiritually, the 'second Eve' and second heir in the 'covenant
of life': 'I am *Anne the Word!*'. During the 1780s and 1790s, Shakerism
developed from being a charismatic movement to a structured
organisation, characterised by the tenets of communal ownership,
celibacy, pacifism and the establishment of parallel men and
women's orders.[67] By the time of the sect's peak in the 1800s, the
number of Shaker communities in America reached a total of
eighteen, each with approximately 6,000 members.[68]

THE SOCIETY FOR THE ABOLITION OF THE SLAVE TRADE

In August 1782, acting on behalf of the Quakers in that state, the
Philadelphia Meeting for Sufferings dispatched a letter to its London
counterpart, urging it to use its influence to bring about a cessation
of the slave trade. In the summer of 1783, the London Meeting for
Sufferings approved a petition calling on Parliament to declare the
slave trade illegal. In an effort to advance this cause, the London
Quakers set up two embryonic antislavery societies whose main task
over the next four years was to promote the antislavery campaign.
This they achieved through the distribution within the metropolis
and the provinces of abolitionist material and the circulation of
petitions and tracts, including Joseph Wood's *Thoughts on the Slavery of
the Negroes* (1786), Anthony Benezet's *A Caution and Warning to Great
Britain and her Colonies* (1766) and the London Meeting for Suffering's
own text, *The Cause of Our Fellow Creatures the Oppressed Africans*
(1784).[69]

Strategically limiting its attentions to the abolition of the slave
trade rather than the abolition of slavery itself, the Society for the
Abolition of the Slave Trade sought to establish active auxiliary

organisations throughout the country in order to supplement the financial support it received from the Quakers.[70] This strategy was championed by Thomas Clarkson's series of lecture tours during 1787–1788 and his collation of extensive information about the slave trade. Having interviewed over two thousand seamen and examined numerous shipholds and naval records, Clarkson presented his evidence to the Privy Council on 27 July 1788, thereby endeavouring to persuade the government to establish other forms of commerce in Africa.[71] Clarkson's lectures, together with the publication of *An Essay on Slavery and the Commerce of the Human Species* (1789) and *An Essay on the Impolicy of the African Slave Trade in Two Parts* (1788), launched the Abolition Society as a significant public campaign.[72] In his *Essay on Slavery*, Clarkson denounced the African trade as 'injustice and inhumane' while his *Essay on Impolicy* undertook to demonstrate that such a trade was as 'impolitick' as it was inefficient:

I shall shew first, that it is in the power of the planters, if they please, to do without fresh supplies from the coast: I shall then shew, that if the importation of slaves is prohibited, no such want will be found, but on the other hand, that the number of cultivators will *increase*; and, lastly, that both the planters, the slaves, and the islands, will be *benefited* by the change.[73]

Two essential elements informing the success of the Society's campaign were firstly, its *internationalist* agenda and secondly, its links with the increasingly popular tenets of radical dissenting Protestantism. The informal relationship which already existed between British and American abolitionists were consolidated by the Society's correspondence with the leading antislavery groups in Philadelphia and New York, and subsequently with the establishment of Les Amis des Noirs in Paris in 1788.[74] Hence the strength of the Society's parliamentary campaign lay essentially within its 'international' spiritual agenda as advanced by well-educated religious enthusiasts and political philanthropists, such as the Clapham Sect. These 'Saints', as they were also known, consisted of a group of Evangelical Anglicans led by William Wilberforce, who dedicated themselves to the urgent moral and spiritual issues ignored by institutionalised Anglicanism. Wilberforce's own religious conversion, inspired after his reading of Philip Doddridge's *Rise And Progress of Religion in the Soul* (1745), had occurred during his grand tour of the Continent in 1783. In that tract, Doddridge had defined religion as a spiritual 'sense of God on the Soul', an aspect of conscious self-reflection which

Wilberforce was to fuse with political activism.[75] Soon after his conversion, Wilberforce was introduced to Clarkson, a meeting which inspired Wilberforce's collaboration with the abolition committee and culminated in his representation of the African cause to Parliament. On 12 May 1789, therefore, having recovered from a serious illness, Wilberforce presented his first motion for abolition. During his three-hour long presentation, Wilberforce concentrated on the damnation effected by England's participation in the slave-trade, and thereby suggested that the nation's spiritual regeneration might be achieved by its severance from the trade:

We are all guilty – we ought all to plead guilty, and not to exculpate ourselves by throwing the blame on others . . . When we reflect it is we ourselves that have degraded them [the Africans] to that wretched brutishness and barbarity which we now plead as the justification of our guilt . . . What a mortification must we feel at having so long neglected to think of our guilt, or to attempt any reparation![76]

This extension of the 'discourse' of spiritual renewal, on both national and individual terms, was fundamental to the success of the abolition campaign. It formed a sophisticated progression of the focus upon self-examination and articulation popularised by radical dissenting Protestantism, yet maintained an infectious, zealous stance. It was, therefore, a complex strategy; and one consequence of this fusion of spiritual and liberationist discourse within a nationalist framework (a kind of national self-authentication) was the inauguration of a renewed zeal for missionary ideology.

JOHN WESLEY, METHODISM AND ABOLITION

As the son of the Anglican vicar, Samuel Wesley, and grandson of the famous Presbyterian divine, Samuel Annesley, John Wesley's birth-right metaphorically reunited the severance between Anglicans and Dissenters which had occurred at the beginning of the eighteenth century.[77] Raised by his mother as an *elect* son of the Puritans and instilled with his father's Anglican fear of the excesses of enthusiasm, John Wesley was sent to Charterhouse, then Oxford, and was finally ordained as a priest of the Church of England in 1728. At Oxford, Wesley became a member, and subsequently the leader, of a religious society which assembled on a regular basis to read the Greek Testament. Because of the rigorous intensity with which these individuals pursued their studies and performed their religious observances, this group of individuals became known collectively as the 'Methodists'. As a group, these Oxford Methodists did not advance any drastic reformation of the doctrines of the Church. They were, however, strongly opposed to the Calvinist doctrines of predestination and election. Moreover, and most important to the dissemination of the language and ideology of radical dissenting Protestantism, these Methodists placed a vital emphasis upon their belief in the individual's *personal* experience of God's perfecting grace, a trait which was to become a major structural feature of narratives (by slaves and others) which combined polemical tactics with literary expressions of identity.

Wesley's travels amongst the Moravians during a two-year trip to Georgia between 1735 and 1737 highlighted the fact that the English clergyman's own ministry had lacked the dynamic spark of personal salvation. On his return from a visit to the Moravian headquarters in Germany, therefore, Wesley succeeded in persuading other dissenting religious societies in England to adopt a modification of Moravian practice, which involved intense moments of spiritual experience witnessed by 'choirs' or units of around six people of the same sex and marital status.[78] In his essay 'On the Causes of Methodism' (1817), the essayist and critic William Hazlitt satirised the Methodist movement as a form of religion equipped with its own 'slobbering-gib and go-cart'. According to Hazlitt, the 'jargon and nonsense' of Methodism held a peculiar charm for all those who had an 'equal facility in sinning and repenting': 'It is a *carte blanche* for ignorance and folly!'[79] In addition, its proponents were characterised by their ability to 'soar' on the 'wings of divine love' and revel in 'a spiritual sea of boundless nonsense': 'To speak of them as they deserve, they are not well in the flesh, and therefore they take refuge in the spirit'.[80] As Hazlitt's satirical diatribe ironically suggests, the primary emphases of Methodist preaching lay upon the witness of spiritual visitation, the experience of salvation through faith and a belief in the possibility of personal triumph over temptation.[81] In his work, *The New Birth: A Sermon on John 3.7* (1784) Wesley described such a process as an instantaneous transformation of the soul wherein 'we are justified by the grace of God' and '*born of the Spirit*'.[82] Accordingly, his concept of the 'new birth' revolved around Pentecostal images of the descent of the mercurial, indeterminate, nebulous 'breath' of the spirit of God upon his chosen ones:

Being born *in sin*, we must be *born again* . . . But how must a man be born again? . . . *The wind bloweth where it listeth* . . . The precise manner how it begins and ends, rises and falls, no man can tell. *So is every one that is born of the Spirit.*[83]

Wesley was careful to distinguish the various stages of salvation, emphasising that whilst any man was capable of holiness ('grace'), his liberation from sin ('justification') could occur only following an intense period of inner struggle and contrition. Whilst 'sanctification' denoted the restoration of the soul to its original condition of 'liberty', the experience of 'new birth' initiated a conviction in the possibility rather than in the immediate achievement of sanctification.[84]

From the time of his conviction and the 'strange warming of his heart' in 1738, Wesley advanced his belief in salvation by faith by gathering around him an organised, itinerant Evangelical ministry, designed to supplement rather than supplant the role of the established Church.[85] Yet in his *Advice to the People Call'd Methodists* (1745), Wesley defined the Methodists as a 'new people' whose faith and love was wrought by the 'inward Witness' of the spirit of God: that 'Supernatural evidence . . . of things not seen'.[86] Similarly, in his *Character of a Methodist* (1743), Wesley called upon Methodists to live according to the 'method of the Bible' and to direct their lives in accordance with an habitual philanthropic disposition towards all men, a request which was to develop into a demand for blacks' liberation from enslavement:

As he [the Methodist] has Time, he does *Good unto All Men*, unto Neighbours and Strangers, Friends and Enemies. And that, in every possible Kind; not only to their Bodies, by *feeding the Hungry, cloathing the Naked, visiting those that are sick or in Prison*; but much more does he labour to do Good to their Souls, as of the Ability which GOD giveth.[87]

Furthermore, in a subtle critique of the authority of the national church, Wesley defined the written word of God as the 'only and sufficient rule' of belief:

We believe indeed, That *All Scripture is given by Inspiration of GOD*; and herein are we distinguished from *Jews, Turks and Infidels*. We believe this written Word of GOD to be the *Only and Sufficient* Rule, both of Christian Faith and Practice.[88]

With its emphasis on personal salvation made possible by the 'spirit of God', the concept of 'new birth' described by the Scriptures and promoted by Methodism fused easily with a discourse of *self-*

authorisation. In this way, the discourse of spiritual regeneration popularised by radical dissenting Protestants provided an important means of realising the self's unconditional liberation from prescribed socioeconomic boundaries. Moreover, the pragmatic individualism embraced by Methodism and other evangelical revivalist movements played a crucial role in the advancement of abolitionist demands.[89]

As noted in his journal entry of 12 February 1772, Wesley had encountered Anthony Benezet's work less than two years prior to the publication of his own *Thoughts Upon Slavery* (1774).[90] In this tract, widely distributed amongst Methodist societies, Wesley petitioned slaveholders, demanding that they improve their ways in order that they might receive salvation from God. By consolidating the evangelical motif with the plight of the slaves themselves, Wesley prophesied both their spiritual and physical salvation by God's divine providence: 'O burst thou all their chains in sunder; more especially the chains of their sins: Thou, O Saviour of all, make them free, that they may be free indeed!'[91] Wesley's *Thoughts Upon Slavery* presented a powerful critique of the slave ideology upheld in the colonies and condemned what he defined as 'unjust' colonial statutes which legitimised the murder of runaway slaves by any means that a slaveholder thought fit. For Wesley, such legislation contravened the concept of 'natural justice' as defined by Lord Mansfield's ruling, whilst slavery transgressed the 'very principles upon which all sales are founded' since 'no equivalent can be given for life or Liberty'.[92] Wesley's abolitionist text therefore pronounced the superiority of a *divine* system of justice at odds with plantation jurisprudence:

Notwithstanding ten thousand Laws, right is right, and wrong is wrong still . . . Where is the Justice of inflicting the severest evils, on those that have done us no wrong? . . . Of tearing them from their native country, and depriving them of liberty itself?[93]

Since England's economic advancement had been gained from the profits of the slave trade, it carried with it an even higher price, the 'violation of Justice, Mercy and Truth', as determined by God's will:

It were better that all those Islands should remain uncultivated for ever . . . than they should be cultivated at so high a price . . . Liberty is the right of every human creature, as soon as he breathes the vital air. And no human law can deprive him of that right, which he derives from the law of nature.[94]

On a similar note, Wilberforce's *Letter on the Abolition of the Slave Trade to the Freeholders and Other Inhabitants of Yorkshire* (1807) concluded:

Is it not utterly astonishing, that Great Britain should have been one of the prime agents in carrying on this trade of blood? . . . We must believe that a continued course of wickedness, oppression, and cruelty. . . must infallibly bring down upon us the heaviest judgements of the Almighty. . . It cannot be denied, that these are circumstances in the situation of this country, which, reasoning from experience, we must call marks of a *declining empire*, but we have, as I firmly believe, the means within ourselves of arresting the progress of this decline.[95]

Methodism's critique of the slave trade as propounded by Wesley and his followers attracted significant support from other non-conformist sects within the various American colonies and provided an adaptable template of liberationist demands, a template that was later reshaped by others including the slaves themselves. In this way, Methodism distinguished itself from other Evangelical sects which maintained the Calvinistic doctrine of election.[96] In his auto-biographical text, the enigmatic revivalist preacher, George White-field described the 'early Movings of the blessed Spirit' upon his heart, his liberation from sensual appetite and his deliverance by the 'Spirit of God': 'God spake to me by his Spirit, and I was no longer dumb'.[97] The publication of Whitefield's 'Letter to the Inhabitants of Virginia, Maryland, North and South Carolina, Concerning Their Negroes' articulated the preacher's unambiguous denuncia-tion of slave abuse within the context of theological debate: 'I must inform you in the Meekness and Gentleness of Christ, that I think God has a Quarrel with you for your Abuse of and Cruelty to the poor Negroes'.[98] Not suprisingly, Whitefield's proposals were met with vehement attacks from various quarters, including the Bishop of London's (Edmund Gibson's) *Short Preservative Against the Doctrines Rev'd by Mr. Whitefield and his Adherents* (1739) and Tristam Land's *Letter to the Revd Mr. Whitefield Designed to Correct His Mistaken Account of Regeneration, or the New Birth* (1739).[99] Yet Whitefield's text did not, however, articulate any radical demands for abolition; rather, it advanced a definition of blacks as the spiritual equals of their white masters and therefore worthy of conversion:

Enslaving or misusing their [the slaves'] Bodies would, comparatively speaking, be an inconsiderable Evil, was proper care taken of their Souls. But I have great Reason to believe, that most of you, on Purpose, keep your

Negroes ignorant of Christianity. . . I believe . . . these despised Slaves will find the Gospel of Christ to be the Power of God to their Salvation.[100]

By targeting the more vulnerable issue of the conditions of the slaves rather than slavery itself, British and American abolitionists such as Whitefield avoided any serious conflict over the sensitive issue of private property. Rather, they promoted a revised image of the nation's role as 'liberator' of the slaves from spiritual darkness. As a consequence, the Society for the Abolition of the Slave Trade issued a public disclaimer in 1788 which stipulated that the abolition of slavery had 'never formed any part of the Plan of this Society'. Instead the Society insisted that slaves would be treated more humanely if the trade were abolished and the price of slaves increased.[101] Similarly, in his two-volume work, *The History of the Rise, Progress, and Accomplishment of the Abolition of the African Slave Trade by the British Parliament* (1808), Thomas Clarkson reiterated the Society's strategic concern for plantation owners and its distinction between 'the evil of the Slave trade' and 'the evil of slavery itself':

By aiming at the abolition of the Slave-trade, they [the Committee] were *laying the axe at the very root*. By doing this, and this only, they would not incur the objection, that they were meddling with the property of the planters, *and letting loose an irritated race of beings*, who, in consequence of all the vices and infirmities, which a state of slavery entails upon those who undergo it, were *unfit for their freedom*.[102]

Nevertheless, the Quakers played a vital role in the abolition of the slave trade, contributing money, manpower and extremely effective ideas to the cause. On 25 March 1807, the resolution to 'take effectual measures for the abolition' of the trade was passed in both the House of Lords and the Commons. As a result, the Society for the Abolition of the Slave Trade was reformed as the African Institution, one of the primary aims of which was to establish alternative forms of legitimate commerce with Africa. It was not until more than a decade later that the struggle for the abolition of the slave trade developed into a movement abnegating slavery itself. Consequently, in 1823, the Society for the Mitigation and Gradual Abolition of Slavery throughout the British Dominions was formed. It was, however, a society dedicated not to the immediate emancipation of slaves, but to the advancement of *gradual* plans of emancipation and the protection of the slaves' welfare. In keeping with this, Wilberforce's *Appeal to the Religion, Justice and Humanity of the Inhabitants*

of the British Empire in Behalf of the Negro Slaves in the West Indies, declared
slavery a system of 'gross' injustice, 'heathenish irreligion and
immorality' and 'unprecedented degradation'.[103] The appeal was
met with much opposition, including Sir Henry William Martin's
Counter-Appeal in Answer to 'An Appeal' from William Wilberforce (1823)
which claimed that slavery was neither 'injust' nor 'displeasing to
God'; nor could it be 'safely or advantageously abolished in the West
Indies'.[104]

It was not until 14 May 1833 that slavery was finally deemed illegal
throughout the British colonies, with effect from the following year.
The protean discourse of radical dissenting Protestantism had
achieved a successful challenge to slave ideology, yet, as I shall
elucidate below, it also introduced revised forms of colonial expansionism, strategically premised upon the principles of missionary
ideology.

METAMORPHOSIS: THE DISCOURSE OF THE SPIRIT, MISSIONARY
IDEOLOGY AND THE DYNAMICS OF EMPIRE

Descend, bright Spirit of eternal Love
Illumine the dark corners of the earth! [105]

From the time of the crusades, Christian ideology endorsed a
classification of cultural 'otherness' in terms of spiritual deprivation
and inferiority. Taking its cue from the proselyte teachings of the
New Testament, where Jesus commanded his disciples to go and
'teach all nations, baptising them in the name of the Father, and of
the Son, and of the Holy Ghost', the advancement of Christianity
was often infused with missionary zeal.[106] During the late eighteenth
century this desire to propagate the Christian faith by missionary
enterprise was strategically combined with the scientific, ethnographical and commercial motives of colonial expansionism, a
process exemplified by the activities of the Sierra Leone
Company.[107] Indeed, on January 1, 1808, the day that slave-trading
became illegal, Sierra Leone, the British Colony for Ex-Slaves in
West Africa passed from the control of the Directors of the
Company to the British Crown.

Following the decision of the Court of the King's Bench over the
Somerset case of 1772, a significant number of blacks in England had
drifted into destitution and poverty. Similarly, the demobilisation of

blacks who had served with the British forces in the American War further augmented the number of poor blacks already resident in England.[108] In 1786, the year that the Society for Effecting the Abolition of the Slave Trade was founded, members of that Society formed an additional society under the leadership of Jonas Hanway. This 'Committee for the Relief of the Black Poor' was set up to discuss ideas concerning the resettlement of ex-slaves and the establishment of a missionary base for expeditions into the African interior. In the same year, the Committee published Henry Smeathman's manifesto, *Plan of a Settlement to Be Made Near Sierra Leona, on the Grain Coast of Africa* (1786).[109] In 1771, Smeathman had travelled to the Banana Islands off the coast of Sierra Leone, West Africa, in order to collect botanical specimens for Sir Joseph Banks' collection at Kew Gardens.[110] Smeathman's *Plan of a Settlement* outlined plans for the transportation and 'happy establishment of Blacks and People of Colour' in one of the most 'pleasant and fertile countries in the known world' under the direction of the British Government.[111] His text proposed that each repatriated black would be allowed, 'by common consent, to possess as much land' as he or she could cultivate in the mild and fertile climate of the country:

An opportunity so advantageous may perhaps never be offered to them [black persons, people of colour and refugees from America] again; for they and their prosperity may enjoy perfect freedom. Settled in a country congenial to their constitutions, and having the means, by moderate labour, of the most comfortable livelihood, they will find a certain and secure retreat from their former sufferings.[112]

For Clarkson, as for others, the Sierra Leone project presented an embryonic prototype of both a revised colonial plan and the means of establishing civilisation in Africa: those who were to settle there were to 'endeavour to establish a new species of commerce, and to promote cultivation in its neighbourhood by free labour'.[113] Having based his opinion of the Sierra Leone project from the accounts by Smeathman and the former slaver-resident, John Newton, Granville Sharp issued prospective emigrants (including poor blacks rounded up from the streets of London) with certificates to protect them against slave-traders. These documents were intended to guarantee the blacks' status as free citizens of the 'Colony of Sierra Leone or the Land of Freedom'.[114] With the development of schools and places of worship, Africa was to be freed from the vicious and barbarous effects of the slave trade so that it might 'be in a better state *to comprehend and receive the sublime truths of the Christian religion*.[115] Initially, Sharp's idea of forming a company on behalf of the settlers with the aid of his friends on the Relief Committee was met with hostility in Parliament. However, with a shift of emphasis from the philan-thropic concerns of the Sierra Leone Company to the commercial objectives of its directors, a Bill to incorporate the Company was passed in June 1791.[116] The success of this revised Bill indicated the mercurial interchange between abolitionist, missionary and colonial ideologies: not unlike plantocracy, Sierra Leone was to function as a Province of Freedom governed by absentees in England.

Reports discrediting the motives behind the Sierra Leone expedi-tion, however, dramatically undermined the original enthusiasm of the settlers, and by November 1786, of the 700 who had originally signed up, only 259 had boarded the departing vessels. At this point, the Committee persuaded the City authorities to round up any black beggars or destitute ex-slaves found on the streets, and under the command of Captain Thompson, the allotted 'repatriation' ships finally left London on 8 April 1787 with 350 black settlers.[117] Within three months of their arrival in Sierra Leone, one third of the prospective settlers had died: eighty-four as a result of the difficult voyage and the remainder from the effects of fever and dysentery to which they were exposed upon their arrival in the colony. Even when the relentless and unexpected rainy season ceased, early attempts to cultivate the land proved disastrous. The 'promised' land which Smeathman had declared to be sufficiently fertile to sustain a whole agricultural community proved in reality to be thinly covered with soil. However, both the author of the Sierra Leone plan and Captain Thompson claimed that the high mortality rate was due to the inadequacy of the settlers and in 1792, the Sierra Leone Company embarked on its second venture, which involved the transference of over 1,000 men and women of African descent from Nova Scotia.[118]

In her *Narrative of Two Voyages to the River Sierra Leone, During the Years 1791–1792–1793* (1794), Anna Maria Falconbridge, who in 1791 had accompanied her surgeon husband, Alexander Falconbridge, to Sierra Leone, dismissed the Clapham Sect's 'philanthropic' colonial plan as 'premature, hair-brained and ill-digested'.[119] As Moira Ferguson notes in her analysis of Falconbridge's text, her *Narrative* disclosed a proud commitment to abolition.[120] However, whereas Falconbridge's text presents a critique of the quiet alliance between colonial ideology and missionary enterprise – 'Be assured, however disinterested and friendly they [the British] appear at this moment, they are aiming at some selfish purposes' – her *Narrative* simultaneously reveals a destabilising fear of cultural 'subalterity' which threatened to undermine the legitimacy of her presence in Africa.[121] Hence, having witnessed the Africans' symbolic public burning of effigies of the 'radical' champions of the west, 'Mr. W-ll-ce and Tom Paine' – an act which she identifies as hideous, uncontrollable and anarchic – Falconbridge's *Narrative* concludes with a note of destabilised cultural hierarchy and deep-seated anxieties of insurrection. Dismissing her previous abolitionist tendencies as manifestations of her youthful naivety, Falconbridge reprioritises her former loyalties and (re)determines the slave trade as an evil 'necessary' for the development of Africa's sense of religious morality: 'I must think favourably of the Slave Trade, while those innate prejudices, *ignorance, superstition, and savageness, overspread Africa*'.[122] Therefore, although Falconbridge's text appears at times to transcend the restrictive requirements of colonial discourse and indeed, to reject stereotypical portrayals of Africans, her *Narrative* is informed by an overriding endeavour to locate the spiritual regeneration of Africa on distinctly western terms, a condition against which slaves were to struggle.

As Falconbridge's text suggests, by the turn of the century, the dynamics of missionary enterprise were often inseparable from the distinctly political aims of British imperial ideology. Following the establishment of the Sierra Leone Company, the Eclectic Society, whose members included John Newton and Richard Cecil, discussed ideas concerning the most efficient methods of propagating the gospel throughout Africa. As a result, the Baptist and London Missionary Society and the Society for Missions to Africa and the East (later the 'Church Missionary Society') were formed.[123] With the adaptation of Bell's 'national system' of education, the schools of the Church Missionary Society endeavoured to teach the principles of Evangelical Christianity and the virtue of hard work in Sierra Leone.[124] As Wilberforce's parliamentary debate of 22 June 1813 confirmed, these missionaries vigorously promoted Christian ideology as the only available pathway to spiritual and temporal well-being: 'That remedy, Sir, is Christianity . . . for Christianity assumes her true character . . . when she takes under her protection those poor degraded beings'.[125] Four decades later, in the preface accompanying his treatise, *A Brief History of the Wesleyan Missions on the Western Coast of Africa* (1851), William Fox defined Africa as a land of 'danger, of dissolution, and of death . . . with its brutal rites and ceremonies, its devil-worship [and] sanguinary superstition'.[126] For Fox, the 'history' of West Africa was primarily an account of the 'valuable lives' of those missionaries who had attempted to spread the 'blessings of a Saviour's love' among the numerous tribes living along the western coast.[127] Yet as these 'modern missionaries' functioned as 'successors of the apostles' they simultaneously advanced England's colonial sovereignty, 'the envy and admiration of the world':

> The 'signs' which have followed the labours of the missionaries of various denominations on the Western coast of Africa, are such as to warrant, not only the hope, but the absolute certainty, that . . . *results still more great and glorious will follow.*[128]

Thomas Coke's *History of the West Indies* (1808–1811) similarly translated the biblical concept of 'redemption' into a narrative delineating the mechanisms of colonial expansionism and the 'necessary' suppression of anti-imperial insurrections in the West Indies:

> *And yet it is to the gospel, that Great Britain, in all probability, stands indebted for the preservation of many of her richest colonial possessions* even to the present day; that her swarthy subjects have not revolted like those of a neighbouring island; and committed those depredations on the white inhabitants, which humanity even shudders to name.[129]

According to Coke, the 'benefits' which were to result from Britain's 'intercourse with distant parts', depended upon the establishment of a *civilised* state amongst the native inhabitants and their 'habitual indulgence' in violent passions.[130] In fact, in its account of the dissemination of the gospel of Jesus Christ, Coke's 'history' of the West Indies fuses territorial expansionism with missionary ideology by presenting a *sacred* history of those islands on revised Christian terms:

> But for the unerring page of *sacred History,* we should have known nothing of the conduct of God towards the human race . . . The origin of justice and of law would have been alike unknown; and our moral and intellectual condition would have been somewhat similar to that of the swarthy inhabitants of those islands which we are about to explore . . . History in general, may be considered as a science without which all others would be useless; and without much impropriety we may denominate it the *memory of the world.*[131]

Three decades later, Thomas Fowell Buxton's *The African Slave Trade and Its Remedy* (1839) emphasised the Christian missionaries' role in establishing the universal abolition of the slave trade. This narrative of abolition promoted a vision of England's redemptive role, rather than its culpability and envisaged a dissolution of the boundaries separating the distinct categories of 'legitimate commerce', agricultural development and Africa's conversion within a single, unified imperial schema: 'The merchant, the philanthropist, the patriot, and the Christian, may unite'.[132] Buxton's text effected a strategic translation of the embryonic prototype of spiritual regeneration into a 'mutant' discourse of national ideology, the 'deliverance' of a thousand nations under the 'divine' aegis of the British Empire:

A nobler achievement now invites us. I believe that Great Britain can, if she will, under the favour of the Almighty, confer a blessing on the human race. It may be that at her bidding *a thousand nations now steeped in wretchedness, in brutal ignorance, in devouring superstitions* . . . [shall] emerge from their debasement, enjoy a long life of blessings – education, agriculture, commerce, peace, industry and the wealth that springs from it; and, far above all, shall willingly receive that religion which, while it confers innumerable temporal blessings, opens the way to an eternal futurity of happiness.[133]

According to commentators such as Buxton, Britain's unquestionable responsibility had been to transform and redeem the African continent of its former cultural epistemologies: 'to take up the cause upon Christian grounds'. This discourse of spiritual regeneration on national colonialist terms was, however, ultimately dependent upon a genre of spiritual autobiography which emerged in the late eighteenth century under the influence of radical dissenting Protestantism. While Buxton's text envisaged the 'deliverance' (and indeed, the appropriation) of one culturally distinct nation by another, the autobiographical narratives reflected and resisted this paradigm of the self by the agency of an indeterminate, 'nebulous', spiritual other.

CHAPTER TWO

Radical dissent and spiritual autobiography
Joanna Southcott, John Newton and William Cowper

Taking their cue from the Puritan legacy of literary testimony and self-scrutiny in spiritual narratives such as John Bunyan's *Grace Abounding to the Chief of Sinners* (1666), Edward Taylor's *Spiritual Relation* (1679), and Increase and Cotton Mather's respective biographical accounts of 1670 and 1724, those authors in eighteenth-century England and America who felt impelled to record the workings of the divine upon their souls were predominantly recent converts to dissenting religious groups such as the Quakers, Methodists and Shakers.[1] Indeed, the founder of Methodism, John Wesley, specifically requested that itinerant preachers employed under his sanction should 'give him in writing an account of their personal history'. This would incorporate a detailed personalised account of their conversion, 'the circumstances under which they were led to minister the word of life' and the 'principal events connected with their public labours'.[2] In these composite forms of autobiographical testimony, select events from the author's past were singled out and posited within a framework of spiritual autobiography, the central features of which were to have a predominant influence on narratives by eighteenth-century dissenters, Romantics and Africans who had either escaped or managed to buy their freedom from slavery. Taking their lead from Wesley's famous 'Witness of the Spirit' sermon of April 1767, in which the Spirit of God was identified as an 'inward impression on the soul', these spiritual 'narratives' provided an important literary paradigm in their focus upon significant moments of conversion, spiritual rebirth and miraculous *liberation* from the sinful burden of the 'self'.[3]

The 'best' of these autobiographical testimonies, which originally appeared in *The Arminian Magazine*, were collected by Thomas Jackson and republished as *The Lives of the Early Methodist Preachers* (1837).[4] These conversion narratives by individuals such as John

Pritchard and Benjamin Rhodes presented details of the authors' 'self-examination' or soul-searching, commencing with recollections of childhood, accounts of various transgressions, repentance and finally, rededication to the service of God via the Pentecostal gifts of the Holy Spirit.[5] The dynamics of these 'spiritual' visitations were variously figured as evidence of the 'unspeakable joy' of God's extraordinary love and as moments witnessing the divine manifestation of gifts of tongues and of prophecy.[6] Moreover, as exemplified by the concluding narrative of *The Lives of the Early Methodist Preachers*, the 'spiritual' awakening of John Pritchard transcribed a complex process of metamorphosis, representing both a liberation from 'enslavement' and a *transformation* of spiritual sterility into ecstatic bliss:

I would not be yet healed, until I heard Mr. Jacob preach from these words, 'There is a river, the streams whereof shall make glad the city of God'. O, how did my heart bound! 'My chains fell off at a stroke! my soul was free; and found redemption, Lord, in thee!' My wilderness soul became a pleasant field, and my desert heart like the garden of the Lord; the promises flowed in upon me.[7]

The model informing these spiritual autobiographies lent itself to a variety of narratives of identity, polemic and dissent texts not included within Jackson's predominantly male collection of authors. Indeed, the immense popularity of this particular trope of discourse or mode of articulation rested upon its fundamentally heterogeneous and protean nature, a versatility which not only allowed but encouraged an indulgence in symbolic reading. As such, it authorised the articulation of disparate autobiographies, alternative fictions and lucid utterances of sociopolitical dissent in an acceptable form. This versatile schema of spiritual discourse not only endorsed an acceptable genre of autobiographical writing, but also strategically disclosed a paradigm of *paradox* in terms of the individual's configuration of identity. Hence, whereas the tightly structured framework of spiritual autobiography appeared to impose a strict codification upon the narrative, the spirit's descent upon the author marked a radical condition of excess and disorder, volatility and chaos. This powerful interplay between the self and a spiritual other simultaneously revealed the absolute loss of the individual self to another and the quintessential inauguration of that individual as an autonomous (and indeed, redeemed) being. In so doing, the 'spirit' was posited as an authoritative challenge to established mechanisms of control and sociopolitical orthodoxy. While appearing to observe the confines of acceptable discourse, the centre of these narratives of spiritual regeneration divulged a radical, autonomous self-evolution both from within and without the sociopolitical sphere, thus determining the 'spirit' as a volatile metaphor (or extension) of the individual's emergent self-consciousness and powerful dissent.

JOANNA SOUTHCOTT AND THE EVOLUTION OF FEMINISED
SPIRITUAL DISCOURSE

I live with Him – I see His face –
I go no more away.[8]

Within these narratives the acquisition of subjectivity or subject identity necessitated a form of creative resistance to the symbolic order. But 'subjectivity', as the term implies, not only denoted a philosophical or abstract ethical position but also a *subjection* to another's system – a voluntary adoption of subject positions to some other 'Absolute' Subject or Being.[9] For the radical prophets and slaves alike, this 'Absolute' Subject was defined as 'the' spirit. Submission to this authoritative entity relocated the self at the centre of the text/prophecy as nothingness, absence, a 'manifestation' of the concept of zero. However, by some curious and mystical process, subjection to the spirit initiated a power that was beyond, before and *within* the self. It was a discourse which identified the self as absolute 'presence' and demanded a transformation of societal boundaries. For those possessed by this spirit, the sentient body in possession inscribed an important form of cultural memory, power and dissent. Incorporated within the prophetic confessional writings and slave texts of the eighteenth century, the discourse of the spirit hence implicated a discourse of the self, a metaphysical thought system in which the self functioned as the first principle. In other words, it was a system in which the self was presented as the unimpeachable ground within which the whole hierarchy of meanings might be constructed.[10] For authors such as Joanna Southcott and Richard Brothers, excess in terms of literary language, fervour, prophecy, passion and obsession, signified an energy or volatility which troubled the boundaries of the dominant symbolic order – such as the law, state, church or patriarchal code. As a disruption of authoritarian discourse, the language of spiritual excess introduced a subversive or semiotic openness across the 'closed' symbolic order.[11]

Following on from the prophetic writings of the mid-seventeenth century, the discourse of the spirit embodied within the prophetic narratives and spiritual autobiographies of the eighteenth century presented vivid claims of hypostatic experience, inspired utterance, rhythmic rapture, literal and metaphysical mergings and an important prioritisation of the concept of the prophet as God's agent.[12] Such manifestations of 'supernatural' inspiration carried with them a subversive, millenarian content by their departure from the established political and religious order. Dreams and visions were identified in terms of their relation to the biblical prophecies of the Book of Daniel and Revelation, whilst the 'prophetic' individual was determined as a valid vehicle for divine authority and spiritual utterance. For women and slaves alike, the dynamic language of dreams, prophecy and spiritual/linguistic excess evoked an aura of performance which articulated and transformed their position of estrangement and isolation.[13] Responsibility for the narrative was never assumed by the 'speaker', but by the 'spirit' for whom the shaman performed or mediated.[14] It was a linguistic zone which 'spoke' of liberation from both socioeconomic and linguistic confinement; it was a 'speaking in tongues' which both described and prohibited entry into the secrets and mysteries of language.

At this point it is useful to refer to Kristeva's idea of the loss of the self in the intertextual experience and the semiotic/symbolic sites of articulation. For Kristeva, the discovery of the self depends on an act of submission to another – hence the bewilderment, confusion and terror of submission is a necessary condition of self-discovery and self-recognition. For the slaves, 'loss' of the self simultaneously denoted their submission to another culture and their reemergence and relocation as 'intertextual' selves oscillating between the narratives of Africa and the west. As the narrators (both slave and otherwise) of these spiritual autobiographies looked outward toward nature for signs of providential direction, they also looked inward in order to register the effects of the divine spirit upon their (past) lives. Autobiographical 'recollections' were therefore used to identify moments of divine intervention and forewarning which, according to these authors, had protected them from irreversible damnation and inaugurated their subsequent reorientation along the path of deliverance. In many cases, as with the Puritan narratives of the sixteenth and seventeenth century, the configuration of dreamscape provided a suitable framework for (apocalyptical) revelations of divine authority and radical critiques of the established order.[15] For the slaves, the language of dreams and visions proffered a displaced reference to spiritual possession characteristic of African belief systems.

If the language of salvation and prophetic narrative promoted by radical dissenting Protestantism provided a significant means of 'liberation' of some kind, it also provided an important means of identity formation and expression for eighteenth-century women. In its early years, Methodism did not object to the emergence of a female ministry, but rather encouraged an extended relationship with female ministers.[16] By the 1800s however, most Methodist organisations refused to recognise female 'spiritual' leadership, with the exception of the Primitive Methodists and the Bible Christians, a fact that makes the popularity of the Devonshire upholstress and domestic servant, Joanna Southcott, all the more remarkable. Born in 1750 and baptised at the parish church of Ottery St. Mary, in 1792 Joanna Southcott claimed that a mysterious Voice ('the Spirit of Prophecy') had informed her that she was to become the New Saviour, the 'woman cloth'd with the Sun' from the Book of Revelations, sent to redeem mankind from the Fall.[17] Joanna therefore presented herself to the various communities of Devon and London as the chosen prophetess, the 'second Eve' who had been selected by God to prophesy the end of Satan's reign on earth. Jeered at and ostracised by local Methodists, Southcott published a tract prophesying the approaching apocalypse, immediately prior to her departure for London. In this text, entitled *The Strange Effects of Faith; With Remarkable Prophecies, Made in 1792, of Things Which Are To Come: Also, Some Account of My Life* (1801–1802), Southcott outlined the emergence of a transgressively apocalyptic, distinctly female prophetic tradition, a declaration which for some confirmed her role as Wesley's successor and identified the speculative quality of her work as a radical critique of eighteenth-century forms of control, knowledge, opportunity and freedom:

Quench not the Spirit; despise not prophecy; for the time is come, that your women shall prophesy, your young men shall dream dreams, your old men shall see visions; for the day of the Lord is at hand.[18]

Within eighteen months and following an intense period of propagandising activity, 8,000 persons declared themselves Southcottian converts. By 1808, over 14,000 tokens of the Joannite, a folded slip of paper inscribed with Southcott's signature, had been purchased, a figure which in London alone had risen to some 100,000 by the time of her death in 1814.[19]

In the 'Preface' to her *Strange Effects of Faith*, Southcott expounded a radical revision of conventional spiritual autobiography on gender terms which, in its explicit defence of woman's spiritual equality, if not her superiority, inscribed radical proposals for social reform under the aegis of divine revelation. The text which followed fulfilled the structural requirements of the redemption narrative by tracing details of the author's visitations from the Holy Spirit, events which Southcott construed as unquestionable confirmations of her divine election:

The word of God is as a book that is sealed, so that neither the learned nor unlearned can read (that is to say, understand) it; for it was sealed up in the bosom of the Father, till he thought proper to break the seals, and reveal it to a *Woman*, as it is written in the Revelations.[20]

Similarly, Southcott described penetration by the Spirit as intense moments of possession, during which her own individuality was given over to another, as she was filled with divine power:

All of a sudden the Spirit entered in me with such power and fury, that my senses seemed lost; I felt as though I had power to shake the house down, and yet I felt as though I could walk in air, at the time the Spirit remained in me; but did not remember many words I said, as they were delivered with such fury that took my senses; but as soon as the Spirit had left me, I grew weak as before.[21]

Southcott's revisionary female theology implicitly challenged the established religious and patriarchal traditions of late eighteenth-century England and redetermined the female body as an important textual medium. Her claims to gnostic authority provided her with a means of transcending religious dogma while her own relationship with the 'spirit' compared favourably with that which had 'inspired all the Prophets' throughout the Bible: 'Without the Spirit I am nothing, without the Spirit I know nothing, and without the Spirit I can do nothing'.[22]

Taking her cue from the prognostic writings of Richard Brothers and other millennial authors, Southcott's *A Dispute Between the Woman and the Powers of Darkness* (1802) and *The Answer of the Lord to the Powers of Darkness* (1802) extended her claims for spiritual receptivity and elucidated the specific role of women within the fulfilment of the prophecies.[23] Prior to this, in his *Revealed Knowledge of the Prophecies and Times Wrote under the Direction of the Lord God, and Published by His Second in Command* (1794), Brothers, a retired naval captain, had prophesied the defeat of the monarchy and the ruin of the empire in a language which combined the 'combustible matter' of poor man's dissent with that of the paraphernalia of the Book of Revelation.[24] Like Southcott, Brothers declared that he had been selected as the true prophet who would lead the chosen ones toward the Promised Land:

The following are the words which the Lord God spoke to me in a vision, soon after I was commanded to write and make known his judgments, for the good of London and general benefit of all nations: – '*There is no other man under the whole heaven that I discover the errors of the Bible to, and reveal a knowledge how to correct them, so that they may be restored as they were in the beginning, but yourself.*'[25]

On 4 March 1795, Brothers was charged with 'unlawful. . . dissension and other disturbances within the realm'. From his confinement in a lunatic asylum, Brothers published his *Description of Jerusalem* (1801) a text which reiterated his self-identification as the preordained King and Restorer of the Hebrews and endeavoured to establish an intimate relationship between the Word of God and his own writings:

God commands me to write to you, and say, – *You see what I have published* – read it with attention, and treat it with respect; for *it is God's word* . . . When I am revealed, then indeed, we become an independent people, and the Hebrew language will be immediately adopted.[26]

As with Brothers, the appeal of Joanna Southcott's prophecies lay in their vivacious combination of desire for personal salvation, self-authorisation, prophetic idioms and critiques of the church and gentry.[27] Moreover, Southcott's textual defence, *A Communication Given to Joanna In Answer to Mr. Brothers' Last Book, Published the End of this Year, 1802* suggests that a deep sense of rivalry over prophetic dominance existed between these individuals. Yet the mercurial format of spiritual and prophetic discourse enabled a relatively unproblematic manifestation of their ideologically opposed schemas. Hence Southcott was able to determine her own power as a revised, and therefore more effective version, of her male predecessor's, and identify her own authority as proceeding from an internal rather than external source of spiritual power:

My heart was deeply wounded to hear read the blasphemy of this last book [by Richard Brothers] . . . But I was answered in the following manner . . . Prophecies have ceased in the manner they were given to the Prophets of old, *ever since* My coming into the world. For then I told them they should be warned by *the inward moving of My Spirit*: and by words being given, *like the sound of the wind*, that ye know not from whence it come, or whither it goeth . . . WOMAN is a type of ME! whose blood was shed for all men to bring the fruits of the spirit to man.[28]

Southcott's text redetermined the metaphorical 'bride' of Revelation as a physical, sociohistoric female entity: the author herself, whose arrival on earth had initiated a severance of womankind's connection with the curse of the Fall. By using the mechanisms of *spiritual* discourse to counter ideologies of female inferiority and sexual vulnerability based on *bodily* determinism, Southcott's counter-hegemonic narrative claimed that through her, women might be redeemed and granted their rightful position within the priesthood of believers.[29] The dream-framework of her narrative not only enabled the exposition of a resolutely female-based model of Christian redemption, but also endorsed a schema in which the discourse of the spirit was fused with an erotic discourse of the 'flesh'. Hence the autobiographical accounts of her 'visitations' by the spirit figured simultaneously as the physical gratifications of a divine lover who shared her bed:

She felt herself laying as it were, in Heaven, in the hands of the Lord . . . He arose, and turned himself backwards towards the feet of the bed . . . His hair was a flaxen colour, all in disorder around his face . . . his locks were wet like the dew of night, as though they had been taken out of a river. The collar of his shirt appeared unbuttoned, and the skin of his bosom appeared white as the driven snow. Such was the beauty of the heavenly figure that appeared before me in a disordered state . . . He put out one of his legs to me . . . [30]

Southcott's feminised and autobiographical exegesis of the Book of Revelation – 'And there appeared a great wonder in heaven: a woman clothed with the sun, and the moon under her feet; and upon her head a crown of twelve stars' – strategically reinstated the apocalyptical marriage within the erotic framework of the biblical

Song of Songs and redefined her own role as both Bride of Christ
and messenger of the Messiah's second coming:

When I came at first it was like man *alone* . . . I left it for my second coming
in the woman . . . to *complete* MY FATHER'S *will*; so must I come in the
body as *perfect* man at first, and in the SPIRIT at my second coming, I must
come *made of a woman*, made under the law to redeem those that were under
the Law.[31]

In an effort to ascertain the validity of Southcott's self-proclaimed
prophetic superiority, *A Warning to the Whole World from the Sealed
Prophecies of Joanna Southcott* (1804) sought to relocate the prophecies
fulfilled by 'The Book of Joanna' as the most recent 'addition' to the
Book of Revelation. It reported that on 19 January 1803, Southcott's
followers concluded unanimously that 'her Calling was of God'.[32] In
the seven-day 'trial' which took place during December, 1804 at
Neckinger House in Bermondsey, London, a court of twelve judges,
twelve jury men and twenty-four elders confirmed their continued
faith in Southcott's prophecies and the transcriptions of her spiritual
communications with the 'Spirit of the living Lord'.[33] The account
of the 'trial' recorded in *The Life and Prophecies of Joanna Southcott* (*c.*
1815) likened Southcott to Anne Lee, the spiritual leader of the
Shakers and presented her possession by the Spirit (she 'felt the
Spirit of the Lord enter within her') as a dissolution of Southcott's
individuality, a necessary precursor to her subsequent emergence as
an autonomous individual – 'she was as a giant refreshed with new
wine' – endowed with divine power: 'A woman is now visited by the
Sun of Righteousness, the Spirit of Truth'.[34]

As Southcott predicted in *The Strange Effects of Faith*, her alleged
powers of prophecy (and indeed, female self-determination) were
vehemently rejected by critics as blasphemous and false, and the
author accused of witchcraft:

> So if a Prophet is deny'd
>   Then say the Witch is come,
> Who can foretel what will befal;
>   I'm jesting now with man.
> After their manner I do speak,
>   As I have often done,
> But soon my fury it will break,
>   And to the purpose come.
> And then you'll find I am no witch,
>   Nor do the lines agree,

But when my hand begins to touch,
Your witchcraft you will see.[35]

Accordingly, in his *Remarkable Life, Entertaining History and Surprising Adventures of Joanna Southcott, The Prophetess* (1810), R. Hann identified Southcott's spirit of prophecy as 'a pretended Mission' of delusion.[36] Hann refuted Southcott's proclaimed visionary powers as 'hazardous and very dangerous' and contrary to the 'written word of God': 'I will further affirm, that whatever visions and dreams support Joanna's Mission, are not from God, because the doctrines that Joanna holds forth are diametrically opposed to the doctrines of the Gospel'.[37] Similarly, William Howard's *Letter to Joanna Southcott, the Pretended Prophetess* (1810) commenced with a warning to those 20,000 Christians who believed Southcott's 'seal' to be a passport to eternal bliss and that 'many false Prophets' were gone out into the World.[38]

Taking into account Wesley's (metaphorical) emphasis upon the 'new birth' of spiritual renewal, it is not surprising that Southcott grafted such images of regeneration on to a personalised account of biological reproduction. Hence, four years later, in 1814, following the publication of over sixty volumes of prophetic writing and the (profitable) results of numerous tours around the country, Southcott's *The Book of Wonders, Announcing the Coming of Shiloh with a Call to the Hebrews* (1814) announced the forthcoming birth of the New Messiah: 'Let us be glad and rejoice, and give honour to him; for the marriage of the Lamb is come and his wife hath made herself ready'.[39] According to Southcott, now that the spirit had brought woman to full perfection, 'equal with MAN', its seed had impregnated the female prophet and planted itself within her virgin womb, thus fulfilling the prophecy that a 'man-child', to be named Shiloh, would be brought forth to 'rule the nations with a rod of iron': 'As the woman bore ME into the world, so she shall bear the FRUITS of the SPIRIT, and the strongest testimony of ME'.[40] To all appearances, Joanna did indeed appear to be pregnant, a 'fact' suggested by the large number of gifts sent by her followers and 'confirmed' by seventeen of the twenty-one physicians who examined her. Joanna was in fact not pregnant but dying. The report of the autopsy which followed her death in December 1814 suggested however that 'no Visible appearance of disease' had been found sufficient to have occasioned her death. Her most ardent followers and severe critics were therefore left to debate the implications of her mysterious 'pregnancy', and the 'spiritual' rather than temporal birth of the Shiloh.[41]

Southcott's use of the 'spiritual narrative' underscores the highly pliable nature of such a discourse and its paradoxical transformation from a site of ethereal asexuality into a distinct radical framework of sexual discourse, female equality and anti-clerical critique. A similar use of the central structural features of radical dissenting Protestantism emerges from the lesser-known autobiographical narrative, *The Extraordinary Life and Christian Experience of Margaret Davidson, As Dictated By Herself* published in Dublin, 1782. In his preface to the *Extraordinary Life*, Edward Smyth explained that the text which followed would appear to some as the fanaticism of the 'defaming tongues of ungodly men'.[42] In its adherence to the requirements of spiritual autobiography, Davidson's narrative traces the author's various stages of spiritual development amidst adverse conditions, including her parents' refusal to allow her to attend Methodist meetings and their threats to commit her to the madhouse at Bedlam. Davidson's resolute desire to receive the Holy Spirit in spite of her suffering and emotional paralysis was, however, eventually rewarded: by an uninhibited salvation of her soul on the one hand – 'Oh the ecstasy of the joy I then felt!' – and more importantly perhaps, by her endowment of the *power of articulation* – the 'spirit of poetry' – on the other.[43] As Davidson's *Extraordinary Life* describes a curve of liberation from a confined and restricted environment, her newly gained freedom is symbolically reflected by her reinscription on to the limitless dimensions of the written page. As with Southcott's narrative, Davidson's 'spiritual' autobiography is by no means entirely isolated from a discourse of the body. As she narrates her successful escape from an attempted rape by an elderly neighbour, Davidson's discourse of the spirit advances a powerful challenge to her rapist's physical (patriarchal) superiority and fuses a narrative of sexual abuse with the dynamics of spiritual discourse: 'Being fast imprisoned in his arms, without a possibility, by my own strength, of getting free . . . I had no other weapon but the *Sword of the Spirit*'.[44]

For Margaret Davidson, the genre of spiritual autobiography clearly enabled a revised articulation of self-empowerment in its account of the preservation of the narrator's virginity from 'pollution' by the powerful agency of the Spirit. Conversely, however, the trope of female 'salvation' adopted within the little-known *Narrative of the Life of Miss Sophia Leece* (1820), recorded 'by' the Reverend Hugh

Stowell, achieves a very different resolution.[45] In this text, the dynamics of female self-empowerment are superseded by a framework of submission and self-erasure and a privileging of male-centred ideology. As the 'spirit' inscribes its presence upon the author's soul, individuality, autonomy and the power of articulation are obliterated as Miss Leece is affected by 'a solemnity of look and manner' which leaves her silent. The Reverend Stowell thus assumes editorial control, (re)writing and indeed, reclaiming the mechanisms of autobiography to advance a didactic tract of conditioned female duty: 'This awful sense of the Divine presence . . . gave serenity to her mind and stability to her conduct. Her views of the doctrines and duties of religion were remarkably correct'.[46] The Reverend's obituary to the 'saintly' young Miss Sophia prioritises a lesson in established sexual hierarchy to be absorbed by 'every class of females' who read his text, in terms of how they too may become 'heavenly in temper, patient in tribulation, holy in life, and happy in death'. Thus Leece's *Narrative* raises important questions over editorial control and audience expectation in relation to the role of spiritual autobiography: for whom were such texts written and why? Stowell's editorial reinscription of Miss Leece's spiritual narrative presents a process of double erasure, as he requests that his female readers similarly adopt the 'lovely features' of self-denial and submission which they have been contemplating.[47]

   While the above-mentioned texts demonstrate the expansion of spiritual disclosure on to diverse literary paradigms of female emancipation (and conversely, female servitude) these gender-orientated texts remain detached from any direct interrelationship with abolitionist demands. Other texts, however, such as John Newton's *An Authentic Narrative* (1764) and William Cowper's *The Task: A Poem in Six Books* (1785), witnessed the coalescence of abolitionist, liberationist ideology with the discourse of spiritual autobiography. As such, these texts occupy an important site in the development of Romantic ideology in that they anticipate the latter's (discrete) relationship with both radical dissenting Protestantism and England's involvement in the slave trade. As these texts reveal, this coalescence of antislavery concern and spiritual discourse was often far from unproblematic: the syntheses which frequently emerged disclosed an ambiguous relationship between the autobiographers' belief in spiritual equality and established schemas of cultural difference. However, in their detailed accounts of rites of passage and spiritual salvation, the work of Newton and Cowper provide important precursors to the rise of self-conscious and counter-hegemonic demands contained within the slave narratives.

In 1748, a former captain of the slave trade, John Newton, converted to evangelical Christianity and became Rector of St Mary Woolnoth. Sixteen years later, in 1764, Newton published his *An Authentic Narrative of Some Remarkable and Interesting Particulars in the Life of John Newton Communicated in a Series of Letters to the Reverend Mr. Haweis* (1764). In this narrative Newton traced the story of his adventurous life prior to and following his conversion and presented a narrative of spiritual salvation from a 'long series of dangers' by the agency and grace of Divine Providence: 'He delivered me from the pit of corruption, and cast all my aggravated sins behind his back'.[48] In the Preface to the work, the Reverend Haweis verified the authenticity of Newton's 'plain' narrative, claiming that he had asked the author to prepare a 'more connected account' of his extraordinary spiritual experiences. According to Haweis, Newton had originally had 'no intention' of publishing such a personal account.[49] Haweis' validation of the private thoughts presented in Newton's 'autobiographical narrative' (a similar emphasis often characterised the Prefaces to the slave narratives) and his focus upon its authenticity, simplicity and unworldly motives locates an important intertextual relationship between the 'authenticity' of autobiographical narrative and divine text. Almost two decades later, in his sermon 'The Nature of Spiritual Revelation, and who are Favoured with it' contained within his collection of *Letters, Sermons, and a Review of Ecclesiastical History* (1780), Newton offered a selective definition of the concept of 'truth'.[50] Posing the question, 'what are we to understand by revelation?', Newton identified revelation as the unveiling of designs hitherto 'neither heard nor thought of' on the one hand, and, as the disclosure of that which was *real and certain before, but unknown* on the other: 'Revelation is not the creation or invention of something new, but the manifestation of what was till then unknown'. For Newton, God's spirit possessed the power to break 'down the walls which prevented and confined' man's perception of truth and thereby reveal 'new' and 'unthought-of prospect[s]'.[51]

The design of Newton's *Authentic Narrative* (presented as a series of letters) resituates the biblical paradigm of pilgrimage, intention ('They frequently lost sight of God's gracious purposes in their favour'), and deliverance (as exemplified by the Israelites' escape from Egypt and their arrival in the promised land) within an autobiographical narrative of spiritual salvation: 'There was a future happy time drawing near, when their journey and warfare should be finished; that they should soon be put in possession of the promised land, and have rest from all their fears and troubles'.[52] In the letter of 12 January 1763 which begins the *Authentic Narrative*, Newton paraphrases the promise of salvation made to the Israelites (Deut. 8: 2) which had prefaced Bunyan's *The Pilgrim's Progress: From this World, to that which is to Come: Delivered under the Similitude of a Dream*:

They were then in the wilderness, surrounded with difficulties [and yet] they should soon be put in *possession of the promised land*, and have rest from all their fears and troubles; and then it would give them pleasure to *look back upon* what they now found so uneasy to bear.[53]

This formulaic emphasis upon pilgrimage as recorded in the scriptures describes the spiritual journey of the soul, its departure from a barren 'wilderness' and its movement towards the salvation contained within the promised land. In its response to the requisite framework of spiritual autobiography, Newton's text delineates a complex interrelation between autobiographical text and scriptural text, past and present self. Whereas the linear narrative is continuously interrupted by retrograde moments of spiritual degeneration, the progressive momentum of the design is never entirely forsaken:

If we look upon the years of our past life . . . if we consider how wonderfully one thing has been connected with another . . . incidents which we thought hardly worth our notice . . . when we compare and consider these things by the light afforded us in the holy Scripture, we may collect indisputable proof . . . [that] God watches over his people from the earliest moment of their life, over-rules and guards them through all their wanderings.[54]

Yet as Newton's text suggests, an individual's spiritual pilgrimage is fundamentally 'unknowable': the sequence of events and impressions which presents Newton with a '*knowledge of Him*' is essentially a 'way' he knows 'not'.[55] Witness of God's grace and providence inaugurates a penetration of knowledge, or 'truth' that is otherwise impenetrable. For Newton, the development of the 'spiritual self' or what he terms 'the Lord's dealings with me', involves the witness and *articulation* of that which is complex and obscure. Therefore, the discourse of the spirit manifested in Newton's text registers the shortcomings of language within the parameters of autobiographical and historical narrative: that is, 'the great difficulty of writing properly where the *Self* is concerned'.[56] It is a 'difficulty' which paradoxically validates and undermines the status of autobiographical narrative and its reliance upon structural design. As with other spiritual autobiographies, it is a difficulty partially resolved by the author's relocation of the discourse of the *self* to the realms of dreamscape and prophecy:

Those who acknowledge scripture, will allow that there have been monitory and supernatural dreams, evident communications from heaven, either directing or foretelling future events.[57]

Recalling his spiritual heritage as the only son of dissenting parents, Newton, pre-empting Wordsworth's concept of 'spots of time', recollects the importance of his memories of 'valuable pieces, chapters and portions of scripture, catechisms, hymns and poems' which return 'again and again' to restore and sustain his spiritual self.[58] Interestingly, whilst these fragments of text maintain an important sense of self, Newton's spiritual degeneration is also identified as having emerged from a textual source: according to Newton, it was the second volume of Lord Shaftesbury's *Characteristics* which 'seduced' and deluded him with pseudo-beliefs: 'I loved sin, and was unwilling to forsake it . . . my simple heart was beguiled'.[59] The autobiographical account of the author's maritime adventures provide a second site of transgression, yet his participation in the slave trade is not specifically identified as a source of spiritual decline. As with the slave narratives, the sea determines a site of isolation and severance from established beliefs. Newton's 'violent and commanding passion' for the daughter of his late mother's friend (an infatuation disclosed neither to the female herself, nor to his friends) is discerned as the cause of his abandonment of all sense of religion and his 'remonstrances of conscience and prudence', a displacement which decentres the focus on his activities as a slave-trader.[60]

According to the *Authentic Narrative*, Newton's 'large strides towards a total apostasy from God' are checked by the forceful impressions of a prophetic dream in which he is given charge of a ring which he is told would bring him happiness. Doubting its powers, Newton rejects this gift and throws it back into the water: 'No sooner [had it] touched [the water], than I saw, the same instant, a terrible fire burst out from a range of the mountains'.[61] Newton interprets this as a visual narrative of his spiritual malaise and rejection of God's mercy ('I perceived . . . my folly') and so, 'deserving no pity', repents.[62] Newton claims that his confession was rewarded by a vision of the restored ring, a vision which he believes indicated his own possible spiritual liberation and salvation: 'The prey taken from the hand of the mighty, and the lawful captive delivered.' In the period which follows, Newton encounters circumstances 'very nearly resembling' those suggested by his extraordinary dream, yet fails to recognise them as manifestations of his earlier vision. Hence standing 'helpless and hopeless upon *the brink of an awful eternity*', the author remains unconscious of the 'grand enemy' and on his return to Kent in December 1743, obtains the post of midshipman upon the *Harwich* man-of-war bound for the East Indies.[63] On board this vessel Newton, 'like an unwary sailor who quits his port just before a rising storm', makes the acquaintance of other sailors whose corrupt influence he claims accelerated the ruin of his principles and led to his total abandonment of the hopes and comforts of the gospel. When the *Harwich* is forced to sail back to Plymouth, having encountered a severe storm off the coast of Cornwall, Newton deserts ship and attempts to secure a position with the merchants of the slave-trade, the Royal African Company. He is, however, recaptured and forced to return to the ship where he is publicly stripped and whipped, a form of punishment frequently experienced by slaves: 'I was now in my turn brought down to a level with the lowest, and exposed to the insults of all'.[64] Yet even at this stage of the *Authentic Narrative*, Newton's 'transgression' is not identified as his collusion with proslavery ideology, but rather his moral (eroticised) lapses, his unacceptable desertion and his degradation in the hands of other sailors.

While the details of the five-year voyage which follow remain opaque (a silence which possibly indicates his own involvement in the slave trade), Newton's *Narrative* suggests that every hour of the sea voyage exposed him to some new degradation and wretchedness: 'Whether I looked inward or outward, I could perceive nothing but darkness and misery'.[65] It is however his severance from his beloved, 'the object of [his] affections' which precipitates 'the most excruciating passions' of bitter rage and black despair and culminates in his attempt to commit suicide by throwing himself overboard.

According to African slave belief systems, for those slaves who threw themselves overboard during the transatlantic crossings, such an act manifested an effort to return to the homeland of their deceased ancestors. Newton's attempted suicide is however miraculously prevented by the 'secret hand of God'.[66] During his subsequent voyage to Madeira and his transference to the Guinea ship bound for Sierra Leone and the Windward Coast of Africa, Newton's depression brings him close to suicide once more. In terms of the spiritual framework, this (non)event (and not his withdrawal from slave ideology) marks the climactical crux of the narrative, a moment which Newton identifies as an unquestionable display of the Lord's 'providence and care'.[67] Yet despite these various miraculous interventions, Newton's spiritual dissolution continues and his 'utterly abandoned' behaviour corrupts the other shipmates on board the *Guinea*: 'I not only sinned with a high hand myself, but made it my study to tempt and seduce others upon every occasion'.[68] When the Captain of the *Guinea* dies, Newton decides to remain in Africa in order to amuse himself 'with many golden dreams' of improving his fortune. He enters the service of a few white settlers 'whose business it was to purchase slaves . . . and sell them to the ships at an advanced price', an event which marks the beginning of his involvement in the slave trade.[69]

As he travels along the slave-trading coast, from the most western point of Africa, Cape Verde, to Cape Mount via Gambia, Sierra Leone and the small 'Bananoes and Plantanes Islands', Newton's autobiographical *Narrative* presents the author as a spiritually-malignant and repugnant 'self', an outcast 'lying in blood', shunned by settlers and Negroes alike. On one of the Platanes islands, Newton becomes seriously ill and is left under the care of his master's black mistress. It is at this stage that his 'spiritual' narrative begins to read like a slave narrative in which the power relations are set in reverse: insulted and humiliated, Newton is kept like a slave to this cruel black mistress:

When I was slowly recovering, this woman would sometimes pay me a visit, not to pity or relieve, but to insult me. She would call me worthless and indolent, and compel me to walk, which, when I could hardly do, she would set her attendants to mimic my motion.[70]

Whereas her attendants ridicule and abuse him, the enchained slaves on the settlement bring him food to keep him alive. Yet their

actions do little to persuade Newton to renounce his trade, nor to
consider the spiritual nor indeed, intellectual equality of the Africans. Rather, as the entry of 26 May 1751 in his subsequent *Journal of
a Slave Trader, 1750–1754* reveals, the Africans' attempted insurrection
on board Newton's own slave-trading vessel is condemned as an
outlandish and unjustifiable attack.[71] Similarly, his journal entry of
26 January 1753 expresses his complete dismissal of African culture
and his unwillingness to consider the Africans' potential ability to
grasp western concepts of freedom or Christianity:

The three greatest blessings of which human nature is capable are
undoubtedly religion, liberty, and love. In each of these how highly has God
distinguished me! But here in Africa are whole nations around me, whose
languages are entirely different from each other, yet I believe they all agree
in this, that *they have no words among them expressive of these engaging ideas* . . .
These poor creatures are not only strangers to the advantages which I enjoy,
but are *plunged in all the contrary evils . . . [that] ignorance, can produce in the mind.*[72]

The return of Newton's captain and their joint departure from the
Plantanes brings him temporary relief until another trader persuades
the captain that Newton is a thief. On this occasion, Newton is
imprisoned upon the deck of the ship, exposed for 'perhaps near 40
hours together in incessant rains' and forced to work on the
plantations like a slave. His narrative of spiritual deterioration and
his subsequent deliverance 'from the pit of corruption' by the
'blessing of the Lord's grace' is however resolutely distinguished
from the *absolute* degeneration experienced by some settlers.[73] Whilst
he admits that he has 'erred', Newton determinedly distances
himself from those colonisers who have succumbed to a Kurtz-type
of debasement.[74] He condemns those colonials who have yielded to
what he terms a 'spirit of infatuation', that is, those who have
abandoned their sense of Christian duty and moral decorum and
participated instead in an unrestrained indulgence in African religious ceremonies, emotional and sexual excess:

There is a significant phrase frequently used in those parts, That such a
white man is grown *black*. It does not intend an alteration of complexion,
but disposition. I have known several who, settling in *Africa* after the age of
30 or 40, have, at that time of life, been gradually assimilated to the
tempers, customs, and ceremonies of the natives, so far as to prefer that
country to *England*.[75]

Such settlers, Newton argues, have sold their souls by embracing
African belief systems and hence become dupes to 'all the *pretended*

charms, necromancies, amulets, and divinations of the blinded Negroes'.
According to him it is a 'fate' which would have also been his, had
he continued to live in *'closer engagement'* with the natives. The
Lord's will, however, or so he claims, has saved him from becoming
'a wretch amongst them', divine providence having prevented an
irreversible *'yield to the whole'*; a deplorable subjection to cultural
alterity.

Whilst Newton's text maintains a narrative of cultural segregation,
the little-known *An Authentic Narrative of Four Years' Residence at
Tongataboo, one of the Friendly Islands, in the South Sea* (1810) by George
Vason (edited by the Revd Piggott), presents a lucid account of the
so-called 'pernicious' influence of heathen customs upon the missionaries based at Tongataboo. In so doing, the author's disclosure
of his submission to unrestrained indulgence, luxury and pleasure
initiates a 'torrent of iniquity' and spiritual neglect:

I began to indulge in foolish imaginations, and to neglect the needful
exercises of private prayer. . . I began to dislike the means of grace, I never
visited the brethren, found delight in the company, manners and
amusements of the natives; and soon took too large a part in them . . . My
evil inclinations, now unchecked by law, and by the reverential sense of the
Divine Being, gradually gained the dominion . . . *After a time, I was induced to
yield to their allurements, to imitate their manners, and to join them in their sins.*[76]

Although Vason claims that the primary motive behind his 'autobiographical' *Authentic Narrative* is to offer some 'useful hints' to future
missionary organisations by advising that *'married'* rather than single
men be sent to less 'tremendously alluring scenes', his text presents
an early type of titillating nineteenth-century soft pornography: that
is, his redeployment of the principal features of Methodism advances
an articulation of sexual and bicultural exposure.[77] For this reason,
the occasion of the 'anonymous author's interracial marriage to a
young relative of the chief of the Tongataboo Island is presented as a
moment which opens 'the door to every indulgence' and throws
'down every barrier of restraint':

I lament to say, that I now entered, with the utmost eagerness, into every
pleasure and entertainment of the natives; and endeavoured to forget that I
was once called a christian, and had left a christian land to evangelise the
heathen. Into such excesses is man ready to run when once he has violated
his conscience, and given way to temptation.[78]

Consequently, Vason's 'deliverance' is identified as an *exodus* from
sexual paradise and racial integration ('may penitence ever bow my

soul in humility') and a reorientation along the path that leads towards 'the narrow way'; that of Eurocentric ideology and cultural (especially sexual) apartheid: 'Had it not been for the arrival of this ship, and my sudden escape to it, it is most probable I should at this moment have been lifting up mine eyes in a *dark world of despair*'.[79]

The subtextual message of Newton's spiritual autobiography is similarly hinged upon a discourse of cross-cultural contact, an experience which threatens to irreversibly divide him, culturally and morally, from his native land. In accordance with this, his confessional text simultaneously reveals and conceals the depths of degradation to which he is subjected. Whilst the 'tempers, customs, and ceremonies of the native' are presented as pernicious agents of degeneration, Newton's text continues to focus on interracial relations, obliquely dealt with in the earlier account of his master's black mistress. Indeed, Newton's *Authentic Narrative* unequivocally equates spiritual degeneration with contact with cultural alterity: ultimate degradation is presented as synonymous with interracial sexual contact. Newton's deliverance from the negroes is, however, close at hand: with the help of a fellow traveller, he is 'freed from a captivity of about fifteen months'.[80] Even so, the various disasters which befall the ship during the author's continued involvement in the trade, persuade the Captain that Newton is a 'cursed Jonah' (not dissimilar to Coleridge's poem, *The Ancient Mariner*) and that all the troubles met with en route are owing to his having 'taken me [Newton] into the vessel'.[81] Meanwhile, although the author experiences several timely 'deliverances' from disaster, he remains ignorant of their providential meaning – that is, until the 'Lord's time was come', and the ship is wrecked by a violent storm. In the days leading up to this catastrophe, Newton's encounter with the ideas articulated within Stanhope's *Thomas à Kempis* have prepared him for spiritual salvation.[82] Moreover, during the storm itself, it is the literal abandonment of the signifiers of colonial trade, the produce of the African continent such as beeswax, ivory and dyers-wood, together with Newton's own plea for mercy, 'spoken with little reflection', which saves most of the crew from the effects of the storm. This miraculous deliverance instigates a structured reordering of hitherto neglected warnings and culminates in Newton's spiritual salvation and the ship's safe arrival, blown by providential winds, in Ireland four weeks later – 'I began to know that there is a God that hears and answers prayers'.[83]

In keeping with this image of pilgrimage and rites of passage, letter X of the *Authentic Narrative* outlines the author's own metaphorical 'pilgrimage' as a voyage undertaken by numerous vessels, 'at different times, and from different places', yet all '*bound to the same port*' and guided by the same spirit (or 'breath') of God:

Some we see set out with a prosperous gale, and when they almost think their passage secured, they are checked by adverse blasts . . . Others meet the greatest difficulties at first . . . Some are hard beset with cruisers and enemies, and obliged to fight their way through . . . The word of God is their compass, *Jesus* is both their polar star and their sun of righteousness; their hearts and faces are all set *Sion*-ward. Thus far they are as one body, *animated by one spirit;* yet their experience, formed upon these common principles, is far from uniform.[84]

Interestingly, this narrative of voyaging and pilgrimage functions as a scriptural exegesis to Newton's autobiographical text and anticipates the discourse of missionary expansionist ideology advanced during the late eighteenth century. Spiritual pilgrimage and slave-trading are not seen as diametrically opposed; the letter concludes with an account of his renewed visits to Sierra Leone and the Plantanes and his continued determination to purchase slaves.[85] In the following letter (XI), Newton records his decision to 'keep a sort of diary' during his subsequent voyages to Guinea. In this he (unashamedly) presents his various escapes from slave mutinies and insurrections as 'deliverances' firmly located within the parameters of spiritual discourse.[86] Similarly, his criticism of the trade, expounded in the penultimate letter XIII of 1 February 1763, focuses, somewhat lamely, upon the icons of enslavement – the chains, bolts and shackles – rather than upon slave ideology or the condition of the slaves themselves. As these textual absences (and their deafening silence) remain eclipsed by the author's own narrative of spiritual evolution, his desire for a more 'humane calling' ultimately suggests his yearning to return to his Christian homeland and his desire for ordination, rather than a concern for the wretched African slaves, or even the possibility of misinterpreting the workings of divine Providence:

During the time I was engaged in the slave trade, I never had the least scruple as to its lawfulness; I was upon the whole satisfied with it, as the appointment Providence had marked out for me; yet it was, in many respects, far from eligible . . . I was sometimes shocked with an employment that was perpetually conversant with chains, bolts, and shackles. In this view I had often petitioned in my prayers, that the Lord (in his own time) would be pleased to fix me in a more humane calling, and (if it might be) place me where I might have more frequent converse with his people and his ordinances, and be freed from those long separations from home, which very often were hard to bear.[87]

So far as his *Authentic Narrative* is concerned, this completes the author's critique of the trade. Ultimately, it is an apoplectic fit, rather than a moment of either remorse or spiritual illumination which finally severs Newton's links with slavery and instigates his ordination within the established church. The emergent narrative of self-consciousness described by Newton's text remains severed from a discourse proclaiming the needs of others.

Twenty-four years after the publication of his *Authentic Narrative* (1764), Newton published his *Thoughts upon the African Slave Trade* (1788), a work which relocated the former text's schema of salvation within an antislavery context: 'I was in effect, though without the name, a Captive and a Slave myself; and was depressed to the lowest degree of human wretchedness'.[88] In this revised testimony of *'public confession'*, Newton recalled what he now considered his shameful participation in a 'business at which my heart now shudders', the 'wretched' activity of purchasing and collecting slaves.[89] His 'testimony' of the workings of the holy spirit thus reformulated as a public disclosure his experiences as a trader over a period of nine years, experiences which, he asserted, confirmed his role as a competent witness of the consequences of the trade – 'I . . . offer nothing in writing, as from my knowledge, which I could not carefully, if requisite, confirm upon oath'.[90] Nevertheless, even in this later text, criticism of the trade is strategically absorbed within a framework of individual spiritual development:

I think I should have quitted it [the slave trade] sooner, had I considered it, as I now do, to be unlawful and wrong. But I never had a scruple upon this head, at the time; nor was such a thought once suggested to me, by any friend. What I did, *I did ignorantly*; considering it as the line of life which Divine Providence had allotted me.[91]

In this subsequent version of Newton's *Narrative* the disclosure of 'truth', described in the 'illumination' episodes of earlier spiritual autobiographies, is reinscribed as the author's efforts 'to throw what light' he can upon the slave trade, 'now that it is likely to become a point of parliamentary investigation'. In so doing, Newton's text anticipates the strategic transformation of spiritual discourse as a significant mode of subversion, most especially via its penetration of the political sphere:

Though unwilling to give offence to a single person: in such a cause, I ought not to be afraid of offending many, by declaring the truth. If, indeed, there can be many, whom even interest can prevail upon to contradict the common sense of mankind, by pleading for a commerce so iniquitous, so cruel, so oppressive, so destructive, as the African Slave Trade! [92]

In his *Thoughts Upon the Slave Trade*, therefore, the autobiographical disclosure of divine 'truth', characteristic of the spiritual narratives, is translated into an exposure of another kind, that is, to a socio-political critique of Britain's 'iniquitous' involvement in the trade, 'this stain on our national character'.[93] Newton's text thus illustrates the developing correspondence between evangelicism, British abolitionism and parliamentary debate, a relationship which underlines the works of one of his 'disciples', the autobiographer and poet, William Cowper.

WILLIAM COWPER'S AMBIGUOUS DELIVERANCE

As an important precursor to the Romantic poets, William Cowper, son of the Rector of Great Berkhampstead in Hertfordshire, was a key voice in the development of the discourse of the spirit which emerged under the influence of radical dissenting Protestantism. In addition, Cowper's concern over the issue of slavery marks the inauguration of a vital tripartite relationship between spiritual discourse, Romantic ideology and the dynamics of abolitionism. Cowper not only anticipates the Romantics' evolution of a heterogeneous form of spiritual discourse but extends the abolitionist demands made (albeit tenuously) by Cowper's mentor, John Newton, and functions as a precursor to the appropriation of spiritual autobiography by English ex-slaves. In line with the emergence of missionary ideology discussed above, his work reveals a coalescence of abolitionist and colonial discourse. Yet as it translates the structural framework of the evangelical motif into a narrative of melancholic excess (or 'psychosis') Cowper's work problematises the traditional 'salvation' crux of the conversion genre.

Possibly inspired by Newton's conversion text, *An Authentic Narrative*, William Cowper's *Memoirs* or 'Adelphi' as he originally conceived his autobiographical narrative, traces the history of the author's 'spiritual' development from the time of his birth in November 1731 until his conversion to Evangelicalism in July 1764. As with Newton's text, Cowper's *Memoirs* are interspersed throughout by poignant accounts of the author's chronic bouts of depression and melancholy. From the time that he was called to the Bar in 1754 (aged 23), Cowper led the typical life of a Temple barrister until his nomination in 1763 for the post of Clerk of the Journals to the House of Lords. Whilst the traumatic effects of his mother's premature death, his bullied childhood at Market Street Boarding School and his thwarted love affair with his cousin, Theodora, had already combined to aggravate a melancholic disposition within the poet, the fear of undergoing a public examination in order to confirm his right of appointment to the Clerkship triggered a severe state of mental instability.[94] According to John Morris and Charles Ryskamp, Cowper's psychological state was compounded by his belief in an 'imagined' defect (hermaphroditic) in his sexual organs which made the prospect of examination of any kind a constant fear.[95] After three attempted suicides and a series of depressive bouts, Cowper was taken to Dr. Cotton's mental asylum in St Albans where he remained from 1763 to 1765.[96]

On his recovery, Cowper took lodgings in Huntingdon in order to be near his younger brother, John, and soon became friends with, and subsequently a lodger, with the Unwin household. Mrs Unwin, the 'Mary' of Cowper's poems, effected a salutary influence upon the author's mind, and in her society Cowper began to lose the conviction that he was forsaken by God. With the death of her husband in 1767, Mrs Unwin and Cowper moved to Olney in Buckinghamshire. Here he formed an acquaintance with the author of the *Authentic Narrative*, John Newton, who had by this time established a reputation as one of the most renowned clergymen of the Evangelical movement. During the first years of his residency at Olney, however, Cowper's fits of depression and insanity returned, possibly triggered by Newton's gloomy teachings of self-accusation and the death of Cowper's younger brother, John, in 1770.[97]

In 1771 Newton suggested that Cowper assist him with the composition of a volume of hymns. Eight years later, in 1779, the *Olney Hymns*, containing 348 hymns in all, were published. In the sixty-eight hymns composed by Cowper, 'deliverance' for adherents of God's ways is celebrated as a process of spiritual salvation /

liberation experienced within the 'calm retreats' of domestic bliss,
far removed from the chaotic world of strife. This model coincided
with the deliverance narratives published by slaves and anticipated
the autobiographical 'conversation' genre favoured by Romantic
poets, such as Coleridge and Wordsworth.[98] In hymnal poems such
as 'Retirement' and 'Light Shining Out of Darkness' Cowper
attempted to articulate the spiritual experience of ecstatic communion with God – an experience profoundly felt yet not necessarily
understood:

> There if thy Spirit touch the soul,
>   And grace her mean abode;
> Oh with what peace, and joy, and love
>   She communes with her GOD!
>
> There like the nightingale she pours
>   Her solitary lays.[99]

With this objective in mind, the poems reveal the poet's unstinting
faith in the Lord's promise to disclose meaning ('GOD moves in a
mysterious way, / His wonders to perform . . . / The bud may have
a bitter taste, / But sweet will be the flow'r') and thereby reveal the
design behind suffering and chaos: 'GOD is his own interpreter, /
And he will make it plain'.[100] Such a schema similarly influenced the
original manuscript of Cowper's *Memoirs* which was read by Martin
Madan in 1767.[101] In addition to Madan, the itinerant preacher who
befriended distinguished Methodists (including the Wesleys, George
Whitefield and Lady Huntingdon) Cowper's manuscript was also
read by Lady Hesketh (Harriet Cowper), Mrs Madan and John
Newton in 1768 and all versions (dating from 1803 onwards) and
printed copies of the *Memoirs* were derived from this.[102] In the
Memoirs of the Life and Writings of William Cowper which appeared in
London in 1814, 'revised, corrected and recommended' by the Revd
S. Greatheed, the editor 'willingly' prefixed his attestation of the
text's authenticity. Greatheed claimed that his edition would 'serve
to correct' those misrepresentations which had presented Cowper's
'deplorable malady' as symptomatic of his dissenting 'religious
sentiments'. According to Greatheed, Cowper's conversion had
precipitated his 'recovery' from his first severe attack of insanity.
Likewise Greatheed's 'unbiased testimony' – 'I avow myself to be no
partisan for the theological system which Mr Cowper imbibed' –
suggested that Cowper's instability was in fact a consequence of his

adherence to a totally different sentiment, 'utterly *incompatible* with his religious creed'.[103]

Subsequent revisions of Cowper's text, such as the *Memoirs of the Remarkable and Interesting Parts of the Life of William Cowper* (1816) and the *Memoir of the Early Life of William Cowper* (1816) similarly claimed complete textual authenticity.[104] While such texts sought to prioritise the poet's spiritual development, they also attempted to counter suggestions which had connected Cowper's (excessive) religious fervour with his 'mental malady'. The first of these texts therefore, identified *'personal religion'* as the only effective cure for a 'wounded conscience' and claimed that this communion with the deity would enable the soul to 'approach the judgment seat of Christ with serenity and confidence'.[105] Likewise, the Preface to the latter text ascribed the origin of Cowper's deranged faculties to 'an excessive sensibility, to which he was by nature subject' rather than to his adherence to any specific kind of religious zeal:

Religion was so far from causing that disturbance in the first instance, either directly or indirectly, that, even in his earliest depressions, it was the only source from which any feelings of a counteractive or consolatory nature were derived.[106]

Accordingly, these various renditions of Cowper's narrative incorporated great efforts to emphasise the spiritual 'solace' experienced by the author, following his admittance into the mental institution at St Albans:

At length his despair was effectually removed by reading the sacred scriptures, that 'God hath set forth Jesus Christ to be a propitiation, through faith in his blood, to declare his righteousness for the remission of sins that are past, through the forbearance of God.' (Rom. 3:25) While meditating on this passage, he obtained a view of the gospel, which was attended with unspeakable joy.[107]

At the outset of the *Memoir of the Early Life*, Cowper's visitations were identified as a 'gift in whom [he] trusted', a power which filled him with 'a degree of trust and confidence in God, that would have been no disgrace to a much more experienced Christian'.[108] For Cowper, however, these spiritualised confirmations of individual election proved to be 'the first and last instance' of such a kind 'between infancy and manhood'.[109] These memoirs described his puberty and late adolescence as miserable periods of emotional volatility which culminated in his blasphemous rejection of the deity, his 'rancorous reproach', his descent into madness ('my ears rang with the sound of torments') and as with Newton's text, frequent contemplations of suicide:

Perhaps, thought I, there is no God; or if there be, the scriptures may be false; if so, then God has no where forbidden suicide. I considered life as my property, and therefore at my disposal. Men of great name, I observed, had destroyed themselves; and the world still retained the profoundest respect for their memories.[110]

After several failed suicide attempts (including an attempt to drown himself in the Thames), Cowper experienced a spiritual awakening during which the atrocity of his actions were revealed to him in colours 'inconceivably strong', hence inaugurating a trans-formation of Newton's captivity theme in terms of emancipatory discourse:

The happy period which was to shake off my fetters, and afford me a clear opening to the free mercy of God in Christ Jesus, was now arrived. . . and the full beams of the Sun of Righteousness shone upon me. . . *In a moment I believed, and received the gospel.*[111]

For most spiritual autobiographers and their editors in the late eighteenth century, the discourse of the spirit provided an acceptable medium of self-confirmation (either real or imagined) and self-empowerment. Yet whilst most editors were eager to present Cow-per's autobiography as a confessional narrative of deliverance, as it was recorded in the *Memoirs*, conversion to Evangelicalism failed to 'cure' Cowper of his depressive tendencies. For this reason the translation of the framework of spiritual regeneration to a narrative detailing Cowper's medical history proved to be problematic in its 'failure' to contain the complex mechanisms of psychosis. As periods of depression continued to plague the author during the composition of the *Olney Hymns* (1779), *The Task* (1785) and *The Cast-Away* (1799), Cowper's narratives may be seen to highlight some of the major limitations of prescribed spiritual discourse: that is, the ever-increas-ing gap between spiritual, fictional and autobiographical modes of articulation. This disjuncture between narratives of spiritual regen-eration and psychosis / depression is partially resolved by the insistence, within Cowper's longest poetical work, *The Task*, that the configuration of identity is a continuous process. Abandoning the crescendo-like momentum and resolute climax of other conversion narratives, *The Task* redetermines spiritual revivification, or 'new birth', as a never-ending process of illumination and thereby high-lights the complex processes of the autobiographical genre. In addition, the poet's text extends the motif of conscious 'awakening' on to a trope of nationalistic dialogue concerning the abolition of the slave trade. To a certain extent therefore, Cowper's work coalesces with the narratives of self-consciousness (cultural and individual) contained within the autobiographical texts by ex-slaves.

POEMS OF LIBERTY AND DELUGE

In his essay of 1979, Joseph Musser declared that those critics who had endeavoured to make claims for the structural unity of *The Task* had had to resort to 'logical and verbal contortion'. Likewise, he argued that the poem's 'lack of formal unity' reflected the frag-mented insanity of the poet himself, a condition at odds with the cohesive unity expected of a 'sane' integrated self. For Musser therefore, the poem's lack of structure revealed the poet's psycho-logical inability to discover, within his own personality, the integra-tion of the self required for sanity.[112] In an effort to counter Musser's claims, I would suggest that Cowper's poem sensitively and success-fully traces the complex process of autobiographical narration. In its refusal to succumb to 'closure' in terms of narrative structure, the poem identifies the on-going dynamics of identity-formation and epiphanic spiritual illumination and thus anticipates the condition of 'diaspora' revealed in the slave narratives. Moreover, in its concern with abolitionist demands, *The Task* confirms Cowper's position as an important precursor to the Romantic poets' autobiographical enterprise *and* as a key influence in the development of spiritual discourse.

In an effort to counter his religious melancholia, Cowper pub-lished a volume of poetry in 1782 which included poems such as 'The Progress of Error', 'Conversation', 'The Negro's Complaint', 'Retire-ment' and 'Verses written by the Scottish sailor Alexander Selkirk'.[113] Although this volume was not a huge success, the domestic, conversational style of the poems presented a form of intimate autobiography and abolitionist defiance that was to signifi-cantly influence the framework of *The Task*. In the same year, Cowper's poem *Charity* (1782) condemned the slave trade, 'the most degrading of all ills', as an aberration of the social bond which united the human race ('God, working ever on a social plan, / By

various ties attaches man to man') and foregrounded the poet's belief
in the spiritual *equality* of the races: 'A Briton knows . . . / That souls
have no discriminating hue, / Alike important in their Maker's
view'.[114] Likewise, in his poem 'The Negro's Complaint' (1788),
Cowper hinted at the divine retribution which he believed would
ensue if England continued its support of the slave trade:

> Hark! he answers – Wild tornadoes,
>   Strewing yonder sea with wrecks;
> Wasting towns, plantations, meadows,
>   Are the voice with which he speaks.
> He, foreseeing what vexations
>   Afric's sons should undergo,
> Fix'd their tyrants' habitations
>   Where his whirlwinds answer – No.[115]

The popularity and accessibility of Cowper's 'merchantable' critique
of the national agenda was established and confirmed when thousands of copies of this poem were distributed throughout England by
the Abolitionist Committee. Indeed, his poems 'The Morning
Dream' (1788) and 'Sweet Meat for Sour Sauce' (1788) anticipated
(or rather prophesied) Britain's withdrawal from the slave trade:

> I saw him [the Demon of Slavery] both sicken and die . . .
> Heard shouts that ascended the sky . . .
> Awaking, how could I but muse
>   At what such a dream should betide?
> But soon my ear caught the glad news
>   Which serv'd my weak thought for a guide –
> That Britannia, renown'd o'er the waves
>   For the hatred she ever has shown
> To the black-sceptred rulers of slaves,
>   Resolves to have none of her own.[116]

In its fusion of spiritual narrative and abolitionist critique, Cowper's major poem, *The Task* endeavours to demonstrate the beneficial
effects of nature upon a 'lost soul' whose wanderings, like those of
the River Ouse, are reflected in the poem's continuum of digressions.
Cowper's poetical project presents a paradigm of spiritual pilgrimage
and redemption in which domestic happiness is identified as a
paradisiacal state wherein man might best discover the 'lineaments
divine'.[117] Predating the embryonic version of Wordsworth's autobiographical poem *The Prelude* by over a decade, Cowper's search for
a contemporary Eden commences with a narrative of liberation in

which communion with God is reinforced rather than severed, suggesting a fusion of the dynamics of the self with those of the divine self. In Book III of *The Task*, entitled 'The Garden', the moment of spiritual salvation is presented as a discrete disclosure of the complex relationship between the poet's own suffering and that experienced by the humanised deity: 'There was I found by one who had himself / Been hurt by th'archers . . . / With gentle force soliciting the darts / He drew them forth, and heal'd and bade me live'.[118] Cowper's synchronisation of the divine within the poetical self inaugurates a validation of the poet's own visionary powers, which enables him to distinguish between divine visitations and the false delusions of wanderers gone astray ('Each in his own delusions; they are lost / In chase of fancied happiness, still woo'd / And never won'). Such claims for visionary powers were later reciprocated by Wordsworth's claims for the infinite powers of the human mind: 'Of first, and last, and midst, and without end'.[119] According to Cowper, for those who searched for truth using the powers of rational intellect, disclosure would remain a continual absence. For those who did not seek it, however, divine illumination would be granted suddenly, powerfully and unmistakably: 'But if his word once teach us, shoot a ray / Through all the heart's dark chambers, and *reveal / Truths undiscern'd but by that holy light, / Then all is plain*'.[120]

Cowper's *Task* therefore prioritises the acquisition of spiritual knowledge over that of empirical science. Since God, he declares, never meant that man should scale the heavens 'by strides of human wisdom', scientific discoveries ('some drill and bore / the solid earth'), or geographical conquests ([some] 'travel nature up / to the sharp peak of her sublimest height'), philosophical dictums and hypotheses merely function as buckets dropped into empty wells, 'growing old in drawing nothing up!'[121] Furthermore the poet suggests that in their use of elaborate and delusive rhetoric, such investigations insidiously destroy the natural international *brotherhood* of man: 'What edge of subtlety canst thou suppose / Keen enough, wise and skilful as thou art, / To cut the link of brotherhood, by which / One common Maker bound me to the kind?'[122]

Prompted by recent 'portentous, unexampled, unexplained' meteorological activity (such as the terrible earthquakes in Sicily in February 1782), the poet argues that in its discrimination against one half of mankind, the slave trade will precipitate the approaching hour of millenarian apocalypse:

And crazy earth has had her shaking fits . . .
What solid was, by transformation strange
Grows fluid, and the fixt and rooted earth
Tormented into billows heaves and swells,
Or with vortiginous and hideous whirl
Sucks down its prey insatiable.[123]

Having endeavoured to relocate the abolitionist concern within the parameters of spiritual illumination, Cowper's text prophesies a national severance from any association with the trade, two years prior to the establishment of the Society for Abolition: 'We have no slaves at home . . . / Slaves cannot breathe in England; if their lungs / Receive our air, that moment they are free, / They touch our country and their shackles fall'.[124] Yet the poet's abolitionist ideology vies unresolvedly with his propagation of colonial ideology and despite his critique of the trade, the concept of empire still looms large. He therefore criticises the 'dissipation and effeminacy' which he believes has reduced the arch of the British Empire to a 'mutilated structure, soon to fall' and advances a mythic valorisation of Britain's redemptive role amongst the pagan nations.[125] Omai, the South Sea islander employed by Captain Cook during his travels, is hence depicted as a patriotic native who weeps honest tears for his benevolent coloniser, 'a patriot's for his country'.[126] Transformation of the island into a civilised paradise, has, to all intents and purposes been merely partial; moreover, it is a transformation which has taken place without the islanders' participation: 'Thou art sad / At thought of her [his island's] forlorn and abject state, / From which no power of thine can raise her up'.[127] Cowper's poem thus establishes the concept of the 'task' on individual *and* national terms and in so doing, prescribes both the salvation of the individual soul and the inauguration of missionary ideology beyond the western hemisphere.

In the first four books of *The Task*, Cowper employs the paradigm of 'journeying', in terms of his walk in the garden and his 'mental' wanderings from the sofa, as a suitable metaphor for spiritual development.[128] Likewise, in the remaining books of *The Task*, this image is transferred to the fluid meanderings of a stream, which projects the influence of the spirit upon the soul as an unstoppable and tireless process, akin to the demands of liberty – 'scornful of a check it leaps . . . / No frost can bind it there'.[129] Having envisaged Britain's redemptive role in the 'liberation' of the slaves (or rather its detachment from the slave trade) Cowper's text posits spiritual liberty as a daring prototype for emancipation: 'be enslaved no more':

> But there is yet a liberty unsung . . .
> Tis liberty of heart, derived from heav'n,
> Bought with HIS blood who gave it to mankind,
> And seal'd with the same token.[130]

Concurrent with this discourse of spiritual emancipation, Cowper's text describes a paradigm of dissolution – the absorption and negation of the individual self within the divine. As with the complex synthesis of the Empress of Russia's ice-palace, which 'was a stream' but soon must 'slide into a stream again', Cowper's poem articulates a submersion of the individual by the cleansing waters of divine deluge. In the ultimate moment of spiritual salvation, therefore, the subject identity is engulfed by that of another, in order that the subject may be *re*formed anew. In the case of the slaves, however, such a process involved an involuntary subjection to a new nation-state (Britain's 'Self') and to its Christian epistemological and colonial discourse:

> Acquaint thyself with God if thou would'st taste
> His works. Admitted once to his embrace,
> Thou shalt perceive that thou wast blind before;
> Thine eye shall be instructed, and thine heart
> Made pure, shall relish with divine delight
> 'Till then unfelt, what hands divine have wrought.[131]

The poet's metaphor of the 'task' hence functions as a search for revelation on both linguistic and spiritual terms – an attempted disclosure of 'the lamp of truth', 'Thy lamp, mysterious Word!' His text identifies the complex relationship between the dynamics of discourse (utterance and ellipse) and the configurations of identity, a principle concern of the slave narratives. *The Task* thereby reveals identity as a continued series of revelations, illuminations and erasures of the self. It is a process which reciprocates the fragmented disclosures of divine truth, the 'unseen' Word, and the problematics of writing the self into text. Autobiographical narrative, and this is especially true of the slave narratives, is seen to proceed via a complex sequence of revelations, ellipses and erasures – epistemological, socioeconomic and historical – of the self:

> In that blest moment, nature throwing wide
> Her veil opaque, discloses with a smile

> The author of her beauties, who retired
> Behind his own creation, works unseen
> By the impure, and hears his pow'r denied.
> *Thou art the source and centre of all minds,*
> *Their only point of rest, eternal word!*[132]

Whilst the promise of spiritual illumination and disclosure in Cowper's narrative suggests the possibility of individual consummation and emancipation – 'Then we are free. Then liberty like day / Breaks on the soul' – subjectivity is determined as necessarily unfinished, incomplete, for ever in transit.[133] As the deity performs that silent 'task', which is also 'himself' ('there lies and works a soul in all things, and that soul is God'), the endless cycle of renewal and regeneration, 'From dearth to plenty, and from death to life', is reciprocated by the poet's own experience of spiritual despair and deliverance.[134]

The 'pilgrimage' traced within *The Task* thus differs strategically from the pattern established by traditional spiritual autobiographies, in that it suggests that despair is *not* always relieved by salvation; hence the uniform transfer of self-articulation to the structural framework of spiritual salvation is denied. This negation of 'closure' recurs in Cowper's final poetical work, *The Cast-Away* (1799), a poem which explores the repeated compulsion to revisit and relive traumatic experience – in this case, the isolation and estrangement felt by the poet himself. In its poignant evocation of abandonment, Cowper's poem presents a disturbing articulation of the experiences of exile and transportation that are marginalised and/or silenced within the narratives of former slaves. However, whilst the slaves' capture severed them culturally and socially from their native epistemological beliefs, the 'unutterable despair' of Cowper's '*destined wretch*' cannot be explained on these terms. The possibility of salvation, a principal tenet of radical dissenting Protestantism, is in fact denied and the probability of divine intervention negated *in totalis*: 'No voice divine the storm allay'd, / No light propitious shone'.[135] Possibly influenced by Richard Walker's description of a seaman swept overboard whilst sailing round Cape Horn in Book I of Lord George Anson's *A Voyage Round the World in the Years 1740–1744* (1748), the metaphors of inundation which in *The Task* had signified the necessary precursors to the deliverance of the individual are abandoned in Cowper's *Cast-Away* and replaced instead by desperate images of desolation and isolation: 'Of friends, of hope, of all bereft:

> When, snatch'd from all effectual aid,
>   We perish'd, each, alone;
> But I, beneath a rougher sea,
> And whelm'd in deeper gulphs than he.[136]

Whereas Cowper's early poems displayed a confident trans-formation of the dynamics of spiritual discourse on to poetical autobiography and thus determined the poet as an important precursor to the Romantic poets, the liberationist ideology of spiritual salvation contained in Cowper's final poems is qualified and replaced by an acute sense of uncertainty and failure, a characteristic which strategically distinguishes his works from those of the Romantic poets.

CHAPTER THREE

Romanticism and abolitionism: Mary Wollstonecraft, William Blake, Samuel Taylor Coleridge and William Wordsworth

Over the past two decades the concept of Romanticism as an homogenised 'project' has been rigorously challenged from both sides of the Atlantic. Leading representatives of Romantic criticism have presented sophisticated critiques of the established hierarchy of the Romantic 'canon' and have applied illuminating deconstructive and poststructuralist analyses of Romantic literature; others have provided lucid interdisciplinary accounts of Romanticism in terms of class, gender and new historicism.[1] As a result, Romanticism is no longer perceived as simply a 'European phenomenon', informed solely by the political and philosophical legacy of the French Revolution and the German Empire. The ahistorical, close readings provided by New Criticism gave way to a study of Romanticism within the context of a history of ideas informed by western liberalism. Paul de Man's deconstructive approach offered a way of reading that resisted 'authoritarian complacency' or a belief in 'timeless truths' and highlighted the inevitable failure of Romanticism's rhetoric of conscious intent and self-representation.[2] Work focusing upon eighteenth-century concepts of sexuality and representations of gender by scholars including Mary Jacobus, Anne Mellor, Marjorie Levinson and Helen Vendler revisited this rhetoric of 'failure' and enlarged the scope of Romantic Studies in terms of feminist literary history.[3] As Mary Favret and Nicola Watson have indicated, Romanticism's increased identification with critical theory prompted interest in new areas of previously excluded material and concerns, including medical treatises, political pamphlets, conduct books and Jacobin novels.[4] Jerome McGann's *Romantic Ideology* (1983) registered a critical shift in Britain and America in its critique of the isolation of the self-conscious Romantic poet from the agents of 'real history' and cultural materialism. According to McGann, the role of the critic of Romantic poetry is to 'make a determined effort to elucidate the subject matter of such poems historically: to define the specific ways in which stylistic forms intersect and join with factual and cognitive points of reference'.[5] More recent critical essays (including those anthologies edited by Alan Richardson and Sonia Hofkosh, and by Tim Fulford and Peter Kitson) have extended the study of Romanticism to the wider contexts of colonialism, education, racial policy, imperialist practice and international trade.[6] This critical interest in the material conditions and sociopolitical constructs within and against which Romantic authors and poets were placed, has brought about an important revaluation of the literature produced during the period 1770 to 1830. In addition to these more recent investigations, this book explores the period's cultural productions from a revised historical and ideological context. Romanticism is analysed in terms of its connection with eighteenth-century dissent and enthusiasm and the use of the discourse of the spirit by leading Romantic figures is examined in the context of abolition and the emergence of literary expressions of liberation, identity and self-consciousness. In its application of some of the major strands of postcolonial, cultural and poststructural theory, this study relocates the Romantic era within a highly complex period that witnessed both the culmination of England's participation in the slave trade and the emergence of pervasive theories of racial difference, alongside the most vigorous spate of abolitionist demands.[7] Indeed, prominent blacks such as Ottobah Cugoano and Olaudah Equiano (discussed in Chapters 6 and 8), in many instances had friends, associations and acquaintances in common with the Romantics such as Thomas Clarkson, Granville Sharp and James Ramsay.[8] By highlighting the relation between the use of the discourse of the spirit employed by Romantic writers, including Wordsworth, Coleridge and Blake, and the uncanonical eighteenth-century dissenting figures discussed in Chapter 2, this study proposes an analysis of eighteenth-century spiritual discourse popularised by radical dissenting Protestantism and contained within the prophetic, confessional and abolitionist works published in both America and England at this time. Moreover, in its relocation of Romanticism within such a context, this chapter prepares the groundwork for an important juxtaposition between Romantic writing and the autobiographical narratives by African slaves published in England; a juxtaposition which not only locates a point of cultural contact between two disparate cultures (Africa and the west) but identifies a

significant translation and subsequent fusion of African epistemology
with Christian ideology and its expression.

The discourse of the spirit employed within a selection of works by
the first generation Romantic poets, Coleridge, Wordsworth and
Blake, suggests that the language of radical dissenting Protestantism
played a major role in the development of Romantic poetry.
Together with the radical liberationist demands contained within
Mary Wollstonecraft's texts, these works indicate Romanticism's
heterogeneous interaction with liberationist and, at times, abolitionist ideology. With their emphasis on spiritual discourse, epiphanic moments of 'divine' witness and actual and figural concepts
of 'captivity' and 'emancipation', these texts demonstrate an intricate relationship with the literary framework appropriated by the
slave narratives. In a sense, therefore, these seemingly disparate
literary movements may be seen as products of the same historical
influences. However, whilst the works by the Romantics and the
slaves determined an inscription of a self-authorised sociohistorical
self, they prescribed two very different kinds of literary enterprise
and motives, and were intended for radically different audiences.
Whereas the language of radical dissenting Protestantism provided
the Romantics with convenient tropes of metaphorical captivity and
liberation, the narratives by the slaves registered the very real
experience of transportation and enslavement and carried with them
overt political messages of emancipation.

With the exception of the poems included in the *Lyrical Ballads*
first published in 1798, the Romantic poems discussed below were
originally exposed to a relatively small audience comprised of close
friends and acquaintances, including Charles Lamb, Dorothy
Wordsworth and Robert Southey.[9] Wordsworth's two-part *Prelude*,
transcribed in December 1799, was not published until 1974; the
Prelude of 1805 remained a manuscript until 1926 and the *Prelude* of
1850 was not printed until ten weeks after Wordsworth's death on 23
April 1850.[10] Similarly, the manuscript version of Coleridge's *Letter to
Sara Hutchinson* differed significantly from the published version,
Dejection: An Ode, and was not published until 1963.[11] Blake's single
bid for public recognition, a one-man exhibition in 1809, proved a
total failure; only when he was in his sixties did he attract a small
group of painters to serve as an audience for his work.[12] In contrast,
the slave narratives were on the whole aimed at a wider audience as
a means of providing financial support for their authors and

advancing abolitionist ideology. Many of their works were immensely popular and were reissued in numerous editions and under various titles throughout Great Britain and America during the seventy years or so following their publication.[13] One other major difference between the production and consumption of the works by the slave narrators was economic: most slave narratives were published by subscription; buyers were committed to paying something towards the book prior to its publication. As a consequence, the subscription lists which preceded the texts functioned as a means of promotion and credibility and often included the names of socially and politically prominent figures, members of the aristocracy, key abolitionists and bluestocking authors. The texts themselves, often edited or rewritten by dissenting editors and philanthropists, attracted a wide spectrum of readers who welcomed the narratives' adventurous plots, their 'conversion' frameworks and their pro-abolitionist ideology.

Therefore, whilst it is true that the writings by slaves and the Romantics employed similar tropes of liberation and spiritual discourse, it is also clear that a considerable ideological distance separated them. In the works of the Romantics, the trope of isolation and/or alienation tended to be at most a temporary, fairly domestic, 'literary' device which established the poets' sense of election, isolation and subsequent reassimilation into society. For the slaves however, the narrative tropes of 'captivity' and 'liberation' designated actual rather than figurative traumatic processes of cultural severance and estrangement, an experience shared by many thousands of other slaves by virtue of their removal from their native lands, their transportation across the Atlantic to the plantations of the West Indies and America and (for a significant few) their subsequent journeys to the slave-trading ports of England and their reemergence as identities in the diaspora. For the slave narrators, the discourse of the spirit described a process by which the slave's former cultural self was redetermined within the parameters of Christian ideology and expression. This reconfiguration of identity involved a delicate negotiation in which cultural *alterity* was inscribed and contained within the popularised discourse of radical dissenting Protestantism. For both the Romantics and the slave narrators, however, the 'non-linguistic' moments of spiritual witness provided cryptic paradigms of liberationist, and sometimes abolitionist, ideology wherein the concept of memory inaugurated a complex discourse of identity configuration within a literary framework.

MARY WOLLSTONECRAFT: FEMINISM AND ABOLITIONISM

> If they are really capable of acting like rational creatures, let
> them not be treated as slaves.[14]

On the margins of canonical Romanticism, yet highly significant in
its relationship with Romanticism's paradigms of liberationist ideology, the work of Mary Wollstonecraft provides an invaluable link
between the discourse of racial and gendered inequality in its
employment of abolitionist rhetoric. Published by Johnson, the same
publisher of works by William Blake and John Stedman, Mary
Wollstonecraft's *Vindication of the Rights of Men* (1790) and *Vindication of
the Rights of Woman: With Strictures on Political and Moral Subjects* (1792)
provide key components in the development of liberationist discourse in the context of colonial and slave ideology. Written as a
repudiation of Edmund Burke's defence of the monarchy and the
aristocracy contained within his *Reflections on the Revolution in France*,
Mary Wollstonecraft's *Vindication of the Rights of Men* identified the
inalienable right to liberty as a necessary prerequisite to the creation
of a society based upon the principles of reason and justice.
Wollstonecraft's text denounced Burke's three main hypotheses: that
all legal and political authority should be derived from the past; that
the alliance between the church and civil government was a
condition of civil society; and that the class system, as determined by
property ownership, was 'natural'.[15] It condemned Burke's un-
ashamed conservatism and denounced slavery as an atrocious and
inhuman traffic that contravened 'every suggestion of reason and
religion'.[16] Likewise, Wollstonecraft defined the slave trade as a
pernicious cause of spiritual deterioration, a trade which fed 'upon
human flesh' and consumed the 'very soul' of society.[17]

> But is it not consonant with justice, with the common principles of
> humanity, not to mention Christianity, to abolish this abominable
> inveterate mischief . . . If it [Parliament] gloriously dared to shew the world
> that British senators were men: if the natural feelings of humanity silenced
> the cold cautions of timidity . . . and all men were allowed to enjoy their
> birth-right – liberty.[18]

Wollstonecraft's *Vindication of the Rights of Men* concluded with an
utopian vision of land redistribution, the new 'Eden' that would be
achieved if large estates were divided into smaller farms. Such a
concept had informed the millenarian prophetic writings of the New

Jerusalem, including those by Richard Brothers, and indeed the more extreme demands of slaves, maroons and radical abolitionists. A rather more philosophical justification was given within William Godwin's *Enquiry Concerning Political Justice* (1793).[19] In that text, Godwin (later Wollstonecraft's lover and the source of Wordsworth's anxiety in Book XI of the *Prelude*) prophesied society's inevitable but peaceful progression, achieved by equal land distribution and the eradication of government. Such radical notions of land redistribution must have haunted English absentee landlords and plantocratic owners, especially in the wake of recent slave rebellions in the colonies and parliamentary debates on abolition.

Published in the year following the successful insurrection by slaves in the French colony of St Domingue, Wollstonecraft's *Vindication of the Rights of Woman: With Strictures on Political and Moral Subjects* (1792) hinged upon a discourse of property rights.[20] In this text, Wollstonecraft identified the condition of women with that of the oppressed slaves and further emphasised the morally undesirable effects of sexism/slavery upon slaveholders and husbands: 'They [women] may be convenient slaves, but slavery will have its constant effect, degrading the master and the abject dependent'.[21] Wollstonecraft emphasised the violation of the 'sacred rights of humanity' effected by women's subordination and placed a significant stress on the enforced sexual abuse suffered by female slaves at the hands of their plantocratic masters: 'Is one half of the human species, like the poor African slaves, to be subject to prejudices that brutalise them?'[22] According to Wollstonecraft, 'marriage', in the form that it existed in England in 1792, was a form of legal slavery not dissimilar to that endured by Africans in the British West Indies. In legal and sociopolitical terms, a wife could not own property, bring legal suits, or expect guaranteed custody of her own children.[23] Hence Wollstonecraft's discussion of female subjugation rested fundamentally upon the dynamics of emancipatory and abolitionist discourse. Economic and psychological dependence had, according to Wollstonecraft, deprived women of their rights to liberty and autonomy:

Liberty is the mother of virtue, and if women are, by their very constitution, slaves, and not allowed to breathe the sharp invigorating air of freedom, they must ever languish like exotics, and be reckoned beautiful flaws in nature.[24]

A woman's value, she argued, was judged not in terms of her

spiritual or intellectual capacities, but upon her external and reproductive potential – a process not dissimilar to the way in which a slave's value was assessed. This subjugated women to the 'pride, sensuality and desire' of their tyrants and confined them to a perpetually dependent state of childhood and ignorance: 'Taught from their infancy that beauty is woman's sceptre, the mind shapes itself to the body, and, roaming round its gilt cage, only seeks to adorn its prison'.[25] If instead, she argued, a woman's understanding was 'emancipated' from its condition of servitude, then claims advocating her biological and rational inferiority would be overturned: rational education would lead to rational love and egalitarian marriages based upon companionship rather than purely sexual desire.[26]

Wollstonecraft's *Vindication of the Rights of Woman* therefore strategically correlated tenets of emancipation with concepts of social freedom and intellectual stimulation. In addition, her text radically suggested that given the conditions of women's/slaves' servitude, their cunning methods of rebellion and independence were, in a sense, justified: 'Women, it is true, obtaining power by unjust means, by practising or fostering vice, evidently lose the rank which reason would assign them, and they become either abject slaves or capricious tyrants'.[27] Similarly, in her *Historical and Moral View of the Origin and Progress of the French Revolution* (1794), Wollstonecraft argued that the deprivation of natural, equal, civil and political rights established a dichotomy between 'tyrants and slaves' and forced otherwise respectable individuals to resort to theft, 'atrocious robberies and murder'. Such a pernicious hierarchy, she suggested, would always result in volatile, 'always terrible', insurrection.[28]

However, her parallel between black slaves and white females was not unproblematic, especially when one considers the complex nature of the power relationships between white colonial mistresses and their female slaves, vividly described in Mary Prince's *History of Mary Prince* (1831) and Moses Roper's *Narrative of the Adventures and Escape of Moses Roper, from American Slavery* (1837).[29] In terms of structure and content, Wollstonecraft's work represented a strategic detachment from any overt relation to autobiographical or 'spiritual' discourse and advanced instead an effective rational, objective rhetoric. Indeed, her account of the *Interesting Narrative* by Olaudah Equiano in the *Analytical Review* of May 1789, suggested that the slave's rendition of his conversion to Methodism was 'rather tiresome' and that his narrative should have concluded with his acquisition of freedom.[30] Thus, whereas Wollstonecraft's work promoted a liberationist schema in terms of gender, her texts remain resolutely detached from the mode of discourse popularised by radical dissenting Protestants and emancipatory ideology. Conversely, the poetical works by Wollstonecraft's contemporary, Samuel Taylor Coleridge, prescribed narratives of 'emancipation' wherein the influence of the dynamics of spiritual discourse were barely concealed. Coleridge's work extended the abolitionist and evangelical design, established by William Cowper, into the public forum as demonstrated by his *Lecture on the Slave Trade*. His poems, especially those referred to as the 'conversation poems', maintained the personalised, autobiographical framework of conversion narratives, yet proffered a significantly revised version of both the confessional motif and the discourse of the spirit.

COLERIDGE'S BITTER SWEET 'LECTURE ON THE SLAVE TRADE'

On 16 June 1795, Samuel Taylor Coleridge delivered his *Lecture on the Slave Trade* at the Assembly Coffee House at the Quay in Bristol, one of England's major slave-trading ports. The text of the *Lecture* was subsequently printed in a condensed and revised form in the fourth issue of the poet's short-lived journal, *The Watchman*, on 25 March 1796.[31] Given that the height of abolitionist protest occurred during the period 1789–1792 and was followed by a climate of suspicion and fear under the Pitt government, Coleridge's lecture took place at a time when 'abolitionism' had begun to lose respectability.[32] Seven years earlier, in March 1788, in the same city, Wesley had preached his famous sermon on the immorality of slavery at the New Room in Bristol. In 1792, three years prior to his *Lecture*, Coleridge, then still at Cambridge, had been awarded the Browne Gold Medal for his 'Ode on the Slave Trade', a poem which had invoked Nemesis to send punishment to those who were 'sated with the persecution' of a miserable people.[33] Coleridge may well have read Blumenbach's 'On the Varieties of Mankind' (1775), a text which repudiated claims which suggested that blacks and whites were two distinct species (see Chapter 5), as three years after the delivery of this *Lecture on the Slave Trade*, Coleridge went to study under Blumenbach in 1798–1799.

The day before the delivery of the *Lecture*, Coleridge consulted the

Bristol Library's copy of Clarkson's *Essay on the Impolicy of the African Slave Trade* (1788) and Carl Bernhard Wadstrom's *Essay on Coloniza- tion, Particularly Applied to the Western Coast of Africa, with Some Free Thoughts on Cultivation and Commerce* (1794), along with notes gathered by his friend and colleague, Robert Southey, from Antony Benezet's *Some Historical Account of Guinea* (1781).[34] Clarkson's text referred to the work of the female slave, Phillis Wheatley (discussed in Chapter 7 below), as an example of 'African intellectual potential' and provided a synopsis of her life as a slave and extracts from three of the poems included in her poetical volume, *Poems on Various Subjects* (1773), a 'Hymn to Evening', a 'Hymn to Morning' and 'Thoughts on Imagination'.[35] Wheatley's work had also been celebrated in the long poem, *The Female Advocate* (1774) by Mary Scott, the Unitarian poet and in Mary Deverell's 'On Reading the Poems of Phillis Wheatley', a poem in the latter's *Miscellanies in Prose and Verse* (1781) which described Wheatley as a representative of 'a race divine; / Like marble that in quarries lies conceal'd'.[36] Coleridge's text may also have been influenced by the testimonial narratives delivered at abolitionist gatherings by former slave-traders and African slaves alike, as well as by denunciations of the trade contained within published narratives, including Ottobah Cugoano's pamphlet of 1787 and Olaudah Equiano's (Gustavus Vassa's) autobiographical text of 1789. In his two-volume *Essay on Colonization*, which contained the now famous cross-section of a typical slave ship, Wadstrom had denounced the trade as an 'European iniquity' which had hindered the superior benefits of colonisation:

Thus Asia and America became the principal theatres of the ambition and avidity of the Europeans; and happy had it been for Africa if they had so continued. But it is distressing to recollect the rapid progress of European iniquity among the simple and untutored nations inhabiting the other quarters of the world . . . It was soon found that the aborigines of the former [America] could not endure the toils imposed on them by their new masters . . . Here commenced the *Slave-trade*.[37]

For Wadstrom, the slave trade, 'that scourge of the human race which has kept down a great part of the Africans in a state of anarchy and blood', had not only impeded the expanding forces of civilisation within Africa, but had prevented plantocratic merchants from 'countenancing the colonisation of that continent'.[38] Wad- strom's text thus proposed commercialisation of Africa as an alter- native to the transportation of West African slaves to the West

Indies. During his *Lecture on the Slave Trade*, Coleridge advanced a critique of the trade in terms of its creation and maintenance of unnecessary, or 'artificial wants'. He defined the produce of others' labour, such as the 'Sugars, Rum, Cotton, log-wood, cocoa, coffee, pimento, ginger, indigo, mahogany, and conserves' imported from the colonies, as a major source of the nation's miseries and vices.[39] If, argued Coleridge, English consumers were to confine their wishes to the 'actual necessaries and real comfort of Life', all causes of complaint and iniquity would be removed: 'What Nature demands Nature everywhere amply supplies – asking for it that portion only of Toil, which would have been otherwise necessary, as Exercise'.[40] Coleridge criticised government policy concerning the slave trade, higlighting the fact that the import duties of such 'slave' produce contributed a substantial amount to the government's revenue.[41] Paradoxically, however, it was precisely the marketing of such 'artificial wants' which had precipitated the increasing popularity of coffee houses throughout Britain, including that in which Coleridge's own lecture took place.

Nevertheless, Coleridge's text developed a narrative which juxtaposed the development of a spiritual capacity with the gratification of 'bodily' wants. Composed in the same year as the *Lecture*, Coleridge's *Six Lectures on Revealed Religion* (1795) had established a critique of the defects of the established Church and its clergy, and cited psychological evidence of truth as offered by David Hartley's *Observations on Man* (1749).[42] Likewise, his *Lecture* prioritised the transcendental potential of the mind and its pilgrimage towards an 'ever-widening prospect': 'the mind must enlarge the sphere of its activity'.[43] By fusing, perhaps unknowingly, Joseph Addison's principal ideas of the imagination stated in *The Spectator* (21 June 1712) and Mark Akenside's blank-verse poem, *Pleasures of Imagination* (1744), Coleridge's text advanced a prototype of liberationist ideology subtly synchronised with a diluted (or indeed, muted) form of spiritual discourse and individual autonomy:

To develope the powers of the Creator is our proper employment – and *to imitate Creativeness* by combination our most exalted and self-satisfying Delight. But we are progressive and must not rest content with present Blessings. Our Almighty Parent hath therefore given to us Imagination that stimulates to the attainment of *real* excellence by the contemplation of splendid Possibilities that still revivifies the dying motive within us, and fixing our eye on the *glittering Summits* that rise one above the other in *Alpine endlessness* still urges us up the ascent of Being, amusing the ruggedness of the road with the beauty and grandeur of the *ever-widening Prospect.*[44]

In the condensed form of the *Lecture on the Slave Trade* which appeared in the *Watchman* one year later, Coleridge made explicit man's dependence upon this faculty of the imagination in determining his position upon the Great Chain of Being: 'But Providence which has distinguished Man from the lower orders of Being by the progressiveness of his nature, forbids him to be contented. It has given us the faculty of the *Imagination*'. In so doing, Coleridge minimised his critique of slavery, or indeed the slave trade, and advanced instead the metamorphic translation of the discourse of the spirit into Romantic ideology's concept of the 'imagination'. As far as his criticism of the 'pestilent invention' of 'unreal wants' was concerned, Coleridge's analysis of the trade implied that without the demand for luxurious goods, the problem of London's poor would be eradicated. His lecture hence presented a shift in focus away from the plight of the African victims and highlighted instead the fate of those English citizens who, 'unwary or in greater distress', had been tricked into employment on board a slave-trading vessel. By prioritising the deplorable 'loss of liberty' encountered by these slave-trading seamen and their horrific experience amidst the 'unwholesomeness of the climate' of both the African continent and the middle passage, Coleridge's text relocated the traumatic experience of slavery onto the hardships suffered by locals:

From the brutality of their Captain and the unwholesomeness of the Climate through which they pass, it has been calculated that every Slave Vessel from the Port of Bristol loses on an average almost a fourth of the whole Crew – and so far is this Trade from being a nursery for Seamen, that the Survivors are rather shadows in their appearance than men and frequently perish in Hospitals after the completion of the Voyage.[45]

Coleridge's endeavour to avoid too direct a reference to the trade, alongside the omission from the published text of his vehement attack on the Pitt administration, reflected both the growing suppression of anti-state criticism in the 1790s and the continued reverberations of the public response to the St Domingue slave insurrections of 1791–1892. Yet the transcript of the original (now lost) manuscript of the *Lecture on the Slave Trade* by E. H. Coleridge suggests that the contributions made by Coleridge's colleague, Robert Southey, to the text strategically differed from Coleridge's focus on luxury and the sufferings of England's poor.[46] Drawing heavily on Benezet's account of his voyage to the coast of Guinea and the reports by the Dutch traveller, William Bosman, Southey's contribution to the narrative focused on the slaves themselves and presented a sexualised (and somewhat titillating) account of the slaves' experience during the Middle Passage, possibly in an attempt to heighten his audience's sympathy:

The wretched slaves . . . are examined *stark naked male and female*, and after being marked on the breast with a red hot iron, with the arms and names of the company or owner, who are the purchasers; they are *thrust promiscuously* into the ship – when on board they are always fettered with leg-shack[l]es and handcuffs, two and two – right and left – they lie in a crowded and cramped state, having neither their length nor breadth.[47]

These intertextual, co-editorial relations between Southey and Coleridge, and indeed between their work and Newton's *Authentic Narrative* were reinforced in Southey's 'The Sailor Who Had Served in the Slave Trade' (1790), a poem not dissimilar to Coleridge's ballad poem, 'The Rime of the Ancient Mariner' (1798). Based on the story of a dissenting minister in Bristol who discovered a sailor in a perplexed state of mind, Southey's and Coleridge's poetical compositions reworked the autobiographical narrative of the conscience-haunted sailor in Newton's text. Yet whereas in Coleridge's text, direct references to the slave trade were removed, in Southey's account, these were foregrounded and specified.[48] Thus whilst Coleridge's 'Rime of the Ancient Mariner' describes the journey of a guilt-ridden sailor who seeks forgiveness for his involuntary killing of an albatross, Southey's 'Sailor' relates the tale of his journeying on board a 'Guinea-man' towards the slave coast, the capture of a cargo of 300 negro slaves and their refusal to eat. One of these enslaved Africans, a 'woman sulkier than the rest', is singled out by the captain of the ship, who orders the sailor to 'tie her up' and flog her to death in front of the crew and the other captives. Her body is flung overboard and Southey's sailor, traumatised, repeatedly revisits the scene in his conscience:

> I saw the sea close over her,
>   Yet she was still in sight;
> I see her thrashing every where;
>   I see her day and night.[49]

The sailor's efforts to purge himself of guilt culminate in a moving confessional account of his cruel treatment of a female slave, an account similar to that found in the *Interesting Narrative* (1789) by the ex-slave, Olaudah Equiano (discussed in Chapter 8 below).[50] The casting of black slaves overboard into the Atlantic, whether healthy or dying, was not a rare occurrence; the most infamous example being that which occurred on board the slave ship *Zong*. During its return voyage to England in 1781, a debilitating illness wiped out a significant number of slaves on board. In an effort to recover the slavers' initial investment via the legal insurance provision for slaves 'irretrievably' lost at sea, 133 healthy slaves were cast overboard at the orders of Luke Collingwood, the *Zong*'s captain.[51] In court (*Gregson* v. *Gilbert*), the owners of the *Zong* pleaded successfully that the slaves' presence had endangered the water supply. As the note at the end of 'The Sailor' suggests, Southey felt that such accounts of inhumane treatment 'ought to be made as public as possible'. This was precisely the motivation behind the actions of the ex-slave, Olaudah Equiano, who, in March 1783, informed Granville Sharp of the *Zong* incident.[52] Sharp's initial response was to pursue the prosecution of the *Zong* sailors themselves. Although Sharp abandoned this approach, it was, in a sense, continued within the poems produced by Coleridge and Southey. In Coleridge's poem, however, specific identification of the slave trade as a 'sin' is absent; the unmotivated killing of the albatross is mitigated by the involuntary blessing of the slimy serpents of the sea. Indeed in both poems, deliverance is granted, or at least secured, by the respective mariners' pleas for forgiveness. Nevertheless, the issue of forgiveness on a scale that implicates the error at the heart of Britain's legal and economic practice, is not, and indeed could not be addressed so long as slaves were considered as forms of property.

Taking his cue from William Fox's famous pamphlet, *A Short Account of the African Slave Trade, and an Address to the People of Great Britain on the Propriety of Abstaining from West Indian Sugar and Rum*, Coleridge's *Lecture on the Slave Trade* proposed abstinence from slave-grown produce, 'sweetened with the Blood of the Murdered', as an effective means of achieving a cessation of the trade – a method which he considered preferable to the circulation of petitions by what he termed 'the vanity of pretended Sensibility': that is, well-educated philanthropic females.[53] Yet Coleridge's concluding inflammatory lines daringly correlated the volatile insurrections and 'justified rebellions' of West Indian slaves in the colonies with the desperate plight of the British peasantry:

For I appeal to common sense whether to affirm that the Slaves are as well off as our Peasantry, be not the same as to assert that our Peasantry are as bad off as Negro Slaves – and whether if the Peasantry believed it there is a man amongst them *who [would] not rebel? and be justified in Rebellion?*[54]

Thus Coleridge's lecture 'on' rather than 'against' the slave trade strategically avoided a discussion of the slaves themselves; rather, it centred upon a discussion of the concept of luxury and the sufferings of the English peasantry, and hinted at the threat which he felt had been posed to his creative 'empire' by the females of 'pretended sensibility'. Yet despite its shortcomings, Coleridge's *Lecture* provides ample evidence of the poet's awareness and involvement in abolitionist activity. It was, however, within the 'conversation poems', composed during the late 1790s, that the poet presented a sensitive exploration of the conditions of estrangement, captivity and liberty, and in so doing, revealed the influence of the discourse of radical dissenting Protestantism on his own contribution to Romantic poetry.

COLERIDGE'S DISCOURSE OF THE SPIRIT: THE 'CONVERSATION POEMS'

During the period of his closest friendship with Wordsworth, Coleridge composed a letter to Thomas Poole (6 February 1797), the first in a series of five autobiographical letters written at Poole's request. In that letter the poet expressed his admiration for the power of the spiritual autobiographies composed by dissenting Protestants, published by *The Gospel Magazine and Theological Review*, which had made its first appearance the year before:

I could inform the dullest author how he might write an interesting book – let him relate the events of his own Life with honesty, not disguising the feelings that accompanied them. – I never yet read even a Methodist's 'Experience' in the Gospel Magazine without receiving instruction & amusement: & I should almost despair of that Man, who could peruse the Life of John Woolman without an amelioration of Heart.[55]

Although there is no further evidence to confirm Coleridge's detailed knowledge of these or any other spiritual autobiographies by radical dissenting Protestants, Coleridge's reference to the Quaker-abolitionist and spiritual autobiographer, John Woolman, suggests that his interest in such autobiographies emerged from an antislavery context. Likewise, evidence of his borrowings from the Bristol Library between 1793 and 1798 reveal the poet's thorough investigation of antislavery accounts: in March 1795 Coleridge borrowed the third volume of the library's *Miscellaneous Poems* which contained Hannah More's *Slavery: A Poem* (1788) and Ann Yearsley's *Poems on the Inhumanity of the Slave Trade* (1788).[56] Between March and August 1795, Coleridge also borrowed Raynal's *Philosophical and Political History of the Settlements* (1776), Clarkson's *Essay on the Impolicy of the Slave Trade* (1788), Wadstrom's *Essay on Colonisation* (1794–1795) and Edwards' *The History, Civil and Commercial, of the British Colonies in the West Indies* (1793–1794).

On the front page of the first volume of *The Gospel Magazine*, the editor introduced 'A Word to those Lovers of Truth' in 'these days of blasphemy, rebuke, infidelity, heresy and error' and adamantly claimed that the narratives (including the 'Memoirs of the Life of John James Claude', the 'Remarkable Passages in the Life of Mr Vavasor Powel', and the 'Singular Experience and Great Sufferings of Mrs Agnes') which followed were valid examples of 'sterling truth, in all its brilliancy and glory'.[57] Over two decades earlier, the abolitionist Quaker, John Woolman (1720–1772) had published his *Journal of the Life, Gospel Labours, and Christian Experiences of that Faithful Minister of Jesus Christ, John Woolman* in Philadelphia in 1774, in London in 1775 and in Dublin in 1776. In this *Journal*, the narrative of Woolman's deliverance from the 'depths of misery' by the 'inward principle' demonstrated his concern for the inhuman and iniquitous practice of slavery:

I was so afflicted in my mind, that I said, before my master and the friend, that I believed slave-keeping to be a practice inconsistent with the Christian religion.[58]

Likewise, in his tract, *Some Considerations on the Keeping of Negroes* (1754), Woolman had declared to his Quaker Friends in words not unlike those contained within Coleridge's *Lecture*, that it was their duty as 'creatures accountable to our Creator, to employ rightly the understanding which he hath given us'.[59] Moreover, Woolman had identified the 'spirit which breathes peace and good will' as the agent which would bring about their philanthropic ambitions.[60]

In keeping with the narrative framework of Woolman's text and those contained within the *Gospel Magazine*, Coleridge elucidated in his letter to Poole his own plans for a similar autobiographical project. This, he suggested, would trace the progress of his life with all its 'charms of variety: high Life, & low Life, Vices and Virtues, great Folly & some Wisdom'.[61] Such a 'task' would prove to be invaluable in his effort to 'renew and deepen' his reflections of the past and thereby reveal the 'many untoward circumstances' which had concurred to form those 'weaknesses and defects of his character'.[62] Coleridge's interest in the discourse of radical dissenting Protestantism may have been provoked by his despair at the news of his brother Frank's suicide in 1792, the deaths of six members of his immediate family between 1780 and 1792 and his own feelings of hopelessness following his secret enlistment in the King's Light Dragoons on 2 December 1793: 'Shall I profess an abhorrence of my past conduct? . . . I am lost in the labyrinth, the trackless wilderness of my own bosom'.[63] The fact that Coleridge's father was vicar of the parish church at Ottery St Mary (where Joanna Southcott was baptised) in Devon and that Coleridge visited him and his brother there on a fairly regular basis, suggests that he may have been familiar with reports of the spiritual teachings advanced by Southcott and Wesley. Likewise, his running away after a quarrel with his brother Frank in the autumn of 1779 and his subsequent night spent by the banks of the River Otter during a storm suggests that he would have responded sympathetically to the narratives of salvation and despair presented within spiritual autobiographies, by John Newton, William Cowper and the slaves.

Whatever the actual source of his awareness of this literary trope, the poet's interest in 'spiritual autobiography' occurred alongside his deliberate withdrawal from the sociopolitical, and indeed, abolitionist, sphere. As he explained in his letter to J. P. Estlin, by the summer of 1797 he had become, or so he claimed, 'wearied with politics even to soreness'. One year later, in a letter to his brother of March 1798, Coleridge announced that he had completely detached himself from any consideration of 'immediate causes'. Rather, he announced that he would turn his attentions towards the composition of a style of poetry which he believed would 'elevate the imagination & set the affections in right tune by the beauty of the inanimate impregnated as with the living soul, by the presence of Life'. The works composed during this period, however, reveal a subtle continuation of the concepts of spiritual liberty and self-autonomy, characteristic of both the language of radical dissenting

Protestantism and abolitionist discourse. Likewise, according to Bernard Martin, it was very possible that Coleridge had read Newton's *Authentic Narrative* or had had it brought to his attention by William or Dorothy Wordsworth between 13 November 1797 and 23 March 1798.[64] Indeed it seems that Wordsworth was making use of John Newton's *Authentic Narrative* (most likely the episode in which Newton becomes a slave to a man named Clow on the Guinea Coast of Africa) at the same time that Coleridge was composing 'The Rime of the Ancient Mariner' (1797).[65]

Thomas Clarkson had introduced Coleridge to the Quaker, John Broadhead, and during his time at Leeds, Coleridge reread the works of many of his favourite Quaker authors, including George Fox, William Penn and John Woolman, amply demonstrating the intertextual transatlantic connection between nonconformist religious sentiment, abolitionist ideology and Romantic concerns.[66] Both Coleridge's and Wordsworth's work denotes an important metamorphosis of the captivity and liberationist genre in which the concept of spiritual impregnation, as recorded by Wesley and other radical prophets, is subtly translated into the power of poetry and identified as imagination's power to impregnate and thereby liberate the 'living soul', hence inaugurating (or rather confirming) the poet/prophet's spiritual role. And yet whilst structurally and ideologically these poets continue the trope of liberationist, individual determinism advanced by such spiritual autobiographies, they also determine a severance from and erasure of overt references to abolitionism. Coleridge's 'conversation poems' skilfully establish a composite continuation of, and departure from the discourse of spiritual autobiography articulated within the paradigm of radical dissenting Protestantism.[67]

Dedicated to Sara Fricker, whom Coleridge had married on 4 October 1795, four months following his *Lecture on the Slave Trade*, the first of these 'conversation poems', 'The Eolian Harp' (1795), presented a transformation of Wesley's image of the 'breath of the spirit' as a metaphor delineating the workings of an 'intellectual breeze' which stirred the mind into consciousness:

> And what if all of animated nature
> Be but organic Harps diversely fram'd,
> That tremble into thought, as o'er them sweeps
> Plastic and vast, one intellectual breeze,
> At once the Soul of each, and God of all?[68]

Sara's mild reproof cautions the poet against too scientific a rationale of the 'incomprehensible', that which one 'inly feels'. Yet the poem's authentication of the powers of the spirit (that 'indeterminate breeze' which impregnates all things) and its complex interrelationship with self-knowledge, remains unchallenged. It is a breeze, which like Wesley's breath of the spirit enlivens, animates and in a sense 'reveals' the self. Coleridge's use of the language of radical dissenting Protestantism forges a link with that employed within the slave narratives, yet in Coleridge's version, the self is mapped on to a mode of discourse severed (or seemingly so) from socioeconomic or historical specificity – a self prescribed *by* the self. In the editorial amendments to the poem of 1817, this source of liberation is redetermined as a power, no longer originating exclusively from without, but as a power which emerged from *within* the self: 'O! the one Life within us and abroad, / Which meets all motion and becomes its soul, / A light in sound, a sound-like power in light, / Rhythm in all thought, and joyance every where'.[69] Although the difference is subtle, the implications of this transformation are great: in Coleridge's hands, narratives of spiritual liberation and self-authorisation become centred around the concept of the imagination and the individual, rather than the collective self.

Coleridge's poem, 'This Lime-Tree Bower My Prison', composed in June 1797, inscribes a model of redemption similarly expounded in the autobiographical narratives of spiritual salvation. More importantly perhaps, in this poetical model of deliverance, the powers of the spirit are unambiguously replaced by the liberating powers of the poet's own imagination. His friends William, Dorothy and Charles Lamb are free to wander as they please, yet Coleridge envisages himself as 'imprisoned' within the perimeters of the lime-tree bower, an image which reflects the decrepit or 'stagnant' powers of his own powers of creativity: '. . . I have lost / Beauties and feelings, such as would have been / Most sweet to my remembrance even when age / Had dimm'd mine eyes to blindness!'[70] Whereas the magnificent external landscape revives the 'gentle-hearted' Charles (whose insane sister had stabbed their mother to death ten months earlier), Coleridge's inner self is impregnated by a power that emerges from within. It is a power which enables him to imagine himself liberated from the constraints of his present condition and reunited with his friends: 'A delight / Comes sudden on my heart, and I am glad / As I myself were there!'[71] As with Wesley's resonant utterances of the spirit's revitalising power of 'new birth', the restorative power of the imagination liberates the anguished poetical self from physical and mental confinement and achieves an hypostatic state of illuminated bliss. In this state, akin to sanctification, the bower is transformed from an image of imprisonment and exile to that of 'transparent' and therefore unbinding, luxurious foliage. Hence the poet glimpses a prophetic state of being in which he is able to discover ('gaze', 'perceive'), acknowledge ('henceforth I shall know') and partake in that which is usually unavailable to man ('And sometimes . . . contemplate with lively joy, the joys we cannot share'); a participation within manifestations of infinitude (space) and eternity (time):

> . . . So my friend
> Struck with deep joy may stand, as I have stood,
> Silent with swimming sense; yea, gazing round
> On the wide landscape, gaze till all doth seem
> Less gross than bodily; and of such hues
> As veil the Almighty Spirit, when yet he makes
> Spirits perceive his presence.[72]

As the poet is 'blessed' with a disclosure of the realm inhabited by the 'Almighty Spirit', he is endowed with a mystical power of articulation which enables him to speak of salvation and which fuses his own text with a manifestation of divine logos, the Word.

COLERIDGE'S 'LETTER TO SARA HUTCHINSON'

In line with the early 'conversation poems', Coleridge's 'Letter to Sara Hutchinson' remains distinctly informed by the schema of spiritual autobiography in its elucidation of the poet's acute sense of melancholy, his depressed state of delusion and inactivity, and his subsequent 'deliverance'. Composed on the evening of 4 April 1802 after hearing the first four stanzas of Wordsworth's *Ode: Intimations of Immortality*, the original version of the 340-line verse 'Letter to Sara' underwent a significant series of revisions and deletions over a six month period, the final variant of which (entitled *Dejection: An Ode*) presents a far less autobiographical, less personalised and less critical text. In this subsequent published version, dedicated to Wordsworth under the pseudonym 'Edmund' and printed in the *Morning Post* (4 October 1802) on both Wordsworth's wedding day and the seventh anniversary of Coleridge's own wedding, the earlier references to

Sara Hutchinson (sister of Wordsworth's fiancée with whom Coleridge had fallen in love) and to his disastrous relationship with Sara Fricker were carefully omitted.[73]

In the original form of the 'Letter to Sara', the poet's depressed state isolates him from any solace arising from the soothing landscape and its enigmatic evening sunset: hence he gazes 'in this heartless Mood' with 'how blank an eye!'[74] Identifying himself with the hero of Milton's *Samson Agonistes*, Coleridge's 'genial spirits' fail to deliver him from this state of spiritual malaise or from the erosion of his innate creative powers effected by the oppressive 'smoth'ring Weight' of his 'coarse domestic life' (experiencing no 'mutual mild Enjoyment of its own') with Delilah/Sara Fricker: 'All this long Eve, so balmy & serene, / Have I been gazing on the western Sky . . . / I see them all, so excellently fair! / I see, not feel, how beautiful they [clouds] are!'[75] This 'burden' of a grief 'without a pang', 'stifling, drowsy and unimpassioned', constitutes an emotional and spiritual sterility ('Void, dark, drear') which the poet suffers alone, unconsoled by external forms which, according to him, remain 'lifeless shapes': 'I may not hope from outward Forms to win / The Passion & the Life, *whose Fountains are within!*'[76]

Coleridge's search for spiritual liberation takes him on a retrospective journey through time towards the memory of his younger self, a being similarly 'cloistered in a City school', who gazes with 'secret yearnings' towards an hypothetical maiden, 'a kind of Vision to me!' who exists beyond the boundaries of his imprisonment.[77] Having 'established' a continuum through time between his past and present self, the poet projects a future 'vision' of Sara, whose gaze he imagines as coalescing with his own yearning for spiritual and emotional liberation. As the boundaries of space and time are transcended, the poet's metaphorical blindness is miraculously 'cured' amidst an ecstatic moment of spiritual awakening and emotional deliverance which leaves his spirit 'awe-stricken with the Excess / And trance-like Depth of it's brief Happiness'.

> I feel my spirit moved –
> And wheresoe'er thou be,
> O Sister! O Beloved!
> Those dear mild Eyes, that see
> Even now the Heaven, *I* see –
> There is a Prayer in them! It is for *me* –
> And I, dear Sara – *I* am blessing *thee*![78]

In accordance with the structural framework of former confessional narratives and spiritual autobiographies by radical dissenting Protestants, Coleridge's poetical 'Letter to Sara' underscores the distinction between his former 'blessed' self and his present despairing self: 'For Hope grew round me, like the climbing Vine . . ./ But now Ill Tidings bow me down . . .'.[79] However, despite his emotional wretchedness and anguished inactivity, the poet's text expounds a new-found faith in his own 'shaping Spirit of Imagination'; that gift which, it is claimed, nature gave him at his birth, a powerful and innate capacity to transform his captivity into a condition of liberation.[80] This intense release from emotional deadlock inaugurates a deliverance from spiritual dead(wed)lock and advances instead a phase of confident, self-authorised mobility: 'I too will crown me with a Coronal'.[81] Denying the basis of his earlier belief in the passive role played by the mind (and indeed, the soul), the poet proclaims his new-found faith in the creative potential of the 'shaping spirit' of imagination:

> Ah! from the Soul itself must issue forth
> A Light, a Glory, and a luminous Cloud
>   Enveloping the Earth!
> And from the Soul itself must there be se[nt]
> A sweet & potent Voice, of it's own Bir[th],
> Of all sweet Sounds the Life & Element.[82]

Accordingly the poet imagines a superior 'marriage' between mind and nature which liberates him from his previous state of domestic captivity (the marriage between two 'unequal minds, two discordant wills') and his desperate condition as a *tongueless* (and hence, creatively 'flightless') poet/Philomel. Hence his text celebrates the impregnating power of the mind itself: 'O Sara! we receive but what we give, / And in *our* Life alone does Nature live. / Our's is her Wedding Garment, our's her Shroud'.[83]

As the powers of the 'spirit' and the poet's imagination merge into one, Coleridge's poem presents a prophetic vision of regeneration which resonates with the apocalyptical language of the Book of Revelation. As 'joy' is identified as the dowry which emerges from this imagined 'wedlock', Coleridge endeavours to expound a purely spiritual, unerotic embrace which transcends the conditions of the physical, or indeed 'sensual' world, and 'satisfies' the condition of Sara's continued physical absence:

JOY, Sara! is the *Spirit* & the Power,
  That wedding Nature to us gives in Dower
A new Earth & new Heaven
Undreamt of by the Sensual & the Proud!
Joy is that strong Voice, Joy that luminous Cloud –
  We, *we ourselves rejoice!* [84]

Interestingly, Coleridge's 'Letter' establishes an important shift away
from the voyeuristic Book of Revelation ('And I saw the holy city,
new Jerusalem, coming down out of heaven from God, prepared as
a bride adorned for her husband')[85] and denotes instead a personalised account of the poet's own spiritual marriage as a reciprocation
of that between God/Israel and the New Jerusalem: 'A new Earth &
new Heaven / Undreamt of by the Sensual & the Proud!'[86]
Although the poet's claims for a resolutely unerotic 'spiritual'
embrace signifies an unambiguous severance from the overtly erotic
tone of the Old Testament Song of Songs around which it revolves
('My beloved is mine and I am his . . . Upon my bed by night I
sought him whom my soul loves'), nevertheless such a division sits
problematically amidst the distinctly physical paradigm of the
earlier stanzas.[87] In an effort to complete this process of de-
erotisation, Sara is transformed into a maternal (rather than
sexualised) image of the Holy Spirit ('mother Dove'), who, with
wings 'blessedly outspread', manifests the promise of divine possibility, corresponding to the poet's imaginative potential. Furthermore, as the confessional 'Letter to Sara Hutchinson' advocates the
poet's own 'spiritual' liberation from emotional and domestic
slavery, the poetical ego emerges 'victorious' with a newly formed
(de-eroticised) sense of self, ultimately freed (or rather, almost freed)
from any overt relationship with either the discourse of the spirit or
the language of abolitionism.

Thus Coleridge's poetical schema prescribes both a revival and
revision of spiritual autobiography established by radical dissenting
Protestantism, and reveals the subtle relationship between the emergence of antislavery ideology and the development of the Romantic
genre. The discourse of the spirit, with its connotations of liberationist ideology and identity configuration, had a distinct influence
upon a body of writing which we have come to know as 'Romantic';
as well as the body of lesser-known work referred to as the slave
narratives. Yet, as I shall discuss below, although the Romantic poet,
William Wordsworth continued the liberationist and self-authorising

dialogue advanced by radical dissenting Protestantism, his poems also paradoxically witnessed a deliberate severance from specific tenets of abolitionism and overt manifestations of spiritual discourse.

WORDSWORTH'S SPIRITUAL AUTOBIOGRAPHY

According to Abrams' *Natural Supernaturalism*, Wordsworth's *Prelude* traced a harmonic secularisation of the Judaeo-Christian myth, framed within the parameters of epic biography and thereby described the poet's emergence as a self-elected prophet:

> Wordsworth's is a secular theodicy . . . which translates the painful process of Christian conversion and redemption into a painful process of self-formation, crisis, and self-recognition, which culminates in a stage of self-coherence, self-awareness, and *assured power* that is its own reward.[88]

Likewise, in his book, *Wordsworth's 'Natural Methodism'* (1975), Richard Brantley argued that the poem's emphasis upon self-mastery, spiritual renewal and confessional introspection determined Wordsworth, not only as a 'definable moral and religious poet', but established the connection between Wordsworth's work, Evangelical Anglicanism and Evangelical nonconformism.[89] In an expansion of the ideas put forward by M. H. Abrams and Geoffrey Hartman, Brantley suggested that Wordsworth's faith was strategically influenced by the broad and reverential evangelicalism of the 'first' Evangelical, John Wesley, and the Evangelical philanthropist and abolitionist, William Wilberforce. Indeed, in the lengthy letter which praised Wilberforce's *Practical View of the Prevailing Religious System of Professed Christians Contrasted with Real Christianity* (1798) and which accompanied a complimentary copy of the *Lyrical Ballads*, Wordsworth claimed to be a 'Fellow-labourer' with Wilberforce 'in the same Vineyard'.[90] However, as I shall discuss below, although the poet's praise of Wilberforce suggested an intimate liaison with both the discourse of dissenting Protestantism and abolitionist ideology, Wordsworth's relationship with these movements was deeply ambiguous.

Whilst at Cambridge, Wordsworth encountered concepts of evangelicalism both formally and informally through the activities and beliefs of his friends, Thomas Middleton (later Bishop of Calcutta), John Gisbourne (a convert to Methodism), William Mathews (son of a London Methodist preacher) and the fervent Evangelical ministry of Charles Simeon (vicar of Holy Trinity during the 1780s).[91] Likewise, the poet's appropriation and revision of spiritual discourse and liberationist ideology may have been influenced by Coleridge's plans to develop the autobiographical style of the Methodist narratives and the philanthropic interests and concerns of the poet's sister, Dorothy. In fact, the nature of Dorothy's close friendship with the parliamentary abolitionist, William Wilberforce, prompted Jane Pollard, one of Dorothy's closest friends, to predict a likely marriage between them, an hypothesis adamantly denied by Dorothy in her self-deprecating reply of 30 April 1790:

Your way of accounting for my apparent absence of mind diverted me exceedingly. I will set forward with assuring you that my heart is perfectly disengaged and then endeavour to shew you how very improbable it is that Mr W. would think of me . . . Mr W. would, were he ever to marry, look for a Lady possessed of many more accomplishments than I can boast.[92]

During his stay at her uncle's parsonage, Wilberforce had introduced Dorothy to a variety of 'Great Awakening' texts, including Philip Doddridge's *Family Expositor* (1739–1756).[93] Wordsworth's discussions with Dorothy over the concerns of the 'soul' described in Francis Wrangham's *Thirteen Practical Sermons: Founded on Doddridge's 'Rise and Progress of Religion in the Soul'* (1800) appear to have had a pervasive influence on his poetical compositions, in terms of their emphasis upon intense self-examination, emotional crisis and spiritual illumination.[94] Indeed Wordsworth had met Francis Wrangham *c.* 1795 when Basil Montagu, the bastard son of the fourth Earl of Sandwich and friend to Godwin, had introduced them. Dorothy's role as mediator between William and various sociopolitical and dissenting discourses of the 1790s may be confirmed by her response to the defeat of Wilberforce's Bill proposing the Abolition of the Slave Trade: 'I was indeed greatly mortified on hearing of Mr W.'s bad success, every friend to humanity must applaud his zeal and lament that it failed in its effect'.[95] In a letter of 8 May 1792, Dorothy persuasively and determinedly urged Jane Pollard to participate in the antislavery debate: 'I hope you were an *immediate* abolitionist and are angry with the House of Commons for continuing the traffic in human flesh so long as till 1796 but you will also rejoice that so *much* has been done. I hate Mr Dundas'.[96] Dorothy Wordsworth's transcription of an extract from letter V of Newton's *Authentic Narrative*, was made sometime between 1798–1799 and provides the source of

Book VI of Wordsworth's own *Prelude* of 1805: 'And as I have read of one by shipwreck thrown . . . who having brought to land a single volume and no more' (VI, 160–5). Wordsworth was most likely referring to the passage of the *Authentic Narrative* in which Newton had described his ill-treatment at the hands of his master's African mistress:

> Though destitute of food and clothing, depressed to a degree beyond common wretchedness, I could sometimes collect my mind to mathematical studies. I had bought *Barrow's Euclid* at Plymouth . . . it was the only volume I brought on shore; it was always with me, and I used to take it to remote corners of the island by the seaside, and draw my *diagrams* with a long stick upon the sand. Thus I often beguiled my sorrows, and almost forgot my feeling.[97]

This 'relationship' between Newton's and Wordsworth's texts, as with those of Southey and Coleridge discussed above, suggests a process of intertextuality between these authors. Given the captivity motif which provides the overall framework for Wordsworth's *Prelude*, it seems difficult to imagine that Wordsworth was unaware of Newton's subsequent debates over slavery.[98] Moreover, as I shall elucidate, Wordsworth's poetical spiritual autobiography bears a marked resemblance to the first literary articulations by black slaves.

In the 1798 draft version of the *Prelude*, the poet identified the natural and spiritual forces which he believed had shaped his early years and nourished his poetical propensity. The 'divine' visitations of the spirit are hence translated, in Wordsworth's schema, into a tableau of privileged election, identifying him as one 'chosen' by the 'spirit of nature': 'was it for this / That one, the fairest of all rivers, loved / To blend his murmurs with my nurse's song . . . / And from his fords and shallows, sent a voice / To intertwine my dreams?'[99] As the poet's salvation is presented in terms of his restored sense of purpose, the opening lines of the 1805 version of the *Prelude* refer not only to the concluding lines of Milton's *Paradise Lost*, but (as with the slave narratives) to the Israelites' escape from Egyptian bondage related in Exodus 13:3:

> A captive greets thee, coming from a house
> *Of bondage, from yon city's walls set free,*
> *A prison where he hath been long immured.*
> *Now I am free, enfranchised and at large,*
> *May fix my habitation where I will . . .*

Joyous, *nor scared at its own liberty,*
I look about, and should the guide I chuse
Be nothing better than a wandering cloud
I cannot miss my way.[100]

Wordsworth discerns these spiritual visitations as manifestations of the 'sweet breath' from heaven which, like Coleridge's 'intellectual breeze', 'saturates' his body with a 'vital breeze'.[101] Wesley's 'discourse of the spirit' had, of course, similarly presented images describing the 'breath' of heaven and its blessed visitations, but Wordsworth appropriates this spiritual framework in order to determine himself as a prophet, not only graced with the power of divine tongues, but with the ability to transcribe such oral utterances into text, the written word: 'To the open fields I told / A prophesy; poetic numbers came / Spontaneously, and clothed in priestly robe / My spirit, thus singled out, as it might seem, / For holy services'.[102] For this reason, the 'conviction of sin' episode (an essential tenet of the 'conversion narrative') presented in the *Prelude* identifies the poet's time at Cambridge as a period of transgression from which he must be saved. As with Cowper's poem *The Task*, it describes an indulgence in erring dreams rather than visionary prophecy – 'I was the dreamer, they the dream; I roamed / Delighted through the motley spectacle'.[103] 'Sealed' by the attributes of divine election, however, such lapses fail, or so he claims, to inflict any permanent damage upon his poetic destiny as 'a chosen son'; rather, they serve to confirm his conviction in his own holy powers.

Three further references in the *Prelude* complete the narrative of the poet's spiritual deterioration: his encounter with the 'Babel din' ('barbarian and infernal – 'tis a dream Monstrous in colour, motion, shape, sight, sound') of the city of London; his carefully disguised 'testimony' of *sexual* transgression (which revolves around his encounter with Annette Vallon and the conception of his illegitimate child); and finally, his abandonment of spiritual truths by his embracement of Godwin's philosophical rationalism, his ruthless 'probing' into one of 'Nature's holiest places'.[104] Yet despite these 'lapses', Wordsworth's ultimate self-restoration, disclosed in the final book of the 1805 *Prelude*, represents a magnificent reworking of dissenting Protestantism's model of apocalyptical sanctification – a witness of divine spirit ('a spirit / Living in time and space, and far diffused')[105] which simultaneously obliterates and confirms the poet's identity:

> For instantly a light upon the turf
> Fell like a flash. I looked about, and lo,
> The moon stood naked in the heavens at height
> Immense above my head, and on the shore
> I found myself of a huge sea of mist,
>
> . . . and it appeared to me
> The perfect image of a mighty mind,
> Of one that feeds upon infinity,
> That is exalted by an under-presence,
> The sense of God, or whatsoe'er is dim
> Or vast in its own being – above all.[106]

In accordance with the autobiographical framework of the conversion narratives, therefore, Wordsworth's discourse of spiritual
ecstasy, divine witness and ethereal illumination discloses a process
of self-engendered ecstasy that continues and revises the traditional
schema of spiritual salvation. Indeed, as with Coleridge's texts,
Wordsworth's *Prelude* advances a discourse of spiritual 'under-pres-
ence' which illuminates and exalts, and more importantly, is both
'God-given' and *self*-initiated. In this way, the creation of matter
from the void described in the biblical account of the holy spirit in
Genesis, is envisaged by the poet as similarly informing his *own*
powers of creative imagination.[107] As 'the perfect image of the
mighty mind' reveals the union of God's and the poet's identity,
Wordsworth's 'word' is figured within a syncretic collusion with that
Word which animates the universe. Accordingly, the power to
assimilate, transform and illuminate is described as having been
appropriated by the poet himself: 'Imagination! . . . / Like an
unfathered vapour, here that power, / In all the might of its
endowments, came / Athwart me'.[108] Recovering from the self-
erasure, self-obliteration and spiritual excess typical of spiritual
autobiography, Wordsworth's text recognises not the power of the
divine, but the ethereal powers of the individual's mind over the
dimensions of space and time:

> Tumult and peace, the darkness and the light,
> Were all like workings of one mind, the features
> Of the same face, blossoms upon one tree,
> Characters of the great apocalypse,
> The types and symbols of eternity,
> Of first, and last, and midst, and without end.[109]

Drawing upon the tenets of autobiography popularised by radical dissenting Protestantism, Wordsworth's *Prelude* confirms the inter-relationship between Romanticism and the discourse of the spirit advanced by the confessional narratives of conversion. As with Coleridge's 'conversation poems', Wordsworth's work maintains the liberationist rhetoric of spiritual autobiography, yet reveals a discernible severance from the abolitionist activities of the late eighteenth-century transatlantic forum, especially in his address to the slave insurrectionist, Toussaint L'Ouverture.

WORDSWORTH AND THE SLAVES

On 2 February 1803, *The Morning Post* published the following sonnet by Wordsworth, 'To Toussaint L'Ouverture', the addressee of which was one of the principal commanders of the violent slave uprising of August 1791. During this insurrection (which was celebrated in Southey's 'To the Genius of Africa') approximately 20,000 former slaves abandoned the slave estates of the French owned colony of St Domingue, the largest and most productive slave colony in the Caribbean:

> TOUSSAINT, the most unhappy man of men!
> Whether the whistling Rustic tend his plough
> Within thy hearing, or thy head be now
> Pillowed in some deep dungeon's earless den; –
> O miserable Chieftain! where and when
> Wilt thou find patience! Yet die not; do thou
> Wear rather in thy bonds a cheerful brow:
> Though fallen thyself, never to rise again,
> Live, and take comfort. Thou hast left behind
> Powers that will work for thee; air, earth, and skies;
> There's not a breathing of the common wind
> That will forget thee; thou hast great allies;
> Thy friends are exultations, agonies,
> And love, and man's unconquerable mind.[110]

Toussaint L'Ouverture, whose pseudonym registered his belief in his own self-appointment as 'one who makes an opening' (that is, the source of hiatus or fissure in the sociopolitical and linguistic order) had seen himself as Napoleon Bonaparte's counterpart and had thus referred to himself as 'the First of the Blacks' in a letter addressed to the latter, 'the First of the Whites'.[111] Wordsworth's reference to the 'Chieftain's' confinement within some 'deep dungeon's earless den' alluded to the slave insurrectionist's detention within the icy dungeons of the Fortress of Joux in the Jura mountains where he died after a ten-month imprisonment in April 1803. Toussaint's imprisonment was similarly described in Marcus Rainsford's *Historical Account of the Black Empire of Hayti: Comprehending a View of the Principal Transactions in the Revolution in Saint Domingo* (1805):

He who had been the benefactor of white people in a country where their enormities had provoked hatred, whose power was never stained by malevolence, and who was greater in his fall, than his enemies in their assumed power, was kept in a *damp and cheerless prison*, without the comfort of a single friend, without trial or even examination . . . This prison may be considered the sepulture of Toussaint. France forgot awhile the habits of a civilized nation, to entomb one she should have graced with a public triumph; and England . . . *should have guarded from violation the rights of humanity in its person.*[112]

Wordsworth's sonnet conclusively marks the translation of the slaves' insurrectionist demands (and indeed, the discourse of abolitionism) into Romanticism's claims for the liberationist powers of the mind. It situates the attributes of the black military leader within a schema that avoids any discussion of race and determines the indiscernible spiritual workings of the natural elements as inseparable from the 'natural' progression of man's 'unconquerable mind'. The poet's homage to L'Ouverture, as one of those 'who will not forget thee', consequently presents the great revolutionary leader as a manifestation of that expansionist, 'intellectual' power, the 'unconquerable mind', and as an individual now fused with the spiritual 'breathings of the common wind'. Likewise Wordsworth's conviction that despite his defeat and imprisonment, the slave rebel should retain a 'cheerful brow', reinscribes Addison's belief in the power of the imagination described in *The Spectator* of 21 June 1712:

By this Faculty [the imagination] a Man in a Dungeon is capable of entertaining himself with Scenes and Landscapes more beautiful than any that can be found in the whole Compass of Nature.[113]

Wordsworth's sonnet provides an important example of the appropriation and concealment of abolitionist discourse contained within Romantic poetry, via its gradual withdrawal from its original focus, the great slave rebel, and its subsequent prioritisation of the symbolic emblem of Romanticism – the power of 'man's unconquerable mind', the imagination. This withdrawal from a sociohistoric figure of non-western specificity was similarly described in the *Prelude* by the poet's account of his conscious detachment from the momentum of the abolitionists' caravan 'towards Liberty' which, by the time of his return from France in 1792, had spread its influence across England: 'a contention . . . raised up / Against the traffickers in Negro blood'.[114] During his absence, public support for the Society of the Abolition of the Slave Trade (founded in 1787) had steadily gained momentum and although Wilberforce's Abolition Bill was defeated in 1791, the 'virtuous feeling' of the antislavery campaign continued to escalate. In 1792, 519 petitions bearing almost half a million signatures were presented to Parliament demanding a cessation of the trade. The Bill providing for a gradual abolition of the trade was finally passed in the House of Commons by a narrow margin of 151 to 132 votes and in the House of Lords in 1807.[115]

Conversely, however, in his own autobiographical text, Wordsworth strategically endeavours to sever himself from any overt identification with the abolitionist movement: 'For me that strife had ne'er / fastened on my affections' (Book 10, lines 218–19). Indeed, he suggests, somewhat dubiously, that the progressive force which had inspired revolutionary France would similarly generate a 'natural' cessation of the slave trade:

My sorrow, having laid this faith to heart,
That if France prospered good men would not long
Pay fruitless worship to humanity,
And this most rotten branch of human shame
(Object, as seemed, of a superfluous pains)
Would fall together with its parent tree.[116]

The poet's faith in 'natural progression' underscores his allegiance to gradual rather than immediate abolition and moreover, indicates his reluctance to consider colonial insurrection as an appropriate model of sociopolitical reform. Likewise, his reference to the 'natural' decay of Milton's 'rotten tree' in *Paradise Lost*, offers an inherently western epistemological response to the 'problem' of the trade, an image which attempts to conceal Britain's past role in nurturing the trade and which fails to acknowledge the insurrectionist efforts of the slaves themselves. By positing the French Revolution as a precursor *to* rather than descendant *of* the liberationist ideology promoted by abolitionists (and slaves), Wordsworth's poem demonstrates a shift away from antislavery activities within the colonies (the non-west) and focuses instead upon the revolutions of the western world. This shift suggests a reluctance to consider the parasitic relation between Great Britain and the colonies and reverses the proposals set out in the pro-rebellion pamphlet by James Stephen, Wilberforce's brother-in-law.[117] Whereas the 1789 revolution in France, despite the poet's subsequent disappointment, could still be celebrated as a praiseworthy event, references to the slave insurrections in St Domingue (1791), Jamaica (1795–1796), Grenada (1795–1797) and Virginia (1800) were carefully excluded from his text and its subsequent revisions.

According to Mary Jacobus, Wordsworth's silence about the material conditions upon which his poems and his culture were ultimately founded, indicate the poet's endeavour to maintain the 'fictive representation of the providentially self-shaped mind' within the autobiographical project.[118] This silence may also have been connected to the colonial activities undertaken by the poet's own relatives and the material benefits received by him from participants in the slave trade. In a letter to Jane Pollard of 28 December 1788, Dorothy Wordsworth noted that her brother, John, had embarked on a trip to Barbados, a fact reiterated in her letter of 27 January 1789.[119] Again, in January 1790, Dorothy noted John's involvement in the famous East India Company and his impending voyage to either America or the West Indies.[120] In July 1795, it was agreed that Wordsworth should become a non-paying tenant of Racedown Lodge, a house in North Devon which was owned by the wealthy Bristol merchant and sugar plantation owner, John Pretor Pinney.[121] And according to Dorothy's letter of 1808, another of Wordsworth's relatives, Henry Hutchinson, had been captured whilst travelling on a slave ship.[122] Not surprisingly therefore, Book 12 of Wordsworth's *Prelude* dismissed Adam Smith's *Inquiry into the Nature and Causes of the Wealth of Nations* (1776) as a work of 'utter hollowness', an example of 'plans without thought' founded upon 'false thought and false philosophy'.[123] His vehement rejection of Smith's critique of colonial slavery on sociopolitical and economic terms suggests in particular that his concealment of abolitionist discourse and his reluctance to partake in abolitionist activities stemmed from a complex web of personal loyalties and competitive creativity. The poet's resolute detachment from abolitionism is even more intriguing when one considers that during the composition and subsequent revisions of the *Prelude*, Wordsworth had become close friends with both Coleridge and Thomas Clarkson, the co-founder of the Abolition Society and the author of *The History of the Rise, Progress and Accomplishment of the Abolition of the African Slave Trade* (1808).[124]

This process of 'self-erasure' from abolitionist dialogue is most revealing in Wordsworth's sonnet, 'To Thomas Clarkson, on the Final Passing of the Bill for the Abolition of the Slave Trade, March 1807'. In this poem, the poet presents an egotistical trope of (personal and collective) self-referencing which strategically endeavours to override both Clarkson's success and the issue of slavery *per se*.[125] Hence when Wordsworth refers to Clarkson's parliamentary successes, the latter's achievements are conveniently mapped on to an image of national victory which duplicates images of the poet's own triumphant ascent, described in the (unpublished at this time) *Prelude*: 'CLARKSON! It was an obstinate hill to climb'.[126] In addition, the poet's response to Clarkson's concern for L'Ouverture's relatives, the three black exiles – Madame Christophe and her daughters – generates a satirical, explicitly racist version of Ben Jonson's sonnet, 'Queen and Huntress, Chaste and Fair' which plays, condescendingly and immaturely, upon concepts of enlightenment and excessive black sexuality:

Queen and Negress chaste and fair!

Shine for Clarkson's pure delight
Negro Princess, Ebon Bright!

Hayti's shining Queen was made
To illumine Playford Hall
Bless it then with constant light
Negress excellently bright![127]

Wordsworth's attitude towards abolitionism suggests a disturbingly ambivalent stance, problematised by familial obligation and influenced by the poet's reluctance to accept antislavery ideologies based on concepts of black (spiritual and physical) equality. For him, the schemas of self-determination and 'imaginative' liberation presented within his own autobiographical texts were not interchangeable with the slaves' demands for political emancipation; nor did he envisage that England's responsibility to its subjects necessitated its participation in any emancipatory role. In this respect, Wordsworth's attitude towards slavery was very different from that of other first generation poets and artists, most especially William Blake.[128] Nearly three decades after the composition of Wordsworth's sonnet to Clarkson, in a letter to Benjamin Dockray (25 April 1833),

Wordsworth's conservatism was confirmed by his criticism of the British public's endeavours to bring about an end of the slave trade. In this letter, the poet pledged his support for the rights and powers of the plantocrats and for what he considered the permanent and 'unalterable' nature of English law:

Fanaticism is the disease of these times as much or more than of any other; fanaticism is set, as it has always been, whether moral, religious, or political, upon attainment of its ends with disregard of the means. In this question there are *three* parties, – the slave, the slaveowner and the British people . . . *But by no means does it follow,* from this . . . that the *third* party, the people of England, who through their legislature have sanctioned and even encouraged slavery, *have a right to interfere for its destruction* by a sweeping measure, of which an equivalent to the owner makes no part. This course appears to me unfeeling and unjust.[129]

In the same letter, the poet declared that although he believed that the principle of slavery was indeed 'monstrous', it was not, according to him, 'in itself' or 'under all circumstances' to be deplored. Wordsworth's attempted isolation from the abolition movement was similarly indicated when, in a letter to Benjamin Haydon of 10 September 1840, he identified demands for emancipation on socio-economic (as Smith had done) rather than moral terms: 'Tho' from the first I took a lively interest in the Abolition of Slavery . . . I was too little a Man of business to have an active part in the Work'.[130]

WILLIAM BLAKE: SPIRITUALISM AND ABOLITIONISM

William Blake's tripartite position as a key Romantic artist and poet, as a perceptive critic of colonialist and slave ideology, and as an adamant proponent of the value of the spiritual world confirms his stature in the development of spiritual discourse and abolitionist polemic. Moreover, his expansion of the lineaments of physical, psychological and sexual enslavement presents sophisticated explorations of the complex configurations of individual and national identity, sexuality and subjectivity. Born the son of a London shop-keeper in November 1757, William Blake's initial apprenticeship as an engraver to James Basire was followed by a studentship at the Royal Academy, which began in October 1779 under the tutelage of George Michael Moser, its keeper. In 1791, Joseph Johnson, patron to William Cowper and publisher of Mary Scott's *The Female Advocate* (1774), Stedman's *Narrative, of a Five Year's Expedition* (1796) (see

Chapter 4 below) and William Wordsworth's *Descriptive Sketches* (1793), agreed to publish Mary Wollstonecraft's *Original Stories from Real Life: With Conversations Calculated to Regulate the Affections, and Form the Mind to Truth and Goodness* (1791), which included six illustrations by Blake that Johnson had commissioned.[131] In addition to Blake's connection with the writings of Coleridge, Wordsworth and Woll-stonecraft, it is probable that he had direct knowledge of the works of African writers then living in London. As Lauren Henry and Paul Edwards note, Blake was a good friend of the painter Richard Cosway. Cosway's house servant was the former slave, Ottobah Cugoano (a member of the Fanti people), who published his abolitionist text, *Thoughts and Sentiments on the Evil and Wicked Traffic of the Slavery and Commerce of the Human Species* in 1787.[132] It is possible therefore, that Blake had direct contact with Cugoano, or even his friend Gronniosaw (another former slave – see Chapter 6 below), or at least had been introduced to their narratives by the Cosway household.[133]

In 1787, after the death of his brother, aged nineteen, Blake claimed to see his brother's spirit rise to heaven, a spirit which he later claimed revealed a method of illuminated printing to him in a dream:

Thirteen years ago. I lost a brother & with his spirit I converse daily & hourly in the Spirit. & See him in my remembrance in the regions of my Imagination. I hear his advice & even now write from his Dictate – Forgive me for expressing to you my Enthusiasm which I wish all to partake of Since it is to me a Source of Immortal Joy even in this world by it I am the companion of Angels.[134]

Blake's elaboration upon the language of dissenting Protestantism, as advanced by the evangelicals John Wesley and George Whitefield, was in part influenced by the visionary accounts of the mystic theologian Emmanuel Swedenborg (1688–1772). In 1789, Blake and his wife Catherine became members of the Great Eastcheap Swe-denborg Society in London. Inspired by Swedenborg's belief in the spiritual symbolism of the material world and his corresponding interpretation of the Bible, Blake's poetical and visual compositions redefined the church as a form of spiritual wisdom. Likewise, his letters and prophetic books presented explorations and illuminations of symbolic insight predicated upon individualist mythology.[135] According to Swedenborg, the world of spirits was neither a form of heaven nor hell; rather it was 'a middle place or state between both;

for thither man first comes after death'.[136] Swedenborg had defined
the spiritual world as 'the vision of God', a state which he believed
the biblical prophets had access to.[137] Blake's annotations to Swedenborg's *Wisdom of Angels Concerning Divine Love and Divine Wisdom*,
attested to their mutual belief in spiritual wisdom:

[Swedenborg] Hence it may appear, that Man from a *merely natural* Idea
cannot comprehend that the Divine is every where, and yet not in Space;
and yet that Angels and Spirits clearly comprehend this; consequently *that
Man also may*, if so be he will admit something of Spiritual Light into his
Thought;
[Blake] *Observe the distinction here between Natural & Spiritual as seen by Man* . . .
[Swedenborg] The Negation of God constitutes Hell, and in the Christian
World the Negation of the Lord's Divinity.
[Blake] *the Negation of the Poetic Genius.*[138]

In his letter to Thomas Butts of 25 April 1803, Blake celebrated his
return to London from Felpham in Sussex, where he had taken up
residence in 1800, in terms of the spiritual freedom it provided: there
he believed he could pursue his visionary studies 'unannoyed',
converse with his friends in Eternity and 'See Visions, Dream
Dreams, & prophecy & speak Parables unobserv'd & at liberty from
the Doubts of other Mortals'.[139] On 11 December 1805 Blake wrote
in similarly spiritual terms to William Hayley, thanking him for his
support during what he described as 'the Darkest Years that ever
Mortal Sufferd':

I speak of Spiritual Things. Not of Natural. Of Things known only to
Myself & to Spirits Good & Evil. but Not Known to Men on Earth. It is the
passage thro these Three Years that has brought me into my Present State.
& *I know* that if I had not been with You I must have Perish'd – Those
Dangers are now Passed & I can see them beneath my feet It will not be
long before I shall be able to present the full history of my Spiritual
Sufferings to the Dwellers upon Earth. & of the Spiritual Victories obtain'd
for me by my Friends.[140]

In addition to the prophetic writings of Swedenborg, the work of the
sixteenth-century German cobbler and mystic, Jacob Boehme, had
an even greater influence upon Blake's thinking. In particular,
Boehme's work instigated Blake's subsequent reexamination and
critique of Swedenborg's doctrines, most especially his condemnation of Swedenborg's belief in predestination. Boehme's initial
influence upon Blake can most easily be detected in two illustrated
prints created in 1788 – 'There is No Natural Religion' and 'All

Religions are One' – texts which denounced the failings of the established church and the invidious doctrine of rationalism, and advocated instead a belief in the 'Poetic or Prophetic character':

Conclusion. If it were not for the Poetic or Prophetic character, the Philosophic & Experimental would soon be at the ratio of all things & stand still, unable to do other than repeat the same dull round over again.
Application. He who sees the Infinite in all things sees God. He who sees the Ratio only sees himself only.[141]

Blake's employment and systematic revision of the symbolic and mystical schemas advocated by Swedenborg and Boehme, present constantly shifting narratives which resist chronology and thereby reflect eternal states of visionary transformation. At once unsettling, episodic and disjunctive, Blake's prophetic writings demand an active, visionary mode of perception and readership. This ambiguity and instability reflect the subversive nature of Blake's work, as it both verifies and undermines preconceptions brought to it by its readers.

Subtitled 'The Voice of One Crying in the Wilderness', Blake's 'All Religions are One' (1788) dissolved the boundaries between religious and cultural differences and located the origins of spiritual and prophetic illumination within man himself. According to Blake, the Poetic Genius was the 'True Man', the source of all religions: 'The Religions of all Nations are derived from each Nations different reception of the Poetic Genius which is every where call'd the Spirit of Prophecy'.[142] For him, the doctrines of future reward prescribed by natural religion (deism) and the orthodox church, not only propounded a pernicious control of the individual but also implicated a denial of the eternal, spiritual world. Blake's prophetic stance hence pronounced a gospel of revolution which negated the traditional Christian dichotomy between body and soul. Consequently, Blake's *The Marriage of Heaven and Hell* (engraved *c.* 1790) promoted a balanced dependence upon spiritual and physical perception, a stance informed by Blake's belief in 'eternal delight' or energy:

(1) Man has no Body distinct from his Soul for that calld Body is a portion of Soul discernd by the five Senses. the chief inlets of Soul in this age.
(2) Energy is the only life and is from the Body and Reason is the bound or outward circumference of Energy.
(3) Energy is Eternal Delight.[143]

Fashioned ostensibly as a parody of Swedenborg's 'Memorable Relations' of his visions of Eternity, Blake's text preserved Swedenborg's concept of the Divine Humanity in which human form figured as a vital index of perfection. In an endeavour to restore 'energy' within a world dominated by Reason, Blake employed the figure of Satan as the representative of 'infernal wisdom' or energy:

Without Contraries is no progression. Attraction and Repulsion, Reason and Energy, Love and Hate, are necessary to Human existence . . . God is the passive that obeys Reason. Evil is the active springing from Energy.[144]

As this revised Satanic figure challenged the limits upon perception defined by reason, the 'Proverbs of Hell' reinstated the importance of impulse, imaginative creativity, sensual passion and vision:

> Prudence is a rich ugly maid courted by Incapacity.
> He who desires but acts not, breeds pestilence . . .
> The lust of the goat is the bounty of God . . .
> The nakedness of woman is the work of God.[145]

Furthermore, Blake's revision of Swedenborg's text traced the historical and psychological moment of segregation from God's existence and human experience ('Thus men forget that All deities reside in the human breast') and called for a reintegration of the divine with mankind.[146] Man's inclination to restrain imaginative vision and repress energy is seen by the poet as a contradiction of the prophets of Israel's prioritisation of the Poetic Genius as the 'first principle'. According to Blake, the restoration of infinity 'will come to pass by an improvement of sensual enjoyment', and it was this co-alignment of the sensual and the spiritual which distinguished Blake's work from the restrictions enforced by some of Wesley's successors.[147] As a text thoroughly opposed to the limitations of rationalism and empirical philosophy, Blake's *Marriage of Heaven and Hell* presented a gospel of unorthodox revolution, intense spirituality and imaginative impulse which identified the mind as an active spiritual agent, an expansive agent of consciousness of individuality which struggled against the oppressed or sealed condition of the rational man.

In the prophetic text, *Jerusalem: the Emanation of the Giant Albion* (printed in 1804), the poet recounts the development of the human consciousness from what he calls 'Eternal Death' (or what we call 'life') to authentic life in Eternity: 'Of the Sleep of Ulro! and of the passage through Eternal Death! and of the awaking to Eternal

Life'.[148] Having rejected the imaginative realm signified by Jerusalem (the emanation of Albion), Albion falls into a spiritual stupor. Los, the personification of the imaginative spirit, struggles to resist Albion's perverted vision, yet he becomes afflicted by the imbalance in Albion and is separated from his emanation, Enitharmon.[149] Blake's poem locates the various efforts to reunite Albion with Jerusalem within a context of repressive moralistic and religious epistemologies: 'Jerusalem replied. I am an outcast: Albion is dead! I am left to the trampling foot & the spurning heel! A Harlot I am calld'.[150] Rebellion, embodied by the figures of Los and Vala, incorporates a declaration of self-assertion and revolt against forms of enslavement prescribed by the dominant culture: 'I know of no other Christianity and no other Gospel than the liberty both of body & mind to exercise the Divine Arts of Imagination'.[151] In Plate 52 (subtitled 'To the Deists') of this complex but beautiful poem, the true pathway towards spiritual enlightenment, taken by the Methodists and the poet himself, is juxtaposed with the repressive regimes advocated by Voltaire and Rousseau:

Deism, is the Worship of the God of this World by the means of what you call Natural Religion and Natural Philosophy, and of Natural Morality or Self-Righteousness, the Selfish Virtues of the Natural Heart. This was the Religion of the Pharisees who murderd Jesus. Deism is the same & ends in the same. Voltaire Rousseau Gibbon Hume. charge the Spiritually Religious with Hypocrisy! but how a Monk or a Methodist either, can be a Hypocrite: I cannot conceive . . . The Glory of Christianity is, To Conquer by Forgiveness. All the Destruction therefore, in Christian Europe has arisen from Deism, which is Natural Religion.[152]

Blake's defence of Whitefield in the section entitled 'To the Deists' at the beginning of Chapter 3 of *Jerusalem* ('Foote in calling Whitefield, Hypocrite: was himself one: for Whitefield pretended not to be holier than others') is followed by a description of the exploitation of human resources within the market economy reminiscent of accounts detailing the slaves' transportation on to slave ships – 'We were carried away in 100s from London. . . in ships clos'd up'.[153] Calling for the transformative and inspirational power which Los possesses and which the poet believes will achieve a restoration of Albion: 'Teach me, O Holy Spirit, the Testimony of Jesus', the concluding chapter of *Jerusalem* addresses those Christians who have rejected the tyrannies of institutional and natural religion and celebrates Albion's forthcoming spiritual awakening:

Awake! Awake Jerusalem! O lovely Emanation of Albion
Awake and overspread all Nations as in Ancient Time
For lo! the Night of Death is past and the Eternal Day
Appears upon our hills.[154]

Blake's poem 'The Little Black Boy' in *Songs of Innocence and Experience*, composed as early as 1789 (the same year that he joined the Swedenborg Society) confronts colonial ideology and cultural difference within a simple yet effective spiritual framework:

My mother bore me in the southern wild,
And I am black, but O! my soul is white;
White as an angel is the English child:
But I am black as if bereav'd of light . . .

Thus did my mother say and kissed me,
And thus I say to the little English boy.
When I from black and he from white cloud free,
And round the tent of God like lambs we joy:

I'll shade him from the heat till he can bear,
To lean in joy upon our fathers knee.
And then I'll stand and stroke his silver hair,
And be like him and will then love me.[155]

By drawing parallels between black and white, lamb and Christ, Blake's poem counters pro-slavery discourse and introduces a poignant moment between mother and son, tenderness alongside a clear articulation of racial and spiritual equality. Anne Mellor has argued that Blake's poem affirms the ideological construction of the African as one who benefits from Christianity, but as his antagonistic relationship with institutionalised religion confirms, Blake's concept of Christianity is radically individual.[156]

Between 1788 and 1789, John Caspar Lavater, the lifelong friend of Henri Fuseli, published his *Essays on Physiognomy*, a work which examined the relationship between cranial proportion and character. One edition of Lavater's work contained four plates which were engraved by Blake and attest to an encounter with the science of physiognomy which must have challenged Blake's belief in racial equality. Less than a year later, Blake engraved sixteen plates for John Stedman's *Narrative of a Five Years' Expedition* (1790), described in Chapter 4 below. Blake's engravings included disturbing illustrations of colonial and slave ideology, such as his 'Execution of Breaking on the Rack' and The Flagellation of a Female Samboe Slave', which sought to replace typical depictions of black inferiority and sexual excess with unsettling representations of sufferings endured under the command of white masters. Given the sociopolitical context of the time and the fact that Stedman's text does not negate the necessity of the slave trade nor criticise the violent suppression of a slave insurrection in Dutch Guiana, Blake's illustrations were radically uncompromising. Designed to shock and educate, the intentions behind Blake's visual supplements to and departures from Stedman's *Narrative* were clearly presented at a time when other abolitionist texts remained cautious and circumspect in their approach. As Richard and Sally Price have noted, during the mid-1790s the relationship between Stedman and Blake was fairly close: the two corresponded, dined and sent gifts to each other frequently.[157] Yet Stedman adamantly refused to sign abolition petitions and when he left for Holland he did not free his personal slave but transferred him to another owner.[158] Conversely, Blake's financial contribution of £10 (approximately £1000 in today's terms), despite his impecuniosity, to the London Abolition Society demonstrated his antipathy toward slave ideology. Under Stedman's instructions, Blake engraved an emblematic representation of the interdependence between Africa, America and Europe. In this revised version of the 'Three Graces', entitled 'Europe Supported by Africa and America', Europe, a white female decorated in pearls, stands supported by her colonially and racially oppressed 'sisters', the enslaved African and the marginalised native American. In Blake's hands, the symbol of harmonious colonial venture and intercultural exchange becomes a sinister emblem of debasement and exclusion.[159]

Significantly influenced by Mary Wollstonecraft's *A Vindication of the Rights of Woman* published the previous year (see above), Blake's *Visions of the Daughters of Albion* (1793) questions the permanency of existing power structures. In its attack against the evils of slavery, sexual inequality, colonial expansionism and repressive cults of virginity, Blake's poem examines the conditions of psychological, sexual and racial enslavement prescribed by the ideologies and practices of mystery, idolatry and cultural superiority: 'Stampt with my signet are the swarthy children of the sun: / They are obedient, they resist not, they obey the scourge'.[160] As David Erdman notes, love and slavery prove to be the 'two poles' guiding the axis of the poem.[161] The unresolved debate between Oothoon, Theotormon and Bromion provides a poetic counterpart to the parliamentary and

editorial debates of 1789–1793 which centred upon the Bill for the
Abolition of the Slave Trade. Like those gradual reformists who
deplored the slave trade but could not subscribe to an open
condemnation of slavery itself, Theotormon remains locked in a
psychological impasse. On the poem's frontispiece, Oothoon (the
representative of liberty – 'the soft soul of America') is enveloped by
the restraining manacles of Bromion, rapist and slaver, whilst
Theotormon's 'jealous waters' form a chain 'round the adulterate
pair, bound back to back in Bromion's caves':

> The voice of slaves beneath the sun, and children bought with money.
> That shiver in religious caves beneath the burning fires
> Of lust, that belch incessant from the summits of the earth
> Oothoon weeps not: she cannot weep! her tears are locked up;
> But she can howl incessant writhing her soft snowy limbs.[162]

In Plate 4 Oothoon soars upwards but is held down by a chain as
Theotormon sits rigidly, his hands over his face, 'shut up in cold
despair', degraded by his misguided ethics:

> The moment of desire! the moment of desire! The virgin
> That pines for man; shall awaken her womb to enormous joys
> In the secret shadows of her chamber; the youth shut up from
> The lustful joy. shall forget to generate. & create an amorous image
> In the shadows of his curtains and in the folds of his silent pillow.[163]

Blake's rendition of Theotormon's psychological impasse exposes
one of the most significant flaws in the British constitution. In the
light of French revolutionary idealism, the defeat of the Bill in
Parliament under pressure from the anti-Jacobin attacks staged by
Edmund Burke, Lord Abingdon and various slave agents, determined Britain's continuing involvement in colonial and racial slavery
at a deplorable and fundamentally regressive stage. Likewise, the
announcement in the *London Chronicle* of February 2, 1792 which
disassociated the Abolition Society from any desire to bring about
'the Emancipation of the Negroes in the British Colonies' and
claimed instead that the Society sought merely to bring an end to
the 'trade of the slaves', highlighted the paralysis at the heart of
Britain's parliamentary and 'moral' centre. As a fused embodiment
of America, Africa and Europe, Oothoon coalesces with, yet also
departs from the ideological parameters prescribed by Wollstonecraft and Stedman. Theotormon's love for the 'gentle' Oothoon
appears to be a coded reference to Stedman's account of his love for

the slave 'Joanna'.[164] However, the fact that Oothoon is not freed, nor able to articulate her anger, nor transform her visions into realities suggests that Blake was presenting an intertextual critique of Wollstonecraft's rationalised arguments for female equality. For Blake, colonial ideology, possessive morality and sexual oppression were all fundamental forms of the pernicious enslavement which corrupted the visionary potential of England.[165]

Blake's concern with physical and spiritual enslavement is thus developed into a sophisticated exploration of psychological enslavement and repression. His extension of the spiritual legacy of radical dissenting Protestantism is reworked on his own terms to provide an all-embracing philosophy of redemption and equality for mankind. Advocating his belief in the potential harmony of mind, body and spirit within all individuals, Blake propounds his conviction in man's ability to experience imaginative vision and achieve eternal life. With radical and absolute egalitarianism, Blake celebrates a state of being in which the evils of cultural difference, based on the injustices of racism, the subordination of women and the pernicious effects of materialism and power abuse, are rejected. As a political activist, unafraid to illustrate the brutality and degradation endured by slaves, as a free thinker and as a radical visionary, Blake avoids the strictures of moral and Christian polemic, beyond the confines of material wealth and concepts of ownership towards a state of intense spiritualism. Unfettered by religious doctrine or utilitarian ethics, Blake occupies a crucial position within the development of the discourse of the spirit. Yet Blake's concern with the spiritual is not at the expense of the physical – as his sensual celebration of the human body demonstrates. Whilst Blake's rejection of eighteenth-century rationalist and empiricist epistemology distinguishes him from the line of argument propounded by Mary Wollstonecraft, his artistic and poetic enjoyment of the physical links his work with that of the Scotsman, John Stedman (discussed below).

In their complex interaction with the language of radical dissenting Protestantism and abolitionist demands prevalent in England at the time, the poetical works by Coleridge, Wordsworth and Blake reveal the transient and protean nature of spiritual discourse and its compelling dynamics of (self-)liberation from servitude. A similar appropriation and transformation of this mercurial discourse was likewise articulated both within the narratives by ex-slaves, published contemporaneously during the late eighteenth and early nineteenth century, and within Stedman's semi-autobiographical account of the insurrectionist negroes in Surinam. Chronologically, Stedman's *Narrative of a Five Years' Expedition against the Revolted Negroes of Surinam* (1790) predates some of the earlier work by the Romantic poets examined above. Its place within this discussion reflects its significant departure from traditional forms of spiritual autobiography and its status as a pivotal text which describes an important translation of the discourse of the spirit (and indeed, the corresponding confessional genre) into a schema of *physical*, rather than purely spiritual, redemption. In so doing, Stedman's text corresponds to some of the most important strategic motives behind the slave narratives – emancipation from slavery and liberation from theories of racial difference and inferiority, which had been used to justify and continue the abhorrent trade. In its account of morganatic marriage Stedman's text presents an interesting parallel with Blake's ideas of sexual freedom, yet extends this to provide an enigmatic autobiographical form of colonial narrative which demonstrates the problematics involved in interracial (sexual) encounters between European men and African women. As a consequence, Stedman's text offers a significant narrative of cross-cultural contact and thereby provides a fitting precursor to the discussion in the subsequent chapters of this book of the 'creolised' schema contained within the slave narratives and the legislative prohibitions of miscegenation in the eighteenth century.

CHAPTER FOUR

Cross-cultural contact: John Stedman, Thomas Jefferson and the slaves

JOHN STEDMAN'S REDEMPTION AND THE DYNAMICS OF MISCEGENATION

During the period of composition of the *Visions of the Daughters of Albion* (1793), William Blake was approached by the publisher Joseph Johnson and asked to supply engravings for a work that was to be published as *Narrative, of a Five Years' Expedition, Against the Revolted Negroes of Surinam, in Guiana, on the Wild Coast of South America; From the Year 1772, to 1777* (1796), an enigmatic combination of botanical description, military stories, adventure and interracial love based on an original 1790 manuscript by Captain John Gabriel Stedman.[1] In the forty years following its publication, Stedman's text was translated into German (1797), French (1798), Dutch (1799), Swedish (1800) and Italian (1818) and provided the source for the 1824 version of the story *Joanna or the Female Slave*.[2] According to his diary, Stedman began working on his *Narrative* on 15 June 1778, just one year after returning from military service with the Scots brigade in Surinam (a Dutch colony since 1667), and only a few days following a request from Sir George Strickland for an account of his voyage.[3] Joseph Johnson had agreed to pay Stedman £500 for the manuscript and in 1791 employed engravers including William Blake, Bartolozzi, Holloway and Benedetti to reproduce and work on Stedman's own drawings and watercolours.[4] Following the public reaction to the number of fatalities in the 1791 slave rebellion in St Domingue led by Toussaint L'Ouverture, in 1794 Johnson employed William Thomson to 'rework' Stedman's original copy of the 865-page manuscript, which was published in 1796. Stedman received his first glimpse of this 'revised' version in May 1795. Outraged by the extent of 'editorial' intervention, he determined to restore the original tone of his narrative, a project which he worked on up until his death two years later.[5]

Stedman's diary makes it clear that what emerged as the first edition of 1796 was an awkward compromise. The scope of Thomson's editorial transformations ranged from minor rephrasing to substantial alterations of Stedman's views on race, slavery and social justice. Significant aspects of his Surinam experiences were obliterated, including passages describing his sexual relationships with female slaves, and his provocative critiques, such as his discussion on the chastity of religious orders, were similarly amended. Passages relating to the sadistic behaviour of plantation mistresses towards slaves (an aspect silenced in many of the slave narratives) and the cruelty and sexual power-relations between European masters and African women were similarly deleted. Most importantly, the disclosure of the relationships which developed between Stedman, his mulatto lover, Joanna, and other female slaves were more often than not completely omitted, leaving little correspondence between the published text and the explicit (sexual) entries contained within his unpublished Surinam diaries:

sleep at Mr. Lolkens . . . I f–k one of his negro maids (9 Feb. 1773) . . .
a negro woman offers me the use of her daughter, while here, for a sertain[sic] soom[.] we dont agre[e] about the price (22 Feb. 1773) . . .
soop in me room with two mallato girls (25 Feb. 1773) . . .
B———e comes to me and stays the whole night (26 Mar. 1773) . . .
B———e sleeps with me (13 Apr. 1773) . . .
J———a comes to stay with me (23 Apr. 1773).[6]

Born in 1744, Stedman, a Scotsman, had inherited his father's commission as an officer in the Scots Brigade of the Dutch Army. In 1773 Stedman was sent out to Surinam as a volunteer in a military expedition, a mission organised by the Dutch government as a response to the colonial crisis created there by mass slave defections and the continuing wars between plantation owners and the maroon societies of the Saramakas and the Djukas.[7] When the rebel maroons eventually abandoned the country for French Guiana in 1778, European 'victory' was seriously undermined by the enormously high (80 per cent) mortality rate amongst soldiers, occasioned by a combination of military incompetence and rampant disease. Stedman's *Narrative of Five Years Expedition* presented a critical exposure of the ineffectual jungle warfare used against the maroons, interspersed with botanical descriptions of the fauna and flora native to Surinam.

In addition, Stedman's text incorporated a narrative of 'salvation' tempered by an underlying discourse of colonial desire, abolition and the dynamics of miscegenation.

As the Preface to the original 1790 manuscript suggests, Stedman, although neither an overt radical republican nor an abolitionist sympathiser, determined to publish a narrative of his experiences regardless of the offence its lack of scientific, structural and cultural orthodoxy and moral decorum would cause:

> But boldly will I first plead my Cause & after that like the dying Indian Submit to my doom without a Shrink or a Complaint – To begin then – I am going to be told that my Narrative besides its not being interesting to Great Britain has neither stile, orthography, order, or Connection – Patcht up with superfluous Quotations – Descriptions of Animals without so much as proper names – Trifles – Cruelties – Bombast &c. to all which Accusations I partly plead Guilty . . . Next that some of my Paintings are rather unfinish'd – That my plants fully prove I am nothing of a Botanist.[8]

To the anticipated criticism that 'the history of Joanna deserves no place at all in this Narrative', Stedman replied with characteristic dismissiveness: 'D——m order, D——m matter of fact, D——m ev'rything I'm above you all'.[9] However, whereas his text evokes a sensitive empathy with the plight of the enslaved Africans, a set of 'living automatons . . . a resurrection of skin and bones', the sight of which fills him with humiliation, Stedman's *Narrative of Five Years' Expedition* is not unambiguously abolitionist. Rather, Stedman's text oscillates tenuously between his concern for the negro slaves, 'I love the African Negroes', and the ideological forces determining his presence in Surinam as a Scots Brigade lieutenant sent to quell the insurrection and prevent 'general massacre'.[10] Hence throughout his account, a touching distress for those miserable slaves, 'wretches who deservedly most attracted my Pity' and who were driven 'like Oxen with a Stick' is revealed. Similarly his admiration for the African slaves' intellectual abilities is indicated by his praise of the African slave, Phillis Wheatley's poetical genius and the inclusion of an extract from her poem, 'Thoughts On Imagination'.[11] At other times, Stedman's narrative appears anti-abolitionist in its concern for the planters and its support of the slave trade itself – '*This trade, or buying of negroe Slaves, is not so bad a thing as some try to support* . . . It is a perfect truth, that from a private evil, is derived a general good'.[12]

Besides I cannot help thinking it ungenerous thus wishing to deprive the West India *Planters* of their Property, by a Sudden abolition of the Slave Trade, who after their many hazards, and their loss of health, Wealth, and time, have no other Method of procuring a Subsistence for their families.[13]

Indeed, Stedman declared he was as much opposed to men such as Thomas Clarkson, the co-founder of the Society for Abolition, as those slaveholders who would 'preserve the most unjust and diabolical barbarity' for the sake of drinking rum.[14] Interestingly, his antagonism towards figures such as Clarkson appears to have stemmed from his intolerance of Europe's resolute, yet hypocritical, mission to convert the Africans to Christianity:

And as to theyr becoming Christians, they may / a few of them Excepted / have a Chance of becoming a parcel of canting Hypocritical Rascals, like too many of theyr protecttors, and use it as a Cloak to impose upon the ignorant, but will never *chuse* to know more of that Sacred Institution, than they already do of Snow.[15]

Stedman's text acknowledges the potential incompatibility or disjuncture between the colonialists' advancement of Christian ideology and the slaves' maintenance of African culture and their continued observance of African ceremonies and libations, most especially the rituals of spirit possession performed by obeahs and female prophets:

Amongst them [the Sibils] who deal in Oracles, these Sage Matrons Dancing And Whirling Round in the Middle of an Audience, till Absolutely they froath at the mouth And drop down in the middle of them; Whatever She says to be done during this fit of Madness is Sacredly Performed by the Surrounding Multitude, which makes these meetings Exceedingly dangerous Amongst the Slaves, who are often told to murder their Masters or Desert to The Woods, & on which account the Excessive of this piece of Fanatisim, is forbid in the Colony of Surinam on Pain of the Most Rigourous Punishment, Yet it is often Put in Execution in Private Places, And Verry Commen Amongst the Owca, & Sarameca Negroes.[16]

His *Narrative* therefore presents a radical challenge to the 'conversion' enterprise inherent within most abolitionist activities and, more daringly, advocates the intrinsic value of the Africans' own belief systems: 'Their [the Africans] own religion being much more Commodious, and not so much divested of Common Sence [sic] as numberless Stupid Europeans imagine'.[17] Stedman's editor replaced statements which vindicated the African's racial and moral equality, with sensationalist propaganda premised on the threatening spectre of potential slave insurrections and excessive violence: 'It must be observed that LIBERTY, nay even too much leanity, when *suddenly* granted to illiterate and unprincipled men, must be to *all* parties dangerous, if not pernicious'.[18] This process of textual erasure and editorial intervention similarly corresponded to those forces to which the slaves' narratives were subjected.

In terms of its relationship with the language of radical dissenting Protestantism, the framework of spiritual autobiography in Stedman's text of 1790 is so dramatically revised that it is scarcely recognisable. Yet Stedman's narrative *is* a narrative of deliverance, albeit an unorthodox one; for his text describes not a deliverance from sin into the grace of God, but a release into sexual redemption via the mulatto female slave, Joanna: 'Never two People were more Completely happy – Not Adam and Eve in Paradise'. The centre of Stedman's text presented a personalised, and indeed, sexualised account of the author's concern for an individual, that 'Unfortunate Mulatto Maid'. For him, she is as a 'forsaken plant / now exposed to every rude blast without protection', and it is *her* sufferings – rather than his own – which generate his state of spiritual dejection and emotional turmoil characteristic of confessional narratives: 'My Spirits were deprest, and in the Space of twenty-four hours I was very ill indeed'.[19]

Stedman's account of his encounter at the beginning of his expedition with the black mistress at Mr Lolken's house provides an amusing paradigm of the author's naivety, in terms of his lack of sexual experience and his immature understanding of his own role within the colonial forum. He claims, retrospectively, that his encounter with Mr Lolken's mistress may serve (as in George Vason's *Authentic Narrative*) as an invaluable example to those young Europeans, who in their close contact with young black females on the plantation estates, may 'not always escape with impunity'. Once Stedman has described his initiation into the licentious world of plantation society –

I was fatigued and longed for some rest – thus made a signal that I wanted to sleep – but here I was truly brought into great Distress – for she [Mr Lolkens' female slave] again misunderstanding me had the unaccountable assurance to give me such a hearty kiss – as had made my Nose as flat as her own.[20]

– a feigned sense of etiquette prompts him to 'draw a Sable Curtain' over the details of this particular sexual encounter, hence making the act of miscegenation itself almost unutterable.[21] When Stedman meets the fifteen-year-old mulatto slave, Joanna, he identifies her as the product of a liaison between a 'respectable *Gentleman*' and a slave woman. This appears to endorse Joanna's status in terms of her (partial) racial compatibility. Given the socioeconomic context of Surinam at the time, however, the dynamics behind the girl's miscegenetic parentage are as problematic as Stedman's own relationship with Joanna, and indeed, with Surinam itself.[22] In his *Philosophical and Political History* (1776), Guillame Raynal defined white males' preference for black women, a condition 'so depraved in the European', as a consequence of the 'nature of the climate':

> The torrid zone irresistibly excites men to the pleasures of love; the facility of gratifying this insurmountable inclination without restraint, and without trouble of long pursuit; from a certain captivating attraction of beauty, discoverable in black women, as soon as custom hath once reconciled the eye to their colour.[23]

As Mary Louise Pratt notes, Stedman's transracial love affair with Joanna is a 'romantic transformation of a particular form of colonial sexual exploitation' in which Europeans bought local women to serve as sexual and domestic partners during their stay in the colonies.[24] However Stedman's desire for Joanna is as much premised upon her (sexual) *accessibility* (as a slave woman) as it is upon her non-availability (in that she belongs to another master), a situation symptomatic of the master/mistress/slave triangle itself:

> My ears being Stund with the Clang of the Whip and the dismal Yels of the wretched Negroes on whom it was inflicted . . . considering that this might one day be the fate of the Unfortunate Mulatto Maid . . . should she chance to fall in the hands of a Tirrannical Master or Mistress.[25]

Such a dichotomy is endorsed by the ambiguous nature of Joanna's mulatto identity, a complexity which posits a continuum of both African and European physical traits and which by inference indicates her synchronous assimilation to and departure from European ideologies. She is therefore, 'rather more than middle Size' whilst her face is 'full of *native* Modesty'; her eyes are 'black as Ebony' yet her cheeks '*glow* in spite of her olive Complexion'; her lips are a 'little prominent', and as a 'Shaul of finest Indian Muslin gracefully' reveals a part of her 'lovely bosom', she shines with a '*double* lustre', a duplicity which exposes her position on the interface between European and African aesthetics.[26]

Against the backdrop of war-besieged Surinam, there is a definite sense that Stedman is particularly conscious of the role he is playing in this luxuriously fecund 'remake' of Milton's *Paradise Lost*, a text with which Blake and Wordsworth (in their respective renditions of the fall and concepts of innocence and experience) also poetically engaged.[27] As he and Joanna, 'free like the roes in the forest and disentangled from every care and fashion' breathe the 'purest Ether' and refresh their limbs in 'Cooling limpid Streams', their physical ecstasy appears to transcend and defy the parameters of the colonial dictum: 'Health and Vigour were now again my portion, while my Mulatto flourished in youth and beauty'. This textual emphasis upon Surinam's abundant fertility discretely corresponds to the commercial objectives of the colonial project. Hence, whereas Stedman's *Narrative of Five Years Expedition* portrays a trope of unrestrained sexual liberty, Joanna herself, like Annette in the *Prelude* is a shadowy, inarticulate, bodily presence, notably silenced by the male author's autobiography of deliverance. The comparison between Joanna and Stedman in Surinam and Adam and Eve in Paradise presents an unconscious, or indeed, suppressed recognition of the necessarily transient (and inappropriate) nature of such a relationship, and the impending effect of colonial dictates upon the dynamics of unrestrained sexual freedom and cross-cultural contact.

According to the *Narrative of Five Years Expedition*, the couple 'married' in Surinam because Joanna was 'unwilling' to accompany Stedman back to England. Yet Stedman could not have been ignorant of the fact that his relationship with Joanna made a mockery of the very struggles he had been sent out to resolve. On the one hand, his relationship with Joanna fulfils an essential requirement of the colonial adventure in its physical manifestation of colonial expansion as Europe's 'redemptive' mission is inscribed on to the body of Joanna herself. On the other hand, however, Stedman's sexual penetration of those painstakingly constructed barriers of cultural/racial difference reciprocates the challenge posed by the rebellious Surinanese maroon societies to such artificial cultural boundaries. In Milton's epic, Adam and Eve retreat from the paradisiacal garden 'hand in hand', yet Stedman's narrative describes its author's solitary withdrawal from the garden of Eden and situates his subsequent quest for a 'paradise regained' *within* that European world he had previously left behind. For Mary Louise Pratt, Stedman's relationship with Joanna is one of 'romantic love rather than filial servitude': it is a relationship which enacts a 'wilful submission of the colonised' and therefore demonstrates the possibility of 'cultural harmony through romance'.[28] Conversely, however, Stedman's narrative demonstrates the process by which cultural integration in its most explicit form – i.e. miscegenation – is *refused* permanence, even when articulated within the paradigm of 'fictionalised' autobiography. Manifestations of miscegenation, cross-cultural contact, and hybridity (symbolised by the existence of their 'mutant', bastard son, Johnny) are carefully marginalised; redetermined as sites existing beyond the fictional and therefore unspeakable. Joanna and her son must remain in Surinam in order that Stedman may be reintegrated with his former cultural self, via his legally and culturally sanctioned marriage in England.

Stedman's return to England and his subsequent marriage hence portray the author's ultimate loyalty to both his nation and his employers. As his former transgressions of both cultural and racial barriers succumb to national duty, his allegiance to the coloniser (Holland) and his rejection of the colonised (Joanna/Surinam) is confirmed. In a sense, the extension of Stedman's earlier 'self' via geographical exploration and sexualised cross-cultural contact enacts the old meaning of the term 'revolution': that is, the re-articulation of European hegemony rather than its overthrow. And as if that were not enough, the 'news' of Joanna's and Johnny's mysterious deaths satisfies an essential structural requirement by effectively silencing any abolitionist and emancipatory dialogue. Their 'erasure' enables a literal concealment of the only remaining evidence of the miscegenetic act and facilitates the author's reintegration/salvation upon culturally acceptable terms:

From Mr. *Gourlay* in August did I receive the melancholy tidings which pierc'd me to the Very Soul that on the Fatal 5 day of Last November / a day ever Remarkable for treason in the Annals of this Island / this virtuous young Creature had died by *poison*, administered by the hand of Jealousy & Envy on Account of her prosperity & the marks of distinction, which her Superior merit so Justly Attracted from the Respectable part of Mankind – While others insisted that her death was the Consequence of a Broken heart.[29]

Such an 'erasure' endorses a trope of cultural amnesia, or severance from the dynamics of cultural miscegenation, similarly evaded by the Romantic texts. The above lines witness a return of the 'conversion' trope of radical dissenting Protestantism, as Stedman's narrative of the negroes' revolt becomes an autobiographical confession describing his own subversive act of sexual/cultural betrayal and his subsequent salvation via a 'muted' dialogue of repentance. Joanna's death, on the anniversary of Guy Fawkes' failed insurrection, symbolically confirms both the effacement and negation of Stedman's own act of (cultural) treason.

Like the above-mentioned poetic schemas of Coleridge's and Wordsworth's texts, Stedman's *Narrative* represents a significant departure from overtly abolitionist discourse. However, it radically deviates from the parameters of the Romantic poets' later work in its graphic disclosure of the highly ambiguous (and physical) inter-relationship between colonials and their colonised 'others'. Stedman's *Narrative* thus heralds the emergence of a paradigm of spiritual autobiography infused with the dynamics of miscegenation and cross-cultural contact. As such, his text provides a fitting precursor to an analysis of the theories of racial difference and similitude prevalent at the time and to the narratives produced by the slaves themselves, accounts which delineate the emergence of a culturally hybrid consciousness of the black diaspora.

THEORIES OF DIFFERENCE / SIMILITUDE

In his attempt to situate historic relationships between civilisations, the German philosopher, George Wilhelm Friedrich Hegel (1770–1831) identified the dichotomy between the African and Asiatic civilisations and the civilisations of ancient Greece, ancient Rome and the modern world, as being determined by the latter's emphasis upon the significance of 'individual freedom' and self-determination.[30] According to Hegel, whereas the emergence of Christianity in the western world confirmed the evolution of self-consciousness, spiritual development and individual freedom, Africa was an 'unhistorical continent, with no movement or development of its own'.[31] For Hegel, therefore, the history of western civilisation could be envisaged as a gradual translation of the Christian discourse of universal freedom into secular demands for social, political and ethical rights within the modern states.[32] In his 'Philosophical History of the World' (second draft, 1830), Hegel declared that the influence occasioned by the rise of Christianity meant that modern western nations were the first to realise that man was, by nature, free. Heralding Christianity as the essential foundation of self-determined rights of liberty, Hegel identified Christian ideology as *the* world narrative of cultural liberation, hence endorsing, albeit indirectly, the interrelationship between missionary activity and colonialism. Similarly, although he acknowledged that slavery was a moral injustice which contravened the very essence of humanity, he suggested that slavery could only become an *actual* injustice if a slave *claimed* his right to be free; a slave who accepted his condition therefore, was as much to blame as his slave owners:

> The only significant relationship between the negroes and the Europeans has been – and still is – that of slavery. The negroes see nothing improper about it, and the English, although they have done most to abolish slavery and the slave trade, are treated as enemies by the negroes themselves . . . The basic principle of all slavery is that man is not yet conscious of his freedom, and consequently sinks to the level of a mere object or worthless article . . . Slavery is unjust in and for itself, for the essence of man is freedom; but he must first become mature before he can be free. Thus, it is more fitting and correct that slavery should be eliminated gradually than that it should be done away with all at once.[33]

Early eighteenth-century travel accounts of voyages to Africa, such as Bosman's *New and Accurate Description of the Coast of Guinea* (1705), William Snelgrave's *New Account of Guinea, and the Slave Trade* (1734) and Atkins' *Voyage to Guinea, Brasil, and the West Indies* (1735) had provided detailed records of African religious practices and doctrines:

> A'most all the Coast *Negroes* believe in one true God, to whom they attribute the creation of the world and all things in it, though . . . [they are not] able to form a just idea of a Deity.[34]

> They [the Africans] went every Morning and Evening to the River side to make *Fetiche* as they call it, that is, to offer Sacrafice to their principal God, which was a particular harmless Snake they adored, and prayed on this occasion, to keep their Enemies from coming over the River.[35]

> [The Snake] is the principle Deity or *Fetish* of the Country. . . They believe an Intercourse with the Snake, to whom they have dedicated their service, capacitates them to stop or promote the plagues that infest them . . . They have *Fetish*-women, or Priestesses, that live separated with a number of Virgins under their care.[36]

Whether Hegel had read any of these accounts, and if so which ones, is difficult to establish. Yet Hegel adamantly asserted that Africans had no understanding of the 'spiritual life': theirs was a nature 'as yet compressed within itself', an undeveloped state with no recogni-

tion of the universal or that which existed 'in and for itself' and
possessed 'absolute validity':

Generally speaking, Africa is a continent enclosed within itself, and this
enclosedness has remained its chief characteristic . . . From the earliest
historical times, Africa has remained cut off from all contacts with the rest
of the world; it is the land of gold, for ever pressing in upon itself, and the
land of childhood, removed from the light of self-conscious history and
wrapped in the dark mantle of night.[37]

Hegel's eurocentric endorsement of the 'glorious light of Christianity' inscribed a binary schema of difference in terms of the
Africans' spiritual non-potential, their intellectual incapacity and
their excessive sensuality. This in turn defined Africa as a land of
absence, a land without religion or consciousness, a land 'enclosed
upon itself'; in other words, the ultimate antithesis of the west's
expansionist and self-constructing self:

This [African] character . . . is difficult to comprehend, because it is so
totally different from our own culture, and so remote and alien in relation to
our own mode of consciousness. We must forget all the categories which are
fundamental to our own spiritual life . . . It must be said in general that, in
the interior of Africa, the consciousness of the inhabitants has not yet
reached an awareness of any substantial and objective existence. Under the
heading of substantial objectivity, we must include God, the eternal, justice,
nature, and all natural things . . . But the Africans have not yet attained this
recognition of the universal; their nature is as yet compressed within itself:
and what we call religion, the state, that which exists in and for itself and
possesses absolute validity – all this is not yet present to them.[38]

In his *Phenomenology of Spirit*, first published in 1807, Hegel
described the concept of the spirit as 'consciousness', a self-knowing
or spiritual essence permeated by a '*self*-consciousness which knows
itself, and knows the essence as an actuality confronting it'.[39]
Likewise, in his account of the 'Phenomenology of Religion', he
examined the ways in which men conceptualised a spirituality that
transcended their own. He identified Christianity as that absolute
and revealed religion by which means men strived to become one
with a spiritual principle unknown to Africans. According to Hegel,
such a process was first manifested within the figure of Jesus, whom
he claimed, communicated the workings of this Divine Spirit to his
believers:

Religion begins with the awareness that there is something higher than
man. But this kind of religion is unknown to the negroes . . . We can sum

up the principle of African religion in his [Herodotus'] declaration that all men in Africa are sorcerers. That is, as a spiritual being, the African arrogates to himself a power over nature, and this is the meaning of his sorcery. . . . *Sorcery* does not entail the idea of a God or of a moral faith, but *implies that man is the highest power and that he alone occupies a position of authority over the power of nature* . . . Man, then, is master of these natural forces. This has nothing whatsoever to do with veneration of God or the recognition of a universal spirit as opposed to the spirit of the individual.[40]

Hegel's analysis of the Africans' 'cult of the dead' (a belief marginalised in the slave narratives) focused upon their belief in the spirits of the dead, their deceased ancestors and forefathers, whom they believed were 'capable of acting against the living': 'They [the Africans] resort to these spirits in the same way as to fetishes, offering them sacrifices and conjuring them up':

They [the Africans] do not invoke God in their ceremonies; they do not turn to any higher power, for they believe that they can accomplish their aims by their own efforts. To prepare themselves for their task, they work themselves into a state of frenzy; by means of singing, convulsive dancing, and intoxicating spirits or potions, they reach a state of extreme delirium in which they proceed to issue their commands.[41]

For Hegel, one important feature which distinguished African epistemology from that of Christianity was the transposition of 'this power of theirs' into a visible form, that is, the projection of 'consciousness' on to an image. This process, however, was not so dissimilar to the Christian emblematisation of various theological concepts such as the 'holy spirit' and the 'sacred heart'. Yet by introducing the term 'fetish' into his discussion of African belief systems, Hegel established a powerful narrative of cultural alterity:

It is a *fetish*, a word to which the Portuguese first gave currency, and which is derived from *fetico*, or magic. Here, in the fetish, the arbitrary will of the individual does seem to be faced with an independent entity, but *since the object in question is nothing more than the will of the individual projected into a visible form*, this will in fact remains master of the image it has adopted.[42]

Paradoxically, Hegel's words provide an interesting paradigm of the Romantic poets' endeavours to project images of the mind on to external forms. As discussed above, Wordsworth's *Prelude* and Coleridge's conversation poems present effective poetical 'mappings' of emblems of consciousness, yet for Hegel such a process, 'the *will of the individual projected into a visible form*', is nothing more than an arbitrary principle of superstition or 'magic'.[43]

Hegel's conviction of Africa's *complete* isolation from the 'developing' world was similarly expressed in Johann Joachim Winckelman's earlier treatise, *The History of Ancient Art*, a text which prioritised the superiority of Greek art 'over that of other nations'.[44] According to Winckelman, Egypt and Greece, in their aesthetic and cultural capacities, were essentially isolated from African influence, whilst 'Africa' itself remained in an eternal state of arrested development:

The art of drawing among the Egyptians is to be compared to a tree which, though well cultivated, has been checked and arrested in its growth by a worm, or other casualties; for it [has] remained unchanged, precisely the same, yet without attaining its perfection, until the period when Greek kings held sway over them.[45]

Hence Winckelman argued that the resemblance between characteristics of Greek and Egyptian art did '*not prove that the Greeks learnt their art from the Egyptians. In fact, they had no opportunity of doing so*'.[46]

Hegel's and Winckelman's claims of difference on cultural and spiritual grounds was similarly upheld by pro-slavery ideology. In the slave states of America and the West Indies, the conversion of slaves to Christianity was opposed on both economic and social grounds: that is, for fear of the rebelliousness that concepts of Christian equality might instil amongst the slaves and the economic crisis that might result. Consequently, anticipating Hegel, slave ideology endorsed a discourse of difference which pivoted upon the claim that since Africans lacked the possession of a soul, or inner spirit, they could be defined as the possessions of others.[47]

Accounts detailing 'proof' of African's racial difference and religion were hence used to support theories of their intellectual inferiority, as demonstrated by David Hume's analysis of the 'negro' in his major essay, 'Of National Characters' (1748) and its revision of 1753:

I am apt to suspect the Negroes to be naturally inferior to the Whites. There scarcely ever was a civilised nation of that complexion, nor even any individual, eminent either in action or speculation . . . Such a uniform and constant difference could not happen, in so many countries and ages, if nature had not made an original distinction between these breeds of men.[48]

Such theories of 'absence' – religious, intellectual and moral – and of difference (aesthetic and racial) contributed to the development of

a complex and often ambiguous discourse of property and justification of slavery, exemplified by Hume's analysis of the origin of
justice and property:

> Our property is nothing but those goods, whose constant possession is
> establish'd by the laws of society; that is, by the laws of justice. Those,
> therefore, who make use of the words *property*, or *right*, or *obligation*, before
> they have explain'd the origin of justice . . . are guilty of a very gross fallacy,
> and can never reason upon any solid foundation. A man's property is some
> object related to him. This relation is not natural, but moral, and founded
> on justice . . . The idea of justice . . . wou'd never have been dream'd of
> among rude and savage men.[49]

Accordingly, theories which negated the presence of Africa's historical or spiritual (or indeed, creative) dimension strategically validated
Europe's concept of itself as (pre)ordained 'saviour' and 'proprietor'
of inferior races. Not surprisingly, such a dichotomy depended upon
the preservation and dissemination of ideologies of cultural difference and racial apartheid, elements formally enshrined within
legislation that prohibited against various forms of 'cultural' miscegenation and informally maintained by means of social beha-
vioural codes in the colonies. Yet despite these efforts to maintain
racial and cultural difference, forces of cultural intertextuality and
racial contact continued to surface.

LAWS OF CONTROL: THE NEGATION OF PROPERTY AND THE
PROHIBITION OF MISCEGENATION

By the end of the seventeenth century, plantation owners had
transported over a quarter of a million slaves from Africa to
Barbados, Jamaica and the Leeward Islands. Over 70 per cent of
those imported by the Royal African Company between 1673 and
1689 came from the Guinea coasts, the remainder originating from
the Senegambia region to the north and from Angola to the south.[50]
In order to undermine the potential of violent insurrections and
thereby ensure the safety of the plantations, English traders deliberately selected slaves from a variety of tribes and languages so that
these slaves, 'not understanding each other languages and customs'
could not 'agree to rebel'.[51] Likewise as part of the effort to negate
the Africans' sense of identity (communal and individual) and
maximise profits derived from sugar, the enslaved Africans were

regarded as chattel and treated as transferable property without rights or redress in the law.

At first, English colonists avoided definitions of slavery by means of a haphazard regulatory structure which governed relations between slaves and masters. Later, however, drawing upon the system of servitude brought to the West Indies by the Spanish, planters developed a network of legal codes and customs designed to maintain a system of binary difference between black 'slaves' and their white 'masters'.[52] In 1637, the Government Council of Barbados decreed that 'Negroes and Indians, that came here to be sold, should serve for life, unless a contract was before made to the contrary'. However, as Alissandra Cummins points out, no such 'contracts' were ever 'made'. Since political power in the British Colonies was dependent upon a relationship between a white elite and the English Crown, the slave system rested upon the legal concept of property in persons, a concept which was later reinforced by the development of West Indian Slave Codes which attempted to define slave status and regulate their activities. As definitions of what constituted a slave were based on lines of descent, reproduction amongst slaves meant an increase in a slaveholders' property:

Slaves . . . shall be judged, deemed, and taken as inheritances and shall accordingly descend; and all children of slaves born in the Possession of Tenant for Life or Years, shall remain, or revert as the Parents do, and should have done.[53]

The category of mulatto was, however, more difficult to define:

And for the better ascertaining who shall be deemed mulattoes . . . no Person who is not above Three Negroes removed in a lineal Descent from the Negroe Ancestor exclusive, shall be allowed to vote or poll in Elections; and no one shall be deemed a Mulatto after the Third Generation, as aforesaid, but that *they shall have the Privileges of this Island, provided they are brought up in the Christian Religion.*[54]

In order to reinforce the constructed dichotomy between masters and slaves, in 1644 the Antigua Assembly composed a law forbidding miscegenation or 'caarnall coppullation [sic] between Christian and Heathen'. Although this law attempted to prohibit interracial sexual contact, it simultaneously defined the product of such an act, the mulatto offspring, as a slave destined to serve until the age of eighteen or twenty-one. It was subsequently revised in 1672 so as to determine the mulatto as a slave for life.[55] In fact, an examination of the Private Acts of Assembly passed in Jamaica indicates that complicated and infrequent efforts were made to secure mulattoes their status as English subjects, as exemplified by the Private Act passed to entitle 'the reputed [Mulatto] Children of Patrick Hanlon, Esquire, deceased . . . to the same Rights and Privileges with English Subjects, under certain Restrictions'.[56]

Attempts (formal and otherwise) to prohibit miscegenation thus strained against the pervasive dynamics of sexual desire, most especially between white masters and females of African descent, and as a result the social structure of the West Indies contained an increasingly large 'coloured' sector (in Jamaica, for example, in the period 1829–1832, of the 4041 coloured children born, at least 2000 had white fathers).[57] In fact, the question of interracial sexual activity reached the House of Commons as early as 1790 when it was admitted by Lt. Dawson that female slaves were frequently let out by their owners 'for Purposes of prostitution'.[58] More sophisticated theoretical endeavours to maintain the distinction between the races included Edward Long's *History of Jamaica: Or, a General Survey of the Antient and Modern State of That Island* (1774). In this text, Long, the son of a Jamaican planter (Samuel Long), claimed that the white and black race were two distinct species and that racial intermixture amongst them would result in a gradual decline in fertility. By combining the concept of polygenesis (many species) – 'must we not conclude, that *they are a different species of the same genus?*' – with religious alterity, Long advanced his theoretical validation of racial difference as a justification of slavery in the West Indies:

I shall next consider their [the Negroes] disparity, in regard to the faculties of the mind. Under this head we are to observe, *that they remain at this time in the same rude situation in which they were found two thousand years ago.* In general, *they are void of genius,* and seem almost incapable of making any progress in civility or science. *They have no plan or system of morality* among them . . . They have *no moral sensations; no taste but for women;* gormondizing, and drinking to excess; no wish but to be idle.[59]

In the following year, the anthropological treatise by Johann Friedrich Blumenbach (under whom Coleridge studied in 1798–1799), 'On the Natural Variety of Mankind' (1775) attempted to repudiate such theories of polygenesis ('the plurality of human species') in terms of their departure from the 'accuracy of *Scripture*' and their lack of scientific analysis:

For on the first discovery of the Ethiopians, or the beardless inhabitants of America, it was much easier to pronounce them different species than to inquire into the structure of the human body, to consult the numerous anatomical authors and travellers . . . When the matter is thoroughly considered, you see that all [species of man] do so run into one another . . . that you cannot work out the limits between them.[60]

Blumenbach's claims for monogenesis were advanced alongside a positive acknowledgement of the Africans' culture and their non-Christian beliefs. In his 'Observations on the Bodily Conformation and Mental Capacity of the Negroes' (1799) and his subsequent 'Contributions to Natural History' (1806), Blumenbach extended his belief in the affinity of the human species to a systematic confirmation of Negro equality, citing the 'good disposition and faculties' of blacks such as the Wesleyan Methodist preacher, Madox, and the ex-slaves, Ignatius Sancho, Gustavus Vassa and Phillis Wheatley.[61] Blumenbach maintained however, in the third edition of the 'Natural Variety' that anatomical differences in the reproductive organs made transracial sexual relationships, especially between black males and white females, difficult and therefore rare.[62] Apart from Coleridge's connection with Blumenbach, these debates concerning racial disparity must have reached the Romantic poets. Book 7 of Wordsworth's *Prelude* displays a significant anxiety in its focus upon racial types ('As we proceed, all specimen of man / Through all the colours which the sun bestows . . . Moors, / Malays, Lascars, the Tartar and Chinese, / And Negro ladies in white muslin gowns'), whilst his poem concerning the three black female exiles, 'Queen and Huntress, Chaste and Fair' (see Chapter 3) emphasises a connection between blackness and (excessive) sexuality.[63] Likewise we know that Blake engraved plates for Lavater's treatise on physiognomy, a text which 'measured' cranial proportions and character.

For Blumenbach, the unity of the species of man was ostensibly delineated by the 'almost insensible and indefinable transition' between the races, from the 'pure white' skin of the Germans, to the yellow and red 'types' and finally, to the 'darkest black' Ethiopians.[64] In 1776 Raynal had claimed that gradual racial intermixture had the 'natural advantage' of preserving 'the species from deteriorating'.[65] According to Blumenbach, evidence of this 'insensible transition' was embodied by the 'hybrid offspring' or 'mulatto' figure provided by the miscegenous act, as its epistemological stem, 'mule', implied:

1. The offspring of a black man and a white woman, or the reverse, is called *Mulatto, Mollaka, Melatta*; by the Italians, *Bertin, Creole* and *Criole*; by the inhabitants of Malabar, *Mestico* . . . 2. The offspring of an European male with a Mulatto female is called *Terceron, Castico*. The son of a European female from a *Metif* is called a *Quarteroon*. The offspring of two Mulattoes is called *Casque*; and of blacks and Mulattoes, *Griffs*.[66]

As far as the monogeneist Blumenbach was concerned, the metamorphosis of colour determined by these 'hybrid' transitions conclusively negated any polygenetic hypotheses of the human species such as those advanced by Long. Conversely, Long's tract, *Candid Reflections* (1775) and the article published in *The Morning Post*, 22 December 1786, by an anonymous author, suggested that 'miscegenation' presented a serious threat to all classes of society and a disturbing contamination of English blood:

When the late Mr Dunning was some forty years ago reasoning against making this country a refuge for all the blacks who chose to come here, he observed, 'that the numerous dingy-coloured faces which crowded our streets, must have their origin in our wives being *terrified* when pregnant, by the numerous Africans who were to be seen in all parts of the town, and if the legislature did not take some method to prevent the introduction of any more, he would venture to prophecy, that London would, in another century, have the appearance of an Ethiopian colony.[67]

In the third edition of 'On the Natural Variety' (1795), Blumenbach's application of critical zoology to the natural history of mankind identified the 'analogous phenomena of degeneration' as a process of biological decline in specialism and function, including the deterioration of a race's intellectual, moral and physical attributes.[68] From the late eighteenth century onwards, the study of 'degeneration', in terms of the physical and physiological characteristics of the human species, became central to definitions of racial variation.[69] Using the example of the mule as their model, those who believed that racial difference was a consequence of polygenesis argued that 'crosses' across the species were rare and that the resulting products were either infertile or would produce infertile offspring. In a development of this discourse of 'degeneration' in his text, *The Animal Kingdom Arranged in Conformity with Its Organisation* (1827), the French scientist Georges Cuvier defined 'degeneracy' in terms of the 'compressed cranium', a signifier of racial inferiority:

In the Ethiopian variety the front of the head is laterally compressed and considerably elongated, so that the length of the whole skull from the teeth to the occiput is great. It forms a complete contrast to the globular head of some Europeans.[70]

Likewise, Cuvier argued that 'degenerate types' would display a constant state of unbridled lascivity and lethargy and would therefore never achieve greatness on physical, mental or moral grounds: 'We may venture to lay it down as a general position, for the truth of which all history may be made to vouch, that the white races are decidedly superior to the dark in intellectual and moral qualities'.[71]

Eighteenth-century theories of evolution and origin – and their rigorous efforts to maintain cultural and/or racial difference between the subject (the west) and its objects (its colonised others) – were essentially problematised by the consequences of assimilation, and more especially, miscegenation. In late seventeenth-century New England, the increasing number of mulattos necessitated the need for distinct laws classifying their otherwise indeterminate status between that of person and property. Likewise, the legal designation of these mixed 'species' by the terms 'mulatto', 'mulatta' or 'molatto' reflected the alarm felt by advocates of racial purity and more general fears concerning the deterioration of slavery itself. By 1664, both Virginia and Maryland had developed harsh laws outlawing interracial marriage; similarly, in December 1705, the legislature of Massachusetts enacted a stringent law for the 'better preventing of a spurious and mix't issue'.[72] In 1768 the ratio between whites and slaves in Jamaica was 17,000:167,000 (approximately 1:10). By the end of West Indian slavery this ratio had become 1:20:2 with a population of 16,000 whites, 310,000 slaves and 31,000 'coloured' persons, the latter constituting a distinct category whose legal status was considered superior to that of slaves but inferior to that of whites. As these population statistics demonstrate, the increasing numbers of mixed race population in colonies constituted an intermediate term which interrupted the master discourse and which constituted a dialogic, turbulent, displaced subject.[73] On a different note, in his *Researches into the Physical History of Man* (1813), the leading authority in England on biological racial theory, James Cowles Prichard, discussed the hypothesis that nature had provided for the preservation of distinct species (which he defined as entities of 'constant and perpetual difference') by means of a system of 'mutual repugnance' between such 'different kinds' of species: 'The hybrid animals, produced by the mixture of any two of them, is unprolific'.[74] Yet for

Prichard, the fact that racial intermixture amongst humans produced offspring that were prolific meant that the 'tribes to which the
parents respectively belong[ed]' could not be proved to be 'specifically different': 'The rule being thus established, there remains no
difficulty with regard to the diversities of mankind. We very easily
conclude that all men are of one and the same species'.[75]

In his *Lectures on Physiology, Zoology, and the Natural History of Man*
(1819), the British anatomist, Sir William Lawrence, identified interracial sexual relations as 'un-natural unions' which he believed
would bring about the physical and moral 'deterioration' of Europeans. Although principally a monogenist, Lawrence, like Prichard,
argued that nature had provided barriers of instinctive aversion and
geographical distance between the races so as to prevent degenera-
tive corruption:

Europeans and Tercerons produce Quarterons or Qaudroons . . . which
are not to be distinguished from whites: but they are not entitled, in
Jamaica at least, to the same legal privileges as the Europeans or white
Creoles, because there is still a contamination of dark blood, although no
longer visible . . . [In] the dark races, and all who are contaminated by any
visible mixture of dark blood . . . all other physical and moral qualities are
equally influenced . . . The intellectual and moral character of the
Europeans is deteriorated by the mixture of black or red blood; while, on
the other hand, an infusion of white blood tends in an equal degree to
improve and ennoble the qualities of the dark varieties.[76]

Three decades later, the nineteenth-century racial theorist Joseph
Arthur de Gobineau outlined the Newtonian laws of attraction and
repulsion between the races in his essay, *The Inequality of Human Races*
(1853–1855). These, he claimed, functioned as key forces governing
the 'secret repulsion from the crossing of blood' between the white,
black and yellow human races, yet he acknowledged the presence of
fertile human hybrids:

The word *degenerate*, when applied to a people, means (as it ought to mean)
that the people has no longer the same intrinsic value as it had before,
because it has no longer the same blood in its veins, continual adulterations
having gradually affected the quality of that blood.[77]

Adopting Gobineau's definition of 'degeneration' as a process of
continual adulteration, Eugene Talbot asserted that the degeneracy
effected by racial intermixture was indicated by the environment;
hence a mulatto was 'better adapted to the white environment than
the pure negro, albeit lesser than the white'.[78] Talbot claimed that

the degeneracy caused by racial intermixture could be confirmed by the 'relapse into voodooism and cannibalism' practised by the Haiti, the Louisiana French hybrids and the Anglo-Saxon hybrids of Liberia. According to Talbot, racial intermixture could not result in the elevation of a race, especially in cases where the female was of an inferior race: 'Given the negro pelvis and the head of a white, results damaging to the offspring cannot but occur . . . hence intermixture with an inferior race . . . would tend to degeneracy'.[79] Gobineau drew a further parallel between his hypotheses of racial inequality and the 'inequality of languages' displayed by Africans. Somewhat paradoxically, he identified the language invented by bushmen as infinitely inferior, even though he suggested that it had been developed as a coded system specifically designed to exclude whites. Hence he concluded that:

All the facts . . . go to prove that, originally, there is a perfect correspondence between the intellectual virtues of a race and those of its native speech; that languages are, in consequence, unequal in value and significance . . . as races are also . . . I may thus lay it down, as a universal axiom, that the hierarchy of languages is in strict correspondence with the hierarchy of races.[80]

Although Gobineau traced the dialectic between the forces of civilisation and the processes of degeneration, he also argued that 'blood mixture' was necessary to the development of primitive society. Cross-cultural contact, he suggested, had provided cultures with conditions necessary for their improvement.[81] Yet he maintained that all civilisations were ultimately derived from the white race; none could 'exist without its help'. For this reason he argued that artistic genius in the black race was merely the result of 'the intermixture' between blacks and whites: that the overall effects of miscegenation were generally unfavourable, since they enervated the noblest elements:

If mixtures of blood are, to a certain extent, beneficial to the mass of mankind, if they raise and ennoble it, this is merely at the expense of mankind itself, which is stunted, abased, enervated, and humiliated . . . There is no greater curse than such disorder, for however bad it may have made the present state of things, it promises still worse for the future.[82]

This confused and ambiguous discourse of hybridisation and degeneration presented by scientists, human biologists and ethnographers alike, served to endorse fears regarding the mulatto's threat to European civilisation. As a consequence of this confusion and ambiguity, the term 'Creole' (discussed in detail in the following chapter) was used to signify a white person born in the colonies and also a person of mixed (European and Indian/native/black) descent.[83] Nonetheless, despite the proliferation of hypotheses advocating the need for racial segregation, the persisting numbers of 'mulattoes', 'quadroons' and 'octoroons' confirmed the increasing mechanisms of desire which functioned at odds with the social and legislative disapproval of interracial contact. As both a physical presence (the product of a socially illicit relationship) and as a metaphor for cultural synchronisation, the mulatto-figure designated a complex site of exchange, of migration and of 'translation' between two cultures, illustrated in Josiah Quincey's journal of 1773:

> The enjoyment of a negro or mulatto woman is spoken of as quite a common thing: no reluctance, delicacy or shame is made about the matter. It is far from being uncommon to see a gentleman at dinner, and his reputed offspring a slave to the master of the table . . . The fathers neither of them blushed or seemed disconcerted. They were called men of worth, politeness and humanity.[84]

Pre-Civil War fears concerning miscegenation had developed into a cohesive system of racist ideology which prioritised the necessity of segregation in order to 'protect' cultural, ethnic and social differences. As Nancy Stepan elucidates, apprehensions relating to the effects of degeneration were increased twofold in the American colonies: firstly, as a consequence of the extensive movement of 'freed' blacks into newly-vacated geographical and social spaces, and secondly, by the threat of biological degeneration upon the white race within the tropical zones appropriated by colonial ideology.[85] Following the Somerset case of 1772, and the final passing of the Bill for Abolition in 1807, a similar situation existed in England and its colonies, where a complex network of suppressive laws were developed which endeavoured to prohibit cultural miscegenation and the education of slaves. For this reason, an intricate series of theories emerged which claimed to endorse the 'natural' division between slaves and their masters on account of the slaves' intellectual inferiority and their failure to embrace the complexities of the written word. For pro-slavery ideologists, racial segregation crucially depended upon the maintenance of a dichotomy constructed around the parameters of literacy. Thus for the slaves, the acquirement of literacy came to represent a crucial means of emancipation.

THE WRITTEN VS. THE SPOKEN WORD

In seventeenth-century England, the absence of (cultural) literacy, and indeed linguistic alterity were identified as signifying the Africans' absence of reason and culture.[86] In Shakespeare's *The Tempest* (*c.* 1611), linguistic colonialism (the propagation of English speech) and the usurpation of the spoken word by the written word (the ultimate signifier of 'humanity') were two decisive factors which informed the struggle over power between Prospero and the 'savage' Caliban. In this play, inspired by Sir George Somer's narrative of his shipwreck in the Bermudas, Prospero's 'white' magic is derived from his claims for the power of the written word which Caliban, the disinherited heir to Sycorax's 'black' magic, recognises as the source and agent of territorial expansionism, colonial ideology and cultural subjugation: 'Remember first to possess his books; for without them/ He's a sot, as I am, nor hath not one spirit to command'.[87] For colonialists and plantocrats alike, the distinction between oral and printed forms of language reflected a systemisation of difference which was to be maintained at all costs. Laws prohibiting the education of slaves, such as the colonial statutes of South Carolina in 1740 thereby confirmed the correlation between political rights and literacy:

Be it enacted, that all and every person and persons whatsoever, who shall hereafter teach, or cause any slave or slaves to be taught to write, or shall use or employ any slave as a scribe in any manner of writing whatsoever, hereafter taught to write; every such person or persons shall, for every offense, forfeith the sum of one hundred pounds current money.[88]

Unsurprisingly, this juxtaposition of literacy and freedom emerged as one of the central tropes of slave narratives published during the late eighteenth and early nineteenth centuries. According to Gates, literacy 'stood as the ultimate parameter by which to measure the humanity of authors struggling to define an African self in Western letters'.[89] In the *Narrative of the Adventures and Escape of Moses Roper, from American Slavery* published in London in 1837, Moses Roper highlighted the inter-relationship between liberation and literacy in an episode describing his acquirement of a forged pass, a document which enabled him to escape from the slave-designated territory of North Carolina and enter the land of 'freedom'. In Roper's text, the written word functioned metaphorically as the slave's passport to freedom and as a literal signifier of his newly acquired identity:

Having heard several freed coloured men read theirs [free passes], I thought I could tell the lad what to write. The lad sat down and wrote what I told him, nearly filling a large sheet of paper for the passport, and another sheet with recommendations.[90]

A slave's 'literary' entrance into the dominant order was, however, also dependent upon his/her appropriation of the established linguistic order. Seventeenth-century linguists such as Sir Thomas Herbert, in his *Some Yeares Travels into Divers Parts of Asia and Afrique* (1638), compared the native languages of Africa with the 'unnatural' sexual practices ('coupling without distinction') between Africans and beasts. This 'beastly copulation or conjuncture', he argued, had caused the Africans' language to be 'rather apishly founded', resulting in a voice 'twixt humane and beast'.[91] Herbert identified this 'unnatural' linguistic mixture as a register of Africans' lack of religion: 'Notwithstanding, though I made all signes, and tried each way possible to discover some spark of devotion, of the knowledge of God, heaven, hell, or immortality; I could not finde any thing that way'.[92]

Alongside the transference of these 'unnatural' linguistic systems and cultural folktales which accompanied the slaves' transatlantic crossings, additional cultural orientations were preserved, the most important of these being the continuation of polytheistic African systems based on a belief in the *spirits* of ancestors and supernatural powers.[93] On the plantation islands and in the colonies, missionaries endeavoured to replace ulterior cultural belief systems with Christian creeds premised upon concepts of original 'sin' and repentance. Yet slaves continued to revere African obeahs and myalists (priests and 'magicians') whom they considered as intermediaries of the spirit world.[94] Many slaves recognised the necessity of appropriating the discourse of Christianity in order to advance abolitionist agendas; others, however, were suspicious of embracing concepts of religious salvation detached from demands for socioeconomic liberation or emancipation. The African slaves' continued reverence for obeahs (who were always African rather than Creole) and myalists reflected a sustained preference for the ecstatic fervour of the spirit rather than the (written) word. This ambivalence towards the written word was recorded during the early stages of seventeenth-century territorial colonialism and described by the Dutch West India Company representative, William Bosman in his account of African coastal societies, *A New and Accurate Description of the Coast of Guinea* (1698):

For a great part of the *Negroes* believe that Man was made by *Anansie*, that is, a great Spider . . . They tell us, that in the beginning God created Black as well as White Men; thereby not only hinting but endeavouring to prove that their Race was as soon in the World as ours; and to bestow a yet greater Honour on themselves, they tell us that God having created these two sorts of Men, offered two sorts of Gifts, *viz.* Gold, and the Knowledge or Arts of Reading and Writing, giving the Blacks the first Election, who chose Gold, and left the Knowledge of Letters to the White. God granted their Request, but being incensed at their Avarice, resolved that the Whites should for ever be their Masters, and they obliged to wait on them as their Slaves.[95]

Interestingly, Bosman's narrative tells us as much about Africa's interpretation of the west as it does about Bosman himself and the culture for which he functioned as an ambassador. When the *New and Accurate Description* was published, Guinea had been firmly established as a major source of slave-based economic wealth. The introduction of the 'guinea' coin confirmed the intricate relationship between the slave trade and England's socioeconomic transformation by means of the industrial revolution.[96] The subtext of Bosman's 'tale' established a paradigm for the critical transference of wealth from Africa to the west, continued in the eighteenth century, and perhaps more importantly, described the pivotal interrelationship between the mechanisms of power and the written word, the whites' 'knowledge of letters'. For the slaves, therefore, 'liberation' depended upon their 'literary' entrance into, or penetration of, the dominant order. At this point, the narratives of insurrection and emancipation inscribed by the slaves coincide with sociopolitical narratives of independence which emerged in England and America during the latter half of the eighteenth century.

DECLARATIONS OF INDEPENDENCE: PAINE, JEFFERSON AND THE SLAVES

For, all men being originally equals, no *one* by *birth* could have a right to set up his own family in perpetual preference to all others for ever: and, though himself might deserve *some* decent degree of honours of his contemporaries, yet his descendants might be far too unworthy to inherit them. One of the strongest *natural* proofs of the folly of hereditary right in kings, is, that nature disapproves it, otherwise she would not so frequently turn it into ridicule, by giving mankind an *ass for a lion*.[97]

On 9 January 1776, Thomas Paine's sensational pamphlet, *Common Sense: Addressed to the Inhabitants of America* appeared. This remarkable text, which in itself manifested a radical departure from time-honoured traditions of political writing, articulated a demand for American independence from Britain, alongside calls for the establishment of a republican government.[98] In this tract, which sold 150,000 copies, Paine passionately and vehemently attacked the English Constitution and the principle of hereditary rule, denouncing them and the English monarchy as 'the base remains of two ancient tyrannies'. Paine, the son of a Quaker and a local attorney's daughter, called for the creation of a republican government based entirely on a representation of the people whereby the rights of persons, property and religion were guaranteed. For him as for other key thinkers of the time, republicanism rested firmly upon a discourse advocating the diffusion of private property amongst citizens. Only this, it was argued, would genuinely establish the conditions necessary for self-government and contribute to the beneficial development of society. Accordingly, the emerging rhetoric of republican discourse centred upon concepts of virtue (the willingness to subordinate selfish interest to the good of the whole); equality (in terms of treatment before the law and wealth distribution): and independence (the ability to resist outside coercion).

On 2 July 1776, the motion put forward by the Virginian Richard Henry Lee, 'That these united Colonies are, and of right ought to be, free and independent States' was carried. Two days later, the signing of Jefferson's 'Declaration of Independence' by delegates of the second Continental Congress, ushered in the appropriation of the Scottish enlightenment philosophical discourse, most especially the 'inalienable rights' to life and liberty advocated by Hutcheson in his *Inquiry into the Original of Our Ideas of Beauty and Virtue* (1725) on a national scale. As a declaration of independence it was written and intended as a persuasive text to be read/heard by an audience resident both within and outside the boundaries of the 'new' nation:

We hold these truths to be self-evident: that *all men* are created *equal*; that they are endowed by their creator with *inherent and* unalienable rights; that among these are life, liberty, & a pursuit of happiness: that to secure these rights, governments are instituted among men, deriving their just powers from the consent of the governed; that whenever any form of government becomes destructive of these ends, it is the right of the people to alter or abolish it, & to institute new government, laying it's foundation on such principles, & organising it's powers in such form, as to them shall seem most likely to effect their safety & happiness.[99]

As a narrative of liberation, America's 'Declaration of Independence' influenced the emergence of a plethora of narratives premised upon declarations of 'independence' and emancipation, conceptually at odds with the master/mother text.[100] This was similarly confirmed by Jefferson's defiant rejection of Quaker ideology and discourse:

A Quaker is, essentially, an Englishman, in whatever part of the earth he is born or lives. The outrages of Great Britain on our navigation and commerce, have kept us in perpetual bickerings with her. The Quakers here have taken side against their own government . . . from devotion to the views of the mother society.[101]

However, Jefferson's revolutionary manifesto, a quasi-legal articulation of civil rights, omitted those racist sentiments derived from ethnographic theory, expressed elsewhere in his writings:

Whether the black of the negro resides in the reticular membrane . . . [or] whether it proceeds from the colour of the blood, . . . the difference is fixed in nature . . . And is this difference of no importance? Is it not the foundation of a greater or less share of beauty in the two races? . . . The circumstance of superior beauty, is thought worthy attention in the propagation of our horses, dogs, and other domestic animals; why not in that of man? . . . They [the negros] have less hair . . . They secrete less by the kidneys, and more by the glands of the skin . . . They seem to require less sleep . . . Love seems with them to be more an eager desire, than a tender delicate mixture of sentiment and sensation . . . It appears to me, that *in memory they are equal to the whites; in reason much inferior . . . and that in imagination they are dull, tasteless, and anomalous.*[102]

Whilst declaring the inalienable rights of life and liberty to *all*, therefore, his 'autobiography' of a nation, a pseudo-narrative of deliverance, implicitly registered a counter-discourse of territorial expansionism, cultural dispossession and enslavement which had made possible the nation's 'innocent' birth. Jefferson's duplicitous position on property rights reflected his awkward attempts to reconcile principle with prejudice:

Whatever be their degree of talent it is no measure of their rights. Because Sir Isaac Newton was superior to others in understanding, he was not therefore lord of the person or property of others.[103]

Across the Atlantic, this important discussion over property rights was further endorsed by the works of Thomas Paine. In 1787, Paine made plans to return to Europe, ostensibly to promote his designs for an iron bridge. Soon however, he became caught up in another political upheaval, the outbreak of the French Revolution in 1789, an event which inspired the Burke-Paine debate over political reform and confirmed the transatlantic intertextual dialogue in which the term 'revolution' simultaneously signified slave emancipation, radical social change and 'postcolonial' reorderings. In November 1790, Edmund Burke published his *Reflections on the Revolution in France*. In this text, Burke denounced the French Revolution as a chaotic bastion of anarchy and extolled instead the virtues of the 'delicate balance' of the British political system, namely the political power of the propertied aristocracy, the 'glorious' benefits of an hereditary line of succession and the necessary alliance between church and state (as opposed to the demands of the 'swinish multitude'). For Paine, events in France heralded a desirable and timely age of revolution and equality. Dedicated to George Washington, Paine's *Rights of Man: Being an Answer to Mr Burke's Attack on the French Revolution* (Part I of which appeared in March 1791) presented a vindication of the events in France and insisted upon the rights and duty of the present generation to act for itself rather than submit to precedent:

Man has no property in man; neither has any generation a property in the generations which are to follow . . . I am not contending for, nor against, any form of government . . . I am contending for the right of the *living*, and against their being willed away, and controuled and contracted for, by the manuscript assumed authority of the dead.[104]

Although Paine was primarily concerned with the rights of the citizen, his rhetoric widely challenged established concepts of 'property', concepts which had crucially been used to define Africans as slaves/objects rather than subjects. Within the legislative and socio-economic discourses of both England and America, a slave's position was intrinsically ambiguous: legal and linguistic definitions continued to vie against each other, determining blacks simultaneously as property and persons before the law: human but not men ('niggers'), 'men' but also property, sexually desirable but not free, 'free(d)' but not equal, equal but not racially compatible. In order to endorse the validity of their own subjectivity and independence, it was essential that a slave's mode of discourse presented an alternative but equally viable discourse, infused with the power to undermine and usurp traditional discourses founded upon plantocratic and racist ideology. The 'discourse of the spirit' provided the slaves with an effective ('creolised') mode of subversion, a persuasive counter-hegemonic mode of articulation via which the culturally hybrid consciousness of a black diaspora could emerge. In other words, the slave narratives provided an illuminating juxtaposition with mainstream Romanticism and hegemonic culture.

PART TWO

CHAPTER FIVE

The diasporic identity: language and the paradigms of liberation

All of it is now it is always now there will never be a time when
I am not crouching and watching others who are crouching too
. . . I cannot fall because there is no room to the men without
skin are making loud noises I am not dead . . . those able to die
are in a pile . . . the little hill of dead people.[1]

Part One of this study has concentrated upon the development of
the discourse of the spirit by (white) western authors, especially in
the context of Romantic and eighteenth-century dissent and enthusiasm. This second part examines the narratives published by slaves
and determines them as important paradigms of cross-cultural
contact: narratives which achieved a complex process of exchange
and negotiation between the discourse of Romanticism as it emerged
out of eighteenth-century dissent and the narratives of displaced
subjects, the slaves from the African diaspora. In so doing it argues
that the slave narratives published at the turn of the century
presented complex literary articulations of the culturally hybrid
consciousness of the black diaspora and thereby achieved an important mixture of conscious stratagem and discursive determination,
non-conformist rhetoric and African epistemology. By charting the
translation of literary and polemic expressions of identity into
abolitionist / non-conformist rhetoric, this latter part locates these
narratives as important disclosures of the slaves' experience of
cultural fragmentation and their emergence into the social and
linguistic order of the west. According to some historians, the
transatlantic journey (or 'middle passage') effected an *erasure* of the
slaves' cultural memory.[2] This study, however, highlights the development of the slaves' sense of cultural identity (defined as a process
of 'becoming' as well as 'being' once history has intervened) and
demonstrates the ways in which their literature presented strategic
endeavours to counteract cultural and historical obliteration. By

examining the gaps and moments of disjuncture contained within these narratives, it determines the poetic and autobiographical narratives of the early black literary tradition as powerful articulations of the diasporic identity, premised upon complex processes of displacement, cultural preservation and miscegenous accommodation.[3] In this study therefore, the use of the term 'slave narrative' extends to a selection of texts (poetical and prosaic) published in England, either composed, dictated or co-edited by slaves and ex-slaves. These were usually accompanied by an engraved portrait of the subject of the narrative, passages of biblical text, poetic epigrams, authenticating testimonials, extracts from legal tracts and newspapers, certificates of manumission and letters and dedications to benefactors, patrons and politicians.[4]

As Hortense Spillers' analysis of the Moynihan Report of the late 1960s suggests, the diasporic plight marked a 'violent severing of the captive body from its motive will, its active desire'.[5] The captive body was hence reduced to an object, a 'being for the captor' whose absence from a subject position provided an index of physical and biological 'otherness' which determined its potential for 'pornotroping' and endorsed its condition of powerlessness:

> That order [the sociopolitical order of slavery], with its human sequence written in blood, *represents* for its African and indigenous peoples a scene of *actual* mutilation, dismemberment, and exile . . . a *theft of the body* . . . The loss of the indigenous name/land provides a metaphor of displacement for other human and cultural features and relations, including displacement of the genitalia, the female's and the male's desire that engenders future.[6]

Spillers argued that the captive body registered a site of dismemberment and exile intrinsically determined by the irreversible effects of cultural dispersal and discontinuity. For Spillers therefore, the slave signified a non-site of suspended identity in which the signifiers of cultural hegemony had been usurped. Conversely, this study locates the slave narratives as important models of cultural preservation which demonstrated a continuation, by means of intrinsic processes of transformation and synthesis, of the preslavery cultural self and proclaimed the emergence of a hybrid, mulatto form.[7]

But what constituted a 'slave' and his/her narrative? According to legal ordinances of the West Indies and the Americas, a child's status (as either slave or free-born) was determined by the status of its mother. Within the plantocratic societies, biological reproduction, whether voluntary or enforced, represented not only the extension of subject hegemony (by the west) but a future investment in the universal mercantile system. This identified the diasporic identity as a site of ambiguity at the interstice of private and public property. The acquirement of two fathers (biological father and captive master) marked the diasporic identity as an intercultural/intertextual space between two narratives, a middle or third term located geographically and metaphorically amidst the middle passage, a term at once dependent upon and independent of both Africa and the west. Such 'interspatial positioning' was replicated by the etymological stems of terms such as 'nigger', 'hybrid' and 'mulatto' – terms which marked the 'unknown' territory between man and animals, Africa and the west.[8]

As a site of constant transformation, the diasporic identity's entry into the western symbolic order effected a confirmation and simultaneous disruption of that established order in terms of its subjection to and destabilisation of manifestations of colonial power. By simultaneously claiming points of cultural *difference* and *similitude*, the diasporic identity transformed the master discourse by significant processes of disturbance and transformation, not in terms of 'otherness', but in terms of an unsettling miscegenation of language and cultural identity:

Across a whole range of cultural forms there is a 'syncretic' dynamic which critically *appropriates* elements from the master-codes of the dominant culture and 'creolises' them, disarticulating given signs and rearticulating their symbolic meaning otherwise. The subversive force of this hybridising tendency is most apparent at the level of language itself where creoles, patois and Black English decentre, destabilise and carnivalise the linguistic domination of 'English' – the nation-language of master-discourse – through strategic inflections, reaccentuations and other performative moves in semantic, syntactic and lexical codes.[9]

This third or 'hybrid' term did not proffer a negation of Hegelian dialectic, nor a process by which the alterity of the other was mitigated by assimilation, but a discourse located within the realm of *hiatus* in which both the subject and object remained intact, albeit transformed. As revealed by the 'mulatto' or hybridised articulations of the eighteenth century, the diasporic identity penetrated the dominant order by means of an intermediary discourse which achieved a fusion of conscious strategem and involuntary translation of abolitionist rhetoric and African epistemology. By interrupting the fixed binary schemas of difference and power, it marked a site of creolised or syncretic discourse which decentred principal tenets of western hegemony. By usurping presuppositions based upon a single historical narrative, the diasporic identity contributed toward a process of adaptation (transformation and synchronisation) which manifested a complex fusion of languages, social order and modes of worship. Ostensibly the diasporic/mulatto figure registered a complicit note of cultural assimilation, yet it simultaneously emerged as a trope of chiasmus, a signifier of disruption and revision which heralded a discourse of resistance and protest.

'WORDS WALKING WITHOUT MASTERS': THE LANGUAGE
OF THE DIASPORA

> I ent have no gun
> I ent have no knife
> but mugging de Queen's English
> is the story of my life
>
> I dont need no axe
> To split / up yu syntax
> I dont need no hammer
> to mash / up yu grammar . . .
> I slashing suffix in self-defence
> I bashing future wit present tense
> and if necessary
> I making de Queen's English accessory to my offence.[10]

In drawing my title for this section from words cited in the novel *Their Eyes Were Watching God* (1937), I hope to invoke and continue the investigative spirit of the vivacious Harlem Renaissance author and anthropologist Zora Neale Hurston (1891–1960), whose efforts during the 1920s to step outside the white hermeneutical circle and enter into the black have proved a pervasive force in the attempt to initiate a dialogue concerned with questions of cultural identity and representation.[11] For Hurston, the search for a black literary language, a language existing on the periphery of a standard English literary tradition yet rooted in a profoundly lyrical, quasi-musical oral tradition, coincided metaphorically with the search for an appropriate mode of articulation for an identity (female and Afro-American) which existed both within and without the dominant (male) discourse. In the context of this study, 'Words walking without masters' suggests not only a quest for a self-reflexive voice, liberated from definitions of identity premised solely upon concepts of race or gender, but corresponds to the diasporic identity's subversive entry into the dominant (symbolic) order via a transformative use and 'abuse' of language.

For the authors of the slave narratives, the emergence of such a voice represented both an individual and collective act, premised upon the mechanisms of self-representation and dissent. In his analysis of the relationship between the African and African-American vernacular traditions and black literature, Henry Louis Gates defined this process as symbolising 'the quest to become a speaking subject'.[12] Two years earlier, William Andrews' *To Tell a Free Story: The First Century of Afro-American Autobiography, 1760–1865* (1986) identified the unity of black autobiographies of the antebellum era as being most apparent in the 'persuasive use of the journey or quest motif' traced within their narratives of spiritual evolution. According to Andrews, the fugitive slave narrator and the black spiritual autobiographer revealed a recognition of their 'fundamental identity with and rightful participation in *logos*, whether understood as reason and its expression in speech or as divine spirit'.[13] Extending the propositions of both Gates' and Andrews' theses, this chapter suggests that in their search for a self-reflexive voice, the first black autobiographers posited a language of cultural identity permeated by the dynamics of the diaspora – that is, as words that walked both with and *without* masters. This informed a sequence of narratives premised upon displacement and recovery, heterogeneity, diversity and hybridity. Uprooted from ancestral soil, stripped of the signifiers of their 'native' culture and transported to the plantocratic societies of the West Indies and the Americas, displaced Africans were forced to maintain their cultural heritage at a *meta* rather than material level, amidst 'the operative metaphysics' of various alien cultures.[14] It is at this point that the interrelationship between Hurston's observation and the quest for freedom which characterises the slave narratives becomes clear, given that the sovereignty of the individual rested primarily upon a (re)possession of language, a linguistic 'mastery' which destabilised the dominant order by means of speech, utterance and protest. Zora Neale Hurston's work provides a renewed interaction with the discourse of the 'spirit', not in terms of unadulterated western Christianity, but in its mutant synthesis of French Catholicism and the religious practices of the Yoruba people of the west coast of Africa.[15]

Bereft of those cultural and political signifiers which had provided them with stable, unchanging and continuous frames of reference and meaning, the slaves' 'autobiographical' publications provided important declarations of cultural identity amidst the traumatic experience of their revised definition in the diaspora and in spite of prohibitions which forbade them to learn to read and write. As these 'autobiographical' narratives manifested the first literary expressions of unprecedented cultural upheaval and revised hierarchies of power, a predominant objective was their endeavour to redress pervasive ideologies which had classified blacks as either non-human or as 'objects' unworthy of subject status. This study elucidates the means by which these slave narratives reveal not only an ambivalence towards the superiority of the written over the spoken word, but register a reluctance to acquire either literacy (and thus cultural identity) on strictly Western terms or to embrace wholesale articulations of western ideology. Premised upon a bilateral assimilation and rejection of dominant hegemony, the diasporic identity emerged as a double-edged discourse, situated both within and outside the parameters of established spiritual discourse.[16] By calling into question the 'spiritual' nature of their European captors, former slaves were treading upon one of the most sensitive areas of 'civilising' ideology.

THE CREOLISATION OF LANGUAGE: CREOLES, BLACK ENGLISH AND PATOIS

Contemporary linguistic studies have shown that languages variously referred to as 'black English' and 'Ebonics' were developed within the complex linguistic arena of the slave plantations. As the visible repositories of African culture were either prohibited or repressed within slave societies, subtle linguistic and communicative syntheses, or 'creolisations' of West African languages and English emerged. In this way the linguistic systems of pidgin, creole and Afro-American retained structural remnants of certain African languages in spite of the imposition of western linguistic models.[17] The emergence of a 'pidgin' language involved a considerable reduction in the grammatical structure of an appropriated language. The emergence of a 'creole' witnessed the moment at which pidgin became the native language of those who used it. A creole, such as the Yoruba-English based 'krio' developed in Sierra Leone, represented a pidgin language that had become a mother tongue. While they employed the language of the respective European colonies, creoles preserved the grammatical structure, pronunciation and translation of African idioms:

> Unlike 'normal languages' a pidgin language usually comes into existence for a specific reason, lasts just as long as the situation that called it into being, and then goes quickly out of use . . . A pidgin acquires a longer lease on life only by becoming the native language of a group of speakers (becoming creolised), and thereby passes over to the status of a 'normal' language. From this point of view, we can speak of pidgins as having 'life-cycles', and of their being 'inherently weak' in that, not their linguistic structure, but their social standing is normally not hardy enough to enable them to be used outside of their original context.[18]

The word 'creole' derives from the seventeenth-century Portuguese term, 'crioulo' (probably from 'criar': to bring up), meaning a slave of African descent born in the New World. Thereafter, the term was extended to include Europeans born in the colonies, and in eighteenth-century Louisiana was used to determine a person of *mixed* European and African ancestry.[19] The Latin stem of 'creole', *creare* meaning 'to create', provides an appropriate metaphor for the creation of slave objects and the complex dynamics of cross-cultural contact. Within this study, the term 'creolisation' refers not only to the creation of new languages at moments of crisis, but also to the revised positions (cultural, geographical and literary) which African subjects took up in Europe and the Americas during the transatlantic slave trade. It was, as Edward Kamau Brathwaite claimed in 1971, a 'two-way process', a cultural transaction which worked in both directions.[20] In this sense therefore, the term creolisation attests to the continuum of African culture which radiated from the slave communities and affected the entire culture of the United States, the Caribbean and the British Isles. In terms of identity (re)formation, the concept of 'creolisation' reflects the critical processes of constant transformation which constituted the slaves' sense of cultural identity in the black diaspora.[21]

On board the slave ships, in the plantations and in the domestic households of the colonies, the syncretic speech patterns, nuances and creolised linguistic formats which emerged amongst the slaves provided a means of communication both with, and to the exclusion of, whites. As these fusions represented an appropriation and revision of the dominant (cultural) discourse, this 'creolisation' of language also marked the first stage in the development of the hybridised discourse contained in the slave narratives. As Molefi Kete Asante explains, the 'English' spoken by the African slaves and their descendants retained the phonological, syntactical structures and pitch tones of African languages:

> Whatever semblance of English they learned had the unmistakable imprint of African languages, much as the English spoken by the average French person is rendered in many instances in terms of French phonology and syntax. These Africans were, for the most part, not linguists learning languages but lay persons acquiring an instrument for their survival. And the limited English vocabulary and few sentences needed for the task of staying alive were extremely useful in dealing with whites. But the mastery of English morphology and syntax lay in the future.[22]

Asante's flow diagram of the development 'from African Languages to Ebonics' illustrates the transformation of West African languages of the Niger and the Congo into what she terms 'ebonics' or black English [Fig. 3]. This process occurs firstly via 'pidginisation', the acquisition of foreign vocabulary in which the original morphology and grammar are maintained; secondly, via 'creolisation', the integration of unrelated languages; and finally, via 'englishization', the emergence of a linguistic schema in which certain lexical terms and the original communicative style are preserved. By means of this complex linguistic process, tenets of African culture were maintained despite the imposition of European values and styles. The significant dichotomies between the 'master language/ideology' and its creolised descendants were most particularly evident in the corresponding verb systems and pronouns. For example, whereas English possesses two perfects (past and present), black English distinguishes between the simple past and present by means of verbal inflection ('I see it' meaning both 'I see it' or 'I saw it', depending on the context) and retains a verb system with four perfects, including a completive perfect, 'I done walked' and a remote time perfect, 'I been walked'. Likewise, the tendency to use several, rather than a single verb to express completed action, 'I took consideration and joined de lawd', dissects the event into its various stages, a process which preserves the predominance of harmonisation as a principal function of black speech behaviour. Conversely, the English equivalent, 'I accepted religion' or 'I became a Christian', reduces the action to a single, main verb hinged upon spontaneity.[23] On another level, African languages and their descendants display a semantic system in which the non-distinctive subject pronoun is retained: for example in Ibo

FROM AFRICAN LANGUAGES TO EBONICS

WEST AFRICAN LANGUAGES
NIGER AND CONGO
|

ACQUISITION OF FOREIGN VOCABULARY
MAINTAINS ORIGINAL MORPHOLOGY, PHONOLOGY, GRAMMAR
|

MORE WORDS AND SOME GRAMMAR
PIDGINIZATION
MAINTAINS ORIGINAL MORPHOLOGY AND GRAMMAR
|

CREOLIZATION
MAINTAINS MORPHOLOGY
|

ENGLISHIZATION   EBONICS
MAINTAINS ORIGINAL COMMUNICATION STYLE
MAINTAINS SOME LEXICAL TERMS

Fig. 3. Molefi Kete Asante, 'African Elements in African-American English', *Africanisms in American Culture*, ed. Joseph Holloway. Bloomington: Indiana University Press, 1990.

language (and often in krio) the third person singular, 'O', signifies both male and female (unlike the gendered English construction which distinguishes between 'he' and 'she'). This disregard for gender with respect to personal pronouns transforms the phrase 'Mary is in the cabin' to 'Mary, he in the cabin'.[24]

PARADIGMS OF LIBERATION: LITERARY AND LINGUISTIC

In the slave narratives which emerged in England and America during the 1780s and 1790s, the manifestation of 'diasporic' self-reflexivity posited a powerful challenge to theories which had determined Africa as 'a land of childhood' lying beyond the day of self-conscious history. The representation and enunciation of 'self-consciousness' within these narratives thereby promoted a *recovery* of the scattered fragments of cultural identity – a process which took place by means of linguistic and literary metamorphoses of form occasioned by cross-cultural contact. As these 'creolised' and 'hybridised' texts asserted their speakers' marginalisation in relation to the 'host' culture, they proclaimed subversive strategies of revision, not only of language, but of the social order itself.[25] As codes of liberation and empowerment, they presented a correlation between discourses of emancipation and conversion and hence disclosed the complex interrelationship between power and literacy, exemplified by the 'Massa' tales:

God let down two bundles 'bout five miles down de road. So de white man and de nigger raced to see who would git there first. Well, de nigger out-run de white man and grabbed de biggest bundle . . . De white man . . . picked up de li'l tee-ninchy bundle layin' in de road. When de nigger opened up his bundle he found a pick and shovel and a hoe and a plow and chop-axe and then de white man opened up his bundle and found a *writin'-pen and ink*. So ever since then de nigger been out in de hot sun, usin' his tools and de white man been sittin' up figgerin, ought's a ought, figger's a figger; all for de white man, none for de nigger.[26]

Heavily encoded with hieroglyphical schemas of displacement, transformation and possibility, the linguistic configurations of the diaspora inaugurated a literary discourse of cultural dispossession and repossession. As the displaced identity recreated itself by a complex system of semantic, syntactical linguistic structures and sub-strata levels of meaning 'unavailable' to 'other' listeners, a body of narratives emerged which determined a paradigm of cultural preservation within the diaspora and testified to African cultural development prior to European contact. As a consequence, the symbolic world of black folklore and African belief systems was maintained. In their preservation of paradigms of defiance amidst cultural hegemony, the tales of Brer Rabbit, Anansi (the Spider), Tortoise and Hare delineated the means by which the dominant order might be transformed and the African cultural legacy sustained.[27] In this way, the folktale victories of Anansi and Brer Rabbit (by means of deceit, evasion and wit) functioned as linguistic models of rebellion and subversion. As with the linguistic process of creolisation itself, the appropriation of these tales by western culture into the (legitimised) forms of 'Spiderman' and Peter Rabbit, implemented a mutual process of exchange and cultural assimilation. The same process of exchange and integration determined the slaves' articulations (constructed and inherent) of the phenomenological operations of the world and their role within it.

CHAPTER SIX

The early slave narratives: Jupiter Hammon, John Marrant and Ottobah Gronniosaw

When Israel was in Egypt's land,
Let my people go.
Oppressed so hard they could not stand,
Let my people go.
Go down, Moses
Way down in Egypt's land,
Tell ole Pharaoh, Let my People go.

(Negro Spiritual)

For those who had never known freedom, the language of the Bible presented a viable discourse of liberation and reform, its metaphors of salvation and freedom providing appropriate paradigms of protest, rebellion and social transformation. However, the challenge posed to those from the African diaspora was to find a way of reappropriating that text, which had played such a significant role in asserting the supremacy of the English language and culture. Championed by the increasingly popular movement of radical dissenting Protestantism, the discourse of the spirit enabled 'authorised' declarations of 'independence' which reached beyond the peripheries of religious orthodoxy. As I shall argue below, this mode of discourse witnessed a moment of cultural synthesis between (rival) hermeneutical discourses, that is, between the west's Christianised concept of the 'holy spirit' and its divine agency, and African spiritual epistemologies, including the belief in the transmigration of souls. Hence, as 'converted' slaves absorbed, or seemed to absorb, the implicit message of impartial spiritual guidance, they transformed Christian tenets of salvation into disruptive strategies for radical social regeneration, claiming 'inspiration' from the spirit and the scriptures as the key influential forces behind their revolutionary activity. Moreover, as religion, often unsuspectingly, 'lent' its voice to revolt and insurrection, slaves exposed the ambiguity behind certain

Christians' support of pro-slavery ideology and in so doing, high-lighted the interrelationship between textual interpretation, herme-neutics and power.

In his article, 'Slave Songs and Slave Consciousness', Lawrence Levine determined the identification of slaves with the chosen people, the children of Israel in Egypt, as 'the most persistent image' of negro spirituals.[1] Indeed, the various references to 'pharaohs' and 'exodus', within this synthesis of discourses of conversion and liberation, harboured coded messages about slave masters and plans for escape into the promised land with the aid of 'Moses' figures such as the underground 'railway' networker, Sojourner Truth.[2] In her essay, 'Spirituals and Neo-Spirituals', Zora Neale Hurston identified the continued significance of such songs in the twentieth century, and defined them as 'genuine spirituals' sung by black groups in America and the Caribbean 'bent on expression of feelings'.[3] In *Tell My Horse* (1938) and *Moses, Man of the Mountain* (1939), Hurston prioritised the cultural significance of references to Moses in both Afro-American folklore and black spirituals. Mosaic legends were not confined to Palestine or Egypt, but were found throughout the Mediterranean and Africa. In tales from Africa Moses figured alternately as 'the fountain of mystic powers', the original conjuror, and as the father of Damballa, his snake-like staff providing a symbol of his power.[4] The revised messages, signs and symbols of the King James Bible therefore functioned as narratives of empowerment rather than servitude. Likewise, when slaves sang their 'spirituals', references to the River Jordan described both the mystical boundary between earth and heaven and the Ohio River which marked the border between the free and the slave states.[5] That boundary registered a critical moment of division and intersec-tion between two distinct cultural schemas: African and Christian epistemology, past and present lives or spirits.

As the framework advanced by dissenting Protestant spiritual autobiographies found a continuum in the slave narratives which appeared in England during the latter half of the eighteenth century, established models of spiritual 'awakening' underwent an essential metamorphosis. The slave 'conversion' narratives transformed the moment of deliverance into a moment of conscious configuration of identity within the diaspora; they translated the paradigm of spiritual deliverance into a schema of secular liberation and insurrection. In their effort to posit the status of their author as 'man', 'brother' and 'truth-teller', slave narratives transformed the discourse of 'spiritual awakening' into a duplicitous discourse of polemical protest and rebellion. Furthermore, they achieved a mapping of African episte-mology on to the dynamics of radical dissenting Protestantism. Consequently, the protean nature of the discourse of the spirit enabled an intermediary dialogue between Africa and the west. Hence the emphasis upon prophetic rapture and spiritual imma-nence, found in the prophetic writings and spiritual autobiographies of the eighteenth century, finds a fascinating counterpart in the indigenous spiritual beliefs of Africa, and indeed their continuation in the slave plantations of America and the West Indies.

Part of the 'cultural baggage' which African slaves brought with them to the New World was informed by their beliefs in the relation-ship between man and man and between man and the gods.[6] The principal features of these included a belief in a remote supreme being, worship of a pantheon of gods (non-human spirits), ancestor worship and belief in the use of dreams and fetishes.[7] In his three-volume work, *A History of the West Indies*, Thomas Coke described the religious worship of the natives of the Leeward Islands in the Caribbean as an 'abyss of mental darkness', which displayed a 'uniform obedience to the injunctions of the zemi':

Like most other savage tribes, these islanders believed in a plurality of gods. They conceived however that there was one, whose power was omnipotent, and whose nature was immortal. To this God they ascribed creation . . . But though they allowed of a supreme God . . . they conceived the government of the world . . . to the management of inferior agents or genii, which they called zemi . . . These malignant deities were not accessible to the multitude without the intervention of the priest and caciques.[8]

Condescending though it is, Coke's discussion of the spiritual world of the 'zemi' identified a key aspect of African epistemology within the diaspora and its focus upon the ancestral spirits of the 'living dead'. Within this system, death signified a process by which a person is gradually removed from the 'Sasa' period (that dimension in which events are either about to happen or have recently occurred) and enters into the 'Zamani' (the final store-house for all phenomena, the 'ocean of time').[9] Hence in African ontology, the deceased is physically dead yet remains alive in the memories of those who knew him. When there is no longer anyone alive who remembers the living dead personally by name – i.e. when such beings have passed out of the Sasa period – then the process of dying is complete and such beings pass into the state of 'collective' immortality as spirits, occupying what Mbiti calls the 'ontological state between God and man'.[10]

Together, Africans enslaved on plantations and runaway slaves who assumed independence (in the West Indies these were known as 'maroons' from the French word *maroon* meaning 'wild, untamed') persisted in keeping the memory of African gods and ritual alive.[11] Within their belief system, a special cast of magicians or physicians claimed control of the supreme powers vested in the gods of healing and the demons of disease. As Thomas Winterbottom, physician to the Sierra Leone Company in 1792 noted, the practice of religious ceremonies ('magical ceremonies and incantations') was often intricately fused with the practice of medicine.[12] Exaltation in language and indulgence in physical and emotional ecstasy were prioritised, a process more recently known as 'receiving the spirit'. In African and West Indian witchcraft, 'myalism' denoted the formal possession by the spirit of a dead ancestor and the dance performed under that possession, whereas 'obi or obeah' signified the person or thing exercising control and the practice of magic derived from it.[13] Central to the religious practices of Africans, therefore, was the ecstatic moment of spirit possession, the domination or control by spirits, 'vodu' being the term used for 'the spirit' by the Fon in Ewe language. Hence tales of 'flying' or possessed Africans provided cultural paradigms of liberation from slavery, in defiance of factual and historical determination.[14] Whilst suicide constituted a cardinal sin in Christian theology (hence its importance in Cowper's and Newton's texts), death by drowning or hanging was considered by many slaves preferable to slavery, as they connected such acts with a belief in a possible return to their homeland, even after death.[15]

Whilst obeah originates from the practice and beliefs of the Ashanti-Fanti tribes, voodoo originates from a system of beliefs with origins in the Fon and Yoruba cultures of the Dahomey or modern Benin region (where Equiano was born). Voodoo (from the Ewe term 'vodu', meaning 'guardian spirit') involved communication by trance with ancestors and animistic deities. Foremost amongst the spiritual gods, or 'loa', was Legba, the interpreter of the will of the gods, then the 'marasa' and the 'dosu/a' (twins and the child born after twins), and the dead. Voodoo ascribed a person two souls: a personal soul ('gros-bon-ange') and the 'm'ait-tete loa' which entered a person during the first possession. These were joined together for life until separated by death, at which time the gros-bon-ange returns to its home in the waters below the earth and the m'ait-tete loa is inherited by the children of the deceased.[16]

As with the moment of spirit possession described by the eighteenth-century radical dissenting Protestants, in voodoo belief, during the mystical experience of possession by the voodoo loa or spirit, the person possessed speaks and acts for that loa. Like the subversive, radical elements of the English tradition of prophetic and confessional writings, voodoo extended to insurrectionary propor-tions. The eighteenth-century voodoo chant ('we sweat to destroy the whites') prescribed a negation of slave ideology, 'changa batio te', as did the voodoo ceremony orchestrated on the eve of the uprising which broke out in the French Caribbean colony of St Domingue in August 1791.[17] In Part Three of the extended *Report of the Lords of the Committee of the Council Appointed for the Consideration of all Matters to Trade and Foreign Plantation* (1789), comprised of over 1200 pages, the means by which obeahs caused death and injury were discussed at length: 'A veil of mystery is studiously thrown over their incantations, to which the midnight hours are allotted, and every precaution is taken to conceal them from the knowledge and discovery of the white people'.[18] According to the *Report*, in 1775 a planter had returned to Jamaica to find that a great many of his slaves had died during his absence and that of those that remained alive, half were 'debilitated, bloated, and in a very deplorable condition'.[19] In an effort to prohibit obeah practice, the first approved *Code Noir* of Jamaica, confirmed in January 1699, suggested that in order to reduce the number of fatal poisonings, the 'bloody and inhuman transactions' which took place during slave gatherings ought to be prohibited.[20] Likewise, clause XLIX of the 'Act to Repeal Several Acts and Clauses' (Dec. 1784) of the *Acts of the Assembly. Passed in the Island of Jamaica, from 1770 to 1783, Inclusive* stated that 'any Negro or other slave' who pretended to 'any supernatural power' would suffer either death or transportation.[21] Accordingly, in his *Twelvemonths Residence in the West Indies, During the Transition from Slavery to Apprenticeship*, R. R. Madden (from the parish of St Andrews) recorded the sentence and subsequent transportation of the female slave, Sarah, for 'having in her possession cat's teeth . . . and other materials, relative to the practice of Obeah, to delude and impose on the mind of the Negroes'.[22] In hoodoo, a variant of voodoo, the major underlying belief is that of a dual division of the

world of causes – that is, a spiritual counterpart to every physical
object and action. Hoodoo belief maintains that to deal with the
physical cause only is to partially administer treatment – the spiritual
reality must be attended to by a root doctor or conjuror whose
exorcising of the lingering spirit will enable complete healing.[23]
Accordingly, the collective terms 'hoodoo' and 'conjure' stem from
traditional beliefs in the magical power of a conjuror, root, or
hoodoo doctor to alter psychic and physical conditions, a system
which ranged from the basic administration of sympathetic magic to
the intricacies of a highly complicated religious system.

In his discussion of obeah and Romantic culture, Alan Richardson
makes it clear that by the end of the eighteenth century, these
religious beliefs as they were practised by black slaves in the British
West Indies had become notoriously familiar to the British reading
and play-going public.[24] Given the prominence and popularity of
works by Africans living in late eighteenth-century Britain (such as
Phillis Wheatley, Olaudah Equiano and others discussed below) *and*
the reference to African religious systems in the works of Robert
Southey, it appears that the 'contact zone' between Romanticism
and black writing had clearly been established by the end of the
century. Popularised by plays such as *Obi; or, Three Finger'd Jack*
(which was first performed at the Theatre Royal in Convent Garden,
London in July 1800), tales such as Charlotte Smith's 'The Story of
Henrietta' (1800) and Maria Edgeworth's 'Belinda' (1790), and lyrics
such as William Shepherd's 'The Negro's Incantation' published in
the *Monthly Magazine* July 1797, these interpretations of West African
religion were translated not only from Africa to the Caribbean but
into the heart of British culture.[25] As Richardson notes, the
Romantic (and indeed British) concern with obeah reflected Britain's
'anxieties regarding power', most especially the fluctuations of
imperial power as Britain, France and Spain vied for dominance in
the Caribbean. Just as importantly, it also registered Britain's
concern over the slaves' power to determine their own fates, as
events in the Caribbean had shown.[26] Like its counterpart, voodoo,
the practice of obeah demonstrated the degree of resistance and
insurrection amongst slaves and their 'continued' forms of cultural
organisation and communication.

One of the most powerful transcriptions of obeah practice by a
British poet occurs in Shepherd's 'Negro Incantation' of 1797.
Shepherd's poem provides a powerful testament to the moment of

colonial conflict, manifested in psychological, cognitive and epistemological terms. Linked directly by the poet to the formidable
insurrections of Jamaican black slaves in 1760 (known as 'Tacky's
Revolt'), Shepherd's poem acknowledges the preservation of African
cults and belief systems within the Caribbean and highlights their
essential role in the slaves' insurrectionary plots. Congo, the repository of obeah power, hails the 'spirits of the swarthy dead' (line 5)
and prepares 'with magic rites the white man's doom' (12), thereby
prophesying an end to British colonial expansionism and slavery via
divine (black) retribution and revolt:

> From mouldering graves we stole this hallow'd earth,
> Which, mix'd with blood, winds up the mystic charm;
> Wide yawns the grave for all of northern birth,
> And soon shall smoke with blood the sable warrior's arm.[27]

In 1863, the American Freedman's Inquiry Commission conducted a vast series of interviews with slaves; and between 1936 and
1938, the Works Progress Administration interviewed over 2,000
former slaves.[28] Many of these interviews confirm the slaves' preservation of African cults on the plantations, and include references
to the 'frolics' and nocturnal prayer meetings which took place
either in slave cabins or in clearings in the woods, during which
slaves would gather to sing, shout and 'get happy'. Slaves such as
Adeline Cunningham, born in Texas, and Ellen Butler (born in
Louisiana, 1859) recollected the interrelationship between spiritual
discourse and linguistic models of emancipation:

No suh, we never goes to church. Times we sneaks in de woods and prays
de Lawd to make us free and times one of the slaves got happy and made a
noise dat dey heerd at da big house and den de overseer come and whip us
'cause we prayed de Lawd to set us free . . . Massa never 'lowed us slaves to
go to church but they have big holes in the fields they gits down in and
prays. They done that way 'cause the white folks didn't want them to pray.
They used to pray for freedom.[29]

Dialogues with spirits and conjure women continued to play an
important role in slave societies of the West Indies and America, as
Harriet Collins, an ex-slave, explained:

Dere been some queer things white folks can't understand. Dere am folkses
can see de spirits, but I can't. My mammy learned me a lots of doctorin',
which she larnt from old folkses from Africy, and some de Indians larnt
her.[30]

Hoodoo and voodoo therefore helped to preserve the precious fragments of cultural legacy within the diaspora and continued a process of resistance against the plantocracy, demonstrated by the Caribbean slave revolt led by a voudoun priest in 1791 and Nat Turner's rebellion of 1831.

In his excellent study of the colony of Jamaica during the first half of the nineteenth century, *Two Jamaicas: The Role of Ideas in a Tropical Colony, 1830–1865,* Philip Curtin traced the historical development of Afro-Christian sects in Jamaica from 1830, when several hundred United Empire Loyalists emigrated from America with their slaves.[31] As syntheses of orthodox Christianity and African cult groups developed, various 'Native Baptist' congregations evolved, the most prominent of which emerged under the leadership of independent black preachers such as Baptist Moses Baker (who had a following of approximately 3,000) and the ex-slaves, George Lisle (or Leile) and George Lewis. Both Lisle and Lewis vehemently opposed traditional Christianity and prioritised their own African-styled belief systems.[32] During these early native Baptist meetings, which were often conducted in patois, African beliefs reappeared in Christian guise. As a result of this 'transition', emphasis lay particularly on the workings of 'the spirit' and upon a corresponding attitude of suspicion towards the written word. As with the call and response and 'shouts' characteristic of African initiation rites, followers were required to be possessed 'of the spirit' before baptism was administered:

This meant that the 'spirit' had to descend on the applicant in a dream, which was then described to the leader. If the dream were satisfactory, the applicant could enter the class. There evolved a regular technique and ceremonial for bringing on spirit-possession.[33]

Missionaries in the colonies faced serious competition from African rival cults as the popularity of African myal religions continued, despite being made illegal, and the practice of myalism and obeah continued to flourish.[34] In this way, the process of Afro-Christian synthesis and the development of what I have termed the 'discourse of the spirit' continued to function as a vehicle of insurrection and cultural preservation. By 1830, Native Baptist sects were established as powerful means of preserving cultural identity within the diaspora, defiantly competing with the ideological framework imposed by Christian missionaries (who occupied a tenuous

position in Jamaican society, simultaneously denounced by plantocrats as slave allies and perceived by slaves as perpetrators of racist
ideology). Nevertheless on the plantations, intrinsic elements of
Christianity such as preaching, hymn-singing, fervent Christian
phraseology and 'prophesying' in the name of the Christian God
were appropriated by African belief systems through a complex
process of 'cultural' miscegenation. By the 1830s, the Wesleyan
Methodist Missionary Society had achieved one of the largest
dissenting slave congregations in Jamaica; however they continued
to maintain an apolitical stance and to preserve strict caste systems
within their chapels. Other sects, such as the Baptists and the
Moravian Brethren were almost entirely devoted to the conversion
of the slave population to orthodox Christianity. By the time of the
final surge of missionary activity, the Great Evangelical Revival of
1860–1861 had, in Curtin's words, '*turned* African' in its complex
fusion of myalism and Christianity.[35] This synthesis had however,
originally occurred over half a century earlier, in the 'discourse of
the spirit' presented in the narratives by ex-slaves and in their
literary articulations of spirit possession, 'prophesying' and initiation
rites.

DISPLACEMENT AND DIASPORA: THE SLAVE NARRATIVES AS AUTOBIOGRAPHIES

As articulations of the complex dialectics involved in the configurations of identity within the diaspora, narratives published by slaves
posited a mulatto-discourse, a third, hybrid term which synchronised
two distinct, and often antithetical, cultural ideologies. From such
'marginalised' sites, these mulatto-texts figured both a process of
assimilation and of counter-language. Sustained by the mechanisms
of imaginative transformation, yet never completely severed from a
remembrance of the past, these literary manifestations of the
diaspora emerged, demanding that they be met, considered, and
evaluated on their own terms.

According to the OED, the term 'autobiography' evolved with
Robert Southey's first usage of it in 1809. However, autobiographi-
cal-style narratives by slaves had been published in England and
America almost three decades earlier, usually prefixed by terms such
as 'Life of', 'History of', 'Adventures of' and so on. As constructed
configurations of identity, these slave narratives established a

relationship between individual *and* cultural 'autobiography' (nation-writing), that is, between narratives of the self/African selves, their cultural past and their position in the diaspora. In the late 1960s, Foucault identified the emergence of the term 'autobiography' as coincidental with what he described as the 'anthropological' processes of western culture. Sigmund Freud's analysis of the unconscious drew upon a discourse which merged tenets of autobiography (life-writing) with anthropological concepts, such as 'fetishisation', and hence translated the dichotomy between an extended framework of the individual self and culturally determined 'others' into a schema of the conscious and the subconscious self. Likewise, the intersection between autobiographical disclosure and the discourse of the spirit disclosed within the slave narratives finds an appropriate site within the world of dreams, that realm of the unconscious (or 'spirit') whose mechanisms cannot be rationally defined.

When one approaches the slave narratives as examples of autobiography, it must be remembered that like all forms of autobiography, these 'confessional' testimonies existed both as unrestrained, personal utterances and as highly self-conscious literary performances. In addition, they were consciously aimed at public consumption and intrinsically shaped by editorial intervention, a factor which destabilises the concept of the 'pure' autobiographical form. Furthermore, the translation of experience into a literary form was also problematised by the peculiarly ambivalent status of the ex-slave author, as an entity both with and without rights (political or editorial) in the diaspora. James Olney's pertinent questions concerning the mysterious and formalised literary genre of autobiography itself must clearly be taken into consideration when applied to the literary productions by slaves emergent in the latter half of the eighteenth century:

What do we mean by the self . . . (*autos*)? What do we mean by life (*bios*)? What significance do we impute to the act of writing (*graphe*) – what is the significance and the effect of transforming life, or *a* life, into a text?[36]

If, as I have argued above, the literary narratives by slaves may be seen as complex articulations of identities enmeshed within the dynamics of the diaspora, as 'creolised' testimonials by 'selves' who had undergone unprecedented historical, psychological and cultural dispossession, then how do we as readers determine an appropriate starting point for our analyses, in terms of both culture and historicity? If autobiography, by its very definition, represents an effort to resolve the problematics of identity, of self-definition and of self-existence, how should we begin to analyse texts proffered by those whose very identity had been erased, linguistically, legally and ideologically from the social order? Likewise, how should we approach such discourses of the 'self', given that the subject status of that articulating 'self' had previously been negated or obliterated by alternate discourses, such as that of the written word or the Law?

As a partial answer, I would suggest that we approach these narratives with caution, as textual configurations of identity, fragmented by upheavals of history and as intricate disclosures of cultural miscegenation, in terms of their syntheses of diverse cultural ideologies and beliefs. If, as Olney has argued, autobiography by definition can never reach completion, since the self or 'bios' must always remain incomplete, that is, 'always in process', then we must in turn see these autobiographical texts as narratives essentially hinged upon the dynamics of a culturally hybrid consciousness of the black diaspora. We must see them, therefore, as complex articulations of incessant migration, continuous flight and ceaseless movement – that is, as narratives of the processes of translation and transference experienced by the suspended status of the diasporic identity. Furthermore, I would suggest that in order to contemplate these 'narratives', we must approach with a caution which allows for the inherent possibilities of irony, counter-discourse and assimilation at the heart of these texts, and which recognises that the collective term 'slave narrative' is used, for want of a better term, to group together narratives written by those born in Africa, in the colonies and indeed, by those for whom 'slavery' was a fiction, or rather a convenient metaphor for post-abolition reality. These narratives were variously edited, dictated or composed 'by' former slaves who had found their way to freedom in conjunction with Christian philanthropists or abolitionist ghostwriters or indeed, by those blacks or anonymous 'white' authors who had themselves never experienced slavery and for whom self-expression involved a mixture of voluntary and involuntary literary and polemical tactics.

By assuming the discourse of the (Christian) spirit, the authenticity and the liberation of both the speaker and his/her narrative was validated under the aegis of self-examination and divine appointment. As the slave narrator posited him/herself as his/her own historian (albeit whose text was 'edited' by another), the 'act' of memory, either fictitious or real, enabled the autobiographer to 'recover and redeem lost time by fixing it forever'. This prioritisation of 'acts of memory' was also demonstrated within the works of the Romantic poets (see Chapter 3). Coleridge's conversation poem, 'This Lime-Tree Bower My Prison', and Wordsworth's *Prelude* signal the role of memory in terms of their authentication of the subject's past, present and future selves. Yet in both these examples, the emphasis is upon the individual rather than the community. 'Memory' therefore, insofar as the Romantics are concerned, is egocentric and solitary; for the slaves however, such acts of memory bore witness to a shared cultural past. This enabled the slave narrator to write his/her life as a unified expression of an entire (cultural and historical) destiny, premised on individual, collective and political liberty (the 'chosen one') and infused with the power to interpret and mediate with the spiritual world.[37] Hence for the slave narrator, the 'act of remembering' constituted a complex act of reconciliation between past and present, a means of situating what one was (culturally and spiritually) with what one had become within the mechanisms of diaspora and personal destiny:

In the act of remembering the past in the present, the autobiographer imagines into existence another person, another world, and surely it is *not* the same, in any real sense, as that past world that does not, under any circumstances, nor however much we may wish it, now exist.[38]

For these slave narrators therefore, 'recollection' constituted an act of cultural historiography: a reassembly of a past extended *self*, within a world that had defined that self as without history and without consciousness. However, as most critics of autobiography would agree, autobiography functions not merely as a recollection of one's life, but as a fiction, an artifact, a construct in which experience is fictionalised and one framework prioritised over all others.[39] For the slave, the climactic point of this prioritised framework, the moment of spiritual/cultural conversion, also figured as a moment of self-liberation in which the narrator broke free from the shackles of his/her father/master *and* past cultural identity, and emerged as a newly formed self.

Consequently, textual analysis of the slave narratives must involve an examination of what is *not* articulated by the text, that is, those textual blindspots, silences and erasures which reveal the highly complex relationship between the reader and the author. In other words, those moments of intersection and radical departure from the reader's (cultural and ideological) assumptions, and those moments of opacity contained within such seemingly transparent narratives of disclosure. Accordingly, whereas I agree generally with Mendel's suggestion that autobiography depends upon 'shared assumptions of culture', I would suggest that the autobiographical narratives by slaves present us with moments when the reverse is true – that is, when such (Christian or African) assumptions cannot be assumed as 'shared', when the very bedrocks of cultural identity are destabilised.[40]

Likewise, such an investigation raises questions over authorship and motive, the dynamics of editorial control, audience expectation and political agenda. And this in turn prompts us to question the motifs behind the considerable number of imitative or 'hoax' slave narratives which emerged in the late eighteenth and early nineteenth centuries, including Thomas Bluett's *Some Memoirs of the Life of Job, the son of Solomon* (1734), Robert Norris' *Memoirs of the Reign of Bossa Ahadee, King of Dahomey* (1789) and *The Narrative of the Travels of John Ishmael Augustus James, an African of the Mandingo Tribe, who was Captured, Sold into Slavery and Subsequently Liberated by a Benevolent English Gentleman* (1836).[41] Certainly texts such as R.W. Loane's *Authentic Narrative of the Late Fortunate Escape of R.W. Loane* (1805) and George Vason's *Authentic Narrative of Four Years' Residence at Tongataboo* (1810)[42] reveal a semi-pornographic and quasi-anthropological agenda under the guise of the 'confessional' captivity genre.[43] Other 'hoax' texts such as *Joanna, or the Female Slave. A West Indian Tale* (1824) provided a platform for anti-emancipatory polemic at odds with the abolitionist agenda characteristic of a majority of the slave narratives:

The Abolition of Slavery bears so much upon Humanity, that to discuss the subject upon principles which *can* be acted upon, seems to infer a want of that divine attribute. Nevertheless, *General Emancipation* must appear to every reflecting mind a measure neither practicable nor advisable; therefore, leaving Emancipation to *time*, which it will take, it is wiser and better to look for a remedy for the present impending evils where it may be found – in the abolition of *cruelty*.[44]

In entering the slave autobiographer's world, we enter a world *conscious* of its need to perform and promote narratives of truths (cultural and historical) under the guise of divine witness. It is at this awkward juncture that the discourse of the 'spirit' comes into play, as the private utterances of the slaves appropriated the framework of 'unorthodox' Evangelical fervour. While these narratives advocated a shared revivalist agenda, they simultaneously advanced a 'counter-commentary' of unsevered allegiance to alterity, and a synthesis of cultural epistemologies based upon systems of belief, space and temporality.

For eighteenth-century radical dissenting prophets, Romantics and slave narrators alike, the act of autobiography manifested an effort to recapture, in words, a lost paradisiacal happiness and to reconcile, however tenuously, that past self with the present self. In writing their selves, the slave narrators endeavoured to transform both a preslavery culture and the 'post-African' diasporic self into a textual form, in narratives both liberated from and imprisoned by the possibilities and limits of western language and ideology. Therefore, as slaves translated the process of 'becoming' from an oral to a written culture, their narratives figured the violent 'unbecomings' of alternative texts which had prescribed their condition as slaves and inferiors. Within these autobiographies, the message of peaceful 'spiritual' transformation vies unresolvedly with subtextual declarations and conflicting hypotheses of radical social transformation. At once dependent upon, and at odds with the very ideology held by their white audience, these hybridised texts presented a trope of miscegenation and cultural assimilation, concurrent with a trope of radical departure from the dominant ideology.[45]

MULATTO DISCOURSES: CHRISTIANITY AND EARLY SLAVE LITERATURE

> To translate:
> To interpret or infer the significance of (gestures, symbols etc.).
> To transform or convert, e.g. to translate hope into reality.
> To move or carry from one place or position to another.
> (Theological) To transfer (a person) from one place or plane of
>   existence to another, as from earth to heaven.
> (Archaic) To bring to a state of spiritual or emotional ecstasy.
>   (*Collins English Dictionary*)

As W. E. B. Du Bois' much quoted passage from *The Souls of Black Folk* suggests, the cultural historiography of the African diaspora has been predominantly influenced by a framework premised upon binary oppositions of cultural difference, which established the diasporic identity as an embodiment of cultural polarity residing within the complex site of dialectical opposition:

The Negro is a sort of seventh son, born with a veil, and gifted with second-sight in this American world, – a world which yields him no true self-consciousness, but only lets him see himself through the revelation of the other world. It is a peculiar sensation, this double-consciousness, this sense of always looking at one's self through the eyes of others, of measuring one's soul by the tape of the world that looks on in amused contempt and pity. One ever feels this two-ness, – an American, a Negro; two souls, two thoughts, two unreconciled strivings; two warring ideals in one dark body, whose dogged strength alone keeps it from being torn asunder.[46]

For Hortense Spillers, the condition of diaspora manifests itself as a reiteration of an unending moment of transition, or middle passage between two cultures, a state of psychological and sensory deprivation, in which one's former identity becomes culturally 'unmade' and autonomous individuals are transformed into captive persons, literally suspended in the 'oceanic', '*nowhere* at all'.[47] For Vévé Clark, the nature of cultural transition finds an appropriate symbolic expression within the 'marasa trois' of voudoun signification. The 'marasa trois' describes the cultural entity which emerges metaphorically as a reformation of form, a revision of the 'marasa', the Haitian term for the twin cult, a mythical theory based on the voudoun sign for the capricious orphans, the *Divine twins*.[48] In traditional West African cults, children born with abnormal characteristics or during any unusual circumstances received very different treatment to their peers: twins born to the Ibo, Delta and Cameron tribes were despised and often killed, whereas within the Yoruba and Guinea coast tribes of Africa they were worshipped.[49] Accordingly, whereas the 'marasa' ostensibly attributes a binary form, generative readings of that sign focus upon the child born sequentially *after* the twins and the creation of the unit termed 'marasa trois'. In Yoruba belief systems, the child born *after* the twins (the *dosu*) emerges as a far more powerful entity than its predecessors. For Clark, therefore, the marasa trois determines 'another form of creativity' which traces a deconstructive path between the binary schema, whilst marasa consciousness provides an appropriate model for cross-cultural contact and configurations of identity within the diaspora.

In an effort to expand and revise Spiller's model of 'undifferentiated identity' and Clark's concept of 'diasporic literacy' – that is, to identify the reformative narrative strategies within literatures of Africa, Afro-America and the Caribbean as 'deconstructions of mastery' – the literary utterances of the diasporic identity are here determined as the products of 'cultural miscegenation'. Therefore, the poetical and prosaic works by slaves published in England during the late eighteenth and early nineteenth century are presented as evidence of the translation of one cultural network into another by a complex process of synchronous assimilation and appropriation.

As identified by the black preacher, John Marrant, who lamented the failure of his 'stammering tongue' and the ex-slave, Henry Bibbs, who despaired of finding a language to 'express adequately' the history of his past and the ambivalence of his present, *language* proved to be both a problematic obstacle and a vehicle of disclosure in the slaves' endeavour to translate the ambiguity of their socio-economic and legal status into 'declarations of independence'.[50] By means of their appropriation of the discourse of the spirit, characteristic of the Evangelical Revival which swept England during the latter half of the eighteenth century, blacks attempted to secure the Bible as a common mythological framework and thereby reestablish its hermeneutical capacity as a primary custodian of Afrocentric cultural ideologies. The aim of the latter part of this study therefore, is to establish the emergent autobiographical voice of the diasporic identity revealed by the slave narratives. In so doing, these texts are located as complex revisions of radical dissenting Protestantism and are identified as revealing an important intersection with the works of radical prophets and the Romantic poets in their poetic articulations of the liberated *self* – sanctified and redeemed – within the parameters of 'spiritualised' discourse.[51]

By engaging with the Scriptures as a form of (cultural) intertext, black autobiographical texts such as Briton Hammon's *Narrative of the Uncommon Sufferings, and Surprising Deliverance* (Boston, 1760) and John Marrant's *A Narrative of the Lord's Wonderful Dealings* (London, 1785), offered a revised paradigm of the spiritual framework and (re)established the biblical pact between Jehovah and the diasporic identity, drawn from the Old Testament. In their complex revision of Scripture, these early black autobiographical texts challenged the hegemonic status of the master discourse (the Law) and its institutionalised form (slavery) by propounding an *intermediate* narrative: that of the discourse of the spirit. Consequently, such texts ushered a radical departure from an ideological (legal and colonial) 'master' discourse which had sought to make them 'dis(re)membered' and disenfranchised, and endeavoured to remaster the symbolic form by duplicating, deconstructing and revising its narrative posture.

Slave narratives, therefore, such as those by the black spiritual evangelists, Jarena Lee, Phillis Wheatley and Olaudah Equiano, (re)presented the lives of their authors as secular figurations of Scriptural *mythoi* within the framework of Protestant redemption narratives. This endeavour to articulate the diasporic identity within the parameters of spiritual autobiography found contemporaneous parallels within the dynamics of early Protestant narratives (most especially those by women such as Southcott), yet also represented an attempt to mitigate boundaries of cultural distance and/or historical alienation.[52] By tracing their authors' journeys towards secular and social freedom, these early 'conversion' narratives posited the acquisition of spiritual awakening as an affirmation of divine election through the unequivocal workings of the Holy Spirit. Hence these narratives registered the diasporic identity's profound sense of dichotomy and duplicity, in terms of its ambivalent status as both object (slave/cultural other) and subject (speaker/assimilated self). This sense of discrepancy anticipates the Romantic poet's focus upon the disjuncture between the internal and external self, and continues the interface between word and text, flesh and spirit presented by eighteenth-century prophets. In an effort to eradicate concepts of difference based on theories of racial hierarchy, these slave narratives heralded their 'dispossessed speakers' as newly 'possessed', as bearers of the Word, as literal embodiments of the (deviant) discourse of the spirit.

JUPITER HAMMON: 'AND YE SHALL KNOW THE TRUTH AND THE TRUTH SHALL MAKE YOU FREE'[53]

Our slavery will be at an end, and . . . we shall sit with God in his kingdom, as Kings and Priests, and rejoice for ever and ever.[54]

In the broadside printed in New York in 1760 entitled 'An Evening Thought: Salvation by Christ with Penitential Cries', the concept of 'salvation' is continuously emphasised throughout the poetical text by the black preacher, Jupiter Hammon, who served the Lloyd family of Long Island as a slave until the death of Henry Lloyd in 1763: 'Salvation comes by Jesus Christ alone, / The only Son of

God; / Redemption now to every one, / That love his holy Word
... / Salvation now comes from the Lord, / He being thy captive
slave . . . / It is firmly fixt his holy Word, / *Ye shall not cry in vain*'.[55]
In the years that witnessed America's bid for independence from
England, Hammon, born a slave on 17 October 1711, composed a
series of poetical works which heralded a merger of the dynamics of
the diasporic identity with Christian tenets of deliverance and
salvation. As Hammon's text was published while he was still the
possession of the Lloyd family of Long Island, any suggestion of an
overt abolitionist schema continued within Hammon's text would
have been mitigated by the conditions enabling the publication of
his work. Hence, although Hammon's texts incorporate an extension
of scriptural mythoi on to the conditions of blacks, they also witness
a fragmented, inchoate transference of salvational rhetoric on to
schemas of abolition.[56] In his second publication, the poetical *Address
to Miss Phillis Wheatley, Ethiopian Poetess in Boston* ('who came from
Africa . . . and soon became acquainted with the Gospel of Jesus
Christ') which was published in August 1778 (five years after the
publication of Wheatley's volume of poems), Hammon posited the
process of 'transition' as both a geographical procedure (from Africa
to America) and a metaphorical movement which brought about a
transformation of cultural signification, the poet's value as a slave,
and her subsequent value as a convert to Christianity. Accordingly,
Hammon's text identified the interrelationship between the commercial apparatus of the middle passage and the various processes of
pilgrimage, salvation and conversion:

> God's tender mercy brought thee here:
>   Tost o'er the raging main;
> In Christian faith thou hast a share,
>   Worth all the gold of Spain.
>
> While thousands tossed by the sea,
>   And others settled down
> God's tender mercy set thee free,
>   From dangers still unknown.[57]

In his final publication, *An Address to the Negroes of the State of New York*
(1787), Hammon combined the dynamics of scriptural discourse with
a distinctly ambiguous liberationist agenda. Whereas on one level,
Hammon's text appeared to advocate a condition of passivity and
unquestioning obedience, on another, his *Address* revealed a subtle

integration of intertextual discourse concerning the inalienable rights of liberty: 'I am certain that while we are slaves, it is our duty to obey our masters in all their lawful commands, and mind them, *unless we are bid to do that which we know to be sin*'. Hammon's text endeavoured to prioritise a common cultural identity between himself and his audience, emphasising his loyalty to his fellow slaves as 'Africans by nation' rather than as representatives of disparate tribes:

I think you will be more likely to listen to what is said, when you know it comes from a Negro, one of your own nation and colour and [sic] therefore can have no interest in deceiving you, or in saying any thing to you but what he really thinks is your interest, and duty to comply with.[58]

At times, Hammon's use of spiritual discourse appears to confirm a distinct complicity with white cultural hegemony in its ambivalent deployment of anti-liberationist propaganda: 'If you become Christians, you will have reason to bless God for ever . . . though you have been slaves'.[59] Hence, although Hammon acknowledges that 'liberty is a great thing' and worth seeking for, he propounds an 'honest' means of securing it: that is, by slaves convincing their masters that their 'good conduct' ought to be rewarded by their freedom.[60] In addition, Hammon asserts, probably as an acknowledgement of the conditions of publication, that he does not wish to be set free, although he would welcome the liberation of other young blacks. Nonetheless, recognising the protean power of Christian discourse, Hammon, like Coleridge, invites his audience to contemplate *spiritual* 'salvation' as a necessary prerequisite to temporal deliverance. By comparing the condition of the slaves in America with that of the Israelites of the Old Testament, Hammon's text prophesies the divine deliverance of the slaves as God's *chosen* people:

Stand still and see the salvation of God, cannot that same power that divided the waters from the waters for the children of Israel to pass through, *make way for your freedom*, and I pray that God would grant your desire, and that he may give you grace to seek that freedom, and I pray that God would grant your freedom which tendeth to eternal life.[61]

At the same time, however, Hammon suggests that both slavery and freedom are preordained, God-given: 'Getting our liberty in this world is nothing to our having the liberty of the children of God':

My Brethren, many of us are seeking a temporal freedom, and *I wish you may obtain it*; remember that all power in heaven and on earth belongs to

God; if we are slaves it is by the permission of God, if we are free it must be by the power of the most high God.[62]

Ultimately, Hammon's tenuous call for social transformation pivots around the belief that whites ought to fulfil their role as enlightened liberators whilst, as God's chosen people, blacks ought to uphold their covenant with God:

> If we should ever get to Heaven, we shall find nobody to reproach us for being black, or for being slaves. Let me beg of you, my dear African brethren, to think very little of your bondage in this life; for your thinking of it will do you no good. If God designs to set us free, he will do it in his own time and way . . . [Yet] I must say that I have hoped that God would open their [white people's] eyes, when they were so much engaged for liberty, to think of the state of the poor blacks, and to pity us. *He has done it in some measure . . . [but] what may be done further, he only knows.*[63]

As a result, his text ambiguously ricochets between a critique of the inconsistencies inherent in white liberationist ideology and an endorsement of passive adherence to black socioeconomic deprivation. Thus Hammon's text describes a crucial yet embryonic phase in the fusion of Christian rhetoric with liberationist ideology. In its emphasis upon the tenets of 'salvation', Hammon's work anticipates the heterogeneous development of the 'discourse of the spirit' contained within the slave narratives published in England in the late eighteenth and early nineteenth century.

JOHN MARRANT: CULTURAL INTERLOCUTOR

Born of free black parents in New York on 15 June 1755, John Marrant's *Narrative of the Lord's Wonderful Dealings with John Marrant, a Black* was published in London in 1785 by the Reverend William Aldridge, the non-conformist minister at the Calvinist-Methodist Jewry Street Chapel who had trained at the Countess of Huntingdon's College in Treveccain, South Wales.[64] The Countess of Huntingdon, Selina Hastings (dedicatee of the slave narratives by Gronniosaw and Phillis Wheatley discussed below) had converted to Methodism in the 1730s and had provided the financial costs of establishing a loose 'connexion' of Methodist congregations in England and Ireland. Three years before Marrant's text was published, she and her follows were declared dissenters and forced to secede from the Anglican Church. Published prior to his departure for Nova Scotia, where he intended to preach the gospel, Marrant's text underwent five successive editions in the same year, with further editions published in London, Dublin, Halifax, Leeds, Wales and Connecticut.[65] In his book, *The Signifying Monkey*, Henry Louis Gates interpreted Marrant's tale principally in terms of its revision of what he terms the 'trope of the talking book'. In this study, I intend to examine Marrant's relationship with what I have termed the 'discourse of the spirit'.

In his Preface to the second edition of *A Narrative of the Lord's Wonderful Dealings with John Marrant*, the Revd Aldridge claimed that Marrant's conversion narrative was 'taken down from his [Marrant's] own Relation', albeit 'Arranged, Corrected and Published' by the good Reverend himself. Indeed, whereas the editor claims to have 'always preserved Mr. Marrant's ideas', Aldridge adds, almost as an after-thought, that he could not reproduce 'his language'.[66] This distinction between the language used by the slave narrator to describe his/her experience and the language used in turn by the amanuensis editor to transcribe, edit and preface the slave's 'autobiography' highlights another form of 'miscegenation' that was involved in the editorial process. As William Andrews points out, this job of 'selecting, arranging and assigning signification' to the facts of the narrator's life lay in the editor's hands.[67] Hence, whilst the protean nature of spiritual discourse presented a convenient site for radical, abolitionist polemic, it also constrained the slave's narrative into a series of conventions. The conversion format presented readers with a familiar, acceptable and easily recognisable form of narrative and therefore established an intricate rapport with its audiences' beliefs. As a result, the narrator/editor relationship shifted and dispersed the centre of the autobiographical text into a pluralised narrative, which sidetracked the issue of slavery or indeed racial miscegenation itself. It was the editor who would decide which 'facts' would be included and how they would be related. Given such constraints, the slaves' own critiques of Christian ideology, and indeed the editorial process itself, are difficult to locate. Where these 'gaps' or chasms do exist they are subdued and muffled. What was clearly highlighted was the religious and abolitionist agenda which the editor/author felt would satisfy the expectations of a certain type of audience.[68]

Examining texts in order to reveal what is 'absent' is, as one would expect, particularly difficult. But I would suggest that these gaps or silenced utterances of the text may be seen to reveal a deviation from Christian epistemology. If this is so, then these narratives may be seen to 'speak' not only to a white Christian audience but to fellow blacks in the diaspora. Therefore, whilst I would agree in part with Andrews' suggestion that the slave narratives were intended to celebrate the 'black's acculturation into the established categories of the white social and literary order', Marrant's texts also hint at a dimension which lies beyond that of the Judeo-Christian tradition.[69] Subtle though it is, Marrant's text begins to speak of an alternative African epistemological system – an aspect which becomes more apparent in some of the later slave texts. There is accordingly a note of tension between the implied author of Marrant's text and its 'actual' author. Although the conversion model endeavoured to encourage a rejection of Marrant's past beliefs, the process is contravened at significant moments in the narrative.

According to Aldridge, Marrant's narrative is 'as plain and artless' as it is 'surprising and extraordinary', and he identifies the text as a narrative of *facts* revealing the author's various 'deliverances', incidences which he claims 'strike the heart' in their display of the 'power, grace and providence of God':

He and his companion enter the meeting at Charles-Town together; but the one is taken, and the other is left. He is struck to the ground, shaken over the mouth of·hell, snatched as a brand from the burning; he is pardoned and justified; he is washed in the atoning blood, and made happy in his God.[70]

At the very outset of the text, Marrant himself, or rather the Marrant 'arranged and corrected' by Aldridge, determines the spiritual motif of his text as an overt continuum of literary Evangelical fervour, declaring that he wished 'these gracious dealings of the Lord with me to be published, in [the] hope that they may be useful to others' and 'to refresh the hearts of true believers'.[71] However, Marrant's spiritual autobiography distinctly conflates conversion with a moment of insurrection, as his 'sanctification' provides him with an empowered discourse of infallibility sanctioned by the 'spirit': 'I now read the Scriptures very much. My master sent often to know how I did, and at last came himself, and finding me well, asked me if I would not come to work again? I answered no'.[72] Marrant's 'spiritual' awakening describes a moment of 'non-articulacy'; or rather, the appropriation of a discourse of alterity situated both on the linguistic parameters of the dominant symbolic order and on the periphery of dissenting Protestantism. Hence as he is struck to the ground,'both speechless and senseless for twenty four minutes' by the words,'PREPARE AND MEET THY GOD, O ISRAEL', spoken by the Reverend George Whitefield (co-founder of Methodism), Marrant's *non-linguistic* (and indeed, culturally deviant) response *disturbs* the meeting at Charles Town: 'I was constrained on the bitterness of my soul *to halloo out* in the midst of the congregation, which disturbing them, they took me away'.[73] By 'hallooing out', Marrant stands apart from the rest of the Methodist congregation – his involvement in spiritual possession exceeds that of the congregation and therefore he is taken away. In fact, his reference to 'hallooing' is more appropriate to African rituals of 'shouting'. Within a condensed and prototypical format, Marrant's text describes the acquirement of a specific discourse which he terms the 'language of Canaan' and the 'song of Moses and of the Lamb', through which blacks were able to enter the white literary arena and therefore the margins of power within the diaspora. For this reason, as with other narratives of spiritual/physical deliverance, the captivity framework of Marrant's *Narrative* pivots essentially upon the 'divine possession' or the gift of tongues; that is, the appropriation of a divinely inspired language which 'delivers' him on separate occasions from the claims of his master and from the hands of the Cherokee Indians who have sentenced him to death:

I prayed in English a considerable time, and about the middle of my prayer, the Lord impressed a strong desire upon my mind to turn into their language, and pray in their tongue. I did so, and with remarkable liberty, which wonderfully affected the people.[74]

Although it is not dwelt upon, it is Marrant's ability to speak in 'tongues' rather than in English which impresses the Cherokees. Yet as far as the overt conversion narrative is concerned, both 'deliverances', spiritual and actual, validate Marrant's entrance into the terrain of white hegemony, and moreover, link his penetration of Cherokee territory with masterdom.[75] Hence, when the Cherokee executioner is unable to carry out his orders to kill Marrant as a trespasser, Marrant's reading from the Bible (possibly an editorial invention) destabilises and indeed, ultimately usurps the power of the Cherokee king. His selection of biblical extracts, from Chapter 53 of Isaiah and Chapter 26 of Matthew's gospel, deserve attention, for they appropriately describe the episodes of revelation and deliverance by the Holy Spirit at the Last Supper, a process which inaugurates the apostles, and indeed Marrant himself, as authorised disciples with the power to baptise and evangelise in the 'name of the Holy Spirit'. Marrant's 'verbal' articulation of this sacred 'written' text appears to precipitate the King's daughter's partial conversion to Christianity, since she takes the sacred book from Marrant's hand and kisses it. Similarly, the executioner falls to his knees and begs the king to let Marrant 'go to prayer':

He arrives among the *Cherokees*, where gross ignorance wore its rudest forms, and savage despotism exercised its most terrifying empire . . . The untutor'd monarch feels the truth, and worships the God of the Christians; the seeds of the Gospel are disseminated among the Indians by a youthful hand, and Jesus is received and obeyed.[76]

Marrant, or rather, the Marrant-Aldridge collaboration, identifies the intense emotional utterings, spiritual ecstasy and passionate physicality demonstrated by the king's subjects, as proof of both the Holy Spirit's power and of Marrant's own divine election: 'In the midst of the prayer some of them cried out, particularly the king's daughter, and the man who ordered me to be executed, and several others seemed under deep conviction of sin'.[77] As if to confirm the authenticity of Marrant's spiritual experience, earlier in the Preface, Aldridge claimed that Marrant had appeared 'to feel most sensibly' when he described the 'most remarkable interpositions of Divine Providence'.[78] One reason for this is the fact that it is a moment which inscribes a memory of a cultural self *other* than that prescribed by radical dissenting Protestantism. The emphasis in Marrant's *Narrative* on the profound enormity of 'the Lord's wonderful Dealings' ('Though I was weak in body, yet was I strong in the spirit') appears to inaugurate an articulation of African epistemology within the continuum of the evangelical momentum established by the Apostles.[79] This in turn enables Marrant's own participation, not only within protean discourse, but in the highest manifestation of Cherokee power, the king's language: 'Here I learnt to speak their tongue in the highest stile'.[80]

Marrant's text presents a revision of the 'captivity' genre, a term conventionally used to describe the immensely popular seventeenth- and early eighteenth-century narratives of female captivity, usually amongst the Native American tribes. Such narratives prescribed a pattern of separation from one's native culture followed by a series of ordeals within Indian society and finally, a return to 'civilisation'.[81] One such example was Mrs Mary Rowlandson's *A True History of the Captivity and Restoration of Mrs Mary Rowlandson, a Minister's Wife in New England*, printed in Boston and London in 1682.[82] This text described Mary Rowlandson's captivity, which resulted from the Indian attack on the English settlement of Lancaster in February 1682 and the slaughter of most of the settlers there. According to the title page, the narrative exposed the 'cruel and inhumane usage' which Mrs Rowlandson underwent, the 'malicious and revengeful' spirit of the heathens and her deliverance as effected by the 'sovraignty of God'.[83] Whilst the author's preservation and salvation form the apex of the narrative, the Lord's providence is seen to have extended to the preservation of her chastity, thereby securing her status as a 'handmaid' amidst the 'roaring lions' and 'Savage Bears': 'Not one of them ever offered the least abuse or unchastity to me, in word or action'.[84]

Marrant's revision of the 'captivity' genre is especially interesting in its reversal of gender roles and its presentation of the diasporic identity as metaphorical interlocutor, the linguistic 'middle passage' of (cultural) intertextuality. Marrant had arrived in London with the cotton merchant John Marsden sometime between 1782 and 1785.[85] His text translates the dynamics of cultural dichotomy between Africa and the west into a revised relationship wherein Cherokee culture, rather than hybridised African diaspora, occupies the site of alterity defined by Hegel. Hence, Marrant's linguistic 'salvation', his acquirement of Cherokee which 'saves' him from death, validates his participation in the transcendental hemispheres of western culture and his appropriation of its discourse. This process witnesses the transference of cultural difference on to another subject. And yet within the framework of his tale, Marrant is not the only 'interlocutor'; the king's daughter also becomes an intermediary, or medium of cultural exchange but her 'conversion' is silenced by Marrant's own overriding discourse. As a result, his 'divine' witness precipitates his physical release from his captors and endorses his career as an evangelical missionary until he returns to his family in Charleston, South Carolina. In May 1785, Marrant was ordained minister for the Countess of Huntington's independent group of Calvinist Methodists and embarked on a subsequent career as itinerant preacher in Bath and Bristol, around the same time that other dissenting Protestants and abolitionists including Coleridge were actively propagandising in that area.[86] Marrant's employment of the non-verbal 'articulations' of the 'spirit' begin, somewhat paradoxically, to present powerful revisions of western cultural hegemony, thus determining spiritual discourse as an alternative model of linguistic fluidity and cultural interchangeability, a process further developed in the slave narrative by James Gronniosaw.

GRONNIOSAW'S 'DELIVERANCE'

The first edition of James Albert Ukawsaw Gronniosaw's *A Narrative of the Most Remarkable Particulars in the Life of James Albert Ukawsaw Gronniosaw, An African Prince, As Related By Himself*, priced at six pence, appeared in Bath in 1770, fifteen years before Marrant's text and six years after John Newton's *Authentic Narrative* was published in 1764.[87] Whilst this latter fact indicates the possible affinity between Gronniosaw's text and that of other prominent eighteenth-century spiritual autobiographers, one other connection exists pertaining to the links between the slave narrators and the Romantics. As Paul Edwards and Lauren Henry point out, Gronniosaw was for a time the house servant of Cosway, who was a good friend of William Blake (see Chapter 3 above).[88]

As Adam Potkay notes, Gronniosaw's text underwent a complicated printing history, with some editions comprised of multiple copies of one issue.[89] Gronniosaw was born between 1710 and 1714 in Borno, Nigeria. He was sold into slavery and became the domestic servant to a wealthy family in New York City. Around 1730 he became a servant to the Dutch Reformed Minister Theodorus Jacobus Frelinghuysen (Mr Freelandhouse). Gronniosaw witnessed the birth of the Great Awakening in New Jersey and sometime between 1747 and 1748 underwent conversion and was subsequently freed by his master. As the title page to Gronniosaw's text suggested, and the dedication to 'The Right Honourable The Countess of Huntingdon' confirmed, the *Narrative of the Most Remarkable Particulars* presented an autobiographical account of deliverance from slavery, thoroughly grounded within the literary genre which emerged from dissenting Protestantism. After his adventurous years as a cook aboard a privateer, as a pirate during the Seven Years' War (1756–1763) and the British sieges of Martinique and Havana, Gronniosaw reached England around 1762. There he visited George

Whitefield and was baptised by the British theologian, Dr Andrew Gifford.[90]

As his choice of epigraph to his *Narrative* implied, Gronniosaw's narrative deployed a critical synthesis of the discourse of spiritual salvation with that of abolitionism:

I will bring the Blind by a Way that they know not, I will lead them in Paths that they have not known: I will make the darkness light before them and crooked things straight. These things will I do unto them and not forsake them. Isaiah 43:16.[91]

Read duplicitously, this quotation from the Old Testament connotes the author's spiritual illumination and conversion to Christianity on the one hand, and on the other, determines the author's definition of himself as 'leader of the people'. He is the one chosen not only to show his *own* people the way to salvation, but to lead the spiritually 'blind', that is, participants and supporters of the slave trade, towards 'a way that they know not', making their crooked ways 'straight'. As the text reveals, this pilgrimage is determined by the literary example of one, the author himself, whose voice is 'inspired' by the spirit and whose words (written and spoken) will initiate the salvation of mankind. At the same time, however, as the subordinate clause of the title suggests, Gronniosaw's narrative of bondage and deliverance pivots upon his reclamation of his disinherited cultural legacy as 'an African prince' to the city of Bournou, the chief city in the kingdom of Zaara.

At the outset of the 1770 edition, the Revd Walter Shirley's 'Preface to the Reader' presents a vigorous effort to ascertain the spiritual focus of Gronniosaw's text and to establish its inherent 'value' for the Christian (white and black) reader. Accordingly, the Preface strategically endeavours to pre-empt any criticism concerning the problematic exposure of personal experience to a public audience and the more sensitive issue concerning the interrelationship between disparate cultural belief systems. Hence, the editor deprioritises the 'fabricated' and overtly politicised nature of Gronniosaw's text and, as with Marrant's text, waves aside criticisms concerning 'pseudo-authorship', the intervention by the female amanuensis from Leominster:

This account of the life and spiritual experience of JAMES ALBERT was taken from his own mouth, and committed to paper by the elegant pen of a young LADY of the town of LEOMINSTER, for her own private satisfaction, and without any intention at first that it should be made public. But now she has been prevail'd on to commit it to the press, as it is apprehended, this little history contains matter well worthy the notice and attention of every Christian reader.[92]

By defining the predominant objective of Gronniosaw's *Narrative* as confirmation of God's omnipotent power over *all* things and *all* lands (including the kingdom of Zaara), the Revd Shirley identifies this slave's text as an attestation of Christianity's 'superiority' over the belief systems held by the Africans. Moreover, in situating the text's focus within the parameters of pilgrimage and conversion, the editor detracts attention away from the unorthodox relationship prior to the text's publication, that is, the transformation of Gronniosaw's oral narrative into a written text, a process which takes place between the female amanuensis from Leominster and 'her' black male 'subject' of enunciation:

Perhaps we have here in some degree a solution of that question that has perplex'd the minds of so many serious persons, viz. *In what manner will GOD deal with those benighted parts of the world where the gospel of Jesus Christ hath never reach'd?* Now it appears from the experience of this remarkable person, that GOD does not save without the knowledge of the truth; but, with respect to those whom he hath fore-known, though born under every disadvantage, and in regions of the grossest darkness and ignorance, he most amazingly acts upon and influences their minds, and in the course of wisely and most wonderfully appointed providences, he brings them to the means of spiritual information, gradually opens to their view the light of his truth, and gives them full possession and enjoyment of the inestimable blessing of his gospel.[93]

In fact, as the above extract suggests, the editor is at pains to inscribe Gronniosaw's former cultural beliefs within the economy of a Christian schema of monotheism, claiming that even as a young boy, the author had felt 'that there was a Being superior to the sun, moon and stars'.[94] Accordingly, the editor suggests that, Gronniosaw, albeit unsuspectingly, 'belong'd to the REDEEMER of lost sinners', and was thus 'delivered' spiritually, an inheritance which he considers far superior to his interrupted (royal) inheritance: 'Though born in an exalted station of life . . . he would rather embrace the dunghill, having CHRIST in his heart, than give up his spiritual possessions and enjoyment, to fill the throne of princes'.[95] Yet Gronniosaw's narrative, commencing as it does with the 'I was born' statement typical of many conversion narratives, is careful to establish the privileged nature of the author's African cultural past, especially his relationship with the royal family of Zaara. This cultural loyalty vies with the ideology informing the very crux of Gronniosaw's conversion narrative and again exposes the miscegenetic nature of the slave narratives in terms of their editorial process. Hence the traumatic and bewildering experiences of capture, transportation and enslavement are reduced or significantly marginalised by the established categories of the conversion narrative. We hear very little, if anything, of his experience as a slave. What is foregrounded is the 'fact' that even at a very young age Gronniosaw felt an intense dissatisfaction with African epistemology, that in the period *prior* to his capture and transportation across the middle passage, he experienced a profound sense of 'hiatus' or disjuncture from his own people and an innate receptivity to a disparate or counter-ideology at odds with his own cultural identity:

Twas certain that I was, at times, very unhappy in myself: it being strongly impressed on my mind that there was some GREAT MAN of power which resided above the sun, moon and stars, the objects of our worship . . . I was frequently lost in wonder at the works of the creation: was afraid, uneasy, and restless, but could not tell for what. I wanted to be inform'd of things that no person could tell me; and was always dissatisfied. – These wonderful impressions *begun in my childhood.*[96]

It is this antagonism towards, or rather betrayal of, his indigenous cultural beliefs which Gronniosaw *claims* precipitated his yearning to depart from the Kingdom of Zaara with the 'aid' of an ivory-merchant from the Gold Coast (a trafficker whom the text identifies as a trader of cultural tokens rather than of slaves) in order to see 'white folks' and 'houses' (ships) that walked 'upon the water with wings to them'. This 'desire' for intercultural determinism establishes Gronniosaw's text as a 'mulatto' or hybridised text, an archetype embodied metaphorically by the physical features of his sister, Logwy, whom he describes as 'quite white and fair, with fine light hair, though my father and mother were black'.[97]

Upon his arrival at the merchant's homeland, the young Gronniosaw is denounced a Zaaran spy and sentenced to death by the king. Interestingly, in his recollection of this dramatic ordeal, the spiritual agent of his deliverance struggles unresolvedly with the signifiers of African culture, those tokens which mark his *dis*inheritance and inspire the king's sympathy towards a fellow royal:

The morning I was to die, I was washed, and *all my gold ornaments made bright and shining*, and then carried to the palace, where the King was to behead me himself . . . I went up to the KING alone, – I went with an undaunted courage, and *it pleased GOD to melt the heart of the KING*, who sat with his scymitar in his hand ready to behead me; yet, being himself so affected, he dropped it out of his hand, and took me upon his knee and wept over me.[98]

As a means of compromise, the king agrees to sell Gronniosaw into slavery, but when the latter overhears of the merchants' plans to throw him overboard should they fail to sell him as a slave, Gronniosaw pleads with a Dutch captain to purchase him, 'though he did not understand my language', in exchange for two yards of checked cloth. Although this reads as a distinctly material trans-action, the author interprets it as a demonstration of the spiritual work of the 'ALMIGHTY'.[99] Whilst with this Dutch master, Gron-niosaw exchanges the elaborate icons of his African heritage, his large gold necklace and pear-shaped gold earrings, for a set of new clothes fashioned in the European style, a transaction which *appears* to symbolise his abandonment of African cultural signifiers and his appropriation of those of the west: 'I found all this troublesome, and was glad when my new Master took it from me'.[100] Likewise, once on board the Dutch ship, the relationship which develops between the Captain and Gronniosaw endorses this assimilation of all things European and guarantees the author's orientation along the path of deliverance. And yet, when his master gives him the Book of Prayers to read, Gronniosaw's cultural exclusion as an African-other resur-faces:

My master grew very fond of me, and I loved him exceedingly . . . He used to read prayers in public to the ship's crew every Sabbath day; and when first I saw him read, I was never so surprised in my life, as when I saw the book talk to my master, for I thought it did, as I observed him to look upon it, and move his lips. – I wished it would do so to me. As soon as my master had done reading, I followed him to the place where he put the book, being mightily delighted with it, and when nobody saw me, I opened it and put my ear down close upon it, in great hopes that it would say something to me; but was very sorry, and greatly disappointed when I found that it would not speak, this thought immediately presented itself to me, that every body and every thing despised me because I was black.[101]

For Gates, the book fails to speak to Gronniosaw because it does not 'recognise his presence' and so refuses to share its secrets or decipher its coded messages.[102] However, Gronniosaw's exclusion from what the book represents is neither absolute nor permanent. Indeed, this passage demarcates the moment *preceding* the cultural interpenetration and assimilation of the western (epistemological) narrative by the mulatto text. It delineates the process of transformation required if Gronniosaw, as a cultural representative, is to be 'delivered' into the realm of the diaspora through a translation of the dynamics of African belief into the tenets of evangelism.

HERMENEUTICS AND CULTURAL BOUNDARIES

Gronniosaw's post-conversion interpretation of the above incident denotes a perception essentially informed by cultural determinism and social aspiration. Whilst the book in question 'seems' to perceive *difference* in terms of its reader, it is exactly at this juncture that the predominant signifier of the western world, the written *word*, and the *oral* articulation of the subject's experience, coalesce. Guided by the 'words' of the spirit, Gronniosaw enters a literary arena sanctified by the grace of God, and the tactile nature of spiritual discourse enables a reappropriation of a literary genre, on both an individual and cultural level. Hence when Mrs Vanhorn, his master's wife, curses her slave for some trifling domestic error, Gronniosaw undermines her social authority with his own religious trump card, a recapitulation of her own Christian ideology: 'Madam, says I, you must not say so. Why, says she? Because there is a black man called the Devil that lives in hell, and he will put you in the fire and burn you, and I shall be very sorry for that'.[103] When Gronniosaw is sold to the minister, Mr Freelandhouse, the latter's doctrinal theological statements are countered by Gronniosaw's own discourse of difference which articulates an *uninterrupted* continuum of preslavery cultural identity and extends the African concept of ancestral 'spirits', thereby bridging the cultural and epistemological divide. Unlike Marrant's text which, to a large extent, echoes the distinct nature of Christian ideology, Gronniosaw's response paves the way for what is the crux of his *Narrative*, the intersection between the origins of his own cultural and epistemological identity and the discourse of radical dissenting Protestantism:

He [Mr Freelandhouse] took great pains with me, and made me understand that he prayed to GOD, who lived in heaven; that He was my Father and BEST Friend. – I told him that this must be a mistake; that *my* father lived at BOURNOU, and that I wanted very much to see him . . . He told me that GOD was a GREAT and GOOD SPIRIT, that He created all the world, and every person and thing in it, in Ethiopia, Africa, and America, and every where. I was delighted when I heard this: There, says I, I always thought so when I lived at home![104]

On hearing his master read from the Book of Revelation, 'Behold, He cometh in the clouds and every eye shall see him, and they that pierced Him' (1:7), Gronniosaw's spiritual pilgrimage towards Christ is inaugurated as he declares himself a sinner ignorant of the *word* of God, and receives a copy of John Bunyan's work, *Grace Abounding to the Chief of Sinners* (1660) and Richard Baxter's *God's Call to the Unconverted* (1719). This journey toward deliverance strategically reiterates the author's 'transcultural' voyage across the middle passage, and his experience of spiritual illumination is simultaneously figured as a deliverance from physical *and* psychic enslavement:

I was one day in a most delightful frame of mind, my heart so overflowed with love and gratitude to the author of all my comforts. – I was so drawn out of myself, and so filled and awed by the presence of GOD, that I saw (or thought I saw) light inexpressible dart down from heaven upon me, and shone around me for the space of a minute. – I continued on my knees, and joy unspeakable took possession of my soul. – The peace and serenity which filled my mind after this, was wonderful, and cannot be told. – I would not have changed situations, or been any one but myself for the world.[105]

However, socioeconomic liberation comes not with conversion to Christianity, but with the death of (and hence deliverance from) his master, whereafter Gronniosaw finds employment on board a ship as a cook. As in John Newton's *Authentic Narrative*, the ship on which Gronniosaw travels is bound for Haiti, one of the largest and most productive colonies of the Caribbean, signifying Gronniosaw's continued, albeit indirect, involvement with the slave trade. Nevertheless, Gronniosaw's sanctified (royal) state continues to 'seal' him from sin, and for this reason the sailor who ridicules his zealous evangelism, dies mysteriously and unexpectedly, thereby confirming God's spiritual powers of retribution and divine election or possibly myal / obeah powers.

In accordance with Daniel Defoe's extremely popular book, *The Life and Strange Suprizing Adventures of Mr. D- De F-* (1719) and Newton's *Authentic Narrative* (1764), Gronniosaw's text describes a series of maritime adventures, including a naval attack on a French fleet, the murder of a French prisoner by the Captain and the theft of the author's savings by various tricksters.[106] Whereas Cowper's texts had prescribed metaphors of water, deluge and inundation, Gronniosaw's text redefines the aqueous zone (of the middle passage and his naval adventures) as one of 'becoming', of assimilation and cultural (re)configuration. Once in England, the author contacts the Evangelical leader, George Whitefield, and so confirms his own spiritual, and indeed 'literary' place within the Great Awakening movement.[107] Later, in Amsterdam, Gronniosaw relates his spiritual experience to a group of Calvinist ministers whom he explains enigmatically, were 'very well satisfied' with his account and were 'persuaded I was *what I pretended to be*':

They wrote down my experience as I spoke it: and the LORD ALMIGHTY was with me at that time in a remarkable manner, and gave me words and enabled me to answer them; so great was his mercy to take me in hand a poor blind heathen.[108]

After a period of twelve months employment with a wealthy merchant in Amsterdam, Gronniosaw returns to England to see his hitherto unmentioned wife, Betty, and their mulatto children. Unlike Marrant's text, which concludes with its author's ordination, here the spiritual focus of the text is abandoned and transformed into a socioeconomic and abolitionist schéma which presents an account of Gronniosaw's family's perpetual state of poverty, starvation and exile as they are forced to move between Essex and London until they receive financial support from a Quaker, Mr Henry Gurney.[109] Even if the experience of slavery is downplayed, this narrative manages to include a personal account of the precarious living conditions experienced by blacks in eighteenth-century England. Hence, whilst Andrews argues that slave narratives such as Gronniosaw's, published between 1760 and 1810, did not articulate any real indication of what it meant to be a black in white society, nevertheless Gronniosaw's text presents a vivid critique of white ideology.[110] What is more, as if to undermine any purely spiritual interpretation of his text, Gronniosaw concludes his *Narrative of the Most Remarkable Particulars* with a blasphemous critique of established religious doctrine, as exemplified by his parish priest's refusal to bury one of his unbaptised children:

At length I resolved to dig a grave in the garden behind the house, and bury her there; when the parson of the parish sent for to tell me he would bury the child, but did not choose to read the burial service over her. *I told him I did not care whether he would go or no, as the child could not hear it.* We met

with a great deal of ill treatment after this, and found it very difficult to live:
We could scarcely get work to do, and were obliged to pawn our cloaths.[111]

This passage clearly identifies the 'hybrid' discourse of Gronniosaw's
text and strategically revises his earlier account of the sacred book's
refusal to speak to him. Gronniosaw's daughter cannot hear the
parson's words not merely because she is dead but because they are
'meaningless' – i.e. situated within the void between religious
discourse and socioeconomic transformation – and secondly,
because as a 'mulatto', his daughter lies on the periphery of cultural
and epistemological boundaries, a 'transmigrated' soul of (self-)exile
and (protean) cultural mutation. Hence, the final paragraph of
Gronniosaw's text encapsulates the point of intersection (a 'non-site'
for advocates of racial segregation) between the discourse of evangelism and the actuality of socioeconomics, in its demands for the
financial alleviation of the black poor, or 'blackbirds', residing in
England during the 1770s. By emphasising his wife's hard labour,
and their dependence upon the charitable donations they periodi-
cally received, Gronniosaw situates socioeconomic discourse within
the framework of pilgrimage and salvation established by Puritan
devotees such as Bunyan and Richard Baxter:

My wife, by hard labour at the loom, does every thing that can be expected
from her towards the maintenance of our family; *and GOD is pleased to incline
the hearts of his people at times to yield us their charitable assistance*, being myself
through age and infirmity able to contribute but little to their support. *As
pilgrims, and very poor pilgrims, we are travelling through many difficulties towards our
HEAVENLY HOME*, and waiting patiently for his gracious call, when the
LORD shall deliver us out of the evils of this present world, and bring us to
the EVERLASTING GLORIES of the world to come. – TO HIM be
PRAISE for EVER and EVER. AMEN. FINIS.[112]

Thus, Gronniosaw's *Narrative* emerges as a protean text of epistemological and cultural indeterminacy: a work which witnesses the
convergence of spiritual discourse with demands for racial and
socioeconomic liberation. His text introduces an appropriate prototype for the juncture between hermeneutical discourse (the science
of interpretation, especially the Scriptures) and the complex mutation of cultural signifiers, a process of self-identification (individual
and cultural) more thoroughly developed within the poetical and
prose work by another slave, Phillis Wheatley.

CHAPTER SEVEN

Phillis Wheatley: poems and letters

Religion indeed, has produced a Phyllis Whately; but it could
not produce a poet.[1]

Three years after the publication of Gronniosaw's *Narrative of the Most
Remarkable Particulars* and long before the publication of Equiano's
autobiographical text of 1789 and Wedderburn's first publication of
c. 1802, *The London Chronicle* (9–11 September 1773) announced the
publication of a volume of *Poems on Various Subjects, Religious and Moral*
(1773) by the black female slave, Phillis Wheatley.[2] Wheatley's
collection of poems (which were included in the 1814 edition of
Equiano's *Interesting Narrative* discussed below) confirm the correlation
between spiritual discourse and radical politics, prescribed within
earlier works by radical dissenting Protestants on both sides of the
Atlantic. In addition, Wheatley's work highlighted the increasingly
antagonistic relationship between England and colonial America, a
debate which was to culminate in the American Revolution of 1783.
In its focus on spiritual development, Wheatley's work (consisting
primarily of poems and letters) provides an appropriate comparison
with the slave narratives discussed above, whilst its emphasis on
concepts of memory, imagination and liberation reveal its literary
relationship with the works of the Romantic poets. Given the
celebrity status bestowed upon Wheatley by London society and the
enthusiastic reviews of her poetry by British periodicals and abolitionists including Thomas Clarkson, it is likely that the Romantics
were aware of her work. Likewise, during her visit to London,
Wheatley was visited by members of some of the best bluestocking
circles and her work was celebrated in poems by prominent British
female writers, including Mary Scott and Mary Deverell.[3] Compiled
in the neoclassical style, against which the Romantics were reacting,
Wheatley's concern with subjectivity, the construction of the self and

Fig. 4. Frontispiece, *Poems on Various Subjects, Religious and Moral* by Phillis Wheatley. London, Bell, 1773.

the power of nature, links her in subject matter, if not in style, to the works of the Romantics. The paradigm of liberation, upon which much of the work of the Romantics was based, finds a precursor in the works of the female slave who demanded liberation from colonial slavery and racial ideology. In this way, Wheatley's work transforms the discourse of 'spiritual awakening' into a duplicitous discourse of protest and rebellion. Moreover, Wheatley's work exemplifies an effective articulation of the dynamics of identity configuration in the black diaspora, together with literary and polemical tactics which serve to expose the antagonistic relationship between Christian ideology and African epistemological belief systems.

Born on the West Coast of Africa, most probably along the Gambia River *c.* 1753–1754, Wheatley was captured and taken aboard a slave ship when she was about seven years old. On her arrival in Boston in 1761, Wheatley was purchased 'for a trifle' by a tailor named John Wheatley, who intended that she would serve as a slave attendant to his wife, Susanna. 'Wheatley' was given the family name of her purchasers and renamed 'Phillis' after the slave-trading vessel that had transported her. This process of renaming was favoured by slave-traders and slave owners in the colonies and represented a succinct form of cultural erasure, whereby African codes were supplanted by European codes, a process which intensified the slaves' endeavours to reestablish configurations of identity in the black diaspora. Yet Wheatley's position as a black female slave was further problematised by the ambiguous status which she held within her master's house and the education she received there. At the Wheatley household, Phillis was taught to read the Bible, Ovid and Latin books of mythology and was probably fourteen years of age when her first poem, 'On Messrs Hussey and Coffin', was published on 21 December 1767. Two years later, in 1769, Wheatley's elegiac poem 'On the Death of Joseph Sewall' was published, a poem which commemorated the death of her most trusted spiritual counsellor. Composed in the neoclassical tradition, Wheatley's poems reflect the profound influence of the meditative Methodist funeral elegy upon the Romantic genre, demonstrated by the popularity of Charlotte Smith's melancholic *Elegiac Sonnets* (1787). Moreover, in their focus on physical loss and spiritual presence, they constitute important poetical representations of the cultural intersection between radical dissenting Protestantism, literary expressions of identity and African beliefs.[4]

Wheatley's poem, 'On the Death of Mr Snider Murder'd by Richardson', composed in the same year as Paine's *Rights of Man* but not published in *Poems on Various Subjects*, celebrated the deceased twelve-year-old son of a German colonist as the 'first martyr of the common good' in the American Revolutionary War. During 1769 and 1770, the aggressive King's Red Coats had enraged citizens of Boston by enforcing oppressive laws previously agreed upon in London without their consultation. Snider had been shot dead on 22 February 1770 when Ebenezer Richardson (a tax informant) had fired indiscriminately into a mob of angry colonials.[5] Living with the Wheatleys, on the corner of King Street and Mackerel Lane, Phillis was almost certainly an eye witness to this momentous outbreak of hostilities between Bostonians and soldiers of the Twenty-Ninth Regiment. Known as the 'Boston Massacre', this event claimed the lives of five Bostonian 'citizens', including the runaway slave, Crispus Attucks, as reported in *The Massachusetts Gazette* and *The Boston Gazette*.[6] Wheatley's poetical account of this important historical episode, 'On the Affray in King St., on the Evening of the 5th of March' (1770) was excluded from the volume of *Poems on Various Subjects*, an omission which highlights the sensitive political climate of the time.[7]

Wheatley's poetry was also distinctly influenced by the complex landscape of eighteenth-century America's liberationist theology, a movement which combined concepts of spiritual illumination with American demands for independence from Britain. Preaching in Boston just a few days after the Massacre, Wheatley's master's son-in-law, John Lathrop, identified the relationship between America and its British oppressors as that between masters and slaves. God, argued Lathrop, had intended that his rational creatures should 'enjoy' those 'natural notions [of liberty]' which had been planted in their breasts:

In those parts of the world where civil government is not established, the inhabitants, no doubt have a right to continue in a state of nature as long as they please . . . One individual can have no right to *compel* another to submit to his authority . . . When men enter into society it must be by voluntary consent . . . Those rulers who take from the people what they please under the notion of a reward for their services, are *tyrants*, and the people *Slaves*.[8]

Three years later, in the last of the artillery election sermons to be preached before the Revolutionary War, Lathrop hinted that 'absolute dominion' belonged 'to the *Lord* of nature' and not to the perpetrators of political power: 'to him alone to rule his creatures with uncontrolled sway'.[9] Lathrop's demands for liberty from colonial oppressors confirmed the liberationist ideology in the years

which led up to America's Declaration of Independence but did not
necessarily indicate a simultaneous commitment to the emancipation
of slaves. Hence, whilst Boston newspapers and preachers attacked
the British ministry, rewards for runaway slaves and slave auction
notices continued to proliferate New England papers.

On 18 August 1771, Wheatley was baptised by the Revd Samuel
Cooper, an Evangelical minister who was at Harvard when George
Whitefield made his first appearance in New England.[10] Ordained
on 21 May 1746, Cooper preached a public sermon of his confession
of faith that set the pattern of his ministry. Cooper (although he had
one slave called 'Glasgow') became one of the poet's most important
spiritual and literary advisors and five months after her baptism
Wheatley published her proposal for a volume of poems.[11] In May
1773, the same year as the 'Boston Tea Party' (during which
Bostonians raided three British ships carrying several hundred tea
chests as a protest against British taxes and the East India Company's trade monopoly) Wheatley set sail for England as the attendant
of Nathaniel Wheatley, her master's son.[12] On her arrival in
London, Wheatley, presumably aided by the influence of the dedicatee of her volume, Selina Hastings (for whom George Whitefield
had served as personal chaplain), continued preparations for the
publication of her *Poems on Various Subjects*. As her letter of 17 July
1773 to David Wooster recorded, once in England Wheatley was
introduced to some of the country's most important abolitionist and
evangelical citizens, including Granville Sharp, later co-founder of
the British Society for the Abolition of the Slave Trade (1787),
Thomas Gibbons, the dissenting minister and composer of devo-
tional verse, Sir Brook Watson, the wealthy merchant who became
the Lord Mayor of London, and William Legge, Earl of Dartmouth
and Secretary of State for the Colonies. During her stay in England,
Wheatley received confirmation that her collection of *Poems on
Various Subjects* would be published by Archibald Bell's of London.

In the original manuscript and prefatory pages of the New
England edition of *Poems on Various Subjects* (1816), the signatures of
eighteen prominent Bostonian citizens attested to the authenticity of
Wheatley's literary talents. These included important evangelical
ministers such as Mather Byles, the poet who renounced his public
career in order to take up the ministry of Hollis Street Church in
Boston, Samuel Cooper, Samuel Mather and John Moorhead:

WE, whose names are underwritten, do assure the world, that the poems specified in the following page, were, as we verily believe, written by Phillis, a young negro girl, who was, but a few years since, brought an uncultivated barbarian from *Africa*, and has ever since been, and now is, under the disadvantage of serving as a slave in a family in this town. She has been examined by some of the best Judges, and is thought qualified to write them.[13]

Other signatories of the 'Letter to the Publick' included Thomas Hutchinson, the governor of Massachusetts Bay, James Bowdoin, founder of Bowdoin College and John Hancock, Declaration of Independence signatory.[14]

Wheatley's premature departure from England on 27 July 1773, necessitated by her mistress' sudden fatal illness, prevented the poet's presence at the launch of her collection of poems and the scheduled meeting with her patroness, Selina Hastings, Countess of Huntingdon.[15] Despite her absence however, Wheatley's *Poems on Various Subjects* received considerable attention from the British press and by authors such as John Stedman.[16] Nine British periodicals cited extracts from her poems as evidence of the sincerity of her piety and the impressive scope of her literary and classical knowledge.[17] Undoubtedly, the evangelical tone of her poems coincided conveniently with the increasing momentum of radical dissenting Protestantism in England and proved an attractive lure to a nation eager to construct a revised (philanthropic) image of itself. A selection of Wheatley's poems were reproduced in the December 1781 issue of the Methodist periodical, *The Arminian Magazine*, a journal which had also included works by William Cowper, Mrs Barbauld and Hannah More.[18] In September 1773, *The Critical Review* heralded the 'African' poetess as a 'literary phenomena' and identified Wheatley's poem, 'To Maecenas', as 'the production of a young Negro, who was, but a few years since, an *illiterate barbarian*'.[19] Similarly, *The London Chronicle* declared the poet an infant prodigy of pronounced linguistic and cultural talent:

Without any assistance from school education, and by only what she was taught in the family, she, in 16 months from her arrival, attained the English language, to which she was an utter stranger before, to such a degree as to read any, but the most difficult parts of the sacred writings, to the great astonishment of all who heard her.[20]

Conversely, however, in October 1773, *The Public Advertiser* adopted a far less favourable tone and reproduced a letter addressed to the paper's editor which (as with Wordsworth's sonnet 'Queen and Huntress, Chaste and Fair') dismissed Wheatley's poetry with a plethora of satirical and sexual (miscegenetic) undertones:

Phillis Wheatley has shone upon us. The figure of the *shining*, I own, is a little unproper, as *Phillis* is of a sable Hue, but I alluded to the Light of her Genius. I know no Way but one to recruit the Lamps of the tuneful Doctors with Oil, so that they may blaze forth upon us again with poetical Lustre. One of them at least has a Hand to give away. Matrimony is the Thing in Poetry as well as in Prose. What may not a male and female genius produce when they are properly joined together.[21]

The editorial voice of *The London Monthly Review* similarly questioned the authenticity of Wheatley's talent, and indeed, the creative potential of the Negro race *per se*, claiming that if genius were the 'natural' offspring of tropical regions, 'we should rather wonder that the sable race have not been more distinguished by it'. In this writer's view, as with other racial theoreticians, proximity to the sun, 'far from heightening the powers of the mind', enfeebled, or rather prohibited, artistic creativity, whereas a cool climate 'naturally' guaranteed an advanced stage of intellectual capability and development:

Thus we find the tropical regions remarkable for nothing but the sloth and languor of their inhabitants, their lascivious disposition and their deadness to invention. The country that gave birth to Alexander and Aristotle, the conqueror of the world, and the greater conqueror of nature, was Macedonia, naturally a cold and ungenial region. Homer and Hesiod breathed the cool and temperate air of the Meles, and the poets and heroes of Greece and Rome had no very intimate commerce with the sun.[22]

The same editor declared that Wheatley's poems bore 'no endemial marks of solar fire or spirit', a remark which strategically endeavoured to sever any relationship between the poet's work and the evangelical concepts of individualism and spiritual sanctification. Nevertheless the anonymous review contained in *The Gentleman's Magazine* (September 1773) praised the abolitionist subtext of Wheatley's *Poems on Various Subjects* and publicly condemned her continued state of servitude. According to that reviewer, it was a 'sad disgrace' to all those who had signed the testimony validating the works of this 'young talented poet':

We are much concerned to find that this ingenious young woman is yet a slave. The people of Boston boast themselves chiefly in their principles of liberty. One such act as the purchase of her freedom, would, in our opinion, have done them more honour than hanging a thousand trees with ribbons and emblems.[23]

Several years later, in his 'Notes on the State of Virginia', Thomas Jefferson, the 'autobiographer' of the American nation, propounded a theory of racial difference based upon a cultural aesthetic dichotomy.[24] In this text, Jefferson described Wheatley's work as a product of religious enthusiasm rather than of poetic talent:

Misery is often the parent of the most affecting touches in poetry. – Among the blacks is misery enough, God knows, but no poetry. Love is the peculiar oestrum of the poet. Their love [blacks] is ardent, but it kindles the senses only, not the imagination. Religion indeed, has produced a Phyllis Whately [sic]; but it could not produce a poet. The compositions published under her name are below the dignity of criticism.[25]

Whilst Jefferson's remark demonstrates the coalescence of ethnographic studies with theoretical justifications of slavery, it must be remembered that Wheatley's poetical work presented an encroachment of the autobiographical forum presided over by Jefferson, a site which conflated the dynamics of autobiography with those of cultural ideology and 'nation' writing.[26]

AN 'ETHIOPIAN SPEAKS'

('America', *Collected Works*, p. 134, line 6).

In her analysis of labouring class women's writing published in Britain between 1739 and 1796, Donna Landry argues that whilst abolitionist discourse facilitated Wheatley's entry into white discursive culture, it also functioned as a constraint upon her literary production in its failure to offer utopian alternatives to her fractured semiotic field or her socioeconomic conditions. According to Landry therefore, Wheatley suffered from a form of 'cultural amnesia' signified by her linguistic entrapment and her appropriation of imperialist culture: 'Wheatley does not "know" what happened, cannot remember, can only envisage within the master's language what her native prehistory might have been'.[27] Such an account does not, however, take into account the complexities of Wheatley's literary configurations of identity, nor her need to solicit rather than alienate potential western (abolitionist) subscribers; to figure as a spokeswoman for other black slaves in the diaspora; and to exercise a 'creolised' literary language that reflects her own contradictory status as a slave owned by an American and writing in Britain. Within her poetry and her letters, Wheatley demonstrates that she understands the problematics involved within configurations of 'homelands'; for blacks in the diaspora, 'new' versions of home must be found to accompany the new subjectivities which slavery and involuntary transportation had produced. Perceptively, Wheatley understands that since language provides the only testament to subjectivity, new ways must be found to make it speak both to her fellow enslaved and her enslavers.

Wheatley's deployment of late eighteenth-century dissenting discourse manifested a complex deconstruction of pro-slavery ideology and heralded an alternative form of cultural interdependence based on symbiosis rather than parasitism. Much of the religious and theological training which Wheatley received from the clergy in New England was thoroughly imbibed with the passionate anti-colonial ideology and revolutionary rhetoric of the 1760s and 1770s, a discourse which Wheatley employed in order to advance her abolitionist and anti-racist demands. Furthermore, her poems emphasised the inalienable rights of all humans to personal liberty as explicated in the theological, philosophical and political theories of Locke, Hume and Montesquieu.[28] As many of her poems' titles suggest – 'On the Death of the Revd Dr Sewall' (1769), 'On the Death of the Revd Mr George Whitefield' (1770) and 'An Elegy Sacred to the Memory of that Great Divine, the Reverend and Learned Mr Samuel Cooper' (1783) – Wheatley maintained an extensive network of connections with prominent members of the New England evangelical establishment. Both Joseph Sewall and Samuel Cooper, author of *Pietas et Gratulatio* (1761), had ministered at the Wheatley family's local church, the Old South Church in Boston. Preachers such as John Lathrop, the Connecticut minister, Timothy Pitkin, Samson Occom (the Indian preacher), the Dartmouth founders, Eleezer Wheelock and Nathaniel Whitaker and the abolitionist, Samuel Hopkins, were often received by the Wheatley household and participated regularly in anti-colonial activities in New England.[29] Indeed, as the tracts and sermons presented by these Boston preachers confirmed, 'slavery' had become a prevalent metaphor for the antagonistic relationship between England and her colonies: 'God has treated us as Children and not as Slaves . . . [and] has called us unto Liberty; and mercifully preserved us from those Chains under which many nations who once were free, are now groaning'.[30] Following this trend, Wheatley's poem 'America' of 1768 (not included in the 1773 *Poems on Various Subjects*) located America's struggle to escape from 'great Britannia's' suffocating grasp, with a powerful image of filial/matriarchal dialectics:

> A certain lady [Britannia] had an only son [Americus]
> He grew up daily virtuous as he grew
> Fearing his Strength which she undoubted knew
> She laid some taxes on her darling son . . .
> By many Scourges she his goodness try'd
> Untill at length the Best of Infants cry'd
> He wept, Britannia turn'd a senseless ear.[31]

Wheatley's image of colonial insurrection translated easily into a model of emancipation, yet the poet herself was caught somewhere in the middle of these conflicting colonial loyalties. For Wheatley 'England' constituted both a colonial oppressor and a surrogate mother, a maternal figure imbued with the power (since the Somerset case of 1772) to facilitate her personal liberation from slavery. The delicate nature of the poet's own sociopolitical demands were therefore presented amidst ambiguous images, which in turn described the complex 'middle passage' of linguistic translation and cultural exchange: 'Thy Power, O Liberty, makes strong the weak / And (wond'rous instinct) *Ethiopians speak / Sometimes by Simile, a victory's won*'.[32]

In the engraving which forms the frontispiece to her *Poems on Various Subjects*, Wheatley is seen poised at a writing desk, a servant's cap on her head, her quill suspended above a leaf of paper. Her eyes are focused on something residing beyond the confines of the etching, beyond the parameters of the western cultural narrative. Her meditative stance suggests not only the poise of an author in the moment of (divine) inspiration, but also registers her active revisionism of European ideologies and scriptural exegesis. That towards which she gazes, but from which she is excluded – the realm of the goddess of liberty – vies unresolvedly with the words of servitude which form the periphery of the print – 'Phillis Wheatley, *Negro Servant* to Mr John Wheatley of Boston'.[33] Likewise, as anticipated by the frontispiece, Wheatley's text identifies a site of intermediation across the ideological divide which separated western culture from that of Africa, its constructed antithesis. Thus the voice of the Ethiopian, contained within her poems, enacted a complex process of intermediation with dominant colonial, racial and radical dissenting ideologies.

In the poem which begins the collection, 'To Maecenas', composed sometime between April 1772 and September 1773, Wheatley commemorates the Roman statesman and patron of the arts, Gaius Maecenas (*c.* 74/64–8 BC) and thereby highlights the importance of her own relationship with her patroness in England, the Countess of Huntingdon. Maecenas, the patron who prided himself in his Etruscan lineage and became known as Caesar's right hand, sponsored poets such as Horace and Virgil, whose artistic works established a glorification of the new regime and celebrated Rome's illustrious historical heritage.[34] Wheatley's own version of the Maecenas/Lady Huntingdon model presents an example of spiritual relationship between the American divine and poet, Mather Byles and his own favourite poet, Pope: 'Does not your [Maecenas'] soul possess the sacred flame? / Their noble strains your equal genius shares / In softer language, and diviner airs'.[35] Yet in her allusion to Book XVI of Pope's translation of *The Iliad*, Wheatley not only signals her appropriation of western mythological figures but reveals her own self-configuration as poetic 'warrior' for her people. In this poem, Wheatley stakes a claim for the potential usurpation of these earlier national figures by her own cultural voice:

> *O could I rival thine and Virgil's page,*
> Or claim the *Muses* with the *Mantuan* Sage;
> *Soon the same beauties should my mind adorn,*
> And the same ardors in my soul should burn:
> *Then should my song in bolder notes arise,*
> And all my numbers pleasingly surprize.[36]

Wheatley's claims for poetical genius are however, immediately superseded by lines which suggest her rhetorical self-effacement: 'But here I sit, and mourn a grov'ling mind, / That fain would mount, and ride upon the wind'.[37] Accordingly, she turns her attention towards the popular comic poet of ancient Rome, 'the happier Terence' (Publius Terentus Afer, *c.* 185–159 BC), the ex-slave and playwright of African descent who composed *The Eunuch* and other plays.[38] Liberated from slavery by the fruits of his pen, Terence presents Wheatley with a much-needed model of emancipation premised upon artistic recognition, a project upon which the publication of her own collection of *Poems on Various Subjects* was equally dependent. In the lines which follow, however, Wheatley questions her idealisation of Terence, arguing that he ought not be the *only* black poet worthy of admiration – in other words, her own poetic merit deserves attention: 'But say, ye *Muses*, why this partial grace, / To one alone of *Afric's* sable race; / From age to age transmitting thus his name / With the first glory in the rolls of fame?'.[39] By highlighting the artistic talent of Terence/Africa – 'from whom those virtues sprung' – she radically champions the continued creative propensity of African culture – a civilisation which *predates* slave-based Roman culture represented by poets such as Homer and Virgil. In so doing, Wheatley consolidates her demands for popular acclaim: 'While blooming wreaths around thy temples spread, / I'll snatch a laurel from thine [Terence's] honour'd head, / While you indulgent smile upon the deed'.[40] Her final plea to Maecenas for protection and patronage thus endorses her recognition of her economic dependence upon her patroness, yet demands that her own poetical talent be acknowledged: 'So long, great Sir, the muse thy praise shall sing, / So long thy praise shall make *Parnassus* ring: / Then grant, *Maecenas*, thy paternal rays, / Hear me propitious, and defend my lays'.[41] While her text acknowledges the dynamics involved in the extension of the self by (cultural) patronal others, her poems demand liberation from servitude for both her 'self' and her people.

TRANSLATION AND SALVATION

In her short poetical piece, 'On Being Brought from Africa to America', composed in 1768, Wheatley achieves an illuminating articulation of miscegenetic identity, in which the meeting point between Africa and the west is located within a synthesis of metaphors of spiritual autobiography and transatlantic translation. As the continuous verb of the title suggests, and the titles of other poems such as 'On Mrs W——'s Voyage to England', 'A Farewell to America' and 'An Elegy on Leaving' confirm, Wheatley's revised concept of the self 'rests' essentially upon an infinite process of transition, transference and translation into new beginnings and configurations of identity within the black diaspora.

In its opening lines, the poet conflates missionary ideology with the transportation of her 'pagan' soul/self by means of a 'pilgrimage' of physical despair, spiritual redemption and finally, conversion: 'Twas mercy brought me from my *Pagan* land, / Taught my benighted soul to understand / That there's a God, that there's a *Saviour* too: / Once I redemption neither sought nor knew'.[42] As the emphases upon the terms 'pagan' and 'saviour' indicate, and the concluding lines reaffirm, the poet's removal from Africa and the 'salvation' of her soul have effected, or indeed, precipitated, her physical and intellectual enslavement, a fact that problematises her use of the term 'redemption'. Whilst her poem strategically evades an explicit disclosure of her own experience of slavery, the linguistic play on the racial and spiritual connotations of the phrase 'benighted soul' and the seemingly obsequious line, 'Once I redemption neither sought nor knew', register a destabilising critique of both the 'conversion' process and Christianity itself, by one who claims to have absorbed those very ideologies.[43] By conflating the moment of salvation with that of her removal from Africa, ('twas mercy brought me from my *Pagan* land'), Wheatley's poem highlights the close proximity between Evangelical, commercial (the slave trade) and colonial ideology. Her ambiguous allusions to the 'salvation' occasioned by her capture (her deliverance from that 'native shore/the land of errors, and *Egyptian* gloom')[44] endeavours to define the audience of her poems as 'saviours' of the African race and thereby constructs an effective shield of 'literary' impunity. Wheatley would have found a far more explicit literary reference to transportation and slavery in Pope's translation of Homer's *Odyssey*.[45] Given the popularity of radical dissenting Protestantism at the time, readers of Wheatley's poems would have had little difficulty in extending the Old Testament account of the Jews' deliverance from Egypt to subtextual demands for emancipation. Likewise, Wheatley's cryptic reference ('Some view our sable race with scornful eye,/"Their colour is a diabolic die"') presented a direct critique of pro-slavery ideology based on theories of aesthetic alterity, (colour/dye), unprecedented genocide (die) and corrupt spirituality (diabolic).[46]

As with the slave narratives by Wedderburn and Equiano who succeed her, Wheatley's scriptural revisionism moves away from a schema based exclusively upon binary opposition. Her poetry highlights the dialectical space existing between antithetical poles, such as that between the internal (mind/spirit) and the external (material/body): 'Remember, *Christians*, *Negros*, black as *Cain*, / May be refin'd, and join th'angelic train'.[47] In this way, the design of her poems coincides with that of William Blake's *Songs of Innocence and Experience*, and indeed, the mind/nature relationship articulated by various Romantic poems.[48] Her reference to the expanding 'angelic train' strategically replaced justifications of racial servitude based on the racial hierarchy contained within the great chain of being. Instead, Wheatley's poems advance a configuration of identity based on concepts of constant flux, transmigration and transmutation; metamorphoses which register an important moment of cross-cultural contact and anticipate the Romantic poets' definition of the imagination and the nature of poetry. Over four decades later, in his *Biographia Literaria: Or, Biographical Sketches of My Literary Life and Opinions* (1817) Coleridge described the 'esemplastic power' of the secondary imagination as that which 'dissolves, diffuses, dissipates, in order to recreate'.[49]

In her elegiac composition, 'On the Death of the Revd Dr Sewall' (1769), Wheatley mourned the death of another of her most trusted spiritual guides, Dr. Joseph Sewall. Son of diarist Chief Justice Samuel Sewall, who had written *The Selling of Joseph* (1700), the first antislavery tract published in New England, Dr Sewall had been the principal minister of the Old South Church in Boston.[50] Wheatley's mythologisation of the late minister presented him as a warning 'prophet' of spiritual liberationist ideology and divine inspiration: 'the Spirit of our God'.[51] However, her lament transcended the prescribed limits of elegy in its prioritisation of Sewall's more radical social vision: 'Come, let us all with the same vigour rise / And take a prospect of the blissful skies; / While on our minds *Christ's* image is imprest, / And the dear Saviour glows in ev'ry breast'.[52] Alongside the sense of loss felt at her mentor's death, Sewall's sanctified state is identified as the same state to which all those who are enslaved may aspire: 'O when shall we to his blest state arrive? / When the same graces in our bosoms thrive'.[53] Hence Wheatley's appropriation of spiritual discourse fuses with an emancipatory design which defines the slave in terms beyond the economic or intellectual.

Continuing this genre of poetic requiem, Wheatley's poem, 'On the Death of that Celebrated Divine, and Eminent Servant of Jesus Christ, the late Reverend, and pious George Whitefield, Chaplain to the Right Honourable Countess of Huntingdon', first appeared as a broadside in Boston in 1770. Dedicated to the 'Voice of the Great Awakening', George Whitefield, the personal chaplain to the poet's own patroness, Wheatley's poem was subsequently printed in *The Massachusetts Spy* (11 October 1770) and later republished in Newport, Boston, New York and Philadelphia.[54] In his controversial 'Letter to the Inhabitants of Maryland, Virginia, North and South Carolina', Whitefield, in his capacity as abolitionist and evangelist, had condemned slaveholders as abhorrent violators of God's law and had, in a significantly radical gesture, condoned pending slave insurrections:

I have wondered, that we have no more instances of Self-Murder among the Negroes, or that they have not more frequently rose up in Arms against their owners . . . And tho' I heartily pray god they may *never* be permitted to get the upper Hand . . . all good Men must acknowledge the Judgement would be just.[55]

As an evangelical crusader, Whitefield made seven journeys to America and may have resided with the Wheatleys in Boston less than a week before his death in Newburyport, Massachusetts.[56] Whitefield's continuous pilgrimages between England and America anticipated Wheatley's own voyaging of 1773, and her elegy may have accompanied the vessel carrying news of Whitefield's death back to England. Likewise, the co-existence of Whitefield's popularity in England and its colonies and the publication of Wheatley's volume of poetry must have intensified the dialogue between abolitionists and dissenting radicals on both sides of the Atlantic.

Wheatley's poem, the first to attract the Countess of Huntingdon's attention, attributed Whitefield's passionate preachings to his desire 'to see *America* excel', a possibility which both he and the poet deemed as incompatible with America's continued involvement in the slave trade.[57] Hence Wheatley extended the minister's vigorous claims for 'impartial' salvation to repentant Americans and to those still enslaved: 'Take him my dear *Americans*, he said, / Be your complaints on his kind bosom laid: / Take him, ye *Africans*, he longs for you, / *Impartial Saviour* is his title due'.[58] By addressing the Countess of Huntingdon directly, Wheatley's poem underscored the slaves' need of 'effective' (Methodist) patronage if abolition was to be achieved without violence: '*Great Countess*, we *Americans* revere / Thy name, and mingle in thy grief sincere; / *New England* deeply feels, the *Orphans* mourn, / Their more than father will no more return'.[59] By situating the Countess as the slaves' surrogate maternal guardian and the Revd Whitefield as their spiritual father, the poet advocated a spiritual economy in which the 'orphans of New England' (its slaves) were to be 'returned' to England's shore by means of a literary and spiritual umbilical cord. In the broadside version circulated in London (known as Variant II), this relationship between evangelicalism and the success of the slaves' struggle for liberation was made unmistakably clear: 'If you will walk in Grace's heavenly Road, / *He'll make you free*, and Kings, and Priests to God'.[60] However, in the version included in the *Poems on Various Subjects*, this fusion of spiritual with physical liberation was subdued and the concept of redemption limited to a spiritual rather than physical realm: 'Wash'd in the fountain of redeeming blood,/ You shall be sons, and kings, and priests to God'.[61]

In October 1773, Wheatley wrote to David Wooster giving him details of her recent manumission, which she defined as the 'desire of my friends in England'. Nevertheless, as the poet acknowledged, whilst political freedom was something to be revered, in the absence of socioeconomic security, such freedom was, in effect, seriously undermined. For this reason, Wheatley confirmed the interrelationship between artistic talent and economic freedom and emphasised her dependence upon her audience's consumerism. In so doing, she acknowledged the complex interaction between her 'autobiographical' narrative and financial market forces:

I beg the favour that you would honour the enclos'd Proposals, & use your interest with Gentlemen & Ladies of your acquaintance to subscribe also, for the more subscribers there are, *the more it will be for my advantage as I am to have half the Sale of the Books*.[62]

Again, the lines which followed the (possibly ghosted) London version of 'On the Death of George Whitefield' unashamedly proclaimed the *economic* aims behind the pamphlet's (re)publication, sold in aid of 'a poor Family burnt out a few weeks since near Shoreditch Church'.[63] For Wheatley, this concern with socioeconomic and political autonomy was significantly interdependent upon an attestation of African culture.

PHILIP QUAQUE AND PHILLIS WHEATLEY

Let us not sell our birthright for a thousand worlds.

In her letter of 30 October 1773 to her close friend Miss Obour Tanner (a slave possibly transported with her aboard the same slave ship), Wheatley constructed a tripartite analogy between her own 'spiritual' salvation, the 'recovery' of her health and what she termed the recovery of her people's 'birthright': 'Let us not sell our birthright for a thousand worlds, which indeed would be as dust upon the balance'. In this text, composed only days after informing Wooster of her manumission and named for inclusion in the proposed volume of 1779, Wheatley's reference to 'the birthright' is significantly ambiguous in its reference to her belief in her right to spiritual and physical liberty and, more importantly, to her continued belief in her people's need to preserve their cultural identity.[64]

In a subsequent letter to the Revd Samuel Hopkins, 6 May 1774, Wheatley noted the failure of Philip Quaque's missionary efforts to convert the indigenous people of the West African Coast: 'I am very sorry to hear, that Philip Quaque has very little or no apparent Success in his mission . . . Let us not be discouraged, but still hope, that God will bring about his great work'.[65] Bearing in mind that Hopkins was one of the most prominent figures of the Great Awakening in New England, Wheatley's comments on Quaque's activities merit further attention. In this letter, Wheatley suggested that Quaque might not provide the most effective means of performing the work of the 'Divine Hand . . . this work of wonder': that is, the redemption of Africa, 'from darkness to light'. Wheatley's recommendations that Quaque use *alternative* methods of 'conversion' underscore the dichotomy existing between Quaque's religious 'orthodoxy' and the fluid, protean and hence more compatible nature of dissenting Protestantism:

Possibly, if Philip would introduce himself properly to them, (I don't know the reverse) he might be more Successful, and in setting a good example which is more powerfully winning than Instruction.[66]

Born in 1741 at 'Cape Coast', a town just outside the principal British settlement and trading station on the West African coast (Cape Coast Castle, Ghana), Quaque, a member of the leading chieftain 'Cudjo' family, was sent to England in 1754 under the sponsorship of the Society for the Propagation of the Gospel in Foreign Parts (the S.P.G.) at the age of thirteen.[67] There, Quaque (whose Fanti name 'Kweku' denoted a male child born on a Wednesday) was placed under the tutorship of Revd John Moore of Charterhouse Street, London, baptised at St Mary's Church, Islington in 1759 and subsequently ordained as a minister of the Church of England.[68] In 1766, nearly eight years before Wheatley's letter, Quaque returned to the Gold Coast as a missionary to his own people at Cape Coast Castle, having married a white woman named Catherine Blunt.[69]

Quaque's appointment as missionary to Cape Coast was sponsored by the S.P.G. in association with the Company of Merchants Trading to Africa, an organised body of British merchants engaged in the slave trade and charged with the management of fortified posts along the African coast. Since their establishment in the late fifteenth century these forts had effectively combined commercial objectives with enterprises hinged upon the dissemination of European culture.[70] Therefore, Wheatley's criticism of Quaque's activities were not confined to a critique of his religious orthodoxy. Rather, it challenged his inherently ambiguous position as a Church of England missionary at a British Fort in Africa and, by implication, condemned the S.P.G.'s continued links with the commercial activities of the slave trade and colonialism. As her letter to John Thornton, dated 30 October 1774, humorously but adamantly indicated, unlike Quaque, Wheatley did not intend to assist the missionary movement in Africa. Rather, she brushed the proposition aside with vague disclaimers which prioritised the probable linguistic difficulties and the possible danger to her health that the 'new' environment would bring:

Upon my arrival [in Ghana, Africa], how like a Barbarian shou'd I look to the Natives; I can promise that my tongue shall be quiet/for a strong reason indeed/being an utter stranger to the language of Anamaboe.[71]

In contrast, Wheatley suggested an alternative means of improving her condition, a solution which combined demands for socioeconomic freedom with the discourse prescribed by radical dissenting Protestantism – 'Let me be a *servant of Christ* and that is the most perfect freedom'. Juxtaposed with Wheatley's poetical design, Quaque's purist approach to Christian propagandising appeared futile in its orthodox inflexibility. By contrast, Wheatley's work stressed that the dynamics of nonconformist dissent held the key to both sociopolitical emancipation and the development of transcultural, 'miscegenetic' epistemologies.

During the next half-century Quaque continued his detailed correspondence with the S.P.G. but it was seven years before he received his first reply (February 1773) and over the next twenty years he received only two others. On 13 March 1765, Quaque's letter to the S.P.G. expressed his desire to bring the 'truth of the glorious light of the Gospel of our Lord and Saviour' to those 'Wretched creatures . . . now languishing under despair'.[72] However, in a letter to Revd Dr Daniel Burton, then Secretary of the S.P.G. (28 September 1766) written from his new post at Cape Coast just eighteen months later, Quaque lamented the failure of his mission, 'All my hopes, I am afraid, are in vain . . . number of communicants none'.[73] Quaque's letter revealed the desperately unhealthy conditions of the British fort ('the third part out of five and twenty Soldiers dead'), 'the fatigue of performing . . . the Service' and his wife's imminent death, just one year after their marriage. In a subsequent letter of 1767, Quaque described the continued polytheism of the indigenous people, those 'illiterate' West Africans, as having grown 'more degenerate than before'.[74] The most serious of all Quaque's missionary difficulties stemmed from the fact that his appropriation of western cultural ideologies had in fact been 'too successful', leaving him alienated from his fellow Africans and bereft of his African 'tongue' which, in a letter of October 1781, he denounced as a 'vile jargon'.[75]

Likewise, in his letter of 17 January 1778, Quaque described the African funeral ceremony of one of his close kinsmen, the Fanti nobleman, government intermediary and linguist, Cudjo Caboceer, as not only laughable but as 'curious withal', 'a horrid and cruel Tradition . . . of infamous Rites'. According to Quaque, this ritual 'absolutely shew[d] the Depravity and Obduracy of their Stubborn Hearts', which for him could only be redeemed by the 'Grace of God . . . and the prevailing operations of the Spirit':

[The] scene appeared to me more like their harvest feasts than that of mourning or sorrow . . . The generality of them equipped with their warlike apparel. Some are covered with a cap of a tiger's skin, others again with deer's, a third the skins of monkeys . . . They likewise paint themselves, both men and women, some with white chalk, others yellow earth . . . But the most detestable scene in all their actions is the barbarous and inhuman practice of *sacrificing innocent lives as attendances to the great folks only in the other world*, which diabolical custom and a mistaken vile notion seems to prevail much with them.[76]

Quaque's hopes for the Africans' deliverance by means of the 'prevailing operations of the spirit' connoted not the dynamics of cultural synthesis, but the imposition of a theological doctrine unaffected by African belief systems. It was little wonder, therefore, that an undeniable pessimism permeated those letters which described his 'unsuccessful mission'.[77]

In a letter of 8 February 1786, Quaque made a rare reference to the slave trade and gave an account of a slave mutiny on board a Dutch trading-vessel, during which over one hundred slaves 'took possession of the vessel' and participated in what he termed a 'scheme of subtlety and art'. Such a paradigm of insurrection was not, however, embraced by Quaque himself, nor did the desertion of the fort by 'castle slaves' months later prompt any radical critique or abandonment of his 'missionary' activities. And yet Quaque's letter denounced the inhumanity of the Dutch Captain's 'indiscriminate' destruction of the ship and the murder of 'upwards of three or four hundred' of its crew. However, Quaque's use of the term 'indiscriminate' was not in itself unproblematic; rather, it suggested a polarisation, at least in his mind, between the rebellious slave insurrectionists and other passive 'victims' of the slave trade. Nor did the problem rest here. If Quaque's letters are regarded as instances of 'textual' autobiography, and if, as Foucault and de Man suggest, autobiography constitutes a literary 'exorcism' of guilt, there is a sense that Quaque's epistles, despite their missionary beliefs, contain a 'confessional' narrative of self-condemnation over his indirect 'involvement' in the activity of British colonialism; his sense of 'guilt' over his voluntary severance from his family and friends and his abandonment of his mother tongue; and, finally, in Wheatley's words, his feelings of shame over his 'betrayal' of his cultural 'birthright'.[78]

RECOLLECTION AND REDEMPTION

On 11 February 1774, Phillis Wheatley composed a letter to her friend, Samson Occom, the famous Mohegan Indian Presbyterian preacher, activist, and author of *A Choice of Hymns and Spiritual Songs* (1766). In this letter, Wheatley employed a linguistic discourse which carefully juggled theological tenets of salvation and redemption with corresponding sociopolitical considerations and critically identified colonisers as redemptive 'invaders' of Africa.[79] Likewise, she implied that the concerns of those colonialist invaders were irreconcilably distinct from 'the divine light' which had come to chase away 'the thick Darkness' of Africa ('the chaos which has reigned so long') and the 'glorious dispensation of civil and religious liberty'. Subtly therefore, Wheatley's text, published in *The Massachusetts Spy* (24 March 1774), *The Boston Post Boy* (21 March 1774) and in *The Connecticut Journal* (1 April 1774) identified the complex interface between spiritual 'conversion' and western narratives of evangelicalism, colonialism and exploitation. In colonial ideology, as in Hegelian terminology, Africa, prior to the dissemination of this divine 'light', figured as a land of darkness and chaos. In Wheatley's text, however, Christianity and its accompanying missionary enterprises remain unnamed referents. What emerges as paramount in her letter, therefore, is not an endorsement of conversion ideology but an advancement of a discourse of what she (extending natural law theories such as those advocated by Rousseau and anticipating Richard Price and Mary Wollstonecraft by over a decade) termed a 'vindication of natural rights'. Contradicting the established pattern of traditional spiritual autobiographies, Wheatley determined spiritual redemption as invalid without its sociopolitical counterpart:

The glorious Dispensation of civil and religious Liberty, which are so inseparably united, that there is little or no Enjoyment of one without the other: Otherwise, perhaps, the Israelites had been less solicitous for their Freedom from Egyptian Slavery.[80]

By drawing an effective comparison between her own struggles and those of the Israelites under Egyptian slavery, Wheatley translated the plight of the diasporic peoples into the dynamics of scriptural narrative and thereby fused the discourse of the spirit with emancipatory rhetoric: 'In every human Breast, God has implanted a Principle, which we call Love of Freedom; it is impatient of Oppression, and pants for deliverance; and by the Leave of our Modern Egyptians I will assert, that the same Principle lives in us'.[81] Her delineation of this principle ('the [soul's] cry for Liberty') anticipated Wordsworth's concern over the 'insurrectionary' power of the imagination as an agent of spiritual and emotional liberation. Similarly, in her poem, 'On Imagination', Wheatley described the poetic process in terms saturated with images of unbounded mental movement and flight, phrases which, as Shields points out, had appeared almost three decades earlier in Mark Akenside's *The Pleasures of Imagination: A Poem. In Three Books* (1744) and Edward Young's *The Complaint, or Night Thoughts* (1742–1745).[82] Mounted upon

the imagination's 'pinions', the poet reaches a state of spiritual
ecstasy which transgresses and surpasses western cultural boundaries. Leaving the 'rolling universe behind' on this imaginative/
spiritual flight, the poet participates in the creative and imaginative
world of the deity:

> Imagination! who can sing thy force?
> Or who describe the swiftness of thy course?
> Soaring through air to find the bright abode,
> Th'empyreal palace of the thund'ring God,
> We on thy pinions can surpass the wind,
> And leave the rolling universe behind:
> From star to star the mental optics rove,
> Measure the skies, and range the realms above.
> There in one view we grasp the mighty whole,
> Or with new worlds amaze th'unbounded soul.[83]

This relationship between the power of imagination and liberation
from the enslavement of the self/mind was to form a recurring
symbolism in Romantic ideology. In Wordsworth's *Prelude*, this
'spiritual' blessing ('a gift that consecrates the joy') would concur
with Wheatley's liberation from spiritual (and physical) bondage:

> Oh there is blessing in this gentle breeze,
> That blows from the green fields and from the clouds . . .
> O welcome messenger! O welcome friend!
> A captive greets thee, coming from a house
> Of bondage, from yon city's walls set free,
> A prison where he hath been long immured.
> *Now I am free, enfranchised and at large* . . .[84]

Similarly, Coleridge's 'Eolian Harp' (1795) would distinguish the
revivifying 'breeze' as a metaphor for poetic inspiration, whilst his
conversation poems, 'This Lime-Tree Bower My Prison' (1797),
'Frost at Midnight' (1798) and 'Dejection: An Ode' (1802) presented
the resurgence of the imagination amidst metaphors describing
escape from domestic captivity and promises of divine possibility:
'But now afflictions bow me down to earth: / Nor care I that they
rob me of my mirth; / But oh! each visitation / Suspends what
nature gave me at my birth, / My shaping spirit of Imagination'.[85]
In Wheatley's poem, the plea for liberation registered abolitionist
discourse as a valid manifestation of imaginative freedom. As a
consequence, and in accordance with the poems by William Cowper,

the power of the imagination was determined as an 'unstoppable' force that would inspire other 'northern tempests' – the violent storms of insurrection / emancipation:

> Though *Winter* frowns to *Fancy's* raptur'd eyes
> The fields may flourish, and gay scenes arise;
> *The frozen deeps may break their iron bands,*
> And bid their waters murmur o'er the sands
>
> Such is thy pow'r [Imagination]
>
> And thine the sceptre o'er the realms of thought.[86]

In her poem, 'To the Right Honourable William (Legge), Earl of Dartmouth', friend of the Countess and supporter of the Methodist Movement in England, Wheatley continued her previous correlation between America's struggle for liberation from British tyranny (1775–1781) and her 'love of *Freedom*': 'I, young in life, by seeming cruel fate / Was snatched from *Afric's* fancy'd happy seat . . . / Steel'd was that soul and by no misery mov'd / That from a father seiz'd his babe belov'd'.[87] Wheatley's choice of addressee, the Secretary of State for the Colonies and President of the Board of Trade and Foreign Plantation ('His Majesty's Principal Secretary of State for North America, &c.') confirms that the poet was deeply aware of the subtle interrelationship between the dynamics of evangelism and the political climate of the 1780s.[88] By figuring the Earl as an important factor in the endeavour to overthrow the 'wanton Tyranny' which had enslaved America, Wheatley skilfully interwove a narrative of England's potential abolitionist role with her own autobiographical narrative of spiritual salvation. As in her earlier poem, 'On Being Brought from Africa to America', Wheatley identified her capture and enslavement as a 'seeming cruel fate', a phrase which paradoxically likened her postlapsarian state to Adam and Eve's 'fortunate fall' and determined her severance from Africa as a state of exile from the Garden of Eden. Whilst she implied that her spiritual development would have remained incomplete without her 'fortunate' encounter with Christianity, cultural severance is nevertheless redetermined as a merciless and intrinsically vicious act – 'Steel'd was that soul and by no misery mov'd'.

For the peoples of the diaspora, as Wheatley seems well aware, the preservation of identity relied essentially upon a conscious and rigorous preservation of individual and cultural memory. Likewise, it

depended upon the maintenance of a counter-discourse to those
ideologies which had determined Africa as an entity without history
or memory. Accordingly, in her poem, 'On Recollection', composed
in late 1771 and included in the *Poems on Various Subjects*, Wheatley
pledges her honour to 'Mneme', a synthesis of Mnemosyme (the
Greek goddess of memory and the muses) and Mneme (the older
goddess of remembrance): 'Mneme begin. Inspire, ye sacred nine, /
Your vent'rous *Afric* in her great design./ *Mneme*, immortal pow'r, I
trace thy spring: / Assist my strains, while I thy glories sing'. Hence,
Wheatley's ostensibly abolitionist text proclaimed the powerful
relationship between cultural memory ('nocturnal visions') and
Mneme's divine vengeance against those who scorned her warnings.
For Wheatley, Mneme, like Keats' Moneta, embodied a permanent
recollection of past sufferings, 'the acts of long departed years, by
thee / Recover'd':

> By her unveil'd each horrid crime appears,
> Her awful hand a cup of wormwood bears.
> Days, years mispent, O what a hell of woe!
> Hers the worst tortures that our souls can know.[89]

Wheatley's 'Mneme' (like Equiano's 'Affoe-wah') forms a continuum
with Achilles' servant, Mnemon, who reminds his master of events
prophesied by the oracle. Consequently, the poet is transported
through the 'ample treasure' of Mneme's secret stores and in this
state of trance-like rapture, cultural memory is identified as the very
essence of 'spiritual' poetry.[90] Furthermore, 'On Recollection'
carries with it coded references to African beliefs in the discontin-
uous link between the self and the community of dead ancestors –
those guardian spirits who protect and guide their descendants.
Hence, Wheatley's poem presents a subtle alternative to white /
western ideologies and epistemology. For her, disremembrance (the
erasure of cultural memory) constitutes an insidious form of self-
imposed amnesia or temporal estrangement. Whereas the travesties
inflicted upon her people, the 'follies of that period', appear to have
been forgotten, Wheatley's poem insists upon their *permanent* inscription on both the personal and collective memory:

> Now eighteen years their destin'd course have run,
> In fast succession round the central sun.
> How did the follies of that period pass
> Unnotic'd, *but behold them writ in brass!*

In Recollection see them fresh return,
And sure 'tis mine to be asham'd, and mourn.[91]

Accordingly, Wheatley extends the power of recollection, the 'pow'r enthron'd in ev'ry breast', to a cultural dimension in line with African belief systems in the diaspora. The power of recollection is also strategically linked to a radical form of sociopolitical transformation, via its relationship with divine retribution, revelation and apocalypse. Wheatley's poem, therefore, prophesied the moment in which the 'thrice blest man' (or slave) would awaken to find himself 'shelter'd from the wrath divine' in 'Recollection's sacred shrine'. Conversely, those wretches who had 'dar'd the vengeance of the skies' would find themselves in an unenviable state of 'horror and surprise'.[92]

For Wheatley, therefore, the act of recollection registers a process not confined to the individual's cerebral sphere but firmly located within the more extensive boundaries of historical and cultural narrative. Her evocation of 'recollection' thus differed significantly from concepts of memory described by the Romantics and their established precursors. Anticipating the work of Toni Morrison, Wheatley's concept of 'recollection' identified the act of 're-membrance' as a crucial form of cultural preservation in the diaspora. According to Margaretta Odell, Wheatley's nineteenth-century biographer, the poet cherished a memory of her mother pouring 'water before the sun at his rising in reference, no doubt, to an ancient African custom'.[93] Wheatley's reinscription of erased cultural memory and her subtle disclosure of African beliefs identifies an African cultural inheritance at odds with tenets of orthodox Christianity. Thus her work offers a poetical assimilation of the discourse of radical dissenting Protestantism by ex-slaves and simultaneously reveals a hybridised text of cultural and epistemological interaction, a form which was to be further developed within the autobiographical narrative by the ex-slave, Olaudah Equiano.

CHAPTER EIGHT

Olaudah Equiano's Interesting Narrative

Two years after the publication of *Thoughts and Sentiments*, Ottobah Cugoano's friend, Olaudah Equiano published his slave narrative, *The Interesting Narrative of the Life of Olaudah Equiano, or Gustavus Vassa, the African, Written By Himself* (1789), a two-volume work which marked a crucial stage in the development of literary autobiographical works by slaves. Equiano's text, which was frequently republished over a period of thirty years, presented a detailed description of displaced cultural identity in the black diaspora previously suggested by Phillis Wheatley's work. Equiano's work represented a fulfilment of the bicultural, creolised tactics of the earlier slave narratives and registered a significant penetration of the political legislature by a black autobiographical voice.[1] As its subtitle, 'Written by Himself', suggested and the signed engraving of the black author holding a Bible upon his lap confirmed, Equiano's text, named by the founder of Methodism, John Wesley, as one of his favourite works, presented a deliberate intersection between the discourse of radical dissenting Protestantism, African culture and the political antislavery milieu which permeated late eighteenth-century England.[2] Equiano was, as Edwards, Dabydeen, Potkay and Hofkosh have suggested, one of a number of politically visible Africans in London in the late 1780s: he was a government employee; he served on the Committee for the Relief of the Black Poor; his letters were frequently published in the *Public Advertiser*; he travelled throughout Britain to advance his abolitionist concerns and liaised with influential political activists, including Granville Sharp.[3]

By assuming the literary structure of the conversion narratives, Equiano's text established a prototype of the slaves' endeavour to recreate identity within the diaspora, by means of a tactical revision of the spiritualised discourse characteristic of the autobiographical genre.[4] In this account of his past, Equiano achieved a creolised

GUSTAVUS VASSA.

the African.

Fig. 5. Frontispiece, *The Interesting Life of Olaudah Equiano, or Gustavus Vassa, the African.*
Halifax: J. Nicholson, 1814.

(re)construction of 'himself' in terms of spiritual and political displacement, and thereby posed a significant challenge to negations of Africans' spiritual capacities and cultural attributes contained within colonial ideology.

Dedicated strategically to 'The Lords Spiritual and Temporal, and the Commons of the Parliament of Great Britain', Equiano's *Interesting Narrative* demonstrated a conscious effort to ascribe spiritual enlightenment to the political arena and hence ascertain the importance of the relationship between spiritual intervention, the 'mysterious ways of Providence' and parliamentary decisions concerning the abolition of the slave trade:

> Permit me, with the greatest deference and respect, to lay at your feet the following genuine Narrative; the chief design of which is to excite in your august assemblies a sense of compassion for the miseries which the Slave-Trade has entailed on my unfortunate countrymen. By the horrors of that trade was I first torn away from all the tender connexions that were naturally dear to my heart; *but these, through the mysterious ways of Providence, I ought to regard as infinitely more than compensated by the introduction I have thence obtained of the knowledge of the Christian religion, and of a nation* which, by its liberal sentiments, its humanity, the glorious *freedom of its government, and its proficiency in arts and sciences, has exalted the dignity of human nature.*[5]

Accordingly, in his role as an itinerant black representative sponsored by the Abolition Committee, Equiano's voice penetrated the stronghold of Parliament through his communication with Granville Sharp, whom he notified of the abhorrent circumstances of the *Zong* incident (in which 132 Africans were deliberately drowned at sea in order to secure insurance compensation). Equiano also rigorously participated in the Abolitionist Committee's intense lobbying of individual members of Parliament; and it was Equiano who, having been appointed as Commissionary of Stores in 1786, initiated an exposure of the corruption implicit in the Government's 'repatriation' scheme of London's black poor to the colony of Sierra Leone.[6] As the list of subscribers cited in the Preface to the 1789 edition of the *Interesting Narrative* suggests, Equiano's efforts were purposefully directed towards a predominantly Evangelical forum, which included the Prince of Wales, the Duke of Marlborough, the Earl of Dartmouth, Lady Ann Erskine, the Countess of Huntingdon, Hannah More, Mrs J. Baillie, Henry Thornton, Thomas Clarkson, and the Revd John Wesley.

Equiano's text, reprinted eight times in Great Britain during the author's lifetime (1745–1797), was reviewed by two London publications. In July 1789, a reviewer in *The Monthly Review* emphasised the 'honest face' of the narrative, proclaiming that he believed the 'sable author' to have been 'guided by principle' and not one of those, who 'having undergone the ceremony of baptism were content with only that part of the Christian Religion'.[7] In July 1789, *The Gentleman's Magazine and Impartial Review* verified the 'truth and simplicity' of Equiano's 'round unvarnished tale' and pledged its support of the author's wish to remove the 'stain on the legislature of Britain' regarding its involvement with the slave trade. Similarly, in the Preface to the 1814 variant published in Leeds by James Nichols (which carried the 'Am I Not a Man or Brother?' motif on the title-page), the editor validated the authenticity of the tale in terms of its affinity to confessional autobiography, defining it as 'a *round unvarnished tale* of sufferings . . . endured' and a 'true relation of occurrences which had taken place'.[8] The editor of that 1814 edition claimed that the authenticity of Equiano's memories of his life as a slave were unquestionable and criticised the 'hostile response of several beneficiaries displayed by the slave trade' in their efforts to invalidate Equiano's testimony 'by accusing him of wilful falsehoods'.[9]

Equiano's *Interesting Narrative* described how its author, transported across the Atlantic to the West Indies at the age of twelve, was renamed Michael and then sold to an American slave-trader, Mr Campbell, who renamed him Jacob and set him to work on a plantation in Virginia until 1756/7. He was then purchased by an English naval officer, Michael Pascal, who substituted the name of a Swedish king, Gustavus Vassa, for the author's Ibo name and took him to England. For many years, Equiano served Pascal both on land and at sea and participated in the Seven Years' War against France and her colonies (1756–1763). He was, however, eventually resold to Captain James Doran, for whom he worked for several years on the island of Montserrat in the West Indies. In 1763, Doran sold Equiano to Robert King (a Quaker merchant); from this time onwards Equiano sailed with Captain Thomas Farmer as a West Indian and North American slaver and trader until he managed to buy his freedom in July 1766, using the capital he had raised by petty trading.[10] Equiano returned to England during 1767 and again ten years later, in January 1777. In Equiano's text, emphasis on the sea (that 'no man's land') functions as a signifier of the author's cultural displacement and territorial dispossession, together with the fluid, protean nature of his efforts to reconstruct his identity within the diaspora. Accordingly, Equiano's detailed account of his naval experiences during Captain Pascal's quick succession of promotions in the Royal Navy, his maritime adventures in 1758 under Admiral Boscawen and during England's Seven Years' War against France, his voyage to the Arctic in 1772 and his travels as a gentleman's valet throughout a tour of the Mediterranean and the Caribbean, all register his continued sense of displacement and 'rootlessness' since the time of his capture.

In an attempt to establish the validity of his autobiographical script and to posit Africa as a veritable paradise exercising its own established system of ethical codes, Equiano's *Interesting Narrative* opens with a detailed account of Ibo life and society in the village of Essaka (now Issake, Nigeria). As Catherine Acholonu comments, Equiano's use of the '-q-' and the '-e-' (which do not exist in Ibo orthography) to transcribe the Ibo sounds '-kw-' and '/i/' confirms his endeavours to transcribe West African language into a written form and to translate tenets of African culture into the apparatus of western discourse.[11] Equiano's correlation of Africa with the biblical Land of Promise hence prescribes an effective transfer of cultural autobiography on to a form of religious dissent, heavily encoded with abolitionist ideology. As his testimony traces the journey of his *own* personal salvation, his text looks forward to the 'salvation' of his people by means of abolition and emancipation. Likewise, as his text attempts to compare African culture with the account of Jewish culture contained in the Scriptures, his efforts to decentre pervasive theories of polygenesis and 'demythologise' narratives which determined Africa as an essentially undeveloped and (sexually) volatile state, rely upon his counter-depiction of African society as a 'civilised' cultural entity:

And here I cannot forbear suggesting what has long struck me very forcibly, namely, the strong analogy which even by this sketch, imperfect as it is, appears to prevail in the manners and customs of my countrymen and those of the Jews, before they reached the Land of Promise, and particularly the patriarchs while they were yet in that pastoral state which is described in Genesis – an analogy, which alone would induce me to think that the *one people had sprung from the other.* Indeed this is the opinion of Dr Gill, who, in his commentary on Genesis, very ably deduces the *pedigree of the Africans* from Afer and Afra, the descendants of Abraham by Keturah his wife and concubine.[12]

As to the colour difference between Iboan Africans and the modern Jews, Equiano does 'not presume to account for it'; rather, he tellingly cites a 'fact as related by Dr. Mitchel' and Thomas Clarkson which proffers a climactic explanation of differences in skin colour. Yet by using such an explanation, Equiano endeavours to destabilise theoretical configurations of polygenesis and racial difference by means of a strategic narrative of cultural hybridity and racial fluidity: 'The Spaniards, who have inhabited America, under the torrid zone, for any time, are become as dark coloured as our native Indians of Virginia'.[13] By highlighting the consequences of the sexual interminglings between Portuguese settlers and natives of the Mitomba settlement in Sierra Leone, whom he declares, have 'now become in their complexion, and in the woolly quality of their hair, *perfect negroes*, retaining, however, a smattering of the Portuguese language', Equiano's words reveal a radical exposé of the dynamics of cultural miscegenation, a process which proves an appropriate paradigm for his own text.

Composed some thirty years after his capture, Equiano's narrative of displacement is framed by what Stuart Hall has defined as an inevitable consequence of cultural dispossession, an 'imaginary plenitude' which recreates an endless desire to return to 'lost origins': a yearning to return to beginnings which 'like the imaginary in Lacan . . . can neither be fulfilled nor acquired'.[14] In accordance with this argument, Equiano's text confirms that the moment *preceding* cultural contact can never again be achieved. His narrative of African culture therefore hinges upon a form of 'symbolic' discourse in which the elements of representation, memory and myth are prioritised. For this reason, whereas his *Interesting Narrative* appears to manifest 'artless' autobiography, his work reveals a close interaction with a variety of established texts, including Constantine Phipps' *A Journey of a Voyage Towards the North Pole* (1774), Anthony Benezet's *Some Historical Account of Guinea* (1771) and Thomas Clarkson's *Essay on Slavery* (1789).[15] This textual interrelationship determines the subtextual agendas of Equiano's text, most especially its correlation with abolitionism, cultural 'autobiography' and its relation with radical dissenting Protestantism. In accordance with Antony Benezet's description of Guinea as that part of Africa which 'extends along the coast three or four thousand miles. Beginning at the river Senegal . . . the land of Guinea . . . [includes] the Grain Coast; the Ivory Coast; the Gold Coast and the Slave Coast, with the large kingdom of Benin' and from which the Negroes are 'sold to be carried into slavery', Equiano's first chapter similarly reads:

That part of Africa, known by the name of Guinea, to which the trade for slaves is carried on, extends along the coast above 3400 miles, from Senegal to Angola, and includes a variety of kingdoms. Of these the most considerable is the kingdom of Benin.[16]

However, whereas Benezet's *Historical Account* presents the natives of Benin as a 'reasonable, good-natured people', Equiano describes them as 'warlike', thereby anticipating the rebellious nature of his own text.[17] Likewise his focus upon the Ibonic rituals of circumcision, sacrificial offerings, washings and purifications ('this necessary habit of decency was with us a part of religion') serves to endorse a comparison between Ibo and Jewish culture, and more importantly, to erode the ideological and epistemological boundaries between African culture and the west. In its effort to establish its position as textual *intermediary* between nonconformist western religious ideologies and the complex landscape of African belief systems, Equiano's *Interesting Narrative* represents the most developed articulation of epistemological and cultural synthesis contained within the slave narratives in England published during the late 1780s.

SYNCHRONISATION: WEST AFRICAN EPISTEMOLOGY AND
RADICAL DISSENTING PROTESTANTISM

'I was named *Olaudah*', declares Equiano at the outset of his text, 'which, in our language, signifies vicissitude or fortunate', as well as 'one favoured, and having a loud voice and well spoken'.[18] This statement establishes the author's select position within the framework of spiritual development advanced by dissenting Protestantism, yet his words also register his identification with Ibo culture and his father's honoured position as an 'Embrenche', a term of 'the highest distinction' and signifying 'in our language a *mark* of grandeur'.[19] Furthermore, the *absence* of this visual signifier of distinction (a thick wale formed by cutting the skin across the top of the forehead) upon his own person, serves to mark Equiano's interrupted cultural destiny. This in turn confirms the correlation between the author's Ibo name and the denial of his privileged status in Benin, 'I also was destined to receive it by my appellation'. It is a status permanently interrupted by his forced enslavement, transportation and subsequent renaming by cultural others.[20]

On one level, Equiano's text endeavours to trace its author's sense of election within a specific cultural arena ('I remember many [people] used to come to see me, and I was carried about to others for that purpose') on to a framework of divine election established by the conversion narratives. Hence, in the opening chapter of his *Interesting Narrative*, Equiano, in the same vein as the dissenting Protestants, Wesley and Newton, exclaims that he regarded himself 'a *particular favourite of Heaven*' who acknowledged the 'mercies of Providence' in every occurrence of his life.[21] This prioritisation of Christian providentialism is, however, antagonised by the author's implicit approval of the Ibo concept of 'chi', the personal spirit of destiny, as maintained by West African epistemology: 'Those spirits, which are not transmigrated, such as their dear friend or relations, they believe always attend them, and guard them from the bad spirits or their foes'.[22] Therefore Equiano's text witnesses a diasporic synchronisation or fusion of the author's 'chi' with dissenting Protestantism's concept of the 'Holy Spirit', a fusion which is maintained, albeit problematically, throughout the text. By appropriating the discourse of dissenting Protestantism, Equiano's text fuses the doctrines of divine grace, mystery and prophecy with essential tenets of African epistemologies and manifests a literary paradigm of cultural symbiosis. Furthermore, Equiano's *Interesting Narrative* functions as a textual prototype of the 'hybrid' black church which emerged in England, America and the Caribbean during the late eighteenth century. His account serves to endorse the essential compatibility or rather, the potential tessellation of aspects of Ibo culture with principles of nonconformist Protestantism. One example of this is the author's correlation of the prophetic and healing qualities of nonconformist ministry with the power of African priests and magicians, the 'Ah-affoe-way-cah', to calculate time, foretell events, heal wounds and expel poisons. Both systems of belief demonstrated a rejection of institutionalised places of worship ('Though we had no places of worship, we had priests and magicians, or wise men')[23] and most important of all, an emphasis upon concepts of spirit possession and divine guidance, exemplified by the intense emotional investment characteristic of dissenting Protestants' confirmations of faith and the ecstatic bodily behaviour of African initiation rites.[24] This creolisation of spiritual discourse traces an

unprecedented moment of cultural intersection between Methodism's concept of divine inspiration and the Ibo belief in its priests'
powers to 'see' and 'discover' that which is hidden and unknown.

As an affirmation of the Ah-affoe-way-cah's powers of spiritual
discernment and revelation, Equiano's *Interesting Narrative* cites an
instance of the disclosure of a young virgin's murderer (the term
'young woman' being substituted for the word 'virgin' in the second
edition by Wilkins) by means of the spirit-possession which over-
powers the bearers of the female corpse:

I hope it will not be deemed impertinent here to insert, as it may serve as a kind of
specimen of the rest, and is still used by the negroes in the West Indies. A virgin had
been poisoned, but it was not known by whom: the doctors ordered the
corpse to be taken up by some persons, and carried to the grave. As soon as
the bearers had raised it on their shoulders, *they seemed seized with some sudden*
impulse, and ran to and fro unable to stop themselves. At last, after having passed
through a number of thorns and prickly bushes unhurt, the corpse fell from
them close to a house, and defaced it in the fall; and, the owner being taken
up, he immediately confessed the poisoning.[25]

Although the authenticity of the Ah-affoe-way-cah's spiritual powers
is ostensibly undermined by the author's marginalisation of the Ibo
priests' 'no doubt . . . unbounded influence over the credulity and
superstition of the [Igbo] people', the footnote which accompanies
the above quotation presents as 'evidence' a similar incident of
spirit-possession at Montserrat in the West Indies in 1763.[26] This
episode, explains Equiano, was not only witnessed by himself, but
experienced by the sceptical crew of the *Charming Sally,* whose
physical autonomy and self-control were overpowered by the possessing spirits:

I then belonged to the Charming Sally, Capt. Doran. – The chief mate, Mr
Mansfield, and some of the crew being one day on shore, were present at
the burying of a poisoned negro girl. Though they had often heard of the
circumstance of the running in such cases, and had even seen it, they
imagined it to be a trick of the corpse-bearers. The mate therefore desired
two of the sailors to take up the coffin, and carry it to the grave. The
sailors, who were all of the same opinion, readily obeyed; but they had
scarcely raised it to their shoulders, before they began to run furiously
about, quite unable to direct themselves, till, at last, without intention, they
came to the hut of him who had poisoned the girl.[27]

It is, however, precisely Equiano's coalescence of the 'heathen'
belief in fortune with the concept of divine (Christian) providence (as

suggested by the explanation he gives for his name) which most disturbed the editor of the Leeds edition of 1814. This prompted him to add an apologetic footnote condemning Equiano's naive and 'indiscreet mode' of referring to God's grace 'by the name of fortune', a trait which he dismisses as 'exceedingly blameworthy' but characteristic of the 'children of men':

It is a conformity to the expressions of a vain world not to be expected from Gustavus, who generally manifests a becoming sense of the benefits which he received, and a knowledge of the Blessed Fountain from whence they issued. After censuring it as *a slip of the pen*, let none venture to attribute it to atheistical motives. The tenor of his conduct and of his words belies such an insinuation. *He had heard the term thus misapplied by others*, and from an imitative habit, he thoughtlessly gave it the same appellation.[28]

The spiritual discourse prescribed by Equiano's *Interesting Narrative* endorses a form of creolised cultural testimony which articulates a critical dissolution of the dichotomy between the inner spiritual being (the soul, or psychic space) and the outer physical entity (the body, or social space) occupied by the slave. Such a dissolution proved crucial to ideologies which advocated inalienable rights to liberty or, more radically, advanced demands for emancipation. Equiano's translation of this discourse of the spiritual/cultural self into the rhetoric of radical dissenting Protestantism participates in a linguistic and cultural exchange between Christian concepts of the holy 'spirit' on the one hand, and Ibo beliefs in the active presence of the spiritual worlds and the transmigration of souls on the other:

As to religion, the natives believe that there is one Creator of all things, and that he lives in the sun . . . They believe he governs events, especially our deaths or captivity; but, as for the doctrine of eternity, I do not remember to have ever heard of it: some however believe in the transmigration of souls in a certain degree.[29]

His autobiographical account of his 'decipherment' of the crew on board the slave ship establishes a decoding of obscured meaning onto 'plain text' and inaugurates a designation of Europeans (and their ideologies) within a context of African epistemology. As part of this process, the author 'interprets' the presence of the slavers in terms of his own native belief system, thereby identifying the traders as 'people full of nothing but magical arts': 'I was in another world, and that everything about me was magic'.[30] This reinterpretation of the Europeans as 'spirits' from another world is continued by the

author's account of his loss of autonomy in their presence, another
form of 'spirit possession':

These filled me with astonishment, which was soon converted into terror
. . . I was immediately handled and tossed up to see if I were sound by
some of the crew; and I was now persuaded that I had gotten into a world
of bad spirits, and that they were going to kill me.[31]

Likewise, when Equiano arrives in Virginia and sees a portrait and a
timepiece for the first time, he interprets these artifacts as the
keepsakes of ancestral spirits, the cultural repositories of history and
time:

The first object that engaged my attention was a watch which hung on the
chimney, and was going. I was quite surprised at the noise it made, and was
afraid it would tell the gentleman any thing I might do amiss: and when I
immediately after observed a picture hanging in the room, which appeared
constantly to look at me, I was still more affrighted, having never seen such
things as these before. At one time *I thought it was something relative to magic*;
and not seeing it move I thought it might be some way the whites had to
keep their great men when they died, and offer them libations as we used to
do to our friendly spirits.[32]

This passage is important, not only because, as Gates observes, it
dramatises the difference between Equiano's earlier self and the self
that narrates his text, but because it witnesses the *transference* of
African concepts of 'spirit possession' on to western ideologies and in
so doing, reveals the intricate interrelationship between spiritual
discourse and literary articulations of power. In addition, Equiano's
interpretations of the spiritual powers contained within the picture
and the watch strategically refer back to his account of the magical
powers of the Ibonic Ah-affoe-way-cah who, as with these western
artifacts, prescribe radically different concepts of vision (real and
prophetic) and time ('they calculated our time').[33]

MOTHERLANDS AND RITES OF PASSAGE

In Chapter 1 of his *Interesting Narrative*, Equiano's recollection of his
mother's libations to those spirits which had not transmigrated,
presents a revised paradigm of spiritual discourse on western terms
and an alternate paradigm of the sublime (an important Romantic
context) within an African context:

I was very fond of my mother, and almost constantly with her. When she
went to make these oblations at her mother's tomb, which was a kind of

small solitary thatched house, I sometimes attended her. There she made her libations, and spent most of the night in cries and lamentations. I have been often extremely terrified on these occasions. The loneliness of the place, the darkness of the night, and the ceremony of libation, naturally awful and gloomy, were heightened by my mother's lamentations; and these, concurring with the cries of doleful birds, by which these places were frequented, gave an inexpressible terror to the scene.[34]

The 'inexpressible terror' of the scene, the darkness and the 'awful' atmosphere which the young Equiano senses during the libation ceremony describe a precious moment in which the presence of some powerful non-material 'other' dominates. In Longinus' treatise *On the Sublime* (translated by the French critic Boileau in 1674), *hypos* or height functions as a predominant metaphor for the experience of sublimity: the reader is uplifted and his soul transported in exultation (in close proximity to the spirit of the deity) as 'though [he] had created what [he] had merely heard'.

Wherefore not even the entire universe suffices for the thought and contemplation within the reach of the human mind, but our imagination often pass beyond the bounds of space, and if we survey our life on every side and see how much more it everywhere abounds in what is striking, and great, and beautiful, we shall discern the purpose of our birth.[35]

In his *Philosophical Enquiry into the Origins of our Ideas of the Sublime and Beautiful* (1757), Edmund Burke reinscribed Longinus' focus on the 'proud flight' of the soul as a moment of infinity and magnificence.[36] Equiano's narrative correlates the sublime, the 'loneliness . . . awful and gloomy', with the Ibonic belief in the transmigration of souls and thereby presents a culturally contextualised account of his peoples' libation ceremonies, their cries and lamentations. Furthermore, Equiano's lucid testimony of his experience of transportation across the middle passage – 'the stench of the hold', the sickness, the 'filth of the necessary tubs', the shrieks of the women (presumably as they were raped) and the groans of the dying – redetermines the terror of the sublime as a scene of 'horror, almost inconceivable', in which the power of the African, now slave, 'self' dissolves under the authority of an 'other' absolute subject (England).[37]

As with Cowper's and Newton's confessional narratives, Equiano's account of his experience during the middle passage unmasks a desire for death/suicide, a textual prerequisite to the mechanisms of divine salvation: 'I began to hope [death] would soon put an end to my miseries'.[38] Equiano's (self-)juxtaposition with the freedom of the 'inhabitants of the deep', '*I envied them the freedom they enjoyed*, and as often wished I could change my condition for theirs', anticipates the post-storm blessing of the sea-creatures in Coleridge's 'The Rime of the Ancient Mariner' (1797) by almost a decade. This form of cultural intertextuality permits a reading of Coleridge's poem as a narrative of dislocation, dispossession and exile:

> Her beams bemocked the sultry main,
> Like April hoar-frost spread;
> But where the ship's huge shadow lay,
> The charmèd water burnt alway
> A still and awful red.[39]

During his transatlantic voyage, Equiano witnesses the suicide of two of his enslaved companions, who, 'preferring death to such a life of misery', throw themselves into the sea.[40] Such a practice was recorded by several slave-traders who, in order to deter the Africans' attempt to return to their spiritual homelands by drowning, would display the mutilated (beheaded) corpses of those who had attempted to escape from the slave ships. Equiano's own form of 'insurrection' takes on a very different guise and inscribes a process of cultural 'translation' as an alternative to cultural erasure. As the passage on the sublime 'oblations' suggests, for Equiano the signifiers of his prediasporic identity are inseparable from his 'recollections' of the maternal figure. This determines the condition of his now diasporic identity as a state of division from both the female and the indigenous culture, a state of hiatus which interrupts the cultural continuum and further problematises the complex processes of (self-) identification. In Equiano's text, this interruption of self-determination/inscription (cultural and sexual) is figured metaphorically by the man who *lies between* the author and his sister during their transportation across the 'middle passage': 'The man, to whom I supposed we belonged, lay with us, he in the middle, while she [my sister] and I held one another by the hands across his breast all night'.[41] Once on board the slave ships, male and female slaves were regularly separated from each other by traders and overseers in an attempt to prevent the terrifying possibility of slave mutinies during the long transatlantic crossings. This division on sexual lines was often continued on the plantations where slaves were often forced to sleep with their masters or with whomsoever their masters ordered. As a consequence, the appropriation and negation of a slave's

sexuality functioned as a symbolic manifestation of Europe's usurpation over Africa, a process continued by the role reversal imposed on
African slaves which forced males to perform traditionally female
roles and vice versa.[42]

Likewise, the *separation* of the child, as in Equiano's case, from the
biological mother's body, posited a metaphor of irreversible division
from the slave's cultural '*motherland*', a severance which represented a
dislocation in language and a significant hiatus in the cultural
continuum.[43] The severing of this umbilical cord inaugurated a
condition of 'fracture' from a specific sociohistorical and cultural
past and hence determined the emergence of a 'fragmented' identity
within the diaspora. In Equiano's text, this relationship with Western
culture figures a complex moment of social and psychological
reorderings: firstly, through the attempted subordination of African
matriarchy by patriarchal European society; and secondly, through
the redetermination of England as both the 'mother country' and
liberator of slaves.

Equiano's narrative therefore reciprocates the conscience-stricken
(sexual) centre of several spiritual autobiographies (including Southcott's *Prophecies* and Wordsworth's *Prelude*), yet his text exceeds the
boundaries of Methodism's confessional framework, as it narrates his
complicity in the sexual violation of female slaves during successive
voyages across the middle passage. It is a practice which he witnesses
and to which he submits, possibly as an active agent, but at the very
least, as a passive observer. As a 'slave'-trader, his status as a 'free'
ir/responsible agent is deeply complex – he is both a subject of, and
subjected to, a complex matrix of desires and restraints:

> I used frequently to have different cargoes of *new negroes in my care* for sale;
> and it was almost a constant practice with our clerks, and other whites, to
> commit violent *depredations on the chastity of the female slaves*; and these
> [atrocities] *I was, though with reluctance, obliged to submit to at all times*, being
> unable to help them [the female slaves] . . . I have even known them [his
> shipmates] gratify their brutal passion with females not ten years old; and
> these abominations some of them practised to such scandalous excess.[44]

Since the predominant processes informing the dynamics of servitude pivoted upon the complex and subtle ideologies of ownership
and its inscription, Equiano's complicity in these sexual assaults
upon the females aboard the slave ships underlines an important
recognition of his own 'lack' of power. His voyeuristic/physical rape
(the exertion of sexual power over female 'others') presents a

concerted attempt to counteract the dispossession which had determined his own condition as a slave. In his authoritative *Commentaries on the Law of England*, William Blackstone had defined rape (*raptus mulierum*) as the carnal knowledge of a woman taken forcibly and against her will.[45] He also recorded that according to English legislation, 'if the rape be charged to be committed on an infant under twelve years of age, she may still be a competent witness'.[46] This legislation made clear the 'crime' of which Equiano's fellow slave traders were, by law, undeniably guilty. However, it also foregrounds the question of Equiano's 'act', whether voluntary, voyeuristic or otherwise. Equiano's 'obligation to civil subjection', whereby an inferior, according to Blackstone, is constrained by his superiors to act 'contrary to what his own reason and inclination would suggest', highlights the complex legislative subject status occupied by slaves at this time. When he complies with his owners' declarations of power, Equiano's actions undergo an intricate process of cultural assimilation and severance from African cultural loyalties. In terms of its confessional framework, his account of these sexual 'plunderings' (to which he claims he was 'though with reluctance, obliged to submit to at all times') satisfies the dynamics of testimony, vindication and absolution contained within the narratives of Cowper, Newton and other spiritual autobiographers.

As discussed above in relation to the early spiritual narratives, the genre of autobiography revolves around a complex configuration of disclosure. In his *Allegories of Reading* (1979), Paul de Man defined the 'confession' as an endeavour to overcome guilt and shame in the name of truth: 'By stating things as they are, the economy of the ethical balance is restored and redemption can start in the clarified atmosphere of truth that does not hesitate to reveal the crime in all its horror'.[47] Likewise, in his study of sexual discourse, *The History of Sexuality*, Michel Foucault defined the confession as 'one of the west's most highly valued techniques for producing truth', a process in which sex and the 'insinuations of the flesh' become a 'privileged theme'.[48] However, as de Man notes with reference to Rousseau, it was not enough for the confessor to tell all: (s)he had to *excuse* as well as confess. This would suggest that no conflict exists between the confession and the excuse, yet language itself cannot constitute a 'reparation in the realm of political justice':

How then are we to know that we are indeed dealing with a *true* confession, since the recognition of guilt implies its exoneration in the name of the same transcendental principle of truth that allowed for the certitude of guilt in the first place?[49]

When applied to Equiano's text, this prompts the reader to question the confessor's narrative of 'absolute truth' and most significantly, the means by which he excuses his guilt. Equiano's text is strategically hinged upon a demand for a representation of the 'principle of truth' (a national, political confession) within the 'realm of political justice'. At the same time, his exposure of his own (sexual) collaboration with the traders demonstrates a complex process of assimilation *with* the host culture. Consequently, it presents a radical exposure of the inherent contradictions and inconsistencies of the English political system itself. Ostensibly, therefore, his 'confessional' disclosure of his collusion with the traders' sexual violations inaugurates a narrative of personal (Christian) salvation, yet his text simultaneously registers a departure from such ideologies, a challenge to the English legislature and an adherence to the African cultural continuum.

As he relates in great detail at the outset of his text, Equiano was destined (like his brothers) to receive the Ibo 'marks' of the 'Embrenche', the visual signifiers of grandeur and distinction, facial marks of scarification which, as I have already noted, would have confirmed his relationship with a great 'chi' (ancestral spirit) and symbolised his transition into physical maturity. However, if, as the anthropologist, Catherine Acholonu suggests, the kidnapping of Olaudah and his sister was no accident, but deliberately arranged by his guardians, then the absence of these markings essentially informs the *cultural* significance of the passage cited above. Lacking the ciphers of manhood and spiritual guidance, Equiano's narrative of displacement and erasure is twofold. Accordingly, his sufferance of the rape of his countrywomen manifests an attempt to inscribe alternative ciphers of his sexual and cultural maturity.[50]

Earlier in the text, Equiano hints at the strong relationship between himself and his mother and his constant accompaniment of her: in her bed, in her hut and during her libations at her mother's tomb.[51] In her analysis of Ibo culture, the anthropologist Ifi Amadiume identifies the temporal space of menstruation as an observed period of gender segregation in African societies:

As women's blood was believed to be polluting both to ancestral spirits and to men, a menstruating woman was forbidden sexual intercourse with her husband and banned from the *obi* areas. *Ino na ezi*, or *ino n'iba*, or *ino na nso*, 'in a state of taboo', were the expressions for being in menses. These expressions were, perhaps, derived from the custom of isolating menstruating women in a little hut at the back of the compound, where they were supposed to remain until the menstrual flow ceased, after which a chick would be killed and the ritual of cleansing performed before they were allowed back into society. The penalty for a woman who broke the rule of trespass or sexual taboo while in her menses was severe.[52]

If Equiano's close ties with his mother during her menstrual cycle were interpreted by his family as evidence of his 'effeminate nature', then the absence of these signifiers of the 'Embrenche' takes on a new dimension. Such a reading would imply that he who was destined to become an 'Embrenche', the epitome of leadership and judgement, was denied these signifiers of masculinity, not because he was transported into slavery but because of the premeditated intervention of his kinsmen. Therefore in Equiano's confessional narrative the paradigm of remorse (in western terms) coalesces with the dishonour (in Ibo terms). His text ultimately identifies not the shame of his sexual transgression/voyeurism but seeks to exonerate the shame accompanying his absent or deficient manhood, together with the shameful betrayal of his family who sold him into slavery.

In fact, Equiano's complicity in the attempt to legitimise 'ownership' by means of 'illegitimate' possession, is redeemed not by an act of repentance, but by the foregrounding of a discourse which 'delegitimises' the very discourse of justice itself. Equiano is beyond repentance, and thus shame, not because he is beyond redemption but because, or so his text suggests, he places himself alternately both without and within the indeterminate, bi-polarised system of English Common Law, a discourse premised upon the basic tenets of property and dispossession, legality and illegality. Equiano's text traces the moment at which language (another system of 'laws') struggles to accommodate the concept of insurrectionary 'possession', or theft, by one who has already been possessed (or stolen): that is, the attempted negation of the female slaves' (sexual) autonomy by one whose own self-determination has been appropriated by others and who, according to the legislature, is powerless.

It is Equiano's complicity in working with slavers, together with his duplicitous appropriation of the signifiers of their culture and his efforts to imbibe their 'spirit', which redeems his transgressions and not an act of self-reproach or contrition. His pretext for being 'unable to help' the female slaves is expressed by means of the ambiguous 'linguistic' tension posed by the indeterminate and interchangeable pronouns, 'us' and 'them': 'us' – slaves/men/ slavers, 'them' – others/females/atrocities. Indeed, Equiano's justification of his submission to the pressures of cultural assimilation/ male bonding, is supported by claims alleging his conscious deferral of 'performance', a hesitancy which correlates with his displaced status: 'though with reluctance [I] was obliged'. Strategically these compact lines outline the irresolution determining Equiano's ambiguous proprietorship of choice and 'non-choice', empowerment and disempowerment. Likewise, in Montserrat, the author witnesses a scene which registers the judicial inconsistencies incurred by sexual relationships between white men and black women on the one hand, and between white women and black men on the other:

And yet in Montserrat I have seen a negro man staked to the ground, and cut most shockingly, and then his ears cut off, bit by bit, *because he had been connected with a white woman, who was a common prostitute: as if it were no crime in the whites to rob an innocent African girl of her virtue; but most heinous in a black man only to gratify a passion of nature, where the temptation was offered by one of a different colour, though the most abandoned woman of her species.*[53]

By exposing the ethical and legislative irregularities related to variants of cross-cultural contact, Equiano's text articulates the ambiguities involved within discourses of ownership and power, set within an ostensibly sexualised framework, and in so doing, further develops the important issue of cultural miscegenation raised in Stedman's and Wheatley's texts.

AQUA VITAE

Ricocheting between poles of cultural difference and cultural similitude, Equiano's *Interesting Narrative* discloses a process of cultural miscegenation and its corresponding concern with the effects of transition, translation and transculturation upon the displaced identity. During his Bible lessons with Daniel Queen on board the *Aetna*, Equiano insists on expounding the parallelisms between the ideologies of the Scriptures and the traditional mores of his native country:

I was wonderfully surprised to see the laws and rules of my country written almost exactly here [in the Bible]; a circumstance which I believe tended to impress our manners and customs more deeply on my memory.[54]

Conversely, when he arrives in Guernsey, Equiano's auto-biographical text registers a crucial moment of cultural and aesthetic difference: 'I then began to be mortified at the difference in our complexions'. It is this oscillation between discourses of perceived difference and declarations of cultural similitude which determine his narrative as a complex articulation of identity in the diaspora and as a significant paradigm of discrete insurrection:

I no longer looked upon them as spirits, but as men superior to us; and therefore I had the stronger desire to resemble them; to imbibe their spirit, and imitate their manners; I therefore embraced every occasion of improvement; and every new thing that I observed I treasured up in my memory. *I had long wished to be able to read and write.*[55]

This progression towards spiritual and personal acculturation ultimately provides the apex of his conversion narrative. It records the moment of intersection between spiritual discourse and hermeneutics, the lucrative site of political revision and reinterpretation of Biblical and legal text: 'In this deep consternation the Lord was pleased to break in upon my soul with his bright beams of heavenly light: and in an instant, as it were, removing the veil, and letting light into a dark place'.[56] Equiano's narrow escapes during expeditions to Cape Lagos in 1759 are accordingly narrated as evidence of the 'particular interposition of heaven'; instances which Equiano identifies as 'plainly' revealing the 'hand of God' and which continue the metaphors of deluge and salvation established by spiritual autobiographers such as Cowper and Newton:

Happily I escaped unhurt, though the shot and splinters flew thick about me during the whole fight . . . Every extraordinary escape, or signal deliverance . . . I looked upon to be effected by the interposition of Providence . . . I began to raise my fear from man to him [God] alone, and to call daily on his holy name with fear and reverence: and I trust he heard my supplications, and graciously condescended to answer me according to his holy word, and to implant the seeds of piety in me, even one of the meanest of his creatures.[57]

Equiano's emphasis upon the aquatic zone does not merely provide the setting for his religious initiation. It also identifies the ocean as a trope of the diaspora itself, a 'no man's land' or middle passage in which 'identity' becomes amorphous and in which epistemological boundaries and cultural ideologies are subjected to processes of instability, transition and miscegenation. As a consequence of this, Equiano comments on the otherwise prohibited interracial marriage between a white man and a free black woman which takes place at sea, redetermining it as an aqueous zone which denies/transcends the peripheries of legal and cultural prohibitions.[58] With the oceanic divide providing an appropriate backdrop for his empowering moments of spiritual illumination, Equiano prays 'anxiously to God' for his liberty. Filled with these 'thoughts of freedom', his identity hangs *'daily in suspense, particularly in the surfs'*, as he prepares himself for the demands of cultural assimilation.[59]

Equiano's baptism at St Margaret's Church, Westminster in February 1759, together with the education provided by the indulgent 'Miss Guerins', function as agents of dissolution, or rather, syntheses of cultural boundaries.[60] Accordingly, conversion to radical dissenting Protestantism establishes a fusion of western and African epistemologies. For this reason, the author's description of the English as a group of 'bad spirits' becomes a declaration of his endeavour to 'imbibe their spirit'. The centre of his 'conversion narrative', his acknowledgement of past transgressions and his 'recollections of [his] past conduct', coincide exactly with his prayers for spiritual and physical deliverance, his denunciation of the 'new slavery' practised by West Indian planters and his demands for revenge:

I therefore, with contrition of heart, acknowledged my transgression to God, and poured out my soul before him with unfeigned repentance, and with earnest supplications I besought him not to abandon me in my distress, nor cast me from his mercy for ever. . . . I rose at last from the deck with dejection and sorrow in my countenance, yet mixed with some faint hope that the *Lord would appear* for my deliverance . . . I called upon God's thunder, and his avenging power, to direct the stroke of death to me, rather than permit me to become a slave, and be sold from lord to lord.[61]

In its focus upon the progeny of interracial sexual relationships, Equiano's 'creolised' or hybrid discourse interrupts and thereby exposes the potential void or self-destructing aspect of the Caribbean's legal narrative. By locating the site occupied by the mulatto-figure, the 'sons and daughters of the French planters', Equiano identifies that point at which the rigidity of definitions distinguishing between slaves and non-slaves, subjects and objects, crumbles:

And what must be the virtue of those legislators, and the feelings of those fathers, who estimate the lives of their sons, however begotten, at no more than fifteen pounds . . . But is not the slave trade entirely a war with the heart of man? And surely that which is begun by *breaking down the barriers of virtue involves in its continuance destruction to every principle, and buries all sentiments in ruin!* ... When you make men slaves you deprive them of half their virtue, you ... compel them to live with you in a state of war ... Are you not hourly in dread of an insurrection?[62]

Equiano's text strategically identifies the paradoxical nature of the colonial legislature, most especially the contradictory aspect of the 329th Act of the Assembly of Barbados. This statute frowned upon the wilful killing of a slave 'out of wantonness, or only out of bloody-mindedness, or cruel intention' yet determined that no person whatsoever, even if it were the master's own child would be liable should a slave or negro 'unfortunately' suffer 'in life or member' as a result of his master's punishment.[63] For Equiano, this constituted a non-text which provided slave owners with absolute impunity from the law.

SALVATION?

When Equiano arrives in Philadelphia in 1766, he chances to pass a meeting house full of Quakers where he is told that the presiding preacher is George Whitefield, the spiritual leader of the Great Awakening. His account of Revd Whitefield 'exhorting the people with the greatest fervour' is, however, curiously dismissive: he describes the Reverend as 'sweating as much' as he did himself whilst a slave on Montserrat beach and declares that he is no longer at a loss to 'account for the thin congregations' to which those divines preached.[64] Concurrent with this ironisation of dissenting Protestantism, Equiano stresses the fact that it was *not* his status as a 'Christian' which had earned him the appellation 'Freeman', but his dabbling in petty trade which had paid for his freedom. Neverthe-less, the framework of the narrative insists that despite his newly obtained economic freedom, his spiritual (and indeed social) devel-opment remains incomplete. On 4 February 1767, therefore, the structural requirement of his spiritual autobiography is fulfilled as the author gives an account of his 'vision'. In this dream, which Equiano interprets as evidence of the spirit's work and as a confirmation of his own divine election, he 'sees' himself save his shipmates from shipwreck 'amidst the surfs and rocks'. In accord-ance with the dream, the remaining text describes how he survived an actual storm and, with the aid of three blacks and a Dutch Creole, was able to transfer the remaining (white) crew back to the safety of an isolated island where they remained until miraculously 'delivered'. In order to reinforce this narrative of redemption, the second volume of Equiano's *Interesting Narrative* included a plate entitled *Nancy Foundering on the Bahama Banks 1767* and cited a passage from the Book of Job which prioritised the importance of the unconscious will, the dream or vision state, and the dreamer's divine 'seal':

Thus God speaketh once, yea, twice, yet Man perceiveth it not. In a Dream, in a Vision of the Night, when deep sleep falleth upon Men, in slumberings upon the Bed: Then he openeth the Ears of Men, & sealeth their instruction. Job. Ch.33 Ver. 14, 15, 16, 29 & 30.[65]

Equiano's subsequent travels take him to England, Turkey, Portugal, Jamaica and even towards the North Pole with a Captain Phipps. During his travels, however, he claims that he remained completely oblivious to the forces occasioning his salvation, despite the symbolic 'fires' in his cabin which (in true conversion narrative-tyle) pre-empt his pending 'deliverance' from the fires of hell. Therefore, whilst Chapter 7 of the *Interesting Narrative* records the climactic point of Equiano's quest for *physical* freedom – 'I, who had been a slave in the morning, trembling at the will of another, was become my own master, and completely free' – Chapter 10 (Volume 2) ultimately serves as the structural zenith of the conversion narrative, where the author reveals his experience of 'the grace of God' and articulates his resolution to achieve the 'salvation' of his soul:

The sense of God's mercies was so great on my mind when I awoke, that my strength entirely failed me for many minutes, and I was exceedingly weak. This was the first spiritual mercy I ever was sensible of.[66]

And so Equiano, 'determined . . . to be a first-rate Christian', travels from church to church, seeking one appropriate to his calling. From the neighbouring churches of St. James, London, however, the author returns 'dissatisfied'; likewise, silent Quaker meetings leave him 'as much in the dark as ever' and as he claims, rather dramatically, he is 'not in the least edified' by the Roman Catholic services which he attends.[67] At length, he determines 'to read the Four Evangelists' and vows to join 'whatever sect or party . . . adhering thereto'. At this point, Equiano's text proceeds to give an account of his disturbingly powerful 'conviction of sin' experiences

and the 'awful visions of the night' which induce him to seek
forgiveness for his past 'follies and vile iniquities'.[68]

Following a series of meetings between himself, Granville Sharp
(the abolitionist politician) and a dissenting minister, Equiano is
eventually taken to an unnamed chapel where he witnesses several
'devotees' speaking of their experiences 'of the providence of God,
and his unspeakable mercies', and of their calling and election to
God.[69] Overcome by the prayer and singing of this 'love-feast',
Equiano undergoes a 'spiritual and temporal' resurrection. On 6
October 1774, whilst reading a description of the descent of the Holy
Spirit upon those 'uneducated, common men', the apostles, Peter
and John, contained in Act 4:12, Equiano's soul is blessed with the
Spirit's 'bright beams of heavenly light':

> I saw clearly with the eye of faith . . . the Scriptures became an unsealed
> book . . . It was given me at that time to know what it was to be born again
> . . . I was sensible of the invisible hand of God, which guided and protected
> me when in truth I knew it not . . . Now the Ethiopian was willing to be
> saved by Jesus Christ . . . Sure I was that the Spirit which indited the word
> opened my heart to receive the truth of it as it is in Jesus . . . the salvation
> of my soul . . . I rejoiced in spirit.[70]

This spiritual visitation not only endorses Equiano's narrative as an
'authentic' tale of divine deliverance, but identifies him as a literal
embodiment of the divine seal, blessed with the power of hermeneutics ('the Scriptures became an unsealed book'), a power previously
attributed to the Ibonic Ah-affoe-way-cah. This moment of divine
vision heralds the translation of the 'African' into Christian discourse
and thus inscribes the inauguration of a creolised discourse, the
discourse of the spirit as a 'gift of many tongues'.

THE SPIRIT AND THE BLACK CHURCH TRADITION

To a significant extent, Equiano's *Interesting Narrative* adheres to the
conversion narrative framework popularised by radical dissenting
Protestantism. Yet in an important departure from this, Equiano's
text presents a narrative of cultural exchange in terms of its subtle
synthesis of African belief systems with the dissenting traditions of
the western world. As a paradigm of cultural miscegenation, therefore, Equiano's 'diasporic' text demarcates a narrative of cultural
hybridity – a text propounding the synthesis of principal tenets of
dissenting Protestantism with West African epistemology. Hence his

text forms a continuum with belief systems which were transported from Africa across the middle passage to the slave plantations of the West Indies and Americas, systems which prioritised a belief in the interactions of lesser gods and ancestral spirits, spirit-possession, kinetic ecstasy and rhythmic oralcy.

Among the Yoruba people, the supreme deity is known as 'Chukwu', from 'Chi-Uku', the 'Great Spirit', whilst the lesser spirits are known as 'abosom' by the Ashanti (Ghana); 'vodun' (hence the term 'voodoo') by the Ewe speaking Fon (Ghana, Togo and Benin) of Dahomey; 'alose' by the Ibo (Nigeria) and 'orisha' by the Yoruba (coastal Nigeria).[71] These ancestral spirits and lesser gods constitute powerful forces which, it is believed, control the mechanisms of the world and intervene in the affairs of men. During initiation ceremonies, novice devotees of these cults are instructed in the rites of the gods and exposed to the secret languages of the spiritual gods. Likewise, established devotees may become the mediums and mouthpieces to ancestral spirits as they experience a phenomenon known as 'spirit possession'. During this time, the identities of the devotees are annihilated or rather 'suspended' as they experience trance-like states of ecstasy or emotional excess.

Composed of some half a million slaves, the French colony of St Domingue constituted the largest and most productive slave colony of the Caribbean during the late eighteenth century. Reciprocated by the process expounded within Equiano's text, the colony provided an appropriate model of the cultural hybridity which emerged as a consequence of the transportation of West African slaves to the Catholic colony, and the resultant fusion of Western Christianity and West African beliefs. The subsequent emergence of the folk religion voodoo hence prescribed a process of religious miscegenation which maintained an emphasis upon the 'spirit world' and oralcy. Accordingly, the 'revelations' inspired by spiritual-ancestors during dreams or voodoo possession rituals functioned to maintain cultural memories of upheaval, slavery and transportation within the African diaspora.[72]

In his systematic analysis of the oral tradition within the African diaspora, Michel Laguerre identified the spirit-inspired songs of voodoo rituals as indicative repositories of preserved fragments of African culture. The words contained within these songs recorded the transportation of African languages across the middle passage and divulged the process by which the slaves created new languages amidst forces of linguistic and cultural dispossession. Furthermore, these songs constituted part of a sacred oral tradition inspired by African ancestral spirits and momentarily recollected by voodoo devotees.[73] As such, they demonstrate the complex process of metamorphosis and syncretism of African belief systems within the diaspora. As an example of this, the voodoo orientation song 'Sin Moiz de zo papa rele loa io pou moin /Sin Moiz de zo papa rele sanble loa io pou moin' ('St Moses, you who live under the sea/ Papa, call upon the spirits for us') redetermined Moses, the Hebrew prophet who led the Israelites out of Egypt, as the messenger called upon by the congregation to gather the spirits into the temple, in order that the ceremony may begin.[74] Likewise, Equiano's text constitutes an embryonic prototype of the cultural hybridity cap- tured by these analogous songs and reciprocated in the development of black church traditions in the diaspora, such as the Revival and Pocomania in Jamaica, the Spiritual Baptists and Shouters in Trinidad and the Black Methodists in the American colonies.[75]

In their emphasis on the emotionally ecstatic initiation rites of the (Holy) 'Spirit', these sects continued the fluid, protean and 'flexible oral stylisations of language' which had characterised radical dis- senting Protestantism.[76] Furthermore, in their application of anti- phonality (call-and-response), polyrhythms, syncopation and repetition, the slaves' spirituals, sermons and songs continued a prioritisation of the spoken word over the written word, the protean power of oral over written culture. Therefore, whereas Philip Quaque's efforts to advance 'Christianity' in its purely western form had ultimately failed, Equiano's text testifies to the success of the *hybrid* syncretic paradigm. In its notable reflection of the fusion between African and Western spiritual discourse and their corre- sponding dynamics of ecstatic bodily behaviour (the passionate physicality of 'spirituality'), Equiano's text presents an endeavour to heal the scars of 'natal alienation', the traumatic experience of unprecedented sociohistorical upheaval.[77] It functions unambigu- ously as both an autobiographical and cultural narrative in which the 'Word of the Spirit' figures as the intermediary mode of discourse between the Word of God, the Christian narrative, and the epistemological cultures of Africa. Moreover, it is precisely this discourse of the 'spirit' which Equiano advances in opposition to the Word of the Law, that constitutional narrative which defined slaves as property (possessions) rather than as subjects (possessors).

Equiano's own spiritual 'conversion' is more or less completed by his account of his attempts (as in Marrant's text) to 'convert' the Musquito Indians on the Dupeupy shore. But this episode, although it occurs near to the end of the *Interesting Narrative*, is not unproblematic; it betrays a necessity to endorse the cultural alterity of another racial type, i.e. Indian rather than African. Therefore, it appears to authenticate a degree of religious expansionism not unlike that displayed by early colonisers, who attributed the superiority of the written word as a power over and beyond the belief systems of the indigenous inhabitants:

> Recollecting a passage I had read in the life of Columbus, when he was amongst the Indians in Mexico or Peru, where on some occasion, he frightened them, by telling them of certain events in the heavens, I had recourse to the same expedient; and it succeeded beyond my most sanguine expectations. When I had formed determination, I went in the midst of them; and, taking hold of the Governor, I pointed up to the heavens . . . I told them God lived there, and that he was angry with them . . . and if they did not leave off [quarrelling] and go away quietly, *I would take the book (pointing to the Bible), read, and tell God to make them dead. This operated on them like magic.*[78]

This incident takes place during Equiano's accompaniment of the 'celebrated Dr Irving' on his extensive travels. At this time, Equiano participates in the selection and purchase of slaves from his own tribe – 'I chose them all of my own countrymen' – in order to establish and cultivate a plantation.[79] The above quotation demonstrates not an innocent desire to convert the Musquito Indians to Christianity but a complex struggle between 'colonised' cultural ideologies. Equiano's attempts to convert these Indian princes to the doctrines of Christianity, are however, undermined by his account of this episode: the 'good seeds' which he sows are rejected at the same rate as he endeavours to 'transplant' them. As a consequence, this chapter describing the '*non*-conversion' of the Indians and his purchase of slaves remains tantalisingly incomplete and prescribes an alternate framework by which Equiano's own conversion narrative may be read.

Equiano's description of the dignified customs and social mores of the Musquito Indians establishes a correlation between this ancient civilisation and his own Ibo culture. In so doing, Equiano's text partakes in a radical alienation of (or even rejection of) Christian ideology. Hence at the very moment at which cultural assimilation achieved by conversion seems most paramount, the very principles of that assimilation are subtly undermined: 'I am sorry to say that there was not one white person in our dwelling . . . that was better or more pious than those unenlightened Indians'.[80] Accordingly, Equiano's *Interesting Narrative* threatens to disrupt the mechanisms of cultural and religious assimilation by exposing their interdependence upon colonial and racist ideology. In other words, his text skilfully discloses the relationship between narratives of cultural/colonial power and language/discourse itself. Consequently, the Bishop of London's refusal to appoint Equiano as a missionary to Africa is attributed to 'some certain scruple of delicacy', a linguistic silence or void which represents the moment at which the inherent correlation between *discourse* and *power* appears to defy words and inhabit a linguistic blindspot.

In fact, by the close of the *Interesting Narrative*, the conversion motif has, to all intents and purposes, been abandoned. In its stead, the reader is presented with a declaration of political activism strategically founded upon the principles of religious dissent. Equiano's text concludes with an exposé of the abuses committed by the Government in its efforts to cleanse London of its black poor by sending them to Sierra Leone:

[The] government were not the only objects of speculation; these poor people suffered infinitely more; their accommodations were most wretched; many of them wanted beds, and many more cloathing and other necessaries . . . Worn out by treatment, perhaps not the most mild, and wasted by sickness, brought on by want of medicine, cloaths, bedding &c. they reached Sierra Leone just at the commencement of the rains. At that season of the year it is impossible to cultivate the lands; their provisions therefore were exhausted before they could derive any benefit from agriculture; and it is not surprising that many, especially the lascars . . . should be so wasted by their confinement as not long to survive it.[81]

Ultimately therefore, in its revision of the 'spiritual' autobiographical framework, Equiano's voice coalesces with that of radical dissent through its unorthodox prioritisation of heterogeneous concepts of 'truth' and election: 'Sure I was that the Spirit which indited the word opened my heart to receive the truth of it as it is in Jesus – that the same Spirit enabled me . . . to believe to [sic] the salvation of my soul'.[82] This paradigm of spiritual illumination inscribes the intrinsic power of *interpretation* as both a critique and challenge to the 'law' of the written and the unspoken word.

Accordingly, the 'revelation' which Equiano receives is not merely a matter of spiritual illumination; it functions as a strategic revelation of the hitherto invisible discourses of power and as an endorsement of his own blessed self-identification as one who, though 'persecuted', now speaks in the political/legislative arena, self-empowered, 'with the spirit'.

The engraving of Equiano reading the passage from Isaiah ('Behold, God is my salvation: I will trust, and not be afraid: for the Lord Jehovah is my strength and my song; he is also my salvation' (12:2.4)) confirms the author's unhesitating critique of the dominant order. This struggle is premised upon a significant investment in the power of both the oral and written 'spiritual' word. As suggested by his petition (on behalf of his brethren) to the Queen, dated 21 March 1788, Equiano initiates an overt penetration of the parliamentary sphere in his request for political salvation: 'I supplicate your Majesty's compassion for millions of my African countrymen, who groan under the lash of tyranny in the West Indies'.[83] The spiritual pilgrimage delineated by Equiano's *Interesting Narrative* concludes, therefore, with a plea to those 'who are possessed of his *spirit*', to disperse that 'auspicious era of expansive freedom' upon black identities in the diaspora:

May the time come . . . when the sable people shall gratefully commemorate the auspicious era of extensive freedom . . . May the blessings of the Lord be upon the heads of all those who commiserated the cases of the oppressed negroes . . . If a system of commerce was established in Africa, the demand for manufactures would most rapidly augment, as the native inhabitants will insensibly adopt the British fashions, manners, customs, &c. *In proportion to the civilisation, so will be the consumption of British manufactures . . . A commercial intercourse with Africa opens an inexhaustible source of wealth to the manufacturing interests of Great Britain, and to all which the slave trade is an objection.*[84]

This concluding religious bribe strategically refuses to close with a paradigm of marriage or ordination, as presented in the slave narratives discussed above. Rather, it proposes a socioeconomic solution which situates the 'British senators' as future advocates of commercial enterprise based in Africa and, by inference, as the spiritually enlightened dismantlers of the slave trade, the 'dispensers of light, liberty, and science'.

A pivotal text in the development of the slave narratives, Equiano's *Interesting Narrative* brings to the fore the bicultural tactics contained within the slave narratives discussed above. This progression ensures that Equiano's text represents an important translation of cultural identity into the framework established by radical dissenting Protestants, prophets and Romantics alike and consequently remains a vital expression of identity in the black diaspora. As a development of the process of 'cultural miscegenation' suggested by Wheatley's work, Equiano's text firmly establishes a crucial synthesis of principal tenets of radical dissent with significant elements of African epistemology. His *Interesting Narrative* hence exposes the mercurial dynamics of possession/dispossession and offers a subtle critique of the relationship between power and the mechanisms of discourse itself. Thus Equiano's text describes the diasporic identity's strategic penetration of the political legislature, an interaction which is radically intensified within the works by the 'mulatto offspring', Robert Wedderburn.

CHAPTER NINE

Robert Wedderburn and mulatto discourse

> But there comes a time, as it came in my life, when a man is
> denied the right to live a normal life, when he can only live the
> life of an outlaw because the government has so decreed to use
> the law to impose a state of outlawry on him.[1]

> Now I have scarcely a drop of black blood left in me, my blood
> having so faded with the blood of a Minister, that I am
> [becoming] as white as a Mulatto.[2]

Whereas Equiano's narrative of spiritual redemption presents a
relatively circumspect demand for political reformation, the accentuation of subversive and millenarian elements of radical dissenting
Protestantism provide an overtly militant and confrontational platform for the black British author and rebel, Robert Wedderburn.[3]
Born in Jamaica around 1761, Wedderburn was the 'mulatto'
offspring of the wealthy Scottish sugar plantation owner, James
Wedderburn and his female slave, Rosanna. Separated from his
rebellious mother as an infant and never acknowledged by his white
father, the near-illiterate Robert was adopted and reared by his
African-born maternal grandmother, the Kingston obeah and smug-
gler, 'Talkee Amy', under whose charge his own prophetic and
oratory powers were developed. As slave plantation societies of the
West Indies endeavoured to maintain remnants of distinctly African
modes of belief, Talkee's position as plantation obeah confirmed her
role as transmitter of preslavery epistemologies. She was revered by
slaves and indeed, by some of their owners, as a chief communicant
with ancestral 'spirits'.[4]

At the age of eleven, Wedderburn witnessed the public flogging of
Talkee allegedly for 'witchcraft' by a young boy she had reared
herself:

My grandmother's new master being a believer in the doctrine of
Witchcraft, conceived that my grandmother had bewitched the vessel

[captured by Spaniards], out of revenge for her not being liberated also. To punish her, therefore, he tied up the poor old woman of seventy years, and flogged her to the degree, that she would have died, but for the interference of a neighbour.[5]

Six years later, in 1778, having served as a fighting seaman in the Royal Navy aboard *HMS Polyphemus* and later as a privateer, Wedderburn arrived in England, aged seventeen.[6] There, he drifted around St Giles as one of the 'London Blackbirds', a community of runaway slaves and immigrants who earned their living as musicians, entertainers, beggars and thieves, until he obtained work as a tailor. According to his semi-autobiographical text, *The Horrors of Slavery: Exemplified in the Life and History of the Revd Robert Wedderburn* (1824), in 1786 Wedderburn underwent what he claims was a profoundly spiritual experience upon hearing the words of a passionate Wesleyan preacher. Having read Thomas Paine's *Rights of Man* (1791), Wedderburn went on to become a licensed Unitarian preacher. The first English Unitarian congregation had been founded seventeen years earlier by Theophilus Lindsey (1723–1808) who, having rejected the Anglican Church's creed restrictions, had established the Essex Street Chapel in London in 1774. These Unitarians practised a system of Christian belief which advocated the unipersonality of God and rejected both the divinity of Christ and the doctrine of the Trinity. Famous Unitarians included Joseph Priestley (1773–1804), the English chemist, political theorist and outstanding Unitarian leader who advocated scriptural rationalism, materialist determinism and humanitarian Christology; Samuel Taylor Coleridge, the poet; and Richard Price (1723–1791), who in 1789 delivered his notorious heretical speech, *A Discourse on the Love of Our Country* at the annual Revolution Society Meeting.

Wedderburn's first publication, a theological tract entitled, *Truth, Self-Supported; Or, A Refutation of Certain Doctrinal Errors, Generally Adopted in the Christian Church* (1790) displayed a complex synthesis of Methodism's principles of redemption and sanctification with elements of West Indian and African culture. His choice of epigraph confirmed his legacy as both a transmitter of (sociopolitical) truths and a creolised voice of radical transformation in the diaspora:

God hath chosen the foolish things of the world, to confound the wise; and God hath chosen the weak things of the world, to confound the things that are mighty; and base things of the world, and things which are despised hath God chosen, &c. 1 Corinthians 1:27–8[7]

Written in the third person rather than the first person characteristic of conversion narratives, Wedderburn's text carefully established a structural framework of spiritual salvation, but with a particular accentuation upon the author's own deliverance from the power of the *law* (the written word of legislation), his empowerment by the *spirit* and the liberty of prophetic oralcy:

Confident that God had *sealed* him unto the day of redemption, not only sealed, but *removed him* by his power from a legal state of mind, into a state of Gospel liberty, that is to say, a deliverance from the power of authority of the law, considering himself not to be under the power of the law.[8]

Given the ambiguous position of slaves in England during the late eighteenth century under English (colonial and local) law, Wedder-burn's claims for self-exclusion from the 'authority of the law' under the aegis of spiritual 'grace' should not be underestimated. William Blackstone's ambitious codification of England's legal constitution, a source of national pride, had been directly encouraged by Lord Mansfield, the Chief Justice. On its publication in 1765, Blackstone's *Commentaries on the Laws of England* was immediately recognised as a lucid and authoritative account of English legislation and govern-ment. Of the social rights enjoyed by the 'free-born Englishman', Blackstone had unhesitatingly declared:

And this spirit of liberty is so implanted in our constitution, and rooted even in our very soil, that a slave or a negro, the moment he lands in England falls under the protection of the laws and becomes *eo instanto* a freeman.[9]

Two years later, having been reminded of the Lord Chancellor's reassurance (formerly the General Attorney, Sir Philip Yorke) to West Indian planters that '*neither baptism nor legislation* could destroy servitude absolutely', Blackstone's unequivocal declaration of English liberty had become one of uncertainty and ambiguity by the time the 1767 edition was printed: 'A slave or negro, the moment he lands in England, falls under the protection of the laws, and so far becomes a freeman; though the master's right to his service may probably still continue'.[10] In spite of this, Blackstone persisted in his attempt to overturn pro-slavery ideologies on the basis that they destroyed the 'very principles upon which all sales are founded'. Yet his systematic and philosophical analysis of the principles of trans-action failed to resolve the dichotomy existing between his own textual consolidation of English legislation and the inconsistencies of a social order in which property, acquired neither by purchase, reciprocity nor original title, continued to be recognised.[11]

Granville Sharp's first pamphlet, *A Representation of the Injustice and Dangerous Tendency of Tolerating Slavery; or Of Admitting the Least Claim of Private Property in the Persons of Men, in England* (London, 1769) argued that slavery, since it depended upon a definition of a person as a possession, was incompatible with English liberty. But it was Granville's involvement in the judicial test case of *James Somerset* (1771–1772) under the adjudication of the Chief Justice, Lord Mansfield, which seemed to confirm once and for all England's legal position regarding slave status at a time when several thousand slaves resided in the metropolis. Somerset had refused to return with his owners and during the trial, he received considerable support from a coalition of fellow blacks and radical artisans, together with free legal aid from barristers. On the other hand, his master received support from self-interested West Indian planters. Initially Lord Mansfield, reluctant to deprive slave owners in Britain of their rights as masters, attempted to postpone this test case several times. However, his final decision of 1772 prohibited the involuntary deportations of slaves by their masters from England:

The state of slavery is of such a nature, that *it is incapable of being introduced on any reasons, moral or political; but only [by] positive law,* which preserves its force long after the reasons, occasion, and time itself from whence it was created, is erased from memory: It is so odious, that nothing can be suffered to support it, but positive law. Whatever inconveniences, therefore, may follow from a decision, I cannot say this case is allowed or approved by the law of England; and therefore the black must be discharged.[12]

Although Mansfield ruled against the deportation of slaves back to the colonies, it did not follow that, on arrival in England, slaves by virtue of English law were deemed autonomous emancipated individuals. It was, however, interpreted as such, and indeed in 1778 the Scottish legislature ruled that no slaveholding rights whatsoever could be upheld within Scotland's borders.

By the time Wedderburn had composed his *Truth, Self-Supported* in 1790, the 'repatriation' Committee for the Relief of the Black Poor (1786) had been in operation for almost four years and Sharp's *Regulation for the New Settlement in Sierra Leone* (1786) had been in circulation for the same amount of time. By 1791, one year after the publication of Wedderburn's tract, slaves had rebelled in the dramatic uprising in St Domingue, the Abolition Bill had been defeated in Parliament and, following the declaration of war between England and France in April 1792, emancipatory demands for slaves were postponed. Although Wedderburn had had no direct experience of slavery, his *Truth, Self-Supported* traced a movement of linguistic and social rebellion by one who considered himself situated on the periphery of a society founded upon principles of binary opposition. For Iain McCalman, Wedderburn's narrative poses a 'crude but sincere attempt to steer an independent course between [the] various doctrinal snags and shoals' of Arminianism, Calvinism and Unitarianism.[13] Yet although Wedderburn's narrative does outline an advancement of radical individualism and nonconformist principles, the route which it follows depends not merely upon a refutation of various theological doctrines, but upon an articulation of cultural ideologies preserved by slave societies in the diaspora.

By situating the journey of his 'desire to become a Christian' alongside his seven year period of transgression 'amongst a set of abandoned reprobates', and his subsequent efforts to abandon 'the road to everlasting ruin', Wedderburn's narrative, in line with that of Equiano, extends the Methodist paradigm of individualism to its furthermost cultural and anarchic extreme. In so doing, Wedderburn's text develops a sustained refutation of established ideological dictates, including that of the legislature by the individual under 'spiritual' inspiration.[14] His interpretation of words by the Wesleyan preacher whom he overhears on passing the Seven Dials in Covent Garden, therefore, functions as a paradigm for the *liberty of grace* (indemnity) prescribed by the suffusion and 'incarnation' of the Holy Spirit:

[The] Mediator through whom and by whom, the Father performs all his Will, by his own Influence or Essence which is called the Spirit . . . *[This] gift of the Spirit is called righteousness* . . . so doth the Spirit *purify and abundantly fill* the soul of the penitent sinner.[15]

Truth, Self-Supported consolidates and imparts an effective paradigm of its author as a prototype of diasporic identity located upon the peripheries of discourse itself, a 'state of Gospel Liberty' situated beyond the authority of the established Church *and* the law. His use of the 'discourse of the spirit' posits a radical *rejection* of the established tenets of the church and society and promotes instead an affirmation of the discourse of the 'self':

If you enquire of a minister of the church of Rome, he is not allowed to think or speak, but as the Pope dictates, and if you should go to the Pope himself, he must of necessity tell you, that, the doctrine of the Trinity is a truth, because it was first broached by the Church of Rome, which pretends to be an infallible Church, and therefore cannot err; so that according to their sentiments, all that do not believe in their tenets must be damned; *therefore you see the necessity of calling upon God for yourselves* . . . Instead of the performances required from us under the Law. . . believing in Jesus Christ, as the Messiah sent of God, and receiving the grace sent by HIM, is *the only work that God requires of every man.*[16]

As a 'mulatto' son with extremely tenuous legal and social rights, the author's affinity with dissenting Protestantism corresponded to his fervent dedication to a series of social and political demands: indeed, conversion to such unorthodoxy depended upon a verbal testimony of desired amelioration – 'for there is salvation in no other'.[17] Wedderburn's 'conversion' encapsulates a significant moment in the development of his religious and political heterodoxy. His appropriation of the discourse of the spirit not only provides him with spiritual indemnity but identifies him with the 'son' of Jehovah, whose 'possession' of the spirit represents a manifestation of power:

The Holy Spirit spoken of in Scripture, is not a Being possessing personality as a Jehovah, but an *Influence of Jehovah*, which is possessed by the Son without measure. By the purpose and good-will of the Father, the Spirit qualifies and possesses Jesus Christ with the ability of God.[18]

Wedderburn's proclaimed adherence to radical dissenting Protestantism's faith in the power of the 'spirit' is also endorsed by his citation of a selection of hymns towards the end of his text, including one by Isaac Watts and another by John Wesley.[19] It is possible that the tonal simplicity of the hymns evoked an impression of the sound of 'negro' spirituals and worksongs reverberating in the plantations. But almost certainly, Methodism's continuum of the African belief in the spirit-world, combined with its obvious antislavery agenda, strategically influenced Wedderburn's claims for 'sanctification' and spiritual indemnity and informed his emphasis upon his *own* powers of exegesis and prophecy, over and beyond those of both the established church and the 'laws' of society. Wedderburn's attestations of 'divine inspiration' and the protection given him by the divine seal thus participate in a paradigm of 'creolised' subversive demands, professing deliverance from the law and 'spiritual immunity' from the perils of sedition and political reformation.

'ACKNOWLEDGE NO KING . . . ACKNOWLEDGE NO PRIEST'[20]

By 1813, Wedderburn had become an ardent follower of Thomas Spence, the leader of an informal political underground, whose doctrines had prophesied an earthly millennium based upon a radical redistribution of land.[21] In 1817, Wedderburn published the first edition of his prophetic *The Axe Laid to the Root, or A Fatal Blow to Oppressors; Being An Address to the Planters and Negroes of the Island of Jamaica* (1817), a text which demanded 'in the name of God, in the name of natural justice and in the name of humanity that all slaves be set free'.[22] Indeed, *The Axe Laid to the Root* advanced claims for land reformation on the plantocratic islands of the West Indies according to Spence's directive and denounced concepts of English liberty as *myths* expounded by priests, kings and lords. Wedderburn's text initially propounds a Spencean vision of *peaceful* sociopolitical transformation by the dissemination of Spencean literature amongst free mulattos –

Oh, ye oppressed, use no violence to your oppressors, convince the world you are rational beings, follow not the example of St Domingo, let not your jubilee, which will take place, be stained with the blood of your oppressors, leave revengeful practices for European kings and ministers.[23]

This contrasts however, with the author's demands for violent slave insurrections, following the model prescribed by the (in)famous St Domingue uprising:

Jamaica will be in the hands of the blacks within twenty years. Prepare for flight, ye planters, for the fate of St Domingo awaits you . . . They [the Maroons] will be victorious in their flight, slaying all before them . . . *Their method of fighting is to be found in the scriptures, which they are now learning to read.* They will slay man, woman, and child, and not spare the virgin, whose interest is connected with slavery, whether black, white, or tawny . . . *My heart glows with revenge, and cannot forgive.*[24]

Wedderburn's call for the emancipation of slaves under the guise of divine guidance ('Wedderburn demands in the name of God . . . that all slaves be set free') and his vehement denunciation of the established church as a tyrannical oppressor, are haunted by his memory of the public flogging of his aged grandmother. For this reason, he portrays himself as a Christ-like but militantly radical saviour who must reject and disobey his earthly father (the Scottish

James Wedderburn), in order to inherit the kingdom destined to be
his: 'Repent ye christians . . . Oh! my father, what do you deserve at
my hands? Your crimes will be visited upon your legitimate offspring
. . . *A black king is capable of wickedness, as well as a white one!*'[25] In
subsequent volumes of his *Axe Laid to the Root*, Wedderburn continued
his antinomian address to the slaves of Jamaica, supplementing it
with drastic calls for a violent transformation of the sociopolitical
sphere and advocating the need for the preservation of cultural
identity within the diaspora:

Dear Countrymen, It is necessary for you to know how you may govern
yourselves without a king, without lords, dukes, earls, or the like; these are
classes of distinction which tend only to afflict society. I would have you
know, with all the proud boasting of Europeans they are yet ignorant of
what political liberty is . . . *Have no white delegate in your assembly . . . Let every
individual learn the art of war, yea, even the females, for they are capable of displaying
courage . . . Teach your children these lines [from the Desponding Negro], let them be
sung on the Sabbath day, in remembrance of your former sufferings, which will show you
what you may expect from the hands of European Christians, by what they have practised
before.*[26]

In the fourth edition of *The Axe Laid to the Root* (1817), Wedderburn
incorporated a letter to a Miss Campbell, the heiress to a sugar
plantation whom he claimed had been censured by the assembly of
Jamaica for freeing her slaves and distributing her land along
Spencean lines. By inferring that this 'Miss Campbell' was a
descendant of an earlier miscegenetic relationship and more daringly, that she and the author shared the same mother, Wedderburn's
text endorsed the paradigm of the mulatto as a radical agent of
socioeconomic transformation premised upon apocalyptic stature:

Dear Miss Campbell . . . I come not to make peace; my fury shall be felt by
princes, bidding defiance to pride and prejudice. Truth is my arrow stained
with Africans' blood, rendered poisonous by guilt, while they hold my
innocent fellow as a slave . . . Fast bound by eternal truth, I have hold of
the God of Israel, like a Jacob, and will not let him go. *I will be made a prince
by prevailing, though a halter be about my neck.* Jacob, I will excell you in
proportion to the present improved state of society. Miss Campbell, though
a goddess, I have a command for thee to obey: like the Christians of old,
you have fallen from the purity of the Maroons, your original.[27]

In 1819 Wedderburn opened a tavern chapel on the corner of
Hopkins Street in Soho, London. In this chapel, which he registered
as a Unitarian meeting house for a sect which he later described as

'Christian Diabolists' or 'Devil Worshippers', up to 300 people converged to listen to his potent mixture of religious zeal and popular radicalism, permeated by scriptural symbolism, prophetic rhetoric and personalised testimonies of his 'sleeping visions'.[28] In what we can assume was a unique interplay between performer and audience during his 'farcical theological debates' with the dwarf shoemaker Samuel Waddington, Wedderburn fused theatrical dia-tribe with anti-clerical blasphemy: he urged his audience to do all that was in their power to overthrow the establishment, even persuading them to participate in dawn drills on Primrose Hill and to tear up iron palisades for use as weapons.[29]

Wedderburn's discourse enigmatically converges with that of the poet and mystic William Blake, whose 'Marriage of Heaven and Hell' (*c.* 1790–3), a 'diabolic' response to Swedenborg, prescribed the 'Voice of the Devil' and the 'Proverbs of Hell' as part of an onslaught against self-righteous members of society and orthodox Christian piety. Blake's account of the ancient poets' receptivity to the gods of nature corresponded closely to the 'animism' of African cults, whilst his text, 'All Religions Are One' (*c.* 1788) stipulated the prime importance of the spirit of prophecy in *all* religions:

The ancient Poets animated all sensible objects with Gods or Geniuses, calling them by the names and adorning them with the properties of woods, rivers, mountains, lakes, cities, nations, and whatever their enlarged & numerous senses could perceive . . . The Religions of all Nations are derived from each Nations different reception of the Poetic Genius which is every where call'd the Spirit of Prophecy . . . The true Man is the source [of all Religions], he being the Poetic Genius.[30]

The emphasis laid by dissenting Protestantism upon the inspira-tional role of song, and upon images of rebirth and transformation, made easy transference to the prophetic belief systems prevalent among West Indians and Africans. However, Wedderburn's radical individualism stretched these elements to extreme limits.[31] In 1820, Wedderburn was tried for blasphemy, a trial in which he represented himself, claiming that even if a barrister were to plead his cause gratuitously, 'he would not dare to do it upon principle'. In the written script which formed his defence, and which the author had intended to be read by the preacher and pornographer George Cannon (alias Erasmus Perkins), Wedderburn ridiculed the inter-relationship between 'the state religion', the enforcement of the 'law of the land', and the former's enforcement at the expense of 'other opinions or laws'. Wedderburn claimed that the established religion propagated such archaic laws and enactments that if they were 'now resorted to, [they] would be instantly erased from the statute-book as absurd, or inhuman, and totally inconsistent with the enlightenment of the present day'.[32]

In the same manner as Phillis Wheatley's 'evangelical' schema, Wedderburn conflated tenets of spiritual illumination with demands for the emancipation of the human mind from 'tyrannical and intolerant laws of darkness, ignorance and the trammels of super- stition':

Therefore I trust that you will not suffer yourselves to be ensnared by that sophistical mode of reasoning which makes me guilty of a crime, merely, because I have offended against opinions or laws originating in times still more bigotted and superstitious than the present. – You will be told that, because christianity, or what *they* choose to call christianity, is a part of the law of the land, or in other words '*the state religion*', that those whose opinions differ materially from it, must necessarily be punished if they circulate those opinions.[33]

Moreover, as with the slave confessional narratives discussed above, Wedderburn promotes his oral defence as a *testimony* to the nature of *truth*, a concept which he identified with freedom of religious opinion and liberty of speech. Wedderburn therefore regarded his trial as part of his mission to expose the 'untruths' of legal and theological discourse:

There is no one who will deny the value and importance of truth, but how is it to be ascertained, if we are not allowed the liberty of free inquiry? Does not Paul tell us to '*prove all things, and to hold fast the best*;' but how are we to be determined in our choice, if we are not allowed to canvas and discuss the merits or demerits of particular systems? . . . I cannot but blush at the weakness and bad policy of those who seek to support their cause by the persecution of an humble individual like myself, when the clergymen of the established church of England alone are 20,000, and their wages amount to two millions annually: in addition to these, there are 50,000 dissenting ministers of different denominations.[34]

In his attempts to identify his own struggles with those of Christ ('He was like myself, one of the lower order, and a genuine radical reformer'), Wedderburn endorses a strategic disassociation of 'genuine Christianity' from the 'state religion' and posits a 're-vision' of Christ as an egalitarian 'who despised the rich for the hardness of their hearts': 'What did he [Jesus Christ] say, "*acknowledge no king.*"

He was a reformer . . . acknowledge no lord . . . acknowledge no rabbi, (no priest:) no! he knew their tricks, and says, *stand it no longer*.[35] Wedderburn's spirited defence (which included statements such as 'if, on the contrary, the spirit of bigotry and religious persecution prevails over you, I shall have this satisfaction, that I suffer like Christ' and 'I shall be far happier in the dungeon to which you may consign me, than my persecutors, on their beds of down') ended with an outrageously ironic 'plea' to (or rather ridicule of) the jury.[36] Not surprisingly, his defence was rejected; Wedderburn was convicted of using 'blasphemous and profane words' and of impiously reviling that book of 'great antiquity' which, it was professed, determined not only the religion of England, but of 'all the civilised and enlightened nations'. The judges severely reprimanded Wedderburn's refusal to repent and consequently denounced his propagation of linguistic and theological deviance as pure 'licentiousness', before proceeding to pass sentence:

It is our duty then to remove you, at least for a time, from society, that you may be prevented doing it a further injury by the dissemination of your dangerous doctrine. The Court do therefore sentence you to be imprisoned for two years in his majesty's jail at Dorchester.[37]

Wedderburn's (albeit temporary) removal from society (by means of his imprisonment) reflected the serious extent to which the court feared the influential disruption that his 'dangerous doctrine' might cause. As such, Wedderburn's text registers a significant departure from the cultural acquiescence suggested by the slave narratives discussed above.

'CAN I CONTAIN MYSELF AT THIS?': WEDDERBURN'S *HORRORS OF SLAVERY*[38]

Seven years after the fourth edition of *Axe Laid to the Root*, Wedderburn published a small pamphlet entitled, *The Horrors of Slavery: Exemplified in the Life and History of the Revd Robert Wedderburn* (1824), dedicated to William Wilberforce. As the subtitle, 'Robert Wedderburn (late Prisoner in his Majesty's Gaol at Dorchester, for Conscience-sake), Son of the Late James Wedderburn, Esq. of Inveresk, Slave Dealer, by One of his Slaves in the Island of Jamaica' explained, Wedderburn had narrowly escaped the more serious charge of high treason. The opening lines of Wedderburn's text suggest a narrative delineating an aged man's humble recollection of past transgressions:

I am now upwards of sixty years of age, and therefore I cannot long expect to be numbered amongst the living. But, before I pass from this vale of tears, I deem it an act of justice to myself, to my children, and to the memory of my mother, to say what I am, and who were the authors of my existence.[39]

However, what follows is an intense declaration of individual freedom, hinged upon Wedderburn's denunciation of his paternal ancestry and promotion of his maternal cultural heritage: 'To shew the world . . . the inhumanity of a MAN, whom I am compelled to call by the name of FATHER. I am the offspring of a slave, it is true; but I am a man of free thought and opinion'.[40] In a letter to the editor of *Bell's Life in London* of February 1824, Wedderburn identified himself as the progeny of the miscegenetic and deplorable actions of the late James Wedderburn, whom he claimed, had 'FORCED' his mother to submit to him 'THOUGH HE KNEW SHE DISLIKED HIM!'[41] The subsequent reply (similarly published in *Bell's Life*) by the author's brother (who had changed his name to A. Colville) dismissed Wedderburn's claims of kinship: 'I have to state, that the person calling himself Robert Wedderburn is NOT a son of the late Mr James Wedderburn, of Inveresk, who never had any child by, or any connection *of that kind* with the mother of that man'.[42]

    As part of this endeavour to reclaim his past, Wedderburn attempts to 'reconstruct' and 'de-stigmatise' his mother, Rosanna (whose memory he claimed had been reviled by his white half-brother, A. Colville), and to align his own (rebellious) nature with hers, even to the extent of endorsing her attempted infanticide:

A younger and more fortunate brother of mine, the aforesaid A. Colville, Esq. has had the insolence to revile her memory in the most abusive language, and to stigmatise her for that which was owing to the deep and dark iniquity of my father . . . I have not the least doubt but that from her rebellious and violent temper during that period, that I have inherited the same disposition – the same desire to see justice overtake the oppressors of my country-men – and the same determination to lose [sic] no stone unturned, to accomplish so desirable an object.[43]

Wedderburn's disenfranchisement had been aggravated by letters to the press which had refuted his claims for inheritance and had sullied his mother's reputation. In a letter to the editor of *Bell's Life in London* it was insinuated that Wedderburn's mother 'was delivered of a mulatto child' and because '*she could not tell who was the father*,' her master, in a foolish joke, named the child Wedderburn'.[44] Consequently, Wedderburn's *Horrors of Slavery* endeavours to reestablish his mother's virtue and integrity; furthermore, it interweaves within the dominant network a fabric articulating the proud and rebellious nature of his mixed ancestral and cultural identity, inherited from his African mother and grandmother, and his white grandfather:

My grandfather was a staunch Jacobite . . . When I first came to England, in the year 1779, I remember seeing the remains of a rebel's skull which had been affixed over Temple Bar; but I never yet could fully ascertain whether it was my dear grandfather's skull, or not.[45]

The text's dedication to William Wilberforce ('Your name stands high in the list of glorious benefactors of the human race; and the slaves of the earth look upon you as a tower of strength') appears to inaugurate an abolitionist polemic in honour of Wilberforce. However, the literary autobiography which follows presents the author as an 'oppressed, insulted and degraded African', whose censure of his paternal father entailed a denunciation of colonialist ideology and of the English legislature.[46] Although ostensibly an autobiographical text, Wedderburn's *Horrors of Slavery* locates addressees other than the 'self' and envisages his audience as including members of the English public, representatives of the powerful propertied class (including the Duke of Queensbury and Lady Douglas) and the legislature, the House of Lords. Wedderburn's 'narrative' therefore not only functions as a striking exposé of a delicate site of taboo (the disclosure of his own sexual genesis) but also as a significant disclosure of the dynamics of miscegenation amongst his audience, the aristocracy and their colonial counterparts, the West Indian planters:

It is a common practice . . . for the planters to have lewd intercourse with their female slaves; and so inhuman are many of these said planters, that many well-authenticated instances are known, of their selling their slaves while pregnant, and making that a pretence to enhance their value.[47]

Wedderburn personalised his account of miscegenation by citing details of the licentious and interracial conduct of his father, whose behaviour is encapsulated by the metaphorical title of 'male-midwife'. According to Wedderburn, as soon as his father became rich, 'he gave loose to his carnal appetites, and indulged himself without moderation . . . [in] libidinous excess'. In so doing, he became 'a perfect parish bull [stud]' whose sexual pleasure was the greater since it simultaneously 'increased his profits' and whose house (or harem) was filled with female slaves, such as his mother. Amongst these 'objects of his lust', he strutted 'like Solomon in his grand seraglio', or rather, 'like a bantam cock upon his own dunghill', and his slaves 'did increase and multiply, like Jacob's kine'.[48]

Interestingly, Wedderburn's narrative wavers between an endeavour to denounce his paternal lineage and to fulfil the paradigm of the mulatto identity by reinstating his birthrights from *both* branches of his parentage. On the one hand, therefore, his text presents an effort to valorise his African legacy and redeem the name of the mother whom his 'father' had 'made the object of his brutal lust' and on the other, it presents a narrative of dispossession in terms of his (dis)inheritance of the Wedderburn estate:

My father's name was JAMES WEDDERBURN, Esq. of Inveresk, in Scotland, an extensive proprietor, of sugar estates in Jamaica, which are now in the possession of a younger brother of mine, by name, A. COLVILLE, Esq. of No. 35, Leadenhall Street . . . From him [my father] I have received no benefit in the world.[49]

Hence Wedderburn's *Horrors of Slavery* can be read not merely as a vilification of slave ideology but as a developed vindication of African cultural legacy. His work registers a further stage of the miscegenetic authenticity and cultural hybridity contained in the works by Wheatley and Equiano. As such, its 'creolised' discourse of fluidity, heterogeneity, movement and change demarcated an illuminating revision of established (static) concepts of power, possession and identity.

Robert's 'brother' changed his name to Colville in order to secure his rights of inheritance on his mother's side; likewise his father changed his name to Wedderburn-Colville. Indeed, a close analysis of Wedderburn's text reveals it to be a narrative saturated with terms of proprietorship – of objects and subjects, slaves and women – and of interrupted inheritance: 'estates . . . now in the possession of a younger brother of mine'; 'my father was restored to his father's property'; 'they [female slaves] being his personal property'; '[he] determined to have possession of her'; 'from the time my mother became the property of my father'; and 'she [my mother] was the property of Lady Douglas'. Wedderburn's claims for 'rightful inheritance', however, are not unproblematic, especially when one considers that his father James Wedderburn had made his fortune as a result of his status as an 'extensive proprietor of sugar [slave] estates in Jamaica', and more dubiously, as a result of his acts of self-reproduction by means of his 'rape' of female slaves, Wedderburn's own mother.

Wedderburn's tract draws loosely upon the genre of abolitionist redemption autobiography established by members of London's black literati, such as Cugoano and Equiano, yet its author could not claim to have suffered directly the 'horrors' implied by the title of his pamphlet. Rather, the 'horrors' he locates are those of cultural disenfranchisement, material dispossession and sociopolitical inequality. The narrative of persecution which follows, therefore, details his continued sufferings and injustices beyond the temporal boundaries of plantocratic societies. Whilst his narrative bears comparison with former autobiographies of evangelical conversion and spiritual illumination, it is hinged essentially upon a paradigm of intervention, exposed and manifested by the product of cultural miscegenation – the mulatto figure itself.

Wedderburn's efforts to ridicule government during entertaining public debates invoking provocative calls for his flock of 'Christian Diabolists' or 'Devil Worshippers' to do all that was in their power to overthrow established authority, undoubtedly unsettled the latter, who, as McCalman records, employed spies in order to keep him under strict surveillance. Even from prison, Wedderburn continued his resolute, radical refutation of cultural orthodoxy, evidenced by his tract, *Cast-Iron Parsons: Or 'Hints to the Public and the Legislature, on Political Economy, Clearly Proving the Clergy Can be Entirely Dispensed With, Without Injury to the Christian Religion, or the Established Church, and to the Great Advantage of the State'*:

State Prison, Dorchester, July 28th, 1820:
My Dear Friend, You will naturally suppose that my solitary hours are much occupied with my favourite *hobby*, THEOLOGY; but a subject has at times engaged my attention, which is equally connected with political economy as with religion . . . I shall now give a slight sketch of the operative part of my scheme, which is as follows: – That the legislature pass an act . . . that the order of persons called Clergy, or Priests, Deacons, Curates, Rectors, Vicars &c. of the Establishment, be totally annihilated, suppressed, and abolished. That every parish shall, immediately after that time, purchase one of the *Cast-Iron Parsons*.[50]

Consequently, Wedderburn's texts and speeches registered a radical challenge to the established authority of England's political legislature and a significant departure from the more subtle 'creolised' strategies contained within the earlier slave narratives.

Wedderburn's last known and most curious tract, 'The Holy Liturgy: Or Divine Science, upon the Principle of Pure Christian Diabolism, Most Strictly Founded upon the Sacred Scriptures', was published before his death at the age of seventy-two (one year before the abolition of slavery in the West Indies) and was partially reproduced on 21 March, 1828 by his fellow inmate, Richard Carlisle, in his journal *The Lion*. Here Wedderburn displayed the same radical demands and parodic anti-establishment critiques which had typified his dynamic performances in his Christian diabolist Chapel in Hopkins Street:

Startle not, gentle Christian reader, at the name DIABOLICAL CHRISTIANS; but carefully *as thou valuest thine Eternal Salvation*, examine the Scriptural principle of this new sect, and say, if they are not justified, by all that is held sacred, in Christian Revelation, and by the most seriously disposed Christians. *It is not a profane hand, it is not the hand of the reviler, that passeth over this page: but the hand of a most sincere Christian* . . . OUR PRAYERS SHALL BE ALL MOST PROPERLY ADDRESSED TO THE *MAJESTY OF HELL*, to the 'GOD OF THIS WORLD', to that IMPERFECT, that OMNIMALEVOLENT, though POWERFUL BEING, *THE DEVIL*. This it is, that will justify our assumed appellation of CHRISTIAN DIABOLISTS . . . THE GOD OF HELL and 'OF THIS WORLD' partakes *in part* of our character and imperfections, and is, consequently. . . a *Being to be feared, to be worshipped, to be cajoled with prayer*.[51]

In an enigmatic, if not disquieting way, the obsessiveness of Wedderburn's 'creolised' antinomian rhetoric elucidated, in no ambiguous terms, the psychological effects that the traumatic processes of sexual violence, cultural disturbance, dispossession, denial of rights and displacement had upon the African (now diasporic) slaves. Whereas the Romantics had displayed varying degrees of affinity with abolitionist and political radicalism, yet had stayed, on the whole, within the confines of the law, Wedderburn took such radicalism to a site of 'illegitimate' anarchy. In his hands, the bicultural tactics presented within the earlier narratives by slaves such as Wheatley and Equiano, reached a volatile climax in terms of his radical negation of church/state authority and his demands for ownership and 'cultural' insurrection. Hence Wedderburn's determined struggle for recognition and justice anticipated the concern over citizenship and civil rights which continued to pre-occupy blacks on both sides of the Atlantic. As his text completed the translation of the discourse of the spirit into the discourse of legislative power, his endeavour to extend the concepts of individual autonomy and divine election in terms of his political demands took the example established by dissenting Protestantism to a heterodox-ical extreme. Accordingly, his work exceeded and, in a sense, exacerbated, the parameters of spiritual discourse contained within the earlier slave narratives and established a conscious fulfilment of the more discrete demands for miscegenetic authenticity and cul-tural hybridity. The 'diabolic' enterprise of Wedderburn's work thereby endorsed the paradigm of 'creolised' dynamics, not merely as a reflection of the fusion of elements of dissenting Protestantism with fundamental elements of African belief systems, but as narra-tives of movement, fluidity and heterogeneity characteristic of identity configuration in the black diaspora. As I hope to have demonstrated, this process coincided with the development of hybrid linguistics (such as creole and patois) and the evolution of cross-cultural epistemologies, hinged upon the dynamics of miscegenation during the late eighteenth century. Articulated within the auto-biographical works by Wedderburn, Equiano, Phillis Wheatley and others, the diasporic identity emerged as a self-conscious trope of cultural hybridity, premised simultaneously upon both the assimila-tion and chiasmus of the dominant social and literary order. Such a process was, by its very nature, hinged upon a narrative of incessant movement, of persistent 'translation' and of indeterminate and ceaseless transformation. Most importantly, the conscious expression of this integral process of fluidity and metamorphosis provided a radical challenge to established concepts of culture and race. In its continuous assimilation of and divergence from diverse cultural epistemologies and hermeneutical schemas, the paradigm of identity in the diaspora provided an appropriate framework for the dynamics of discourse itself.

Notes

INTRODUCTION

1 Letter from Lord Sydney to the Lord Commissioners, 7 December 1786, *Parliamentary Papers* (1789) vol. 89; Nigel File and Chris Power, *Black Settlers in Britain 1555–1958* (1981; repr. Hampshire: Heinemann Educational Press, 1990) 26.

2 Parliamentary Committee on Convict Transportation, 1786. For a more detailed discussion of the colony of Sierra Leone see Christopher Fyfe, *A History of Sierra Leone* (1962; Hampshire: Gregg Revivals, 1993); Joan Anim-Addo, *Sugar Spices and Human Cargo: An Early Black History of Greenwich* (Greenwich: Leisure Services, 1996); Lamin Sanneh, *West African Christianity: Its Religious Impact* (London: George Allen and Unwin, 1983).

3 Proclamation 1786; Letter from Lord Sydney to the Lord Commissioners, 7 December 1786, *Parliamentary Papers*, (1789) vol. 89.

4 Minutes of the Committee for the Black Poor, 9 and 24 October 1786.

5 *The Public Advertiser*, 3 January 1787.

6 Moira Ferguson, *Subject to Others: British Women Writers and Colonial Slavery, 1670–1834* (London: Routledge, 1992) 118.

7 *Ibid.*, 199.

8 A. F. Walls, *The Mission of the Church and the Propagation of the Faith* (Cambridge: Cambridge University Press, 1970) 107–29; Stiv Jakobsson, *Am I Not a Man and a Brother? British Missionaries and the Abolition of the Slave Trade and Slavery in West Africa and the West Indies 1786–1838* (Lund: Gleerup, 1972) 68–9.

9 Ottobah Cugoano, *Thoughts and Sentiments on the Evil and Wicked Traffic of the Slavery and Commerce of the Human Species Humbly Submitted to the Inhabitants of Great Britain* (London, 1787).

10 *The Public Advertiser*, 4 April 1787.

11 See Fyfe, *A History of Sierra Leone*; Paul Edwards and David Dabydeen *Black Writers in Britain, 1760–1890* (1991; Edinburgh: Edinburgh University Press, 1994) 83–98, 87.

12 Mary Louise Pratt, *Imperial Eyes: Travel Writing and Transculturation* (London: Routledge, 1992).

13 This point responds to Richard Wright's request that we attempt to discover such a relation between the two worlds. Richard Wright, *African Philosophy: An Introduction*, 3rd edn. (Lanham, M.D.: University of Toledo, 1984) 26–7.

14 V. Y. Mudimbe, *Tales of Faith: Religion as Political Performance in Central Africa* (London: Athlone Press, 1997).

15 Paul Gilroy, *The Black Atlantic: Modernity and Double Consciousness* (London: Verso, 1993) 4, 12.

16 15 Stuart Hall, 'Cultural Identity and Diaspora', *Identity: Community, Culture, Difference*, ed. Jonathan Rutherford (London: Lawrence and Wishart, 1990) 222–37.

17 Jim Clifford, 'Diasporas', *Cultural Anthropology* 9 (1994): 302–38; Lawrence Grossberg, 'Identity and Cultural Studies – Is That All There Is?', *Questions of Cultural Identity*, ed. Stuart Hall and Paul du Gay (London: Sage, 1996) 92.

18 Homi K. Bhabha, 'The Third Space: Interview with Homi K. Bhabha', *Identity: Community, Culture, Difference*, ed. Jonathan Rutherford, 221.

19 *Ibid.*, 221; see also James Clifford, *The Predicament of Culture, Twentieth-Century Ethnography, Literature, and Art* (Cambridge, Mass.: Harvard University Press, 1988) 1–17.

20 Raman Selden and Peter Widdowson, *A Reader's Guide to Contemporary Literary Theory* (1985; Brighton: Harvester Wheatsheaf, 1993) 127–51; Michel Foucault, *The Archaeology of Knowledge*, trans. Alan Sheridan (London: Tavistock Publications, 1972); Diane Macdonell, *Theories of Discourse: An Introduction* (Oxford: Blackwell, 1986) 1. See also Sara Mills, *Discourses of Difference: An Analysis of Women's Travel Writing and Colonialism* (London: Routledge, 1993) for an interesting study of feminist discourse theory analysis in relation to British women writers of the late nineteenth century.

21 Paul de Man, *Allegories of Reading: Figural Language in Rousseau, Nietzsche, Rilke, and Proust* (New Haven: Yale University Press, 1979); Hall and du Gay, *Questions of Cultural Identity*, 4.

22 Emile Benveniste, *Problems in General Linguistics*, trans. Mary Meek (Coral Gables: University of Miami Press, 1971) 224–5.

23 Paul Gilroy, *'There Ain't No Black in the Union Jack': The Cultural Politics of Race and Nation* (London: Hutchinson, 1987); *Small Acts: Thoughts on the Politics of Black Cultures* (London: Serpent's Tail, 1993); Robert Young, *White Mythologies: Writing History and the West* (London: Routledge, 1990); Carl Plasa and Betty Ring, eds, *The Discourse of Slavery: Aphra Behn to Toni Morrison* (London: Routledge, 1994); Edwards and Dabydeen, eds, *Black Writers in Britain, 1760–1890*; Peter Fryer, *Staying Power: The History of Black People in Britain* (London: Pluto Press, 1984); Keith Sandiford, *Measuring the Moment: Strategies of Protest in Eighteenth-Century Afro-English Writing* (Selinsgrove: Susquehanna Press, 1988); William Andrews, *Sisters of the Spirit: Three Black Women's Autobiographies of the Nineteenth Century*

(Bloomington: Indiana University Press, 1986); *idem, To Tell a Free Story: The First Century of Afro-American Autobiography, 1760–1865* (Urbana: Illinois University Press, 1986); Houston Baker, *Blues, Ideology and Afro-American Literature: A Vernacular Theory* (Chicago: Chicago University Press, 1984); Henry Louis Gates, *The Signifying Monkey: A Theory of African-American Literary Criticism* (New York: Oxford University Press, 1988).

24 John A. Holm, *Pidgin and Creoles*, 2 vols. (Cambridge University Press, 1988) vol. i, 6.

25 Kwame Anthony Appiah, *In My Father's House: Africa in the Philosophy of Culture* (London: Methuen, 1992). I am grateful to Alan Richardson for recommending this text to me.

26 Wright, *African Philosophy: An Introduction*, 35, 43; Henri Maurier, 'Do we Have an African Philosophy?', *African Philosophy* 25–40, 35.

27 Richard Onwuanibe, 'The Human Person and Immortality in Ibo (African) Metaphysics', *African Philosophy* 183–97, 189.

28 Dennis Porter, '*Orientalism* and its Problems', *The Politics of Theory: Proceedings of the Essex Conference on the Sociology of Literature, July 1982*, ed. Francis Barker, Peter Hulme, Margaret Iversen and Diana Loxley (Colchester: University of Essex, 1983) 181. Edward Said, *Orientalism: Western Representations of the Orient* (London: Routledge and Kegan Paul, 1978).

1 THE ENGLISH SLAVE TRADE AND ABOLITIONISM

1 Charles MacInnes, *England and Slavery* (Bristol: Arrowsmith, 1934) 18; Peter Fryer, *Staying Power: The History of Black People in Britain* (London: Pluto, 1984) 8. For further discussion see James Walvin, *Black Ivory: A History of British Slavery* (London: Harper Collins, 1992); Eric Williams, *Capitalism and Slavery* (1945; London: Andre Deutsch, 1964); Anthony Tibbles, ed., *Transatlantic Slavery: Against Human Dignity* (Liverpool: National Museums and Galleries on Merseyside, 1994).

2 Jamaica was seized from Spain in 1655. See David Richardson, 'The Rise of the Atlantic Empires', *Transatlantic Slavery: Against Human Dignity*, ed. Anthony Tibbles, 22.

3 See Philip Curtin, *The Atlantic Slave Trade: A Census* (Madison: Wisconsin University Press, 1969) 122–3, 128–30.

4 Robin Blackburn, *The Overthrow of Colonial Slavery, 1776–1848* (London: Verso, 1990) 5. In his book Blackburn argues that slavery was not overthrown purely for economic reasons but because it became politically untenable. Blackburn also suggests that the progress of abolition depended upon black intervention, upon slave resistance and upon the black 'Jacobin' breakthrough in the 1790s – that is, that without the black contribution to antislavery feeling, the challenge to colonial slavery could not possibly have triumphed. See also Williams, *Capitalism and Slavery*.

5 Blackburn, *Overthrow*, 12–13.
6 Norman McCullough, *The Negro in English Literature: A Critical Introduction* (Ilfracombe: Arthur H. Stockwell, 1962) 55.
7 B.W. Higman, *Slave Populations of the British Caribbean, 1807–1834* (Baltimore: Johns Hopkins University Press, 1984) 72; *idem, Slave Population and Economy in Jamaica, 1807–1834* (Kingston: The University of the West Indies Press, 1995) 15.
8 Elsa Goveia, *Slave Society in the British Leeward Islands at the End of the Eighteenth Century* (New Haven: Yale University Press, 1965) 152.
9 William Blackstone, *Commentaries on the Laws of England in Four Books*, 8th edn., 4 vols. (Oxford, 1779) vol. i, 424. See also David Brion Davis, *The Problem of Slavery in the Age of Revolution, 1770–1823* (Ithaca: Cornell University Press, 1975).
10 For an excellent discussion of British antislavery and emancipation see Howard Temperley, *British Antislavery, 1833–1870* (London: Longman, 1972).
11 Michael Craton, James Walvin and David Wright, eds, *Slavery, Abolition and Emancipation: Black Slaves and the British Empire* (London: Longman, 1972) 170; cited in Moira Ferguson, *Subject to Others: British Women Writers and Colonial Slavery, 1670–1834* (London: Routledge, 1992) 116–17.
12 Edward Long, *Candid Reflections upon the Judgement Lately Awarded by the Court of the King's Bench in Westminster-Hall, on What is Commonly Called 'the Negroe Cause' by a Planter* (London, 1772) iii.
13 *Ibid.*, 24, 4, 39.
14 *The London Chronicle*, 13–16 March 1773; cited in Nigel File and Chris Power, eds, *Black Settlers in Britain, 1555–1958* (1981; repr. Hampshire: Heinemann Educational Press, 1990) 23.
15 Aristotle, *Aristotle's Ethics and Politics Comprising His Practical Philosophy*, ed. John Gillies, 2 vols. (London, 1797) vol. ii, 27. See Sandiford, *Measuring the Moment: Strategies of Protest in Eighteenth-Century Afro-English Writing* (Selinsgrove: Susquehanna Press, 1988) for an excellent discussion of the intellectual milieu surrounding the abolitionist debate.
16 Aristotle, *Ethics*, vol. ii, 29.
17 John Locke, 'Essay Concerning the True Original, Extent, and End of Civil Government', *Two Treatises of Government: In the Former, the False Principles, and Foundation of Sir Robert Filmer, and His Followers, Are Detected and Overthrown. The Latter is an Essay Concerning the True Original, Extent, and End of Civil Government* (London, 1690) 220.
18 *Ibid.*, 220.
19 *Ibid.*, 1.
20 *Ibid.*, 242.
21 *Ibid.*, 242.
22 David Brion Davis, *The Problem of Slavery in Western Culture* (Ithaca: Cornell University Press, 1966) 118.
23 Charles Louis Montesquieu, *De l'espirit des lois*, ed. Anne Cohler, Basia

Miller and Harold Stone (Cambridge University Press, 1989). See also Montesquieu, *The Spirit of Laws*, trans. T. Nugent, 2 vols. (London, 1750); *The Spirit of Laws*, ed. David Wallace Carrithers (Berkeley: University of California Press, 1977) 18–23. Carrithers notes the irony of the fact that it took a Frenchman to explain the British constitution to the British. So authorative was Montesquieu's account, that it was amplified by Blackstone in his *Commentaries on the Laws of England* (1765–1769).

24 Montesquieu, *The Spirit of Laws* (London, 1750) vol. i, 337, 336.

25 *Ibid.*, vol. i, 348, 339.

26 Act 38, Clause 40, *Acts of Assembly, Passed in the Island of Jamaica; from 1681, to 1754, Inclusive* (London, 1756) 63: 'No Slave shall be free by becoming a Christian'.

27 John Atkins, *A Voyage to Guinea, Brasil, and the West Indies; in His Majesty's Ships, the Swallow and Weymouth. Describing the Several Islands and Settlements, the Colour, Diet, Languages, Habits, Manners, Customs and Religions of the Respective Natives, and Inhabitants. With Remarks on the Gold, Ivory, and Slave Trade; and on the Winds, Tides and Currents of the Several Coasts* (London, 1735); Francis Hutcheson, *A System of Moral Philosophy in Three Books*, 2 vols. (Glasgow, 1755); Sir Hans Sloane, *A Voyage to the Islands Madera, Barbados, Nieves, S. Christophers and Jamaica with the Natural History of the Herbs and Trees, Four-footed Beasts, Fishes, Birds, Insects, Reptiles &c. of those Islands: To Which is Prefix'd an Introduction, wherein Is an Account of the Inhabitants, Air, Waters, Diseases, Trade &c. of that Place*, 2 vols. (London, 1707): 'The *Negros* are usually thought to be haters of their own Children, and therefore 'tis believed that they sell and dispose of them to Strangers for Money, but this is not true . . . The Punishments for Crimes of Slaves, are usually for Rebellions burning them, by nailing them down on the ground, and then applying the Fire by degrees from the Feet and Hands, burning them gradually up to the Head, whereby their pains are extravagant. For Crimes of a lesser nature Gelding, or chopping off half of the Foot with an Axe. These Punishments are suffered by them with great Constancy (vol. i, lvi-lvii).'

28 Hutcheson, *System*, vol. i, xvi, 1.

29 *Ibid.*, vol. i, 299.

30 *Ibid.*, vol. i, 293.

31 *Ibid.*, vol. i, 300–1.

32 *Ibid.*, vol. i, 300.

33 George Wallace, *A System of the Principles of the Law of Scotland* (Edinburgh, 1760) 89–90.

34 *Ibid.*, 91.

35 *Ibid.*, 96.

36 Antony Benezet, *A Short Account of That Part of Africa Inhabited by Negroes* (Philadelphia, 1762); Michel Adanson, *A Voyage to Senegal, the Isle of Goree and the River Gambia*, trans. Jean de Fouchy (London, 1759); William

Bosman, *A New and Accurate Description of the Coast of Guinea, Divided into the Gold, the Slave, and the Ivory Coasts. Containing a Geographical, Political and Natural History of the Kingdoms and Countries: With a Particular Account of the Rise, Progress and Present Condition of All the European Settlements upon that Coast; and the Just Measures for Improving the Several Branches of the Guinea Trade* (London, 1705); William Smith, *A New Voyage to Guinea* (London, 1744).

37 Antony Benezet, *Some Historical Account of Guinea, its Situation, Produce and the General Disposition of its Inhabitants. With an Inquiry into the Rise and Progress of the Slave Trade, its Nature and Lamentable Effects. Also a Republication of the Sentiments of Several Authors of Note on This Interesting Subject; Particularly an Extract of a Treatise by G. Sharp* (Philadelphia, 1771) i.

38 Benezet, *Some Historical Account*, 94–5.

39 *Ibid.*, iii.

40 Antony Benezet, *A Caution and Warning to Great Britain and Her Colonies, in a Short Representation of the Calamitous State of the Enslaved Negroes in the British Dominions* (Philadelphia, 1766) 4–5, 23.

41 Benezet, *A Caution and Warning*, 4, 97.

42 Guillaume Thomas Raynal, *A Philosophical and Political History of the Settlements and Trade of the Europeans in the East and West Indies*, trans. J. Justamond, 5 vols. (London, 1776) vol. iii, 422.

43 *Ibid.*, vol. iii, 510.

44 *Ibid.*, vol. iii, 506.

45 Blackburn, *Overthrow of Colonial Slavery*, 55.

46 Adam Smith, *An Inquiry into the Nature and Causes of the Wealth of Nations*, 2 vols. (London, 1776) vol. ii, 587.

47 John Millar, *The Origin of the Distinction of Ranks* (1771; London, 1779) 347.

48 *Ibid.*, 349.

49 James Beattie, *An Essay on the Nature and Immutability of Truth, in Opposition to Sophistry and Scepticism*, 2nd edn. (Edinburgh, 1771); see Sandiford 47–9. David Hume, *A Treatise of Human Nature: Being an Attempt to Introduce the Experimental Method of Reasoning into Moral Subjects*, 3 vols. (London, 1739) and *The Philosophical Works of David Hume*, 4 vols. (Edinburgh: Adam and William Tait, 1826).

50 Beattie, *An Essay on the Nature and Immutability of Truth*, 507, 506, 508. Two decades after this publication, Beattie, in his *Elements of Moral Science* (1790; Edinburgh, 1793) presented an argument against slavery on humanitarian rather than rationalistic grounds.

51 Beattie, *An Essay on the Nature and Immutability of Truth*, 509, 512.

52 David Bebbington, *Evangelicism in Modern Britain: A History from the 1730s to the 1980s* (London: Unwin Hyman, 1989).

53 *Ibid.*, 20; Mark Noll, David Bebbington and George Rawlyk, *Evangelicalism: Comparative Studies of Popular Protestantism in North America, the British Isles, and Beyond, 1700–1990* (Oxford: Oxford University Press, 1994) 6.

54 *Encyclopaedia of Religion*, ed. Mircea Eliade, 20 vols. (London: Macmillan, 1987) vol. v, 32–6, 370.

55 Harry Richardson, *Dark Salvation: The Story of Methodism as it Developed Among Blacks in America* (New York: Anchor Press, 1976) 9.

56 Robert Southey, *The Life of Wesley and the Rise and Progress of Methodism* (London: Warne, 1889) 476.

57 John Wesley, *The Works of John Wesley*, ed. Albert Outler, 5 vols. (Nashville: Abingdon Press, 1984) vol. i, 5. John Wesley's 'strange warming' of the heart on 24 May 1738 signalled the birth of Evangelical Methodism whilst the conversion of William Grimshaw in 1742 and the appointment of William Romaine as lecturer at St. Dunstan's, London, in 1748, marked the birth of Evangelical Anglicanism.

58 It was a style that was to strategically influence the Preface accompanying the second edition of Wordsworth's and Coleridge's collection of *Lyrical Ballads, with a Few Other Poems*, published in London 1800.

59 Wesley, Preface to 'Sermons on Several Occasions' (1746), *Works*, vol. i, 104–6.

60 George Fox, *A Journal, or an Historical Account of the Life, Travels, Sufferings, Christian Experience and Labour of Love in the Ministry of George Fox* (London, 1694); John Woolman, *A Journal of the Life, Gospel Labours and Christian Experience of that Faithful Minister of Jesus Christ, John Woolman, to Which are Added his Works* (Dublin, 1776); William Penn, *No Cross, No Crown: Or Several Sober Reasons against Hat-Honour, Titular Respects, Yon to a Single Person, with the Apparel and Recreations of the Times* (London, 1669); Robert Barclay, *An Apology for the True Christian Divinity, As the Same Is Held Forth by the Quakers* (Aberdeen, 1678).

61 John Woolman, *Some Considerations on the Keeping of Negroes* (1754; Northampton: Gehenna Press, 1970) 13, 84.

62 John Woolman, *A Journal*, 3.

63 *Ibid.*, 19, 43.

64 Anthony Benezet, *The Case of Our Fellow-Creatures, the Oppressed Africans, Respectfully Recommended to the Serious Consideration of the Legislature of Great Britain, by the People Call'd Quakers* (London, 1784) 3.

65 *Ibid.*, 7.

66 Blackburn, *Overthrow of Colonial Slavery*, 137.

67 *Encyclopaedia of Religion*, vol. xv, 200–1.

68 Logie Barrow, *Independent Spirits: Spiritualism and English Plebians, 1850–1960* (London: Routledge and Kegan Paul, 1986) 4.

69 Joseph Wood, *Thoughts on the Slavery of the Negroes* (London, 1786); The London Meeting for Suffering, *The Cause of Our Fellow Creatures the Oppressed Africans* (London, 1784). See Temperley, *British Antislavery*, 2.

70 Granville Sharp, *A Representation of the Injustice and Dangerous Tendency of Admitting the Least Claim of Private Property in the Persons of Man, in England* (London, 1769); idem, *The Just Limitation in the Laws of God, Compared with the Unbounded Claims of the African Traders and British American Slaveholders* (London, 1776); idem, *The Law of Retribution; Or, a Serious Warning to Great Britain and Her Colonies, Founded on Unquestionable Examples of God's*

Temporal Vengeance against Tyrants, Slaveholders and Oppressors (London, 1776).

71 Sandiford, *Measuring the Moment*, 57; Davis 213–54.

72 Thomas Clarkson, *An Essay on Slavery and the Commerce of the Human Species, Particularly the African. Translated from a Latin Dissertation, Which Was Honoured with the First Prize in the University of Cambridge for the Year 1785, with Additions* (London, 1789); idem, *An Essay on the Impolicy of the African Slave Trade in Two Parts*, 2 vols. (London, 1788).

73 Clarkson, *An Essay on the Impolicy*, 3, 81–2.

74 Blackburn, *Overthrow of Colonial Slavery*, 169–76.

75 Philip Doddridge, *The Rise and Progress of Religion in the Soul: Illustrated in a Course of Serious and Practical Addresses* (London, 1745) 1–2.

76 Ernest Marshall Howse, *The Saints in Politics: The 'Clapham Sect' and the Growth of Freedom* (1953; London: Allen and Unwin, 1971) 35.

77 Dissenters included Congregationalists, Baptists and Presbyterians. See Brantley, *Wordsworth's 'Natural Methodism'*, 5; see also F. C. Gill, *The Romantic Movement and Methodism* (London: Epworth Press, 1937) and Thomas Boswell Shepherd, *Methodism and the Literature of the Eighteenth Century* (London: Epworth Press, 1940).

78 *Encyclopaedia of Religion*, vol. xv, 370–1.

79 William Hazlitt, 'On the Causes of Methodism' (1817), *The Complete Works of William Hazlitt*, ed. P. P. Howe, 21 vols. (London: J. M. Dent, 1930–4) vol. iv, 57–61; 58, 60.

80 *Ibid.*, 61, 58.

81 See Bernard Semmel, *The Methodist Revolution* (London: Heinemann, 1974); Eliade vol. ix, 493–5.

82 John Wesley, *The New Birth: A Sermon on John 3.7* (London, 1784) 1.

83 *Ibid.*, 5–6.

84 Davis 386–7; Harold Lindstrom, *Wesley and Sanctification: A Study in the Doctrine of Salvation* (London: Epworth Press, 1950); John Henry Overton, *The Evangelical Revival in the Eighteenth Century*, ed. M. Creighton (1886; London: Longmans, 1898).

85 Richard Brantley, *Wordsworth's Natural Methodism* (New Haven: Yale University Press, 1975) 6.

86 John Wesley, *Advice to the People Call'd Methodists* (London, 1745) 3–4.

87 John Wesley, *The Character of a Methodist* (1743; London, 1745) 17–18.

88 *Ibid.*, 4–5

89 Arnold Rattenbury, 'Methodism and the Tatterdemalions', *Popular Culture and Class Conflict, 1590–1914: Explorations in the History of Labour and Leisure*, ed. Eileen and Stephen Yeo (Brighton: Harvester Press, 1981) 28–61.

90 Sandiford, *Measuring the Moment*, 53.

91 John Wesley, *Thoughts Upon Slavery*, 3rd edn. (London, 1774) 28.

92 *Ibid.*, 17–18.

93 *Ibid.*, 16.

94 *Ibid.*, 20, 27.

95 William Wilberforce, *A Letter on the Abolition of the Slave Trade to the Freeholders and Other Inhabitants of Yorkshire* (London: Hansard, 1807) 345, 350–1.

96 Blackburn, *Overthrow of Colonial Slavery*, 101.

97 George Whitefield, *A Short Account of God's Dealings with the Reverend Mr George Whitefield from His Infancy, to the Time of His Entring into Holy Orders. Written by Himself* (London, 1740) 11, 49, 69.

98 George Whitefield, 'Letter to the Inhabitants of Virginia, Maryland, North and South Carolina, Concerning Their Negroes', *Three Letters from the Reverend George Whitefield* (London, 1740) 5–11, 6.

99 Edmund Gibson, *A Short Preservative Against the Doctrines Rev'd by Mr Whitefield and His Adherents* (London, 1739); Tristam Land, *A Letter to the Revd Mr Whitefield Designed to Correct His Mistaken Account of Regeneration, or the New Birth. Written Before His Departure from London and Now Published to Prevent His Doing Mischief Among the Common People, upon His Return from Georgia* (London, 1739).

100 Whitefield, 'Letter to the Inhabitants', 8, 10.

101 Temperley, *British Antislavery*, 7.

102 Thomas Clarkson, *The History of the Rise, Progress, and Accomplishment of the Abolition of the African Slave Trade by the British Parliament*, 2 vols. (London: Longman, Rees and Orme, 1808) vol. i, 286–7; my emphasis.

103 William Wilberforce, *Appeal to the Religion, Justice and Humanity of the Inhabitants of the British Empire in Behalf of the Negro Slaves in the West Indies* (London: J. Hatchard, 1823) 1.

104 Henry William Martin, Sir, *A Counter-Appeal in Answer to 'An Appeal' from William Wilberforce* (London: J. Rivington, 1823) 2.

105 Mrs Maddocks, *The Female Missionary Advocate, A Poem* (London: J. Holdsworth, 1827) 23–4.

106 Matth. 28: 18–20.

107 Urs Bitterli, *Cultures in Conflict: Encounters Between European and Non-European Cultures, 1492–1800* (Cambridge: Polity Press, 1989) 5, 7–8.

108 Paul Edwards and David Dabydeen, eds, *Black Writers in Britain, 1760–1890* (1991; Edinburgh: Edinburgh University Press, 1994) 83.

109 Henry Smeathman, *The Substance of a Plan of a Settlement to Be Made Near Sierra Leona, on the Grain Coast of Africa* (London, 1786).

110 Philip D. Curtin, *The Image of Africa: British Ideas and Action, 1780–1890* (London: Macmillan, 1965) 15–17. In 1788, Banks founded the exploratory 'Association for Promoting the Discovery of the Interior Parts of Africa' (known as the 'African Association'), the ostensible purpose of which was to collect African geographical, ethnographical and botanical data.

111 Smeathman, *Substance of a Plan*, title page, 24. See also Johnson Asiegbu, *Slavery and the Politics of Liberation* (London: Longman, 1969) 1–34, 160–3.

112 Smeathman, *Substance of a Plan*, 160, 162.
113 Clarkson, *History of the Slave Trade*, vol. ii, 342
114 Asiegbu 5.
115 Clarkson, *History of the Slave Trade*, vol. ii, 585–6; my emphasis.
116 Asiegbu, *Slavery and the Politics*, 11.
117 See Ferguson, *Subject to Others*, 199.
118 A. F. Walls, *The Mission of the Church and the Propagation of the Faith* (Cambridge: Cambridge University Press, 1970) 107–29; Stiv Jakobsson, *Am I Not a Man and a Brother? British Missionaries and the Abolition of the Slave Trade and Slavery in West Africa and the West Indies 1786–1838* (Lund: Gleerup, 1972) 68–9.
119 Anna Maria Falconbridge, *Narrative of Two Voyages to the River Sierra Leone, During the Years 1791, 1792, 1793* (1794; London: L. I. Highman, 1802) 125, 134–5. Alexander Falconbridge, *An Account of the Slave Trade on the Coast of Africa* (London, 1788). For a further discussion of Maria Falconbridge's text, see Ferguson, *Subject to Others*, 200–8.
120 Ferguson, *Subject to Others*, 198.
121 *Ibid.*, 199; Rana Kabbani, *Europe's Myth of Orient, Devise and Rule* (London: Macmillan, 1986) 6.
122 Ferguson, *Subject to Others*, 238–9; my emphasis.
123 Howse, *Saints in Politics*, 73–6.
124 Philip Curtin, *The Image of Africa: British Ideas and Action, 1780–1890* (London: Macmillan, 1965) 262–3; Curtin notes there was an exception to this educational system: interest of a group of Quakers in ethnology and linguistics informed a plan of *phased* acculturation which began with elementary instruction in African languages alone and later advanced into education in English.
125 *Parliamentary Debates*, vol. xxvi, 827–73, 831–72; cited in Howse, *Saints in Politics*, 88.
126 William Fox, *A Brief History of the Wesleyan Missions on the Western Coast of Africa: Including Biographical Sketches of All the Missionaries Who Have Died in that Important Field of Labour. With Some Account of the European Settlements and of the Slave Trade* (London: Aylott and Jones, 1851) v.
127 Fox, *A Brief History*, 5.
128 William Fox, *The Western Coast of Africa, Suggestions on the Best Means of Exterminating the Slave Trade and Some Accounts of the Success of the Gospel and of the Present State and Prospects of the Wesleyan Missions on that Coast* (London: Aylott and Jones, 1851) 101, 87; my emphasis.
129 Thomas Coke, *A History of the West Indies, Containing the Natural Civil and Ecclesiastical History of Each Islands; with an Account of the Missions Instituted in those Islands, from the Commencement of their Civilisation*, 3 vols. (Liverpool: Nuttall, Fisher and Dixon, 1808–1811) vol. i, 20–1; my emphasis. In 1842, the best five texts submitted for an interdominational competition on missionary theory were published, including John Harris, *The Great Commission: Or, the Christian Church*

Constituted and Charged to Convey the Gospel to the World (London: Thomas Ward, 1842) and Baptist Wriothesley Noel, *Christian Missions to Heathen Nations* (London: James Nisbet, 1842). In 1850, Robert Ramsden's text, *Missions: Or, a Word for the Heathen, Being Facts and Anecdotes, Selected from the Journals and Letters of Missionaries* (London: John Nisbet, 1850) concluded with a plea to its readers to assist in the dissemination of the gospel to those millions 'whose spiritual necessities baffle all description': 'O turn not a deaf ear to the poor African and Hindoo, whose cry is, "Come over and help us"'. Ramsden, *Missions*, 464–5. See Curtin, *The Image of Africa*, 267, 415.

130 Coke, *A History of the West Indies*, vol. i, 30.
131 *Ibid.*, vol. i, 19.
132 Thomas Fowell Buxton, *The African Slave Trade and Its Remedy*, 2nd edn. (London: John Murray, 1839) 195–6.
133 *Ibid.*, 305–6, 338–9; my emphasis. Indeed Buxton's conviction greatly influenced, and in a sense, culminated in Dr. Livingstone's belief in his own 'missionary' role in Africa's social, economic and spiritual progress. See also Isaac Schapera, ed., *Livingstone's Missionary Correspondence, 1841–1856*, 2 vols. (London: Chatto and Windus, 1961).

2 RADICAL DISSENT AND SPIRITUAL AUTOBIOGRAPHY: JOANNA SOUTHCOTT, JOHN NEWTON AND WILLIAM COWPER

1 See Malcolm Bradbury and Richard Ruland, *From Puritanism to Postmodernism: A History of American Literature* (London: Routledge, 1991); John Bunyan, *Grace Abounding to the Chief of Sinners: Or, a Brief and Faithful Relation of the Exceeding Mercy of God in Christ to His Poor Servant, John Bunyan* (London, 1666); Edward Taylor, *Spiritual Relation* (Massachusetts, 1679); Increase Mather, *The Life and Death of Richard Mather* (Cambridge, Mass., 1670); Cotton Mather, *Memoirs of Remarkable Events in the Life and Death of Dr Increase Mather, who Expired, August 23, 1723* (Boston, 1724); and Diane Sasson, *The Shaker Spiritual Narrative* (Knoxville: University of Tennessee Press, 1983).
2 Thomas Jackson, *The Lives of the Early Methodist Preachers Chiefly Written by Themselves*, 3 vols. (London: John Mason, 1837–1838) vol. iii, iii.
3 Such testimonies were also influenced by extracts from Bunyan's *The Pilgrim's Progress: From This World, to That Which is to Come: Delivered under the Similitude of a Dream*, 2 vols. (1678; London, 1728) which frequently appeared in *The Arminian Magazine* (later named *The Methodist*).
4 The first volume of *The Arminian Magazine: Consisting of Extracts and Original Treatises on Universal Redemption* appeared in London in 1778.
5 Also included within the first volume of *The Arminian Magazine* were: 'The Life of Arnelle Nicholas' (vol. i: 194–9); 'An Account of Mr

Alexander Mather' (vol.1: 199–207); and 'A Short Account of God's Dealings with Mr John Haime' (vol.1: 207–17).

6 Richard Brantley, *Wordsworth's 'Natural Methodism'* (New Haven: Yale University Press, 1975) 69–75.

7 Jackson, *Lives of the Early Methodist Preachers*, 454.

8 Emily Dickinson, 'Numen Lumen', *The Complete Poems of Emily Dickinson*, ed. Thomas H. Johnson (London: Faber, 1975) 222, lines 1–2.

9 Simone de Beauvoir, *The Second Sex*, trans. and ed. H.M. Parshley (London: Pan Books, 1988) 13–19, 23–4.

10 Jacques Derrida, 'Speech and Phenomena' (1967), *A Derrida Reader, Between the Blinds*, ed. Peggy Kamuf (Hertfordshire: Harvester Wheat-sheaf, 1991) 6–30.

11 For a discussion of the concept of pre-Oedipal semiotic discourse see Julia Kristeva, *Desire in Language: A Semiotic Approach to Literature and Art*, ed. Leon S. Roudiez and trans. Thomas Gora, Alice Jardine and Leon Roudiez (Oxford: Blackwell, 1980) and Toril Moi, ed. and trans., *The Kristeva Reader* (Oxford: Basil Blackwell, 1986).

12 Nigel Smith, *Perfection Proclaimed: Language and Literature in English Radical Religion, 1640–1660* (Oxford: Clarendon Press, 1989) 24–6.

13 For this reason, prophetic or spiritual discourse was in essence most akin to the spoken rather than the written word. It transcribed a form of 'orature' (oral literature) which succeeds in maintaining a subversive quality of performance in that it prioritises the vitality of linguistic energy, flow and excess which defies the boundaries of form. Ngugi Wa Thiong'o, *Decolonising the Mind: The Politics of Language in African Literature* (London: James Curry, 1980) 83, 94–5; Henry Louis Gates, *The Signifying Monkey: A Theory of African-American Literary Criticism* (New York: Oxford University Press 1988) xxii, 63.

14 Roland Barthes, 'The Death of the Author', *Image – Music – Text*, ed. and trans. Stephen Heath (London: Fontana, 1977) 142–8.

15 Sasson, *The Shaker Spiritual Narrative*, 11–16. See also Elizabeth Sampson Ashbridge's Quaker autobiography, *Some Account of the Fore-Part of the Life of Elizabeth Ashbridge, Who Died in Truth's Service. Wrote by Herself* (Nant-wich, 1774).

16 For a further discussion see Barbara Taylor, *Eve and the New Jerusalem: Socialism and Feminism in the Nineteenth Century* (1983; London: Virago, 1991); John Hopkins, *A Woman To Deliver Her People: Joanna Southcott and English Millenarianism in the Era of Revolution* (Austin: University of Texas Press, 1982).

17 Joanna Southcott, *Memoirs of the Life and Mission of Joanna Southcott Interspersed with Authentic Anecdotes, and Elusidated by Interesting Documents Including the Progress of Her Pregnancy, Detailed by Herself* (London: W. Lewis, 1814) 13.

18 Joanna Southcott, *The Strange Effects of Faith; With Remarkable Prophecies, Made in 1792, of Things Which Are To Come: Also, Some Account of My Life in*

Six Parts (Exeter: T. Brice, 1801–1802); Book 1, [Part One] 25. See also Clare Brant and Diane Purkiss, eds, *Women, Texts and Histories, 1575–1760* (London: Routledge, 1992) 103–4.

19 Taylor, *Eve and the New Jerusalem*, 162. See also J. F C. Harrison, *The Second Coming: Popular Millenarianism, 1780–1850* (London: Routledge and Kegan Paul, 1979).

20 Southcott, *Strange Effects*, Book 1, iii; my emphasis.

21 Southcott, *Copies and Parts of Copies of Letters and Communications, Written from Joanna Southcott, and Transmitted by Miss Townley to Mr. W. Sharp, in London* (London: S. Rousseau, 1804) 80–1.

22 Southcott, *Strange Effects*, 75; idem, *A Warning to the Whole World from the Sealed Prophecies of Joanna Southcott* (London: S. Rousseau, 1804) 58.

23 Southcott, *A Dispute Between the Woman and the Powers of Darkness* (London: E. Spragg, 1802); idem, *The Answer of the Lord to the Powers of Darkness* (London: E. Spragg, 1802).

24 E. P. Thompson, *The Making of the English Working Class* (1963; London: Victor and Gollancz, 1990) 127.

25 Richard Brothers, *A Revealed Knowledge of the Prophecies and Times Wrote under the Direction of the Lord God, and Published by His Second in Command, it Being the First Sign of Warning for the Benefit of All Nations Containing with Other Great and Remarkable Things, Not Revealed to Any Other Person on Earth, the Restoration of the Hebrews to Jerusalem, by the Year 1798, under Their Revealed Prince and Prophet, Richard Brothers*, 2 vols. (London, 1794) 54; Preface to Book 2, iii–iv; my emphasis.

26 Brothers, *A Description of Jerusalem: Its Houses and Streets, Squares, Colleges, Markets, and Cathedrals, the Royal and Private Palaces with the Garden of Eden in the Centre As Laid down in the Last Chapters of Ezekiel* (London: George Ribeau, 1801) 142, 139; my emphases. The source of Brother's vision of the perfect city has traditionally been located in the prophetic writings of the Old Testament, especially those of Revelation (21: 9–11) and Ezekiel, in which Jerusalem is described as a city 'prepared as a bride adorned for her husband'.

27 Thompson, *The Making of the English Working Class*, 420–8.

28 Southcott, *A Communication Given to Joanna in Answer to Mr. Brothers' Last Book, Published the End of this Year, 1802* (London: E. Spragg, 1802) 1, 5, 7. My emphasis on 'the inward moving of My Spirit'.

29 Taylor, *Eve and the New Jerusalem* 162; Southcott, *The Answer of the Lord*.

30 Southcott, *The Life of Joanna Southcott, the Prophetess: Containing an Impartial Account of Her Wonderful and Astonishing Writings, Her Miraculous Conception, the Coming of Shiloh, Mr. Seddon*, 9th ed. (London: John Fairburn, 1814) 13; idem, *Letters and Communications of Joanna Southcott, the Prophetess of Exeter, Lately Written to Jane Townley*, ed. Ann Underwood (Stourbridge: J. Heming, 1804) 114.

31 Revd 12:4 and 19:7; Southcott, *The Answer of the Lord*, 120.

32 Southcott, *A Warning to the Whole World*, 1.
33 R. Hann, ed., *The Trial of Joanna Southcott, During Seven Days, Which Commenced on the Fifth and Ended on the Eleventh of December 1804 at Neckinger House, Bermondsey, near London* (London: S. Rousseau, 1804) 79. See also Hann's critique and condemnation of the trial, *Charges Against Joanna Southcott and Her Twelve Judges, the Jury, and Four and Twenty Elders, who Presided at Her Pretended Trial, at the Neckinger, Bermondsey, in the Year 1804* (London: R. Walker, 1804).
34 Southcott, *The Life and Prophecies of Joanna Southcott, from Her Infancy to the Present Time. With an Account of her Miraculous Conception, her Astonishing Writings, the Coming of Shiloh, the Millennium, the Reign of Christ upon the Earth; and the Sealing of the Faithful* (London: Dean and Murray, c. 1815) 13.
35 Southcott, *Strange Effects*, Book 1, 77.
36 R. Hann, *The Remarkable Life, Entertaining History and Surprising Adventures of Joanna Southcott, the Prophetess, Giving an Account of the Familiar Spirit That Attends and Directs Her; Also, an Account of the Seal, the Manner of Sealing the People, and the Manner of Receiving Communication from the Spirit* (London: W. Smith, 1810).
37 *Ibid.*, 2–4. Hann was also the author of *A Letter to the Right Reverend the Lord Bishop of London Concerning the Heresy and Imposture of Joanna the Prophetess* (London: J. Smith, 1810).
38 William Howard, *A Letter to Joanna Southcott, the Pretended Prophetess, with a Fac-Similie of Her Handwriting, as Connected with Her Blasphemous Seal* (London: Watts and Bridgewater, 1810) 3.
39 Joanna Southcott, *The Book of Wonders, Marvellous and True, Announcing the Coming of Shilol with a Call to the Hebrews*, ed. Ann Underwood (London: W. Marchant, 1814) Book 3, 11. See also Harrison, *The Second Coming*, 86–134; Morton Paley, 'William Blake, the Prince of the Hebrews and the Woman Clothed with the Sun', *William Blake: Essays in Honour of Geoffrey Keynes*, ed. Morton Paley and Michael Phillips (Oxford: Clarendon Press, 1973) 260–93; Taylor, *Eve and the New Jerusalem*, 162–7.
40 Southcott, *Prophecies Announcing the Birth of the Prince of Peace, Extracted from the Works of Joanna Southcott: To Which Are Added a Few Remarks Thereon, Made by Herself*, ed. Ann Underwood (London: W. Marchant, 1814) 11, 15.
41 See Richard Reece, *A Correct Statement of the Circumstances That Attended the Last Illness and Death of Mrs. Joanna Southcott with an Account of the Appearances Exhibited on Dissection* (London: Sherwood, Neely and Jones, 1815) and *idem*, *Life and Death of Joanna Southcott; With Particulars of Her Will and An Account of Her Dissection* (London: Sherwood, Neely and Jones, 1814).
42 Margaret Davidson, *The Extraordinary Life and Christian Experience of Margaret Davidson, As Dictated By Herself*, ed. Edward Smyth (Dublin, 1782) 1.
43 *Ibid.*, 17.

44 *Ibid.*, 28–9.

45 Sophia Leece, *A Narrative of the Life of Miss Sophia Leece*, ed. Hugh Stowell (Liverpool: R. Trilling, 1820) 5.

46 *Ibid.*, 15.

47 *Ibid.*, 75.

48 John Newton, *An Authentic Narrative of Some Remarkable and Interesting Particulars in the Life of John Newton Communicated in a Series of Letters to the Reverend Mr. Haweis*, ed. Revd Haweis (London, 1764) 87.

49 *Ibid.*, i-iii.

50 John Newton, *Letters, Sermons, and a Review of Ecclesiastical History. An Authentic Narrative of Some Particulars in the Life of ****, 3 vols. (Edinburgh, 1780).

51 *Ibid.*, vol. ii, 137–8.

52 Newton, *Authentic Narrative*, 1.

53 Bunyan, *Pilgrim's Progress*; Newton, *Authentic Narrative*, 1–2.

54 Newton, *Authentic Narrative*, 4–5.

55 *Ibid.*, 5.

56 *Ibid.*, 11.

57 *Ibid.*, 36.

58 *Ibid.*, 16–7.

59 *Ibid.*, 23, 26: 'I thought the author a most religious person', *ibid.*, 25.

60 *Ibid.*, 30.

61 *Ibid.*, 39.

62 *Ibid.*, 40.

63 *Ibid.*, 42–3.

64 *Ibid.*, 51.

65 *Ibid.*, 53.

66 *Ibid.*, 52.

67 *Ibid.*, 62.

68 *Ibid.*, 64.

69 *Ibid.*, 67.

70 *Ibid.*, 78.

71 John Newton, *The Journal of a Slave-Trader, 1750–1754. With Newton's Thoughts upon the African Slave Trade*, ed. Bernard Martin and Mark Spurrell (London: Epworth Press, 1962): 'Sunday 26th May . . . In the evening, by the favour of Providence, discovered a conspiracy among the men slaves to rise upon us, but a few hours before it was to have been executed', 54–5.

72 *Ibid.*, xii; my emphases.

73 Newton, *Authentic Narrative*, 76–7.

74 Joseph Conrad, *Heart of Darkness and Other Tales*, ed. Cedric Watts (Oxford University Press, 1990).

75 Newton, *Authentic Narrative*, 89–90.

76 George Vason, *An Authentic Narrative of Four Years' Residence at Tongataboo, one of the Friendly Islands, in the South Sea, by – [George Vason] who Went*

Thither in the Duff, Under Captain Wilson, in 1796 (London: Longman, Hurst, Rees and Orme, 1810) 107–8; my emphasis.

77 *Ibid.*, 113–114.
78 *Ibid.*, 112.
79 *Ibid.*, 200; my emphasis.
80 Newton, *Authentic Narrative*, 95.
81 *Ibid.*, 100.
82 *Ibid.*, 107.
83 *Ibid.*, 126.
84 *Ibid.*, 141, 142–3.
85 *Ibid.*, 147.
86 *Ibid.*, 170.
87 *Ibid.*, 192–3, 99.
88 Newton, *Thoughts upon the African Slave Trade* (London, 1788) 1.
89 *Ibid.*, 1.
90 *Ibid.*, 4.
91 *Ibid.*, 4; my emphasis.
92 *Ibid.*, 22.
93 *Ibid.*, 3.
94 Theodora's father had forbidden the marriage between them on the grounds of Cowper's financial state.
95 John Morris, *Versions of the Self: Studies in English Autobiography from John Bunyan to John Mill* (London: Basic Books, 1966) 154; Charles Ryskamp, *William Cowper of the Inner Temple: A Study of His Life and Works to the Year 1768* (Cambridge: Cambridge University Press, 1959) 143–4.
96 For further discussion of Cowper see David Cecil, *The Stricken Deer: Or the Life of Cowper* (London: Constable, 1929); Dustin Griffin, *Regaining Paradise: Milton and the Eighteenth Century* (Cambridge: Cambridge University Press, 1986); Bill Hutchings, *The Poetry of William Cowper* (London: Croom Helm, 1983); and Martin Priestman, *Cowper's Task: Structure and Influence* (Cambridge: Cambridge University Press, 1983).
97 See Cowper, *The Task. A Poem in Six Books: To Which Are Added an Epistle to Joseph Hill, Esq., Tirocinium, or a Review of Schools, and the History of John Gilpin* (London, 1785) Book II, lines 780–7.
98 See Griffin, *Regaining Paradise*, for an excellent discussion of Cowper's concept of a domestic Eden.
99 Cowper, 'Retirement', *Poetical Works*, ed. H. S. Milford, 4th edn. (London: Oxford University Press, 1967) Hymn XLVII, 463, lines 9–14.
100 Cowper, 'Light Shining Out of Darkness', *Poetical Works*, Hymn XXXV, 455 lines 1–2, 19–20, 23–4.
101 See Cowper to Mrs Madan 26 September 1767, *The Letters and Prose Writings of William Cowper, 1750–1781*, ed. James King and Charles Ryskamp, 5 vols. (Oxford: Clarendon Press, 1980) vol. i, xxii, 179–81.

102 See Cowper to Mrs Madan, 18 June 1768, *Letters and Prose* vol. i, 196–8.
103 Cowper, *Memoirs of the Life and Writings of William Cowper*, ed. Samuel Greatheed (London: T. Williams, 1814) vi.
104 Cowper, *Memoirs of the Remarkable and Interesting Parts of the Life of William Cowper* (London: Cox, 1816); idem, *Memoir of the Early Life of William Cowper Esq., Written by Himself and Never Before Published: With an Appendix Containing Some of Cowper's Religious Letters* (London: R. Edwards, 1816).
105 Cowper, *Memoirs of the Remarkable Life*, viii; my emphasis.
106 'Publisher's Preface' to the *Memoir of the Early Life*, vii, viii.
107 Cowper, *Memoirs of the Remarkable Life*, 12.
108 Cowper, *Memoir of the Early Life*, 3.
109 *Ibid.*, 3.
110 *Ibid.*, 58, 27.
111 *Ibid.*, 44, 67. In a letter to Lady Hesketh, dated Huntingdon, July 4, 1765, Cowper wrote: 'I am *only now a convert.* You think I always believed, and I thought so too, but you were deceived, and so was I. I called myself a Christian, but he knows my heart, knows that I never did a right thing, nor abstained from a wrong one, because I was so'.
112 Joseph Musser, 'William Cowper's Rhetoric: The Picturesque and the Personal', *Studies in English Literature* 19 (1979): 515–31.
113 Alexander Selkirk's adventures also provided the prototype of Daniel Defoe's novel, *The Life and Strange Suprizing Adventures of Mr D[aniel De F[oe] of London, Hosier. In a Dialogue between Him, Robinson Crusoe, and His Man, Friday* (London, 1719). Alexander Selkirk, *A Voyage to the South Sea, and Round the World, Perform'd in the Years 1708, 1709 and 1711*, 2 vols. (London, 1712).
114 Cowper, 'Charity', *Poetical Works*, 76, lines 15–16; 80, lines 200–3.
115 Cowper, 'The Negro's Complaint', *Poetical Works*, 372, lines 33–40.
116 Cowper, 'The Morning Dream', *Poetical Works*, 373–4, lines 37–48. See also Ferguson, *Subject to Others*, 210.
117 Cowper, *The Task*, Book III, p. 179, line 722.
118 *Ibid.*, Book III, 97, lines 112–16.
119 *Ibid.*, Book III, 97, p. 166, lines 125–7. William Wordsworth, *The Prelude, 1799, 1805, 1850: Authoritative Texts, Context and Reception, Recent Critical Essays*, ed. Jonathan Wordsworth, M. H. Abrams and Stephen Gill (New York: Norton, 1979) Book VI, 218, line 572. See also Keats' concept of the visionary and the dreamer in 'The Fall of Hyperion: A Dream', *The Poems of John Keats*, ed. Jack Stillinger (London: Heinemann, 1978) 478–90.
120 Cowper, *The Task*, Book III, 103, lines 240–243; my emphasis.
121 *Ibid.*, Book III, 99, line 149; 101, lines 222, 150–1, 156–7, 190.
122 *Ibid.*, Book III, 101–2, lines 206–9.
123 *Ibid.*, Book II, 48, line 60; Book II, 50, lines 99–103.
124 *Ibid.*, Book II, 47, lines 38–42.
125 *Ibid.*, Book I, 41, lines 770–4.

126 *Ibid.*, Book I, 35, line 658.
127 *Ibid.*, Book I, 35, lines 658–60.
128 *Ibid.*, Book VI, 268, lines 719–21.
129 *Ibid.*, Book V, 186, lines 101–4.
130 *Ibid.*, Book V, 208–9, lines 538, 545–7.
131 *Ibid.*, Book V, 221, lines 779–84.
132 *Ibid.*, Book V, 227, lines 891–7; my emphasis.
133 *Ibid.*, Book V, 226, lines 883–4.
134 *Ibid.*, Book VI, 240, line 181.
135 Cowper, *The Cast-Away: The Text of the Original Manuscript and the First Printing of Cowper's Latin Translation*, ed. Charles Ryskamp (New Jersey: Princeton University Press, 1963) 17, lines 61–2.
136 George Anson, *A Voyage Round the World in the Years 1740–1744* (London, 1748); Cowper, *The Cast-Away*, lines 63–6.

3 ROMANTICISM AND ABOLITIONISM: MARY WOLLSTONECRAFT, WILLIAM BLAKE, SAMUEL TAYLOR COLERIDGE AND WILLIAM WORDSWORTH

1 For a comprehensive overview of the development of Romantic Studies see Marilyn Butler, *Romantics, Rebels and Reactionaries: English Literature and Its Background, 1760–1830* (Oxford: Oxford University Press, 1981); Stephen Copley and John Whale, eds, *Beyond Romanticism: New Approaches to Texts and Contexts, 1780–1832* (London: Routledge, 1992); Paul de Man, *Blindness and Insight: Essays on the Rhetoric of Contemporary Criticism* (New York: Oxford University Press, 1971); *idem*, *The Rhetoric of Romanticism* (New York: Columbia University Press, 1984).
2 Mary Favret and Nicola Watson, eds, *At the Limits of Romanticism: Essays in Cultural, Feminist, and Materialist Criticism* (Bloomington: Indiana University Press, 1994) 3.
3 Mary Jacobus, *Romanticism, Writing and Sexual Difference: Essays on the 'Prelude'* (Oxford: Clarendon Press, 1989) 69–97; Marjorie Levinson, *Keats' Life of Allegory: The Origins of a Style* (Oxford: Basil Blackwell, 1988); *idem*, *Romanticism and Feminism* (Bloomington: Indiana University Press, 1988); Ann Mellor, *Romanticism and Gender* (London: Routledge, 1993); Helen Vendler, *The Odes of John Keats* (Cambridge, Mass.: Harvard University Press, 1983).
4 Favret and Mary Watson, *At the Limits of Romanticism*.
5 Jerome McGann, *The Romantic Ideology: A Critical Investigation* (Chicago: Chicago University Press, 1983).
6 Alan Richardson and Sonia Hofkosh, eds, *Romanticism, Race, and Imperial Culture* (Bloomington: Indiana University Press, 1996) and Tim Fulford and Peter Kitson, eds, *Romanticism and Colonialism* (Cambridge: Cambridge University Press, 1998).
7 In her study, *Romanticism, Writing and Sexual Difference*, Jacobus identified

Wordsworth's *Prelude* as a site of historical repression and argued that
the invisible relationship between Wordsworth's poem, Newton's conversion and slavery marked one of the most crucial chapters in
eighteenth-century economic history: see 69–97.

8 Lauren Henry, 'Sunshine and Shady Groves: What Blake's 'Little Black
   Boy' Learned from African Writers', *Romanticism and Colonialism*, ed.
   Fulford and Kitson, 67–86, 70–1.

9 Wordsworth and Coleridge, *Lyrical Ballads with a Few Other Poems*
   (London, 1800).

10 Wordsworth, *The Prelude, 1799, 1805, 1850: Authoritative Texts, Context and
   Reception, Recent Critical Essays*, ed. Jonathan Wordsworth, M. H. Abrams
   and Stephen Gill (New York: Norton, 1979) x-xi. Likewise, William
   Blake sold very little of his work and his exhibitions were ill-attended.

11 Samuel Taylor Coleridge, *The Collected Letters of Samuel Taylor Coleridge*,
   ed. E. L. Griggs, 6 vols. (Oxford: Clarendon Press, 1956–1971) vol. ii,
   790–801.

12 M. H. Abrams, ed., *Norton Anthology of English Literature*, 2 vols. (London:
   Norton, 1993) vol. ii, 18.

13 See Lauren Henry, 'Sunshine and Shady Groves', 69.

14 Mary Wollstonecraft, *A Vindication of the Rights of Men, in a Letter to the
   Right Honourable Edmund Burke Occasioned by His 'Reflections of the Revolutions
   in France'* (London, 1790) 71.

15 Anne Mellor, *Romanticism and Gender*, 66–7.

16 Wollstonecraft, *Rights of Men*, 121–2.

17 Moira Ferguson, *Subject to Others: British Women Writers and Colonial
   Slavery, 1670–1834* (London: Routledge, 1992) 188.

18 Wollstonecraft, *Rights of Men*, 121–2.

19 William Godwin, *An Enquiry Concerning Political Justice and Its Influence on
   General Virtue and Happiness*, 2 vols. (London, 1793).

20 Mary Wollstonecraft, *A Vindication of the Rights of Woman: With Strictures on
   Political and Moral Subjects* (London, 1792).

21 *Ibid.*, x-xi.

22 Anne Mellor, 'Am I Not a Woman, and a Sister?': Slavery, Romanticism,
   and Gender', *Romanticism, Race, and Imperial Culture*, ed. Richardson and
   Hofkosh, 311–329.

23 Katherine Rogers, *Feminism in Eighteenth Century England* (Sussex: Harvester Press, 1982).

24 Wollstonecraft, *Rights of Woman*, 73.

25 *Ibid.*, 90.

26 Mellor, 'Am I Not a Woman?', 318

27 Wollstonecraft, *Rights of Woman*, 92.

28 Mary Wollstonecraft, *The Works of Mary Wollstonecraft*, ed. Janet Todd
   and Marilyn Butler, 7 vols. (London: William Pickering, 1989) vol. vi,
   234.

29 Moses Roper, *A Narrative of the Adventures and Escape of Moses Roper, from*

American Slavery, ed. Revd T. Price (London: Darton, Harvey and Darton, 1837); Mary Prince, *The History of Mary Prince, a West Indian Slave As Related by Herself with a Supplement by the Editor to Which is Added, the Narrative of Asa-Asa, a Captured African*, ed. T. Pringle (London: Westley and Davis, 1831).

30 Wollstonecraft, *The Works of Mary Wollstonecraft*, vol. vii, 100–1.

31 Coleridge, *Lectures 1795 on Politics and Religion*, ed. Lewis Patton and Peter Mann (London: Routledge and Kegan Paul, 1971) 231–52; 'On the Slave Trade', *The Watchman*, ed. Lewis Patton (London: Routledge and Kegan Paul, 1970) 130–140. These editions of Coleridge's *Lectures 1795* and *The Watchman* form volumes one and two of *The Collected Works of Samuel Taylor Coleridge*, 6 vols., ed. Kathleen Coburn (London: Routledge and Kegan Paul, 1983).

32 Deirdre Coleman, 'Conspicuous Consumption: White Abolitionism and English Women's Protest Writing in the 1790s', *English Literary History* 61 (1994): 342.

33 See Eric Williams, *Capitalism and Slavery* (1945; London: Andre Deutsch, 1964) 195. Coleridge's poem also referred to the slaves' epistemological belief in the world of the spirits.

34 Coleridge, *Lectures 1795*, 235, n.3, 240, n.4.

35 Thomas Clarkson, *An Essay on the Implicity of the African Slave Trade in Two Parts*, 2 vols. (London, 1788) 110.

36 Ferguson, *Subject to Others*, 127, 129. Mary Scott, *The Female Advocate: A Poem Occasioned by Reading Mr. Duncombe's Feminead* (London: Joseph Johnson, 1774); Mary Deverell, *Miscellanies in Prose and Verse, Mostly Written in the epistolary Style*, 2 vols. (London, 1781).

37 Carl Bernhard Wadstrom, *An Essay on Colonisation, Particularly Applied to the Western Coast of Africa, with Some Free Thoughts on Cultivation and Commerce* (London, 1794) 3, 4.

38 *Ibid.*, 4, 5.

39 Coleridge, *Lecture on the Slave Trade*, 236.

40 *Ibid.*, 235.

41 Coleman, 'Conspicuous Consumption', 344.

42 David Hartley, *Observations on Man* (London, 1749).

43 Coleridge, *Lecture on the Slave Trade*, 235.

44 *Ibid.*, 235; my emphases except the word 'real'. Mark Akenside, *The Pleasures of Imagination. A Poem in Three Books*, 3rd edn. (London, 1744); *The Spectator*, 21 June 1712. William Hazlitt defined Coleridge's discourse as the type of 'angelic wings': 'He was the first poet I ever knew . . . His genius at that time had angelic wings, and fed on manna. He talked on for ever . . . And shall I, who heeded him then, listen to him now? Not I! . . . That spell is broke; that time is gone for ever'. Hazlitt, 'Lectures on the English Poets', *The Complete Works of William Hazlitt*, ed. P. P. Howe, 21 vols. (London: J. M. Dent, 1930–1934) vol. v, 167.

45 Coleridge, *Lecture on the Slave Trade*, 238.

46 *Ibid.*, 233.

47 *Ibid.*, 241; my emphases.

48 I am grateful to Alan Richardson for highlighting the correspondence between these poems.

49 Southey, 'The Sailor Who Had Served in the Slave Trade', *Poems, by Robert Southey* (London: Longman and Rees, 1799) 103–8, lines 101–4.

50 Southey was also the author of *The Life of Wesley.* See Robert Southey, *The Minor Poems of Robert Southey*, 3 vols. (London: Longman, Hurst, Rees, Orme and Brown, 1823).

51 See James Walvin, *Black Ivory: A History of Black Slavery* (London: Harper Collins, 1992) 16–22; Fryer, *Staying Power: The History of Black People in Britain* (London: Pluto Press, 1984) 127–30; Potkay and Burr, eds, *Black Atlantic Writers of the Eighteenth Century: Living the New Exodus in England and America* (Basingstoke: Macmillan, 1995) 165; Gilroy, *Small Acts: Thoughts on the Politics of Black Cultures* (London: Serpent's Tail, 1993) 81–5.

52 See also Turner's painting 'Slavers Throwing Overboard the Dead and Dying: Typhoon Coming On' (1840).

53 William Fox, *A Short Account of the African Slave Trade, and an Address to the People of Great Britain on the Propriety of Abstaining from West Indian Sugar and Rum* (Sevenoaks, 1791). Coleridge, *Lecture on the Slave Trade*, 248–9.

54 Coleridge, *Lecture on the Slave Trade*, 251; my emphasis.

55 Coleridge, *Collected Letters*, vol. i, 302.

56 George Whalley, *The Bristol Library Borrowings of Southey and Coleridge, 1793–1798* (London: The Bibliographical Society, 1949) 119.

57 *The Gospel Magazine and Theological Review* (1796) vol. i, i; 'The Memoirs of the Life of John James Claude', *The Gospel Magazine* vol. i, 152–7; 'The Remarkable Passages in the Life of Mr Vavasor Powel, Minister of the Gospel in Wales, Written by Himself', *The Gospel Magazine* vol. i, 217–21; and 'The Singular Experience and Great Sufferings of Mrs Agnes', *The Gospel Magazine* vol. i, 297–305.

58 Robert Woolman, *A Journal of the Life, Gospel Labours, and Christian Experience of that Faithful Minister of Jesus Christ, John Woolman, to Which Are Added His Works* (Dublin, 1776) v, 8, 15.

59 John Woolman, *Some Considerations on the Keeping of Negroes* (Philadelphia, 1754) included in *A Journal of the Life*, 251–325; 277.

60 John Woolman, *Some Considerations*, 305.

61 Indeed, Coleridge's later project, *Biographia Literaria* (1817) presented an enigmatic form of autobiographical self-examination. See Coleridge, *Biographia Literaria: Or, Biographical Sketches of My Literary Life and Opinions*, ed. James Engell and W. Jackson Bate, 2 vols. (Princeton: Princeton University Press, 1983).

62 Richard Brantley, *Wordsworth's 'Natural Methodism'* (New Haven: Yale University Press, 1975) 38.

63 See Frank Coleridge's suicide note, 19 Dec. 1791 and Coleridge, *Collected Letters*, vol. i, 63, 68.

64 Bernard Martin, *The Ancient Mariner and the Authentic Narrative* (London: Heinemann, 1949) 37–8.

65 *Ibid.*, 37.

66 For more on Coleridge's relation with the Quakers see Deirdre Coleman, *Coleridge and the Friend, 1809–1810* (Oxford: Clarendon Press, 1988).

67 For further discussion of these poems see Lucy Newlyn's *Coleridge, Wordsworth and the Language of Allusion* (Oxford: Clarendon Press, 1986); Kathleen Wheeler, *The Creative Mind in Coleridge's Poetry* (London: Heinemann, 1981) and Kelvin Everest, *Coleridge's Secret Ministry: The Context of the Conversation Poems, 1795–1798* (Hassocks: Harvester Press, 1979).

68 Coleridge, 'The Eolian Harp', *Poetical Works*, ed. Ernest Hartley Coleridge (Oxford: Oxford University Press, 1969) 102, lines 44–8.

69 *Ibid.*, 101, lines 26–9.

70 Coleridge, 'This Lime-Tree Bower My Prison', *Poetical Works*, 178–9, lines 2–5.

71 *Ibid.*, 180, lines 43–5.

72 *Ibid.*, 180, lines 37–43.

73 See Newlyn, *Language of Allusion*, for an excellent discussion of Coleridge's and Wordsworth's exchange of ideas. In the intervening versions of Coleridge's poem, the addressee underwent several gender transformations, changing from Sara, William, then Edmund, and finally ending with the 'Lady' of the 1817 *Sybilline Leaves* version.

74 Coleridge, 'Letter to Sara', *Collected Letters*, vol. i, 790, line 23; vol. i, 790, line 34.

75 *Ibid.*, 791, lines 31–2, 42–3. I am grateful to Jonathan Wordsworth for his suggestions about this poem.

76 *Ibid.*, 791, lines 50–1; my emphasis.

77 *Ibid.*, 791, line 73. Coleridge had in fact been born in rural Devonshire (Ottery St Mary) but with the death of his father was sent to school at Christ's Hospital, London.

78 *Ibid.*, 793, lines 109–10; 792, lines 92–8.

79 *Ibid.*, 796, lines 236–8.

80 *Ibid.*, 796, line 242.

81 *Ibid.*, 793, line 136.

82 *Ibid.*, 798, lines 302–7.

83 *Ibid.*, 797, lines 296–8.

84 *Ibid.*, 798, lines 315–20; my emphases.

85 Rev. 21:3.

86 Coleridge, 'Letter to Sara', 798, lines 317–18.

87 *Song of Songs* 2:16, 3:1.

88 Meyer Howard Abrams, *Natural Supernaturalism: Tradition and Revolution in Romantic Literature* (London: Oxford University Press, 1971) 95–6; my emphasis.

89 Brantley, *Wordsworth's 'Natural Methodism'*, xi.
90 William Wilberforce, *A Practical View of the Prevailing Religious System of Professed Christians Contrasted with Real Christianity* (London, 1798); Wordsworth to Wilberforce, *The Letters of William and Dorothy Wordsworth: The Early Years, 1787–1805*, 2nd edn., ed. Chester Shaver; gen. ed. Kathleen Coburn, 10 vols. (Oxford: Clarendon Press, 1967) vol. i, 685.
91 Brantley, *Wordsworth's 'Natural Methodism'*, 15–20.
92 Dorothy Wordsworth to Jane Pollard, *Letters of William and Dorothy Wordsworth*, vol. i, 28.
93 Philip Doddridge, *The Family Expositor: Or, a Paraphrase and Version of the New Testament*, ed. J. Orton, 6 vols. (London, 1739–1756).
94 Brantley, *Wordsworth's 'Natural Methodism'*, 24; Doddridge, *Rise and Progress of Religion in the Soul: Illustrated in a Course of Serious and Practical Addresses* (London, 1745); Francis Wrangham, *Thirteen Practical Sermons: Founded upon Doddridge's 'Rise and Progress of Religion in the Soul'* (London: J. Mawman, 1800) 23, 26, 59: 'You must be fully aware of your guilt . . . It is no *small matter* to have transgressed the laws of your Maker . . . *To you is the word of salvation sent*'.
95 Dorothy Wordsworth to Jane Pollard (26 Jun. 1791), *Letters of William and Dorothy Wordsworth* vol. i, 54.
96 Dorothy Wordsworth to Jane Pollard (8 May 1792), *ibid.*, vol. i, 75. Dundas had strongly opposed Wilberforce's first Abolition Bill, 18 Apr. 1791.
97 Martin, *The Ancient Mariner*, 38; Newton *Authentic Narrative*, 82.
98 Cf. Brantley, *Wordsworth's 'Natural Methodism'*, 37–8; Jacobus, *Romanticism, Writing, and Sexual Difference*, 79–82; Duncan Wu, *Wordsworth's Reading, 1770–1799* (Cambridge: Cambridge University Press, 1993).
99 Wordsworth, 'MS JJ, October 1798', *The Prelude: 1799, 1805, 1850*, 487, lines 1–3, 5–6. All subsequent references will be from this edition.
100 Wordsworth, 'Prelude of 1805', 28, Book 1, lines 6–10, 16–19; my emphases.
101 *Ibid.*, 30, Book 1, lines 41–4.
102 *Ibid.*, 32, Book 1, lines 59–63.
103 *Ibid.*, 92, Book 3, line 28–9.
104 *Ibid.*, 233, Book 7, line 157; 262, Book 7, 661–2; 406, Book 10, line 878. See Jonathan Wordsworth, 'Versions of the Fall', *William Wordsworth: The Borders of Vision* (1982; Oxford: Clarendon Press, 1984) 231–78.
105 Wordsworth, 'Prelude of 1805', 306, Book 8, lines 763–4.
106 *Ibid.*, 460–2, Book 13, lines 39–43, 68–73.
107 See William Hazlitt, *Complete Works*, vol. v, 156, 163: 'Mr. Wordsworth is the most original poet now living . . . His powers have been mistaken by the age, nor does he understand them himself . . . He tolerates only what he himself creates . . . He see nothing but himself and the universe'.
108 Wordsworth, 'Prelude of 1805', 216, Book 6, lines 526–9.

109 *Ibid.*, 218, Book 6, lines 567–72.

110 Wordsworth, 'To Toussaint L'Ouverture', *Poetical Works*, ed. Ernest de Selincourt (Oxford University Press, 1969) 242–3. Although it first appeared in the *Morning Post*, 2 Feb. 1803, the poem was probably written between 1 and 29 Aug. 1801.

111 Robin Blackburn, *The Overthrow of Colonial Slavery, 1776–1848* (London: Verso, 1990) 163, 218, 240. For a more detailed account of the slave insurrection see C. L. R. James, *The Black Jacobins: Toussaint L'Ouverture and the San Domingo Revolution* (1938; London: Allison and Busby, 1980).

112 Marcus Rainsford, *An Historical Account of the Black Empire of Hayti: Comprehending a View of the Principal Transactions in the Revolution in Saint Domingo; With its Antient and Modern State* (London: James Cundee, 1805) 323–4; my emphases.

113 Joseph Addison, *The Spectator*, ed. Donald Bond, 5 vols. (Oxford: Clarendon Press, 1965) vol. iii, 537.

114 Wordsworth, 'The Prelude of 1805', 370, Book 10, line 217; 368, Book 10, lines 205–6.

115 Blackburn, *Overthrow of Colonial Slavery*, 144–6.

116 Wordsworth, 'The Prelude of 1805', 370, Book 10, lines 221–226.

117 Cited in Blackburn 252. See also James Stephen, *Crisis of the Sugar Colonies: Or, an Enquiry into the Objects and Probable Effects of the French Expedition to the West Indies and their Connection with the Colonial Interests of the British Empire to Which Are Subjoined, Sketches of a Plan for the Settling of the Vacant Lands of Trinidad* (London: L. J. Hatchard, 1802) 195–7; *The Opportunity: Or, Reasons for an Immediate Alliance with San Domingo* (London: C. Whittingham, 1804) 47.

118 Jacobus, *Romanticism, Writing and Sexual Difference*, 72, 74.

119 Dorothy Wordsworth to Jane Pollard, 27 Jan.1789: 'My Brother John has set sail for Barbados. I hope, poor Lad! that he will be successful and happy, he is much delighted with the profession he has chosen. How we are squandered abroad!', *The Letters of William and Dorothy Wordsworth*, vol. i, 16, 21.

120 Dorothy Wordsworth to Jane Pollard (25–6 Jan. 1790), *The Letters of William and Dorothy Wordsworth*, vol. i, 25.

121 Stephen Gill, *William Wordsworth: A Life* (Oxford: Clarendon Press, 1989) 92.

122 Frank Prentice Rand, *Wordsworth's Mariner Brother* (Amherst, Mass.: Newell Press, 1966) 13–14.

123 Wordsworth, 'Prelude of 1805', 440, Book 12, lines 75–6.

124 Clarkson, *The History of the Rise, Progress and Accomplishment of the Abolition of the African Slave Trade by the British Parliament*, 2 vols. (London: Longman, Reas and Orine, 1808).

125 Wordsworth, 'To Thomas Clarkson, on the Final Passing of the Bill for the Abolition of the Slave Trade, March 1807', *Poetical Works*, 248.

126 Wordsworth, 'To Thomas Clarkson', 248, line 1.

127 Forlarin Shyllon, *Black People in Britain, 1555–1833* (London: Oxford University Press, 1977) 70–1.

128 William Blake, *The Complete Poetry and Prose of William Blake*, ed. David Erdman (New York: Doubleday, 1988) 665. In his annotations to Wordsworth's Poems of 1815, Blake commented: 'I see in Wordsworth the Natural Man rising up against the Spiritual Man Continually and then he is No Poet but a Heathen Philosopher at Enmity against all true Poetry or Inspiration'.

129 Wordsworth, *The Letters of William and Dorothy Wordsworth*, vol. v, 605–6.

130 *Ibid.*, vol. iv, 108–9. See also Norman Lewis Shelley, *The Abolitionist Movement in Sheffield* (Manchester: Manchester University Press, 1934) 15–17.

131 See Anne Mellor, 'Sex, Violence and Slavery: Blake and Wollstonecraft', *Huntington Library Quarterly* 58: 345–360.

132 Ottobah Cugoano, *Thoughts and Sentiments on the Evil and Wicked Traffic of the Slavery and Commerce of the Human Species, Humbly Submitted to the Inhabitants of Great Britain, by Ottobah Cugoano, a Native of Africa* (London, 1787).

133 Lauren Henry, 'Sunshine and Shady Groves', 83; Paul Edwards, *Unreconciled Strivings and Ironic Strategies: Three Afro-British Authors of the Georgian Era: Ignatius Sancho, Olaudah Equiano, Robert Wedderburn* (Edinburgh: Edinburgh University Press, 1992) 181.

134 Blake to William Hayley, 6 May 1800, *The Complete Poetry*, 705.

135 Mona Wilson, *The Life of William Blake* (Hertfordshire: Grenada, 1971) 56–8.

136 Emanuel Swedenborg, *New Jerusalem Tracts* tract 4, 1 in *The True Christian Religion*, 2 vols..

137 *Idem, The True Christian Religion, Containing the Universal Theology of the New Church, Foretold by the Lord* (New York, 1912) 146.

138 Blake, 'Annotations to Swedenborg's *Divine Love and Divine Wisdom*' (London, 1788) *The Complete Poetry*, 603. Blake's annotations are in italics.

139 Blake to Mr. Butts, 25 April 1803, *ibid.*, 728.

140 Blake to Hayley, 11 December 1805, *ibid.*, 767.

141 *Ibid.*, 3; Blake, 'There is No Natural Religion', *ibid.*, 3.

142 Blake, 'All Religions are One', *ibid.*, 1.

143 Blake, Plate 4, 'The Marriage of Heaven and Hell', *ibid.*, 34.

144 Blake, Plate 3, *ibid.*, 34–6.

145 Victor Paananen, *William Blake* (Boston, Mass.: Twayne, 1977), 50.

146 Blake, Plate 11, *ibid.*, 38.

147 *Ibid.*, 39.

148 Blake, 'Jerusalem', 146; Paananen, *Blake*, 141.

149 Bernard Nesfield-Cookson, *William Blake: Prophet of Universal Brotherhood* (England: Crucible, 1987) 342.

150 Blake, 'Jerusalem', *The Complete Poetry*, 212.

151 *Ibid.*, 231.
152 *Ibid.*, 201.
153 *Ibid.*, 201.
154 Blake, 'Jerusalem', Plate 97, lines 1–4, *ibid.*, 256–8.
155 Blake, 'The Little Black Boy', *ibid.*, 9. Mellor, *Romanticism and Feminism*, 94.
156 Mellor, 'Sex, Violence, and Slavery: Blake and Wollstonecraft', 345–62; 360.
157 Richard and Sally Price, 'Introduction', *Stedman's Narrative*, xii. See also Hugh Honour, *Representations of Black People in Western Art* (Cambridge Mass.: Harvard University Press, 1989).
158 Joan Baum, *Mind-Forg'd Manacles: Slavery and the English Romantic Poets* (New Haven, Connecticut: Archun, 1994) n.35, 187.
159 Mellor argues that Blake's visual assimilation of the black female body to the classical western white body is either an attempt to 'humanise' the African or a reflection of his neoclassical artistic training. Mellor, 'Sex, Violence, and Slavery: Blake and Wollstonecraft', 358.
160 Blake, *Visions of the Daughters of Albion*, lines 21–2 *The Complete Poetry*, 46.
161 David Erdman, *Blake: Prophet Against Empire: A Poet's Interpretation of the History of His Own Times* (New Jersey: Princeton University Press, 1977) 228–30.
162 Blake, *Visions of the Daughters of Albion*, lines 8–12, *The Complete Poetry*, 46.
163 *Ibid.*, Plate 7, lines 3–7, 50.
164 Joan Baum, *Mind-Forg'd Manacles*, 14.
165 *Ibid.*, 228–30.

4 CROSS-CULTURAL CONTACT: JOHN STEDMAN, THOMAS JEFFERSON AND THE SLAVES

1 John Gabriel Stedman, *Narrative, of a Five Years' Expedition, Against the Revolted Negroes of Surinam, in Guiana, on the Wild Coast of South America; From the Year 1772, to 1777*, 2 vols. (London, 1796); Stedman, *Narrative of a Five Years Expedition, Against the Revolted Negroes of Surinam Transcribed for the First Time from the Original 1790 Manuscript*, ed. Richard Price and Sally Price (Baltimore: Johns Hopkins University Press, 1988). I shall refer to this edition throughout unless otherwise specified. See also Geoffrey Keynes, *Blake Studies: Essays on His Life and His Work* (Oxford: Clarendon Press, 1971) 98–105. For more details on the Dutch colony of Surinam see Waldo Heilbron, *Colonial Transformations and the Decomposition of Dutch Plantation Slavery in Surinam* (London: Goldsmiths College, 1993).
2 Mary Louise Pratt, *Imperial Eyes: Travel Writing and Transculturation* (London: Routledge, 1992) 91–2.
3 See Richard Price's excellent introduction to the *Narrative*, xiii-xcvii, xvi, xxx.

4 As Erdman notes, we know that Blake was working on these plates during the production of the 'Visions of the Daughters of Albion' because he submitted them in batches dated 1 Dec. 1792 and 2 Dec. 1793. David Erdman, *Blake: Prophet Against Empire: A Poet's Interpretation of the History of His Own Times* (New Jersey: Princeton University Press, 1977).

5 Stedman, *Narrative*, Introduction, xxxvii, xlviii, xlix.

6 *Ibid.*, xxxii.

7 Mary Louise Pratt, *Imperial Eyes*, 90–102, 91.

8 Stedman, *Narrative* (1988), 7.

9 *Ibid.*, 7.

10 *Ibid.*, 173, 27–9.

11 *Ibid.*, 199; Stedman, *Narrative* (1796), vol. ii, 259–60.

12 Stedman, *Narrative* (1988), 171; my emphasis.

13 *Ibid.*, 171.

14 *Ibid.*, 168.

15 *Ibid.*, 171; my emphasis.

16 *Ibid.*, 521.

17 *Ibid.*, 171.

18 Stedman, *Narrative* (1796), vol. i, v; cited in *Narrative* (1988), lxiv.

19 Stedman, *Narrative* (1988), 90, 260.

20 *Ibid.*, 43.

21 See Abena Busia, 'Miscegenation as Metonymy: Sexuality and Power in the Colonial Novel', *Ethnic and Racial Studies* 9 (1986): 360–72.

22 Stedman, *Narrative* (1988), 88.

23 Guillaume Thomas Raynal, *A Philosophical and Political History of the Settlements and Trade of the Europeans in the East and West Indies*, trans. J. Justamond, 5 vols. (London, 1776) vol. iii, 164.

24 Pratt, *Imperial Eyes*, 95–7.

25 Stedman, *Narrative* (1988), 90.

26 *Ibid.*, 87–8; my emphasis.

27 *Ibid.*, 90, 98–100, 260.

> Here in close recess,
> With flowry Garlands and sweet Smelling herbs,
> Espoused Eve did deck her ruptial [nuptial] bed,
> And heavenly Quires the hymeneal Sing;
> What Day the genial Angel to *her friend*
> Brought her in naked Beauty more adorn'd,
> More lovely than Pandora, whom the Gods
> Endow'd with all their Gifts.

John Milton, *Poetical Works, Paradise Lost: A Poem Written in Ten Books* (London, 1667) Book 4, lines 708–15.

28 Pratt, *Imperial Eyes*, 97. See also Peter Hulme, *Colonial Encounters: Europe and the Native Caribbean, 1492–1797* (1986; London: Routledge, 1992).

29 Stedman, *Narrative* (1988), 624.

30 Stephen Houlgate, *Freedom, Truth and History: An Introduction to Hegel's Philosophy* (London: Routledge, 1991) 19.
31 George Wilhelm Friedrich Hegel, 'The Natural Context or the Geographical Basis of World History', *Lectures on the Philosophy of World History*, trans. H.B. Nisbet, ed. Duncan Forbes (Cambridge: Cambridge University Press, 1975) 190.
32 Houlgate, *Freedom, Truth and History*, 20.
33 Hegel, *Lectures*, 183–4.
34 William Bosman, *A New and Accurate Description of the Coast of Guinea, Divided into the Gold, the Slave, and the Ivory Coasts . . .* (London, 1705) 146.
35 William Snelgrave, *A New Account of Guinea, and the Slave Trade* (London, 1734) 10.
36 Atkins, *A Voyage to Guinea, Brasil, and the West Indies; in His Majesty's Ships, the Swallow and Weymouth . . .* (London, 1735) 113–14.
37 Hegel, *Lectures*, 173–4.
38 *Ibid.*, 176–7.
39 George Wilhelm Friedrich Hegel, *Phenomenology of Spirit*, trans. A.V. Miller, ed. J. N. Findlay (Oxford: Clarendon Press, 1977) 297.
40 Hegel, *Lectures*, 178–9; my emphases.
41 *Ibid.*, 181, 180.
42 *Ibid.*, 180–1; my emphases.
43 See Andrew Bowie, *Aesthetics and Subjectivity, from Kant to Nietzsche* (Manchester: Manchester University Press, 1990) for a discussion of the Romantic critique of Hegel.
44 Johann Joachim Winckelman, *The History of Ancient Art*, trans. G. Henry Lodge, 2 vols. (Boston: Little Brown and Co., 1856) vol. ii, 4.
45 *Ibid.*, vol. i, 191–2.
46 *Ibid.*, vol. i, 199.
47 This was a point vehemently contended by Puritan advocates of slave conversion such as Cotton Mather and defied by the first baptism of a slave in New England in 1641. For further discussion, see Lorenzo Greene, *The Negro in Colonial New England, 1620–1770* (New York: Columbia University Press, 1945) 257.
48 David Hume, 'Of National Characters' (1753), *The Philosophical Works of David Hume*, 4 vols. (Edinburgh: Adam Black and William Tait, 1826) vol. iii, 236 (note c).
49 David Hume, *A Treatise of Human Nature: Being an Attempt to Introduce the Experimental Method of Reasoning into Moral Subjects*, 3 vols. (London, 1739) vol. iii, 61, 50.
50 Philip Curtin, *Two Jamaicas: The Role of Ideas in a Tropical Colony, 1830–1865* (Cambridge, Mass.: Harvard University Press, 1955) 123; K. G. Davies, *The Royal African Company* (London: Longman, 1957).
51 See Alissandra Cummins, 'Caribbean Slave Society', *Transatlantic Slavery: Against Human Dignity*, ed. A. J. Tibbles (Liverpool: National Museums and Galleries on Merseyside, 1994) 51–9, 51.

52 Elsa Goveia, *Slave Society in the British Leeward Islands at the End of the Eighteenth Century* (New Haven: Yale University Press, 1965) 152–8.

53 *Acts of the Assembly, Passed in the Island of Jamaica; from 1681, to 1754 Inclusive* (London, 1754) 64, Act 38.

54 *Ibid.*, 181, Act 98, Clause 10; my emphasis.

55 Cummins, 'Carribean Slave Society', 55. Detailed Leeward Islands, MSS Laws, 1644–1673: C.O. 154 / 1 / 49–51.

56 *Acts of the Assembly. Passed in the Island of Jamaica; from 1770, to 1783, Inclusive* (London, 1783), 20.

57 B. W. Higman, *Slave Population and Economy in Jamaica, 1807–1834* (Kingston: The University of the West Indies Press, 1995) 141.

58 Edward Brathwaite and Edward Kamau, *The Development of Creole Society in Jamaica, 1770–1820* (1971; Oxford: Clarendon Press, 1978) 160.

59 Edward Long, *The History of Jamaica: Or, a General Survey of the Antient and Modern State of That Island; with Reflections on its Situation, Settlements, Inhabitants, Climate, Products, Commerce, Laws and Government*, 3 vols. (London, 1774) vol. ii, 353, vol. ii, 356, 353; my emphases.

60 Johann Friedrich Blumenbach, 'On the Natural Variety of Mankind' ['De Generis Humani Varietate Natura'], *The Anthropological Treatises of Johann Friedrich Blumenbach. With Memoirs of Him by Marx and Flourens, and an Account of His Anthropological Museum by Professor R. Wagner, and the Inaugural Dissertation of John Hunter on the Varieties of Man*, ed. and trans. Thomas Bendyshe (London: Longman, Green, Longman, Roberts and Green, 1865) 65–144, 98–9; Robert Young, *Colonial Desire: Hybridity in Theory, Culture and Race* (London: Routledge, 1995) 64.

61 Blumenbach, 'Contributions to Natural History', *Anthropological Treatises*, 277–325, 305–12, 307.

62 Nancy Stepan, 'Biological Degeneration: Races and Proper Places', *Degeneration: The Dark Side of Progress*, ed. Edward Chamberlain and Sander Gilman (New York: Columbia University Press, 1985) 105. In the third edition of 'On the Natural Variety of Mankind' (1795) Blumenbach also discussed the size of the African penis; *Anthropological Treatises*, 145–276, 249.

63 Wordsworth, *The Prelude, 1799, 1805, 1850: Authoritative Texts, Context and Reception, Recent Critical Essays*, ed. Jonathan Wordsworth, M. H. Abrams and Stephen Gill (New York: Norton, 1979) Book 7, 235–43.

64 Blumenbach, 'On the Natural Variety of Mankind', 107.

65 Raynal, *A Philosophical and Political History*, vol. iii, 490.

66 Blumenbach, 'On the Natural Variety of Mankind', 111–12.

67 Long, *Candid Reflections*; *The Morning Post*, 22 Dec. 1786, cited File 27.

68 Blumenbach, 'On the Natural Variety of Mankind' (1795), 47, 188–263.

69 For an excellent discussion of degeneration, see Chamberlain and Gilman, *Degeneration*, 97–121.

70 Georges Leopold Cuvier, *The Animal Kingdom Arranged in Conformity with Its Organisation: With Additional Descriptions of All the Species Hitherto Named,*

and of Many Not Before Noticed, ed. Edward Griffith, 2 vols. (London: George Whittaker, 1827) 165–6.

71 *Ibid.*, 171.

72 Greene, *Negro in Colonial New England*, 207–8.

73 James Walvin, *Black Ivory: A History of British Slavery* (London: Harper Collins, 1992) 225. It was this intermediary group which instigated many of the most destructive of slave revolts.

74 James Cowles Prichard, *Researches into the Physical History of Man*, ed. George W. Stocking (Chicago: Chicago University Press, 1973) 10, 11–13.

75 *Ibid.*, 9–10.

76 William Lawrence, *Lectures on Physiology, Zoology, and the Natural History of Man Delivered to the Royal College of Surgeons* (London: J. Callow, 1819) 296, 300.

77 Joseph Arthur de Gobineau, *The Inequality of Human Races*, trans. Adrian Collins (Los Angeles: Noontide Press, 1966) 25; Young, *Colonial Desire*, 102.

78 Gobineau, *The Inequality of Human Races*, 25; cf. Michael D. Biddiss, *Father of Racist Ideology: The Social and Political Thought of Count Gobineau* (London: Weidenfeld and Nicolson, 1970) 109; Eugene Talbot, *Degeneracy: Its Causes, Signs and Results* (London: Walter Scott, 1898) 99.

79 Talbot 101–3.

80 Gobineau, *The Inequality of Human Races*, 204.

81 Biddiss, *Father of Racist Ideology*, 116.

82 Gobineau, *The Inequality of Human Races*, 210–1.

83 Percy Bysshe Shelley's poetical search for 'origins' in *Alastor, or the Spirit of Solitude* (1815) appears to be informed by the pervasive theories of racial origins prevalent in the late eighteenth and early nineteenth century. On the other hand, Mary Shelley's *Frankenstein; Or, the Modern Prometheus*, 3 vols. (London: Lackington, Hughes, Harding, Mavor and Jones, 1818) presents an investigation of the interrelationship between western aesthetics, racial difference and the ostracised (or 'mutant') entity's efforts to 'master' language. Likewise, Bertha Mason in Charlotte Bronte's *Jane Eyre* (1847) presents the threat posed by the white 'Creole' (a figure who darkens as the novel progresses) who threatens the domestic tranquillity of Thornfield. See Firdous Azim, *The Colonial Rise of the Novel* (London: Routledge, 1993) 182.

84 Josiah Quincey, 'Journal of Josiah Quincey Junior, 1773', *Proceedings from the Massachusetts Historical Society, June 1916* 49 (1916): 424–81, cited in Hazel Carby, *Reconstructing Womanhood: The Emergence of the Afro-American Woman Novelist* (Oxford: Oxford University Press, 1987) 30. See also William and Ellen Craft, *Running a Thousand Miles for Freedom, Or, the Escape of William and Ellen Craft from Slavery* (London: William Tweedie, 1860) and Nella Larsen, *Quicksand and Passing* (New York: Negro University Press, 1928) for examples of a nineteenth-century auto-

biographical account of the consequences of racial intermixture and a fictionalised twentieth-century account.

85 Stepan, 'Biological Degeneration', 99. Less than a century later, the ruthless cleansing process of Nazi Germany witnessed the effective translation of eighteenth-century racialised semantics into anti-semitism.

86 Henry Louis Gates, *The Signifying Monkey: A Theory of African-American Literary Criticism* (New York: Oxford University Press, 1988) 129.

87 William Shakespeare, *The Tempest*, ed. J. R. Sutherland (Oxford: Clarendon Press, 1978) Act III, Scene II, 89–92. See also Stephen Greenblatt, *Learning to Curse: Essays in Early Modern Culture* (London: Routledge, 1990); Peter Hulme, 'Hurricanes in the Caribbees: The Constitution of the Discourse of English Colonialism', *1642: Literature and Power in the Seventeenth Century. Proceedings from the Essex Conference on the Sociology of Literature, July 1980*, ed. Francis Barker et al. (Colchester: University of Essex, 1981) 55–83.

88 From the *American Slave Code* cited in Henry Louis Gates, *Figures in Black. Words, Signs and the 'Racial' Self* (New York: Oxford University Press, 1989) 17.

89 Gates, *Signifying Monkey*, 131.

90 Moses Roper, *A Narrative of the Adventures and Escape of Moses Roper, from American Slavery*, ed. Revd T. Price (London: Darton, Harvey and Darton, 1837) 82.

91 Pete Fryer, *Staying Power: The History of Black People in Britain* (London: Pluto Press, 1984) 137–8; Thomas Herbert, *Some Yeares Travels into Divers Parts of Asia and Afrique. Describing Especially the Two Famous Empires, the Persian, and Great Mogull with the History of These Later Times* (1638; London, 1677) 18.

92 Herbert, *Some Yeares Travels*, 17.

93 Zora Neale Hurston's play, 'The First One: A Play', *Ebony and Topaz*, ed. Charles Johnson (New York: National Urban League, 1926) illustrates the folkloric process by which the Judeo-Christian tradition was Afro-Americanised.

94 See Mary Turner, *Slaves and Missionaries: The Disintegration of Jamaican Slave Society, 1787–1834* (Urbana: University of Illinois Press, 1982) 51–9, 65–95 for a discussion of the development of African polytheistic beliefs in Jamaica.

95 William Bosman, *A New and Accurate Description of the Coast of Guinea*, 146–7. See also William Pierson, *Black Yankees: The Development of an Afro-American Subculture in Eighteenth-Century New England* (Amhurst, Mass.: Massachusetts University Press, 1988) 10.

96 See Eric Williams, *Capitalism and Slavery* (1945; London: Andre Deutsch, 1964) 126–53.

97 Thomas Paine, *Common Sense: Addressed to the Inhabitants of America* (Edinburgh, 1776) 22.

98 Eric Foner, *Thomas Paine and Revolutionary America* (New York: Oxford University Press, 1976).

99 See Stephen Fender's excellent discussion of these key American texts, *American Literature in Context I: 1630–1830* (London: Methuen, 1983) 63–97, 110, 101; Thomas Jefferson, 'A Declaration by the Representatives of the United States of America, in General Congress Assembled', *Writings*, ed. Merrill Peterson (New York: Literary Classics, 1984) 19; my emphases.

100 See Robert Sayer and James Cox, 'Autobiography and the Making of America', 'Recovering Literature's Lost Ground', *Autobiography: Essays Theoretical and Critical*, ed. James Olney (Princeton: Princeton University Press, 1980).

101 Jefferson, 'To Samuel Kercheval', 19 Jan. 1810, *Writings*, 1214.

102 *Ibid.*, 264–6; my emphasis. Following the twelve-year period (1865–1877) of reunion, reconstruction and racial readjustment which followed the American Civil War of 1861–1865 (and which established both the Thirteenth Amendment to the Constitution and the 'forty acres and a mule' motto of land distribution), biracial democracy was abandoned and economic and domestic apartheid legalised by the Supreme Court's overturning of the Civil Rights Act of 1875. This was further endorsed by the *Plessy vs. Ferguson* decision of 1896. For an excellent discussion of the first and second Reconstruction in America, see Manning Marable, *Race, Reform and Rebellion: The Second Reconstruction in Black America, 1945–1982* (London: Macmillan, 1984).

103 Jefferson, 'To Henri Gregoire', 25 Feb. 1809, *Writings*, 1202.

104 Thomas Paine, *Rights of Man: Being an Answer to Mr Burke's Attack on the French Revolution* (London, 1791) 9–10; my emphasis, except for the word 'living'. Eleven months later in Part Two of the *Rights of Man*, Paine's defence of the French Revolution developed into a systematic theory of government and society which contained an economic programme designed to alleviate the plight of the European masses by means of a progressive tax on landed property.

5 THE DIASPORIC IDENTITY: LANGUAGE AND THE PARADIGMS OF LIBERATION

1 Toni Morrison, *Beloved* (1987; London: Chatto and Windus, 1988) 210–13.

2 Hortense Spillers, 'Mama's Baby, Papa's Maybe: An American Grammar Book', *Diacritics* 17 (1987): 67, 72, 73.

3 See Stuart Hall, 'Cultural Identity and Diaspora', *Identity: Community, Culture, Difference*, ed. Jonathan Rutherford (London: Lawrence and Wishart, 1990) 222–37. See also Pierre Macherey, *A Theory of Literary Production*, trans. G. Wall (London: Routledge and Kegan Paul, 1978)

82–93, for Macherey's concept of what is unspoken and repressed in a text.

4 James Olney, '"I Was Born": Slave Narratives, Their Status As Auto-biography and Literature', *The Slave's Narrative*, ed. Charles T. Davis and Henry Louis Gates (Oxford: Oxford University Press, 1985) 151. Accord-ing to W. J. T. Mitchell, the slave narratives enabled an 'ekphrasis of the self', a conscious re-memory of slave times written from the standpoint of freedom. W. J. T. Mitchell, *Picture Theory: Essays on Verbal and Visual Representation* (Chicago: University of Chicago Press, 1994) 184, 190.

5 Spillers, 'Mama's Baby, Papa's Maybe', 67.

6 *Ibid.*, 67, 73. *The Moynihan Report* (The United States Department of Labour, 1965) claimed that the matriarchal structure of the black American family retarded 'the progress of the group as a whole'.

7 My use of the term 'mulatto' is therefore, not intended pejoratively, but as a positive reclamation of that term used to designate a person of mixed racial parentage.

8 Toni Morrison, *Playing in the Dark: Whiteness and the Literary Imagination* (London: Picador, 1992) 70.

9 Kobena Mercer, 'Diaspora Culture and the Dialogic Imagination: The Aesthetics of Black Independent Film in Britain', *Blackframes: Critical Perspectives on Black Independent Cinema*, ed. Mbye B. Cham and Claire Andrade-Watkins (Cambridge, Mass.: M.I.T. Press, 1988) 57. Cited in Stuart Hall, 'Cultural Identity', 236.

10 John Agard, 'Listen Mr Oxford Don', *Mangoes and Bullets* (London: Pluto, 1985).

11 Zora Neale Hurston, *Their Eyes Were Watching God* (1937; London: Virago, 1990).

12 Henry Louis Gates, *Signifying Monkey: A Theory of African-American Literary Criticism* (New York: Oxford University Press, 1988) xix–xxviii.

13 William Andrews, *To Tell A Free Story: The First Century of Afro-American Autobiography, 1760–1865* (Urbana: Illinois University Press, 1986) 7.

14 Houston Baker, *Blues, Ideology and Afro-American Literature: A Vernacular Theory* (Chicago: Chicago University Press, 1984) 17–19, 92–3.

15 I am referring to 'hoodoo' and the 'vodun' rituals of the Yoruba people which I shall discuss below. See Zora Neale Hurston, *Tell My Horse: Voodoo and Life in Haiti and Jamaica*, ed. Ishmael Reed (New York: Harper and Row, 1990); and Michel Laguerre, *Voodoo Heritage* (Beverley Hills: Sage Publications, 1980).

16 I am expanding and revising William Edward Dubois' notion of 'two-ness' in his essay 'Of Our Spiritual Strivings' (1903), *The Souls of Black Folk*, ed. Cadance Ward (New York: Dover Publications, 1994).

17 David Sutcliffe, *British Black English* (Oxford: Basil Blackwell, 1982) 8–13.

18 Robert Anderson Hall, *Pidgin and Creole Languages* (Ithaca: Cornell University Press, 1966) 126; cited in Suzanne Romaine, *Pidgin and Creole Languages* (London: Longman, 1988) 115.

19 Gwendolyn Midlo Hall, *Africans in Colonial Louisiana: The Development of Afro-Creole Culture in the Eighteenth Century* (Baton Rouge: Louisiana State University Press, 1992) 157.

20 Edward Kamau Brathwaite, *The Development of Creole Society in Jamaica, 1770–1820* (Oxford: Clarendon Press, 1971).

21 *Ibid.*, 309–11.

22 Molefi Kete Asante, 'African Elements in African-American English', *Africanisms in American Culture*, ed. Joseph Holloway (Bloomington: Indiana University Press, 1990) 22. See also Mervyn Alleyne, *The Roots of Jamaican Culture* (London: Pluto Press, 1988).

23 Asante, 'African Elements', 27, 17. See also Ifi Amadiume, *Male Daughters, Female Husbands: Gender and Sex in African Society* (1987; London: Zed Books, 1992) 89–91.

24 Eugene Genovese, *Roll, Jordan Roll: The World the Slaves Made* (1974; New York: Vintage Books, 1976) 421.

25 John Reinecke, 'Trade Jargons and Creole Dialects as Marginal Languages', *Language in Culture and Society*, ed. C. Dell Hymes (New York: Harper and Row, 1964) 534–46.

26 Zora Neale Hurston, *Mules and Men*, ed. Franz Boas and Arnold Rampersad (1935; New York: Harper Perennial, 1990) 74–5; my emphasis. See also Karla Holloway, *The Character of the Word: The Texts of Zora Neale Hurston* (Connecticut: Greenwood Press, 1987) 78.

27 See Maria Leach and Jerome Fried, eds, Funk and Wagnalls Standard Dictionary of Folklore, Mythology and Legend (London: New English Library, 1975) 18–24 and Sidney Mintz and Richard Price, *An Anthropological Approach to the Afro-American Past: A Caribbean Perspective* (Philadelphia: Institute for the Study of Human Studies, 1976).

6 THE EARLY SLAVE NARRATIVES: JUPITER HAMMON, JOHN MARRANT AND OTTOBAH GRONNIASAW

1 See Lawrence Levine, 'Slave Songs and Slave Consciousness: An Exploration in Neglected Sources', *Anonymous Americans*, ed. Tamara K. Haveran (New Jersey: Prentice-Hall, 1971) 107; Sterling Brown, 'Spirituals', *The Book of Negro Folklore*, ed. L. H. and Arna Bontemps (New York: Dodd and Mead, 1958) 279–89; Robert Hemenway, *Zora Neale Hurston: A Literary Biography* (1977; London: Camden Press, 1986) 258–9.

2 Cf. Johannes Nederven Pieterse, 'Slavery and the Triangle of Emancipation', *Race and Class* 30 (1988): 1–22.

3 Zora Neale Hurston, 'Spirituals and Neo-Spirituals', *The Negro Anthology*, ed. Nancy Cunard (London: Nancy Cunard, 1934).

4 Zora Neale Hurston, *Tell My Horse: Voodoo and Life in Haiti and Jamaica* (1938; New York: Harper Perennial, 1990); idem, *Moses, Man of the Mountain* (1939; New Jersey: Chatham, 1974).

5 Houston Baker, *Long Black Song* (Chicago: Chicago University Press,

1990) 12, 31–3; W. F. Allen, *Slave Songs of the United States* (New York: Dover, 1867); Brown, 'Spirituals', 279–84; James Weldon Johnson, ed., *A Book of American Negro Spirituals* (London: Chapman and Hall, 1926).

6 Richard Sheridan, *Doctors and Slaves: A Medical and Demographic History of Slavery in the British West Indies, 1680–1834* (Cambridge: Cambridge University Press, 1985) 73.

7 Orlando Patterson, *The Sociology of Slavery: An Analysis of the Origins, Development and Structure of Negro Slave Society in Jamaica* (London: MacGibbon and Kee, 1967) 182–5.

8 Thomas Coke, *A History of the West Indies, Continuing the Natural, Civil and Ecclesiastical History of Each Island: with an Account of the Missions Instituted in those Islands, from the Commencement of their Civilisation*, 3 vols. (Liverpool: Nuttall, Fisher and Dixon, 1808–1811) vol. i, 112–13.

9 John Samuel Mbiti, *African Religions and Philosophy* (1969; London: Heinemann, 1990) 2.

10 *Ibid.*, 26–7.

11 Harry Gilford, *Voodoo: Its Origins and Practices* (London: Franklin Watts, 1976) 9.

12 Thomas Winterbottom, *An Account of the Native Africans in the Neighbourhood of Sierra Leone; To Which is Added, an Account of the Present State of Medicine Among Them*, 2 vols. (London: C. Whittingham, 1803) vol. ii, 10.

13 *Myal*: cf., Hausa *maye*,1. Sorcerer, wizard; 2.Intoxication; Return, *Dictionary of Jamaican English*; *Obi* cf. Efik, *ubio*, 'a thing or mixture of things, put into the ground, as a charm to cause sickness or death', OED.

14 Carolyn Cooper, 'Something Ancestral Recaptured', *Motherlands: Black Women's Writing from Africa, the Caribbean and South Asia*, ed. Sushiela Nasta (London: The Women's Press, 1991) 64–87. See also Toni Morrison, *Song of Solomon* (London: Picador, 1978).

15 William Pierterse, 'White Cannibals, Black Martyrs: Fear, Depression and Religious Faith As Causes of Suicide among New Slaves', *Slave Trade and Migration: Domestic and Foreign*, ed. Paul Finkelman (London: Garland Publications, 1989) 323–35; 148–53.

16 Gilford, *Voodoo*, 30.

17 David Geggus, *Slave Resistance Studies and the Saint Domingo Slave Revolt: Some Considerations* (Miami: Florida International University, 1983) 18.

18 *The Report of the Lords of the Committee of the Council Appointed for the Consideration of all Matters to Trade and Foreign Plantation* (London, 1789); Joseph Williams, *Voodoos and Obeahs: Phases of West India Witchcraft* (London: George Allen and Unwin, 1933) 111.

19 Williams, *Voodoo*, 114.

20 *Acts of the Privy Council*, vol. ii, 834 cited in Williams, *Voodoo*, 161.

21 *Acts of Assembly* (Kingston, 1786) 277; cited in Williams, *Voodoo*, 163–4.

22 R. R. Madden, *A Twelvemonths Residence in the West Indies, During the Transition from Slavery to Apprenticeship*, 2 vols. (London: James Cochrane, 1835); Williams, *Voodoo*, 190.

23 See Harry Hyatt, *Hoodoo, Conjuration, Witchcraft and Rootwork Beliefs Accepted by Many Negroes and White Persons, These Being Orally Recorded Among Blacks and Whites*, 5 vols. (Cambridge, Md.: Western Pub., 1978).

24 Alan Richardson, 'Romantic Voodoo: Obeah and British Culture, 1797–1807', *Studies in Romanticism* vol. 32:1 (1993):3–28.

25 *Obi; or, Three Finger'd Jack: A Melo-Drama, in Two Acts* (London: Thomas Hailes Lacy, n.d. [1800]); Charlotte Smith, 'The Story of Henrietta', *Letters of a Solitary Wanderer: Containing Narratives of Various Descriptions*, 2 vols. (London: Sampson Low, 1800); Maria Edgeworth, 'Belinda', *Popular Tales*, 3 vols. (1790; repr. London: J. Johnson, 1804); William Shepherd, 'The Negro's Incantation', *The Monthly Magazine* July 1797 and *The Poetical Register and Repository of Fugitive Poetry, for 1803*, 2nd edn. (London: Rivington, 1805) 413–15. See also the anonymous 'Negro's Imprecation', *The Meteors* (London: A. & J. Black, 1800).

26 Richardson, 'Romantic Voodoo', 5.

27 Shepherd 'Incantation', lines 34–7.

28 John Blassingame, *Slave Testimony: Two Centuries of Letters, Speeches, Interviews and Autobiographies* (Baton Rouge: Louisiana State University Press, 1979) xlii.

29 William Boscom, 'Acculturation Among the Gullah Negroes', *American Anthropologist* 43 (1941): 44; cited in George Rawick, *The American Slave: A Composite Autobiography*, 6 vols. (Connecticut: Greenwood, 1972) vol. i, 35.

30 Rawick, *The American Slave*, vol. i, 49; Hemenway, *Hurston*, 118–19. One such descendent conjuror was Marie Leveau (*c.* 1819–1881), the legendary Creole conjuror who presided over the Hoodoo world of New Orleans. In *Mules and Men*, ed. Frank Boas and Arnold Rampersad (New York: Harper Perennial, 1999), Hurston claimed that Marie Leveau was a descendant of three generations of hoodoo queens.

31 Philip D. Curtin, *Two Jamaicas: The Role of Ideas in a Tropical Colony, 1830–1865* (Cambridge, Mass.: Harvard University Press, 1955).

32 John Clark, *Memorials of Baptist Missionaries in Jamaica, Including a Sketch of the Labours of Early Religious Instructors in Jamaica* (London: Yates and Alexander, 1869) 12–4.

33 Curtin, *Two Jamaicas*, 33.

34 *Ibid.*, 35, 168–9.

35 *Ibid.*, 171.

36 James Olney, ed., *Autobiography: Essays Theoretical and Critical* (Princeton: Princeton University Press, 1980) 6. See also George Starr, *Defoe and Spiritual Autobiography* (Princeton: Princeton University Press, 1965); John Morris, *Versions of the Self Studies in English Autobiography from John Bunyan to John Mill* (London: Basic Books, 1966); Paul Delany, *British Autobiography in the Seventeenth Century* (London: Routledge and Kegan Paul, 1969); Patricia Meyer Spacks, *Imagining a Self: Autobiography and the Novel in Eighteenth-Century England* (Cambridge, Mass.: Harvard University Press, 1976); Roy Pascal, *Design and Truth in Autobiography* (London: Routledge

and Kegan Paul, 1960) and Elizabeth Bruss, *Autobiographical Acts: The Changing Situation of a Literary Genre* (Baltimore: Johns Hopkins University Press, 1976).

37 Georges Gusdorf, 'Conditions and Limits of Autobiography', *Autobiography: Essays Theoretical and Critical*, ed. Olney, 37.

38 James Olney, 'Some Versions of Memory / Some Versions of Bios: The Ontology of Autobiography', *Autobiography: Essays Theoretical and Critical*, ed. Olney, 241.

39 See Barrett J. Mendell, 'Full of Life Now', *Autobiography: Essays Theoretical and Critical*, ed. Olney, 49–72.

40 *Ibid.*, 72.

41 Philip Curtin, *Africa Remembered: Narratives by West Africans from the Era of the Slave Trade* (Madison: University of Wisconsin, 1967) 1–14; Thomas Bluett, *Some Memoirs of the Life of Job, the Son of Solomon, the High Priest of Boonda in Africa* (London, 1734), Robert Norris, ed., *Memoirs of the Reign of Bossa Ahadee, King of Dahomey to Which are Added; The Author's Journey to Abomey the Capital and a Short Account of the African Slave Trade* (London, 1789); John Ishmael Augustus James, *The Narrative of the Travels of John Ishmael Augustus James, an African of the Mandingo Tribe, who was Captured, Sold into Slavery and Subsequently Liberated by a Benevolent English Gentleman* (Truro: n.d., 1836).

42 R.W. Loane, *Authentic Narrative of the Late Fortunate Escape of R. W. Loane Who, with Captain R. Youl, M. J. Flower and Eleven Natives Was Captured by Aza Arabs in the Persian Gulf* (London: Ferris, 1805); George Vason, *Authentic Narrative of Four Years' Residence at Tongataboo, one of the Friendly Islands, in the South Sea, by [George Vason] who Went Thither in the Duff, Under Captain Wilson, in 1796* (London: Longman, Hurst, Rees and Orme, 1810).

43 Cf. Allan de Sousa and Yong Soon Min's collaborative installation, *Alter Idem: Performing Personae* (London: Camerawork Photographic Gallery, September 1994) presented a visual analysis of the interrelationship between ethnography and photography by means of the concept of the 'native informant'. See also James Clifford, *The Predicament of Culture – Twentieth Century Ethnography, Literature and Art* (Cambridge, Mass.: Harvard University Press, 1988); James Clifford and George Marcus, eds, *Writing Culture – The Poetics and Politics of Ethnography* (Berkeley: University of California, 1986); and Margaret Hodgen, ed., *Early Anthropology in the Sixteenth and Seventeenth Centuries* (Philadelphia: University of Pennsylvania Press, 1964).

44 Joanna, *Joanna, or the Female Slave. A West Indian Tale, Founded on Stedman's Narrative of an Expedition Against the Revolted Negroes of Surinam* (London: S. and B. Bentley, 1824) viii.

45 Sayer, 'Autobiography', 165.

46 William Edward Dubois, *The Souls of Black Folk*, ed. Cadance Ward (New York: Dover Publications, 1994), 2–3.

47 Spillers, 'Mama's Baby, Papa's Maybe', 67, 72, 73.

48 Vévé Clark, 'Developing Diaspora Literacy and *Marasa* Consciousness', *Comparative American Identities: Race, Sex and Nationality in the Modern Text*, ed. Hortense Spillers (New York: Routledge, 1991) 42–4.

49 The Fanti slave Ottobah Cugoano, author of *Thoughts and Sentiments on the Evil and Wicked Traffic of the Slavery and Commerce of the Human Species, Humbly Submitted to the Inhabitants of Great Britain* (London, 1787), emphasised his status as a twin.

50 John Marrant, *Journal of the Revd John Marrant* (London, 1790).

51 See William Hosking Oliver, *Prophets and Millennialists: The Uses of Biblical Prophecy in England from the 1790s to the 1840s* (Auckland: Auckland University Press, 1978) for an excellent study of the millennial movement.

52 Andrews, *To Tell a Free Story*, 62–65.

53 Jupiter Hammon, 'A Winter Piece' (1782), *The Complete Works of Jupiter Hammon*, ed. Stanley Ransom (New York: Kennikat Press, 1970) 73.

54 Jupiter Hammon, 'An Address to the Negroes in the State of New York' (1787), *Magazine of History Series* 114 (1925): 46.

55 Jupiter Hammon, 'An Evening Thought: Salvation by Christ with Penitential Cries: Composed by Jupiter Hammon, A Negro Belonging to Mr. Lloyd, of Queen's Village, on Long Island, the 25th December, 1760', *Jupiter Hammon: American Negro Poet. Selections from His Writings and a Bibliography*, ed. Oscar Wegelin (New York: Heartman, 1915) 29–31, lines 39–40.

56 Jean Ossan, *Henry Lloyd's Salt Box Manor House* (New York: Lloyd Harbour Historical Society, 1982) 20–4, 30, 38; Philip Richards, 'Nationalist Themes in the Preaching of Jupiter Hammon', *Early American Literature* 25 (1990): 123–38.

57 Jupiter Hammon, *An Address to Miss Phillis Wheatley* (Hartford, 4 Aug. 1778), *Jupiter Hammon*, 32–3, lines 13–20.

58 Hammon, *Address to the Negroes*, 107.

59 *Ibid.*, 51.

60 *Ibid.*, 47.

61 *Ibid.*, 73; my emphases. Richards, 'Nationalist Themes', 123–38.

62 *Ibid.*, 73.

63 *Ibid.*, 73, 51, 47; my emphasis.

64 John Marrant, *A Narrative of the Lord's Wonderful Dealings with John Marrant, a Black (Now Going to Preach the Gospel in Nova Scotia) Born in New York, in North America*, 2nd edn. (London: Gilbert and Plummer, 1785). All references will be to this edition.

65 Henry Louis Gates, *The Signifying Monkey*, 142–6. Marrant's text was frequently amended and republished. As Potkay notes, there are multiple copies of single issues and haphazardly reassembled collections of various texts. The first six editions of 1785 were printed by Gilbert

and Plummer; the last 'enlarged by Mr. Marrant' himself. The last two of these editions comprised of the same imprint 'with additions' by Marrant. The 1812 edition, *A Narrative of the Life of John Marrant of New York, in North America: Giving an Account of his Conversion When Only Nine Years of Age* (London, 1812), was edited by J. Nicholson. See Adam Potkay and Sandra Burr, eds, *Black Atlantic Writers of the Eighteenth Century: Living the New Exodus in England and America* (Basingstoke: Macmillan, 1995) 71–3.

66 Marrant, *Narrative*, v.

67 William Andrews, 'The First Fifty Years of the Slave Narrative, 1760–1810', *The Art of the Slave Narrative: Original Essays in Criticism and Theory* (Macomb: Western Illinois University, 1982) 6–24, 7. Aldridge was not the distributor of the fourth edition of Marrant's text, however.

68 Wolfgang Iser, *The Implied Reader: Patterns of Communication in Prose Fiction from Bunyan to Beckett* (Baltimore: Johns Hopkins University Press, 1974) 33, 208.

69 Andrews, 'The First Fifty Years', 18.

70 Marrant, *Narrative*, iii.

71 *Ibid.*, 7.

72 *Ibid.*, 13.

73 *Ibid.*, 11.

74 *Ibid.*, 24.

75 At the time of Marrant's capture, the Cherokee tribe of the Indian South constituted a population of about 15,000. Richard VanDerBeets, ed., *Held Captive by Indians: Selected Narratives, 1642–1836* (Knoxville: University of Tennessee Press, 1994) 178.

76 Marrant, *Narrative*, iv.

77 *Ibid.*, 27.

78 *Ibid.*, iv.

79 *Ibid.*, 27.

80 *Ibid.*, 29.

81 VanDerBeets, *Held Captive by Indians*, x-xii.

82 Mary Rowlandson, *A True History of the Captivity and Restoration of Mrs. Mary Rowlandson, a Minister's Wife in New England* (London, 1682).

83 *Ibid.*, title page, i, iv.

84 *Ibid.*, 32.

85 Potkay and Burr, *Black Atlantic Writers*, 68. In November 1785, Marrant arrived in Nova Scotia as a preacher to blacks, white and native tribes but was accused of erroneous and devilish teachings by the Wesleyan layman Philip Marchantan and R. Garretson.

86 Six years after his return to London in 1790, Marrant was buried in the cemetery on Church Street in Islington.

87 James Albert Ukawsaw Gronniosaw, *A Narrative of the Most Remarkable Particulars in the Life of James Albert Ukawsaw Gronniosaw, An African Prince, As Related By Himself*, ed. Revd Walter Shirley (Bath: S. Hazard, 1770).

88 Lauren Henry, 'Sunshine and Shady Groves: What Blake's 'Little Black Boy' Learned from African Writers', *Romanticism and Colonialism*, ed. Tim Fulford and Peter Kitson (Cambridge: Cambridge University Press, 1998) 83; Paul Edwards, 'An African Literary Source for Blake's 'Little Black Boy?', *Research in African Literatures* 21 (1990) 171–81.

89 Potkay and Burr, eds, *Black Atlantic Writers*, 24–6. There were four Bath editions of Gronniosaw's text in 1770; one Newport edition in 1774; a Welsh translation printed in Aberhonddu, 1779; Clonnel, Ireland, 1786; Dublin, 1790 (which did not contain a dedication to the Countess of Huntingdon); Leeds, 1800.

90 Potkay and Burr, eds, *Black Atlantic Writers*, 23.

91 Gronniosaw, *Narrative of the Most Remarkable Particulars*, i.

92 *Ibid.*, iv. Gronniosaw's female amanuensis may have been the religious author and social reformist, Hannah More; Potkay and Burr, eds, *Black Atlantic Writers*, 26.

93 *Ibid.*, iv.

94 *Ibid.*, iv.

95 *Ibid.*, iv-vi.

96 *Ibid.*, 7–8; my emphasis.

97 *Ibid.*, 14, 11.

98 *Ibid.*, 14–15; my emphases.

99 *Ibid.*, 16.

100 *Ibid.*, 16.

101 *Ibid.*, 16–17.

102 Gates, *Signifying Monkey*, 137.

103 Gronniosaw, *Narrative of the Most Remarkable Particulars*, 18.

104 *Ibid.*, 19.

105 *Ibid.*, 25.

106 Daniel Defoe, *The Life and Strange Suprizing Adventures of Mr D-DeF- of London, Hosier. In a Dialogue between Him, Robinson Crusoe, and his Man, Friday* (London, 1719).

107 Gronniosaw, *Narrative of the Most Remarkable Particulars*, 35.

108 *Ibid.*, 37; my emphasis.

109 *Ibid.*, 38.

110 Andrews, 'The First Fifty Years', 6–8.

111 Gronniosaw, *Narrative of the Most Remarkable Particulars*, 47–8; my emphasis.

112 *Ibid.*, 49; my emphases.

7 PHILLIS WHEATLEY: POEMS AND LETTERS

1 Thomas Jefferson, 'Notes', *Writings*, ed. Merrill Peterson (New York: Literary Classics, 1984) 276.

2 Phillis Wheatley, *Poems on Various Subjects, Religious and Moral*. Printed for Arch. Bell (London, 1773); *The London Chronicle*, 9–11 Sept. 1773. The

American printing of Wheatley's poems did not appear until 1786 in Philadelphia, two years after the poet's death on 5 Dec. 1784.

3 Moira Ferguson, *Subject to Others: British Women Writers and Colonial Slavery, 1670–1834* (London: Routledge, 1992) 127, 129; Lauren Henry, 'Sunshine and Shady Groves: What Blake's 'Little Black Boy' Learned from African Writers', *Romanticism and Colonialism*, ed. Tim Fulford and Peter Kitson (Cambridge: Cambridge University Press, 1998) 69; Wylie Sypher, *Guinea's Captive Kings: British Anti-Slavery Literature of the Eighteenth Century* (Chapel Hill: University of North Carolina Press, 1942) 4.

4 Charlotte Smith, *Elegiac Sonnets* (London, 1787).

5 John Shields, 'Phillis Wheatley's Struggle for Freedom in her Poetry and Prose', *The Collected Works of Phillis Wheatley*, ed. John Shields (New York: Oxford University Press, 1988) 233. All references are from this volume unless otherwise specified. For further discussion on Wheatley see William Robinson, *Phillis Wheatley and Her Writings* (New York: Garland Press, 1984) and *Critical Essays on Phillis Wheatley* (Boston, Mass.: G. K. Hall, 1982).

6 Sidney Kaplan, *The Black Presence in the Era of the American Revolution, 1700–1800* (Amherst, Mass.: University of Massachusetts, 1989) 6–8; Shields, *Collected Works*, 233. For a further discussion on the reasons which most likely hindered the publication of Wheatley's poetry, see William Robinson, *Black New England Letters* (Boston: Boston Public Library, 1977) 50–1 and Mukhtar Ali Isani, 'The First Proposed Edition of *Poems on Various Subjects* and the Phillis Wheatley Canon', *Early American Literature* 49 (1977): 97–103.

7 It was, however, cited amongst the list of titles for the proposed 1772 Boston volume.

8 John Lathrop, *Innocent Blood Crying to God from the Streets of Boston* (Boston, 1771) 8; John Levernier, 'Phillis Wheatley and the New England Clergy', *Early American Literature* 26 (1991): 26, 15–16.

9 John Lathrop, *A Sermon Preached to the Ancient and Honourable Artillery-Company in Boston, New England, 6th June 1774* (Boston, 1774) 13, 15.

10 Charles W. Akers, *The Divine Politician: Samuel Cooper and the American Revolution in Boston* (Boston: Northeastern University Press, 1982) 124.

11 *Ibid.*, 123–4.

12 On 5 Mar. 1771, Samson Occom, the West Indian minister sent a request to Susanna Wheatley, asking her to send Wheatley back to Africa as a lay preacher: 'Pray Madam, what harm would it be to send Phillis to her Native Country as a Female Preacher to her kindred, you know Quaker women are alow'd to Preach, and why not others, in an Extraordinary Case': see also Harold Blodgett, *Samson Occom* (Hanover: Dartmouth College Publications, 1935).

13 Wheatley, *Poems on Various Subjects, Religious and Moral* (New England, Mass.: n.p. 1816) vii. John Moorhead was the pastor of the Scotch Presbyterian Church in Boston and master of Scipio Moorhead, the

black servant to whom Wheatley addressed some of her poems. See Shields, 'Phillis Wheatley's Struggle', 300 and Betsy Erkila, 'Revolutionary Women', *Tulsa Studies in Women's Literature* 6 (1987): 201–21.

14 Shields, 'Phillis Wheatley's Struggle', 229.

15 *Ibid.*, 230.

16 John Gabriel Stedman, *A Narrative, of a Five Years' Expedition, Against the Revolted Negroes of Surinam, in Guiana, on the Wild Coast of South America; From the Year 1772, to 1777*, 2 vols. (London, 1796) 520. For an informal reception of Wheatley's poetry see Philip Vickers Fithian, *The Journal and Letters of Philip Vickers Fithian 1773–1774: A Plantation Tutor of the Old Dominion* (Virginia: Colonial Williamsburg, 1957) 72–3.

17 Mukhtar Ali Isani, 'The British Reception of Phillis Wheatley's *Poems on Various Subjects*', *Journal of Negro History* 66 (1981): 144–9. Wheatley was one of three American slaves who managed to publish literary works whilst still in bondage, the other two being Jupiter Hammon (1711–179?) and George Moses Horton (1797–1883).

18 Anna Barbauld, author of *Epistle to William Wilberforce* (London, 1791) and Hannah More, author of *Slavery: A Poem* (London, 1788).

19 *The Critical Review* (36) Sept. 1773; Isani, 'The British Reception', 145–6.

20 *The London Chronicle* (34) 16–8 Sept. 1773; Isani, 'The British Reception', 146.

21 *The Public Advertiser* Oct. 1773; William Scheick, 'Phillis Wheatley and Oliver Goldsmith: A Fugitive Satire', *Early American Literature* 19 (1984): 82–4.

22 *The London Monthly Review* (49) Dec. 1773, 457–9; Isani, 'The British Reception', 147–8.

23 *The Gentleman's Magazine* (43) Sept. 1773; Isani, 'The British Reception', 146.

24 Robert Sayer, 'Autobiography and the Making of America', *Autobiography: Essays Theoretical and Critical*, ed. James Olney (Princeton: Princeton University Press, 1980) 146–68.

25 Jefferson, *Writings*, vol. i, 266–7.

26 Jefferson, 'Autobiography', *Writings*, 3–101.

27 Donna Landry, *The Muses of Resistance: Labouring-Class Women's Poetry in Britain, 1739–1796* (Cambridge: Cambridge University Press, 1990) 244.

28 Levernier, 'Phillis Wheatley', 25.

29 Robinson, *Critical Essays* 181–9; Levernier, 'Phillis Wheatley', 24.

30 Akers, *The Divine Politician*, 36.

31 Wheatley, 'America' (1768) lines 8–11, 15–17.

32 *Ibid.*, lines 38–40; my emphasis.

33 For an excellent discussion of Abigail Adams and Phillis Wheatley within the matrix of revolutionary America, see Erkila, 'Revolutionary Women', 202.

34 Maecenas' own prose and verse, however, were ridiculed by Augustus for their undisciplined style; *The New Encyclopaedia Britannica*, ed. Warren

Preece, 15th edn., 30 vols. (London: Encyclopaedia Britannica, 1974) vol. xiv, 563.

35 Wheatley, 'To Maecenas', *Poems*, 9–12, lines 4–6. See John Shields, 'Phillis Wheatley and Mather Byles: A Study in Literary Relationships', *The College Language Association Journal* 23 (1980): 337–90.

36 Wheatley, 'To Maecenas', *Poems*, 10, lines 23–8; my emphases.

37 *Ibid.*, 9, 11, lines 29–30.

38 Julia Stewart, ed., *African Names* (New York: Citadel Press, 1994) 133. Wheatley, 'To Maecenas', *Poems*, line 37.

39 Wheatley, 'To Maecenas', *Poems*, 11, lines 39–42.

40 *Ibid.*, 11–12, lines 45–7.

41 *Ibid.*, 12, lines 52–5.

42 Wheatley, 'On Being Brought from Africa to America', *Poems*, 18, lines 1–4.

43 *Ibid.*, 18, line 4.

44 Wheatley, 'To the University of Cambridge in New England', *Poems*, 15, lines 4–6.

45 Homer, *The Odyssey*, trans. Alexander Pope, 4 vols. (London, 1773) Book 18, line 25.

46 Wheatley, 'On Being Brought from Africa to America', *Poems*, 18, lines 5–6.

47 *Ibid.*, 18, lines 7–8.

48 Blake's poem 'The Little Black Boy' emphasised the *spiritual* capacity of Africans rather than the connotations associated with their physical exterior.

49 Samuel Taylor Coleridge, *Biographia Literaria: Or, Biographical Sketches of My Literary Life and Opinions*, 2 vols., ed. James Engell and W. Jackson Bate, 2 vols. (Princeton: Princeton University Press, 1983).

50 Levernier, 'Phillis Wheatley', 24; Kaplan, *Selling of Joseph*, 27–52.

51 Wheatley, 'On the Death of the Revd Dr Sewall', *Poems*, 19–21, line 9.

52 *Ibid.*, 19, lines 11–14; 20.

53 *Ibid.*, 21, lines 50–1.

54 Henry Louis Gates, *Figures in Black: Words, Signs and the 'Racial' Self*, 74; Dorothy Porter, 'Early American Negro Writings: A Bibliographical Study', *PBSA* 39 (1945): 261–3; Levernier, 'Phillis Wheatley', 31; Shields, 'Phillis Wheatley and Mather Byles', 282.

55 Whitefield, 'Letter to the Inhabitants of Virginia, Maryland, North and South Carolina, Concerning Their Negroes', *Three Letters from the Reverend Mr G. Whitefield* (London, 1740) 14.

56 Shields, 'Phillis Wheatley and Mather Byles', 282.

57 Wheatley, 'On the Death of George Whitefield', *Poems*, 23, line 21.

58 *Ibid.*, 23, lines 32–5.

59 *Ibid.*, 24, lines 38–41.

60 *Ibid.*, 210, lines 43–4; my emphasis.

61 *Ibid.*, 23, lines 36–7.

62 Wheatley, *Collected Works*, 170; my emphasis.
63 For further discussion of some variants of Phillis Wheatley's poems, see Isani, 'The Methodist Connection: New Variants in Some of Phillis Wheatley's Poems', *Early American Literature* 22 (1987): 108–13.
64 Wheatley, *Collected Works*, 172.
65 *Ibid.*, 181–2.
66 *Ibid.*, 181–2.
67 Paul Edwards and David Dabydeen, eds, *Black Writers in Britain, 1760–1890* (1991; Edinburgh: Edinburgh University Press, 1994) 101.
68 See Margaret Priestley, 'Philip Quaque of the Cape Coast', *Africa Remembered: Narratives by West Africans from the Era of the Slave Trade*, ed. Philip Curtin (Madison: University of Wisconsin Press, 1967) 99.
69 Two years earlier, another 'Cudjo' member, 'William' who had also travelled with Quaque under the auspices of the S.P.G., was 'put out of reach of instruction by a Lunacy' which seized him in December 1764 and led to his confinement in St Luke's Hospital and subsequent death in Guy's Hospital.
70 Priestley, 'Philip Quaque of the Cape Coast', 99–106.
71 Wheatley, Letter to John Thornton, 30 Oct. 1774, *Collected Works*, 184.
72 Priestley, 'Philip Quaque', 109.
73 *Ibid.*, 113–7.
74 *Ibid.*, 121.
75 See Curtin, *Africa Remembered*, 123, note 55; 131. Quaque, 20 Oct. 1781.
76 Quaque, 17 Jan. 1778; Priestley, 'Philip Quaque', 129; my emphasis.
77 Quaque, 13 Oct. 1811; Priestley, 'Philip Quaque', 109.
78 Michel Foucault, *The History of Sexuality. Volume One: An Introduction*, trans. Robert Hurley (Harmondsworth: Penguin, 1990) 53–73; de Man, *The Rhetoric of Romanticism* (New York: Columbia University Press, 1984). 278–302.
79 Henry Louis Gates, *Figures in Black*, 76. See Blodgett, *Samson Ocean*, 119, 148.
80 Wheatley, letter to Revd Samson Occom, 11 February 1774, *Collected Works*, 176–7, 176; *The Boston Post Boy*, 21 March 1774, Erkila, 'Revolutionary Women', 201–23; Gates, *Figures in Black*, 77; *The Connecticut Journal*, 1 April 1774, 1.
81 Wheatley, letter to Revd Samson Occom, 11 Feb. 1774, *Collected Works*, 177.
82 Mark Akenside, *The Pleasures of Imagination. A Poem. In Three Books*, 3rd edn. (London, 1744): 'The silken fetters of delicious ease' (Book II, line 562); Edward Young, *The Complaint, or Night Thoughts* (London, 1742–1745).
83 Wheatley, 'On Imagination', *Poems*, 66, lines 13–22.
84 William Wordsworth, *The Prelude*, ed. Jonathan Wordsworth, M. H. Abrams and Stephen Gill (New York: Norton, 1979) Book 1, 28, lines 1–2, 5–9; my emphasis.
85 Coleridge, 'The Eolian Harp', *Poetical Works*, ed. Ernest Hartley

Coleridge (Oxford: Oxford University press, 1969) 100–2; 'This Lime-Tree Bower My Prison', *Poetical Works*, 178–81; 'Frost at Midnight', *Poetical Works*, 240–2; 'Dejection: An Ode', *Poetical Works*, 362–8, lines 82–6.

86 Wheatley, 'On Imagination' *Poems*, 66, lines 23–6, 33, 36.

87 Wheatley, 'To the Right Honourable William, Earl of Dartmouth', *Poems*, 74, lines 25–31.

88 Erkila suggests that during these years the Earl incited slave rebellions against plantation masters: 'Revolutionary Women', 207.

89 Wheatley, *Collected Works*, 285; 'On Recollection', *Poems*, 63, lines 5–6, 27–30.

90 Wheatley, 'On Recollection', *Poems*, 62, lines 15–16.

91 *Ibid.*, 63–4, lines 31–6; my emphasis.

92 *Ibid.*, 64, lines 37–50.

93 Margaretta Odell, *Memoir and Poems of Phillis Wheatley: A Native African and a Slave. Also Poems by a Slave* (Boston: Geo. W. Light, 1834) 10. Wheatley's 'Thoughts on the Works of Providence' similarly depicted the sun as a supreme symbol of divinity.

8 OLAUDAH EQUIANO'S *INTERESTING NARRATIVE*

1 Olaudah Equiano, *The Interesting Narrative of the Life of Olaudah Equiano, or Gustavus Vassa, the African. Written By Himself*, 2 vols. Printed and sold by the author (London, 1789). All references will be from this edition unless otherwise specified. In 1789 there were two further editions of Equiano's text, both of which were printed by T. Wilkins. A fourth edition was published in 1790; a fifth in 1791 and a sixth in 1793. A London edition of 1809 was printed by S. Mason. In 1814 further editions were printed by James Nichols of Leeds and J. Nicholson of Halifax. Other editions included one printed in Norwich in 1794 and Penryn (printed by W. Cock) in 1816. Subscribers to Equiano's text included Hannah More, Revd Aldridge, Ottabah Cogoano and T. Clarkson. For further publication details see Adam Potkay and Sandra Burr, eds, *Black Atlantic Writers of the Eighteenth Century: Living the New Exodus in England and America* (Basingstoke: Macmillan, 1995) 162–3 and for a discussion of Equiano's text, see Keith Sandiford, *Measuring the Moment: Strategies of Protest in Eighteenth-Century Afro-English Writing* (Selinsgrove: Susquehanna Press, 1988) 118–48.

2 Angelo Costanzo, *Surprising Narrative: Olaudah Equiano and the Beginnings of Black Autobiography* (New York: Greenwood Press, 1987) 125–6, n. 9.

3 Sonia Hofkosh, 'Tradition and the *Interesting Narrative*: Capitalism, Abolition, and the Romantic Individual', *Romanticism, Race, and Imperial Culture*, ed. Alan Richardson and Sonia Hofkosh (Bloomington: Indiana University Press, 1996) 330–43, 332.

4 Sandiford, *Measuring the Moment*, 126–8.
5 Equiano, *Interesting Narrative*, vol. I, iii–iv; my emphases. Joanna Southcott presented a similar petition to the 'spiritual' dimension of the Houses of Parliament in her request that Richard Brothers be freed from prison. Joanna Southcott, *Joanna Southcott to the Lords Spiritual and Temporal and to the Gentlemen of the House of Commons in Parliament, May 29 1802* (London: E. Spragg, 1802) I.
6 During the court proceedings, an insurance lawyer summarised English law as follows: 'The insurer takes upon him the risk of the loss, capture, and death of slaves, or any other unavoidable accident to them: but natural death is always understood to be expected: – by natural death is meant, not only when it happens by disease or sickness, but also when the captive destroys himself through despair, which often happens: but when slaves are killed . . . to quell an insurrection . . . then the insurers must answer.' See Susanne Everett, *The Slaves* (London: Bison Books, 1978) 60.
7 Costanzo, Surprising Narrative, 43–4; *The Monthly Review*, June 1789, 551–2.
8 Equiano, *The Interesting Narrative of the Life of Olaudah Equiano: Or Gustavus Vassa, the African, Written by Himself*. A new edition, corrected (Leeds: James Nichols, 1814) v. The other new 1814 edition was the J. Nicholson reprint (Halifax) which included Wheatley's *Poems on Various Subjects, Religious and Moral* (London: Arch. Bell, 1773).
9 Equiano, *Interesting Narrative* (1814), vi.
10 Hofkosh argues that Equiano's text demonstrates that the economic structure of property and power undermines the very possibility of individual freedom. His manumission indicates that individualism is double-edged: capitalism and abolition are 'two sides of the same cognitive coin'; Hofkosh, 'Tradition and the *Interesting Narrative*', 335.
11 See Catherine Obianuju Acholonu, *The Igbo Roots of Olaudah Equiano: An Anthropological Research* (Owerri, Nigeria: AFA Publications, 1989).
12 Equiano, *Interesting Narrative*, vol. I, 38; my emphases.
13 *Ibid.*, vol. I, 41; Dr Mitchell, *Philos*, no. 476; sect. 4.
14 Stuart Hall, 'Cultural Identity and Diaspora', *Identity: Community, Culture, Difference*, ed. Jonathan Rutherford (London: Lawrence and Wishart, 1990) 402.
15 Constantine Phipps, *A Journey of a Voyage Towards the North Pole* (London, 1774); Benezet, *Some Historical Account of Guinea, its Situation, Produce and the General Disposition of its Inhabitants* . . . (Philadelphia, 1771) and Clarkson, *An Essay on Slavery and the Commerce of the Human Species* . . . (London, 1789); Gates 153.
16 Benezet, *Some Historical Account*, 6–7; Equiano, *Interesting Narrative*, vol. I, 4.
17 Benezet, *Some Historical Account*, 35.
18 Equiano, vol. I, 31.
19 *Ibid.*, vol. I, 5–6.

20 See James Arthur Baldwin, *The Fire Next Time* (London: Michael Joseph, 1963) for a contemporary account of renaming in the diaspora.

21 Equiano, *Interesting Narrative*, vol. 1, 3.

22 *Ibid.*, vol. 1, 28; See Paul Edwards, *Unreconciled Strivings and Ironic Strategies: Three Afro-British Authors of the Georgian Era: Ignatius Sancho, Olaudah Equiano, Robert Wedderburn* (Edinburgh: Edinburgh University Press, 1992) 9.

23 Equiano, *Interesting Narrative*, vol. 1, 32.

24 For a discussion of the emergence of the prophetic black church tradition in Afro-America, see Cornel West, *Prophetic Fragments* (Michigan: Ferdmans, 1988).

25 Equiano, *Interesting Narrative*, vol. 1, 34–5; my emphases.

26 *Ibid.*, vol. 1, 35.

27 *Ibid.*, vol. 1, 35–6.

28 Equiano, *Interesting Narrative* (Leeds, 1814) Chap. 2, vol. 1, 33; my emphases.

29 Equiano, *Interesting Narrative*, vol. 1, 27–8; See also Toni Morrison, *Beloved* (1987; London: Chatto and Windus, 1988), and Ben Okri, *The Famished Road* (London: Cape, 1991).

30 Equiano, *Interesting Narrative*, vol. 1, 83.

31 *Ibid.*, vol. 1, 70.

32 *Ibid.*, vol. 1, 92–3; my emphasis.

33 Henry Louis Gates, *The Signifying Monkey: A Theory of African-American Literary Criticism* (New York: Oxford University Press, 1988), 155; Equiano, *Interesting Narrative*, vol. 1, 33. The young Equiano's initial response to these cultural signifiers of control anticipates the Africans' fear of possession *of* the spirit *by* the camera, which reached the continent in 1839. Nicholas Monti, *Africa Then: Photographs, 1840–1918* (New York: Alfred Knopf, 1987) 5–11.

34 Equiano, *Interesting Narrative*, vol. i, 28–9.

35 Longinus, *Longinus on the Sublime*, ed. and trans. W. Rhys Roberts (Cambridge: Cambridge University Press, 1987) 7, 2, 3–4; Thomas Weiskel, *The Romantic Sublime: Studies in the Structure and Psychology of Transcendence* (Baltimore: Johns Hopkins University Press, 1986) 4.

36 Edmund Burke, *A Philosophical Enquiry into the Origins of our Ideas of the Sublime and Beautiful*, ed. Adam Phillips (Oxford: Oxford University Press, 1990).

37 Equiano, *Interesting Narrative*, 79.

38 *Ibid.*, vol. 1, 80.

39 *Ibid.*, 80. Samuel Taylor Coleridge, 'The Rime of the Ancient Mariner', *Poetical Works*, ed. Ernest Hartley Coleridge (Oxford: Oxford University Press, 1969) 197, lines 267–81.

40 Equiano, *Interesting Narrative*, vol. 1, 81.

41 *Ibid.*, vol. 1, 60.

42 bell hooks, *Ain't I a Woman?: Black Women and Feminism* (1981; London: Pluto Press, 1992) 20–2.

43 See Elaine Savory Fido, 'Mother/lands: Self and Separation in the Work of Buchi Emecheta, Bessie Head and Jean Rhys', *Motherlands: Black Women's Writing from Africa, the Caribbean and South Asia*, ed. Sushiela Nasta (London: The Women's Press, 1991) 330–49.
44 Equiano, *Interesting Narrative*, vol. 1, 205–6; my emphases. For a discussion of legal constraints, desires and deconstruction see Stanley Fish, *Doing What Comes Naturally: Change, Rhetoric and the Practice of Theory in Legal Studies* (Oxford: Clarendon Press, 1989) 12.
45 William Blackstone, *Commentaries on the Laws of England in Four Books*, eighth edn., 4 vols. (Oxford, 1779), vol. iv, 210.
46 *Ibid.*, vol. iv, 214.
47 Paul de Man, *Allegories of Reading: Figural Language in Rousseau, Nietzsche, Rilke, and Proust* (New Haven: Yale University Press, 1979) 279.
48 Michel Foucault, *History of Sexuality*, trans. Robert Hurley (Harmondsworth: Penguin, 1990) vol. i. 61–3, 19–21.
49 De Man, *Allegories of Reading*, 280.
50 Acholonu, *The Igbo Roots*, 16–7.
51 Equiano, *Interesting Narrative*, vol. 1, 28–9;.
52 Ifi Amadiume, *Male Daughters, Female Husbands: Gender and Sex in African Society* (1987; London: Zed Books, 1992) 92–3. See also Chinua Achebe, *Things Fall Apart* (1958; London: David Campbell, 1992).
53 Equiano, *Interesting Narrative*, vol. 1, 206–7.
54 *Ibid.*, vol. 1, 172.
55 *Ibid.*, vol. 1, 132–3; my emphases.
56 Equiano, *Interesting Narrative*, vol. 1, 131–6, 151.
57 Equiano, *Interesting Narrative*, vol. 1, 148–9, 154, 160.
58 *Ibid.*, vol. 1, 241–2.
59 *Ibid.*, vol. 1, 244.
60 *Ibid.*, vol. 1, 134.
61 *Ibid.*, vol. 1, 181–3, 190.
62 *Ibid.*, vol. 1, 219–20, 224, 225–6; my emphasis.
63 *Ibid.*, vol. 1, 217–18.
64 Equiano, *Interesting Narrative*, vol. 2, 5.
65 *Ibid.*, vol. 2, Frontispiece.
66 *Ibid.*, vol. 2, 126.
67 *Ibid.*, vol. 2, 117–18.
68 *Ibid.*, vol. 2, 125.
69 *Ibid.*, vol. 2, 130.
70 *Ibid.*, vol. 2, 146–7, 148, 150–1, 154.
71 Albert J. Raboteau, *Slave Religion: The 'Invisible Institution' in the Antebellum South* (1978; Oxford: Oxford University Press, 1980) 7–10.
72 Laguerre, *Voodoo Heritage*, 21–7.
73 *Ibid.*, 27–8.
74 *Ibid.*, 150.
75 By 1797, blacks constituted 25 per cent of the total Methodist population

in the United States, the majority of which were located in Maryland, Virginia and North Carolina. Raboteau, *Slave Religion*, 131. See Frederick Law Olmsted's account of the ecstatic behaviour displayed during an evangelical sermon in a black church in New Orleans: 'Sometimes the outcries and responses were not confined to ejaculations of this kind, but shouts, and groans, terrific shrieks, and indescribable expressions of ecstasy – of pleasure or agony – and even stamping, jumping, and clapping of hands . . . I was once surprised to find my own muscles all stretched, as if ready for a struggle – my face glowing, and my feet stamping . . . I could not, when my mind reverted to itself, find any connection or meaning in the phrases of the speaker that remained in my memory.' Raboteau *Slave Religion*, 62.

76 Paul Gilroy, *Small Acts: Thoughts on the Politics of Black Cultures* (London: Serpent's Tail, 1993) 138.

77 I am using the term 'natal alienation' as coined by Orlando Paterson (*The Sociology of Slavery* (New Jersey: Rutherford, 1969)), to infer the loss of ties at birth experienced by slaves in both ascending and descending generations; the severance of ties to the past and to progeny; and the attempted erasure of African language, culture and religion.

78 Equiano, *Interesting Narrative*, vol. 2, 186–7; my emphasis.

79 *Ibid.*, vol. 2, 178.

80 *Ibid.*, vol. 2, 182–3.

81 *Ibid.*, vol. 2, 235, 237. Equiano had been appointed Commissionary for Provisions for the New Colony in Sierra Leone but was dismissed on 24 Mar. 1787 for exposing the misuse of the projects funds.

82 *Ibid.*, vol. 2, 150–1.

83 *Ibid.*, vol. 2, 244.

84 *Ibid.*, vol. 2, 247–50; my emphases.

9 ROBBERT WEDDERBURN AND MULATTO DISCOURSE

1 Nelson Mandela at his first trial in 1962.

2 Furbush, *Dying Confessions*, cited in William Andrews, *To Tell a Free Story: The First Century of Afro-American Autobiography, 1760–1865* (Urbana: Illinois University Press, 1986) 49.

3 See Iain McCalman's edition, *The Horrors of Slavery and Other Writings by Robert Wedderburn* (Edinburgh: Edinburgh University Press, 1991) and *idem, The Radical Underworld: Prophets, Revolutionaries and Pornographers in London, 1795–1840* (Cambridge: Cambridge University Press, 1988) 5–7, 28–9, 50–3,149. See also Paul Edwards, *Unreconciled Strivings and Ironic Strategies: Three Afro-British Authors of the Georgian Era: Ignatius Sancho, Olaudah Equiano, Robert Wedderburn* (Edinburgh: Edinburgh University Press, 1992).

4 McCalman, *The Horrors of Slavery*, 52–3.

5 Robert Wedderburn, *The Horrors of Slavery: Exemplified in the Life and*

History of the Revd Robert Wedderburn in Which is Included the Correspondence of Robert Wedderburn and His Brother A[ndrew] Colville, alias Wedderburn. Printed and published by Robert Wedderburn (London, 1824) 11.

6 Edwards, *Unreconciled Strivings*, 15–19.
7 Wedderburn, *Truth, Self-Supported; Or, A Refutation of Certain Doctrinal Errors, Generally Adopted in the Christian Church, by Robert Wedderburn (A Creole from Jamaica)* (London, 1790), title page.
8 *Ibid.*, 5–6.
9 Blackstone, *Commentaries on the Laws of England in Four Books*, eighth edn., 4 vols. (Oxford, 1779) cited in Blackburn, *The Overthrow of Colonial Slavery, 1776–1848* (London: Verso, 1990) 81.
10 Blackburn, *The Overthrow*, 81; Fryer, *Staying Power: The History of Black People in Britain* (London: Pluto, 1984) 114–15; Blackstone, *Commentaries*, vol. i, 123. In the second edition of 1767 the revised formula appears on page 127.
11 Blackburn, *The Overthrow*, 81.
12 Michael Craton, James Walvin and David Wright, eds, *Slavery, Abolition and Emancipation: Black Slaves and the British Empire* (London: Longman, 1976) 170; cited in Moira Ferguson, *Subject to Others: British Women Writers and Colonial Slavery, 1670–1834* (London: Routledge, 1992) 116–17; my emphasis.
13 McCalman, *The Horrors of Slavery*, 58.
14 Wedderburn, *Truth, Self-Supported*, 3–4.
15 *Ibid.*, 12, 14–15; my emphases.
16 *Ibid.*, 13–14; my emphases.
17 *Ibid.*, 8–10.
18 *Ibid.*, 8–9.
19 Wesley's hymn is identified by McCalman as number 340. John Wesley, *The Works of John Wesley*, ed. Albert Outler, 5 vols. (Nashville: Abingdon Press, 1984).
20 Wedderburn, *The Trial of the Revd Robert Wedderburn, a Dissenting Minister of the Unitarian Persuasion, for Blasphemy in the Court of the Kings Bench, Westminster, the Sittings after Hilary Term, 1820*, ed. E. Perkins (London: W. Mason, 1820) 5.
21 See McCalman, *Radical Underworld*. Four years later, the Government arrested Thomas Evans, the founding member of the Society of Spencean Philanthropists set up in 1814.
22 Wedderburn, *The Axe Laid to the Root, or A Fatal Blow to Oppressors; Being An Address to the Planters and Negroes of the Island of Jamaica* (London, 1817) 4 parts; cited in Ian McCalman ed, *The Horrors of Slavery and Other Writings by Robert Wedderburn* (Edinburgh: Edinburgh University Press, 1991) 81–105.
23 *Ibid.*, Part 1, 81.
24 *Ibid.*, Part 1, 86; my emphases.
25 *Ibid.*, Part 1, 86–7; my emphasis.

26 *ibid.*, Part 2 (1817) 89–90 my emphases.

27 *Ibid.*, Part 4 (1817): 96–7; my emphasis.

28 McCalman, *The Horrors of Slavery*, 132.

29 *Ibid.*, 136.

30 William Blake, 'The Marriage of Heaven and Hell', *The Complete Poems of William Blake*, ed. W. H. Stevenson (London: Longman, 1989) 111, Plate 11. Although it is not known whether Wedderburn knew anything of Blake's writings, Wedderburn's work established a relation to the prophetic example set by his Soho neighbour, Richard Brothers, a contemporary of Blake's who was sent to Bedlam in 1795.

31 McCalman, *The Horrors of Slavery*, 56. See also Arnold Rattenbury, 'Methodism and the Tatterdemalions', *Popular Culture and Class Conflict, 1590–1914: Explorations in the History of Labour and Leisure*, ed. Eileen and Stephen Yeo (Brighton: Harvester Press, 1981) 28–61; J. Obelkevich, *Religion and Rural Society: South Lindsey, 1825–1875* (Oxford: Clarendon Press, 1976); William Hosking Oliver, *Prophets and Millennialists: The Uses of Biblical Prophecy in England from the 1790s to the 1840s* (Auckland: Auckland University Press, 1978) 11–24, 34–5, 45–7, 50–6.

32 Wedderburn, *The Trial*, 9.

33 *Ibid.*, 10.

34 *Ibid.*, 10–12.

35 *Ibid.*, 5; my emphases.

36 *Ibid.*, 19.

37 Wedderburn, *The Address of the Revd R. Wedderburn, to the Court of the King's Bench at Westminster, on Appealing to Receive Judgement for Blasphemy when he was Sentenced to Two Years Imprisonment in Dorchester Jail on Tuesday 9th of May 1820*, ed. Erasmus Perkins (London, 1820); McCalman, *The Horrors of Slavery*, 141.

38 Wedderburn, *Horrors of Slavery*, 5.

39 *Ibid.*, 4.

40 *Ibid.*, 4.

41 *Ibid.*, 13.

42 *Ibid.*, 15.

43 *Ibid.*, 5, 9. See also Toni Morrison's *Beloved* (1987; London: Chatto and Windus, 1988) for an examination of infanticide in the post-slavery America.

44 Wedderburn, *The Horrors of Slavery*, 15–16.

45 *Ibid.*, 5.

46 *Ibid.*, 3.

47 *Ibid.*, 6.

48 *Ibid.*, 6–8.

49 *Ibid.*, 5.

50 Wedderburn, *Cast-Iron Parsons: Or 'Hints to the Public and the Legislature, on Political Economy, Clearly Proving the Clergy Can be Entirely Dispensed With, Without Injury to the Christian Religion, or the Established Church, and to the*

Great Advantage of the State' (London, 1820); cited in McCalman, *The Horrors of Slavery*, 143, 147.

51 Wedderburn, 'The Holy Liturgy: Or Divine Science, upon the Principle of Pure Christian Diabolism, Most Strictly Founded upon the Sacred Scriptures', *The Lion*, 21 March 1828; cited in McCalman, *The Horrors of Slavery*, 153, 154; my emphases except final sentence. Wedderburn's Christian Diabolist Liturgy found its way to New York where it appeared in *The Correspondent*, ed. George Houston, 4 Oct. 1828, 168–70; McCalman, *The Horrors of Slavery*, 34.

Index

CAMBRIDGE STUDIES IN ROMANTICISM

Titles published

33458414R00209

Made in the USA
Lexington, KY
27 June 2014